THE HOMESTEADING HANDBOOK

A Back to Basics Guide to
Growing Your Own Food • Canning
Keeping Chickens • Generating Your Own Energy
Crafting • Herbal Medicine • and More

Abigail R. Gehring

Skyhorse Publishing

THE HOMESTEADING HANDBOOK

Skyhorse Publishing books may be purchased in bulk at special discounts for sales promotion, corporate gifts, fund-raising, or educational purposes. Special editions can also be created to specifications. For details, contact the Special Sales Department, Skyhorse Publishing, 307 West 36th Street, 11th Floor, New York, NY 10018 or info@skyhorsepublishing.com.

Skyhorse® and Skyhorse Publishing® are registered trademarks of Skyhorse Publishing, Inc.®, a Delaware corporation.

www.skyhorsepublishing.com

20 19 18 17 16 15 14 13

Library of Congress Cataloging-in-Publication Data

Gehring, Abigail R.
  The homesteading handbook : back to basics guide to growing your own food, canning, keeping chickens, generating your own energy, crafting, herbal medicine, and more / Abigail R. Gehring.
    p. cm.
  ISBN 978-1-61608-265-9 (alk. paper)
 1. Agriculture--Handbooks, manuals, etc. 2. Family farms--Handbooks, manuals, etc.
3. Home economics, Rural--Handbooks, manuals, etc. 4. Sustainable living--Handbooks, manuals, etc. 5. Agriculture--United States--Handbooks, manuals, etc. I. Title.
  S501.2.G44 2011
  640--dc22

                                        2011017263

Printed in China

Contents

The Home Garden

Creating a garden—whether it's a single tomato plant in a pot on your windowsill or a full acre chock-full of flowers and veggies—takes imagination, hard work, a bit of planning, patience, and a willingness to take risks. There are some factors you can control, like the condition of the soil you bury your seeds in, the time of year you start planting, and what plants you put where. But there will always be situations you can't predict; you might get a frost in June, an old discarded pumpkin seed might sprout up in the middle of your magnolias, or the cat could knock your basil plant off the counter to its demise on the kitchen floor. This element of surprise is one of the joys and challenges of gardening. If you can learn to skillfully navigate the factors in your control and accept the unpredictable circumstances with patience and a sense of humor, you'll have mastered a great life lesson. The following pages are meant to help you with that first part: gaining the knowledge and insight you need to give your garden the best chance of thriving. From understanding a plant's basic needs, to properly preparing soil, to protecting against weeds and harmful insects, this section covers all the gardening basics. Beyond that, you'll find information on growing plants without soil, tips for keeping your garden organic, and inspiration for gardening in urban environments. There is little in life as rewarding as enjoying a salad composed entirely of things you've picked from your own garden. But gardening is also about the process: If you can learn to love the feel of the dirt between your fingers, the burn in your muscles as you dig, and the quiet, slow way in which sprouts reach toward the sun, no moment of your labor will have been a waste, regardless of the end results.

Planning a Garden

Basic Plant Requirements

Before you start a garden, it's helpful to understand what plants need in order to thrive. Some plants, like dandelions, are tolerant of a wide variety of conditions, while others, such as orchids, have very specific requirements in order to grow successfully. Before spending time, effort, and money attempting to grow a new plant in a garden, to do some research to learn about the conditions that a particular plant needs in order to grow properly.

Environmental factors play a key role in the proper growth of plants. Some of the essential factors that influence this natural process are as follows:

1. Length of Day

The amount of time between sunrise and sunset is the most critical factor in regulating vegetative growth, blooming, flower development, and the initiation of dormancy. Plants utilize increasing day length as a cue to promote their growth in spring, while decreasing day length in fall prompts them to prepare for the impending cold weather. Many plants require specific day length conditions in order to bloom and flower.

2. Light

Light is the energy source for all plants. Cloudy, rainy days or any shade cast by nearby plants and structures can significantly reduce the amount of light available to the plant. In addition, plants adapted to thrive in shady spaces cannot tolerate full sunlight. In general, plants will only be able to survive where adequate sunlight reaches them at levels they are able to tolerate.

3. Temperature

Plants grow best within an optimal range of temperatures. This temperature range may vary drastically depending on the plant species. Some plants

Some gardens require more planning than others. Flower gardens can be carefully arranged to create patterns or to contain a specific range of colors, or they can be more casual, as this garden is. However, always keep in mind a plant's specific environmental needs before choosing a place for it.

Some plants, like cacti, thrive in hot, dry conditions.

thrive in environments where the temperature range is quite wide; others can only survive within a very narrow temperature variance. Plants can only survive where temperatures allow them to carry on life-sustaining chemical reactions.

4. Cold

Plants differ by species in their ability to survive cold temperatures. Temperatures below 60°F injure some tropical plants. Conversely, arctic species can tolerate temperatures well below zero. The ability of a plant to withstand cold is a function of the degree of dormancy present in the plant, its water status, and its general health. Exposure to wind, bright sunlight, or rapidly changing temperatures can also compromise a plant's tolerance to the cold.

5. Heat

A plant's ability to tolerate heat also varies widely from species to species. Many plants that evolved to grow in arid, tropical regions are naturally very heat tolerant, while sub-arctic and alpine plants show very little tolerance for heat.

6. Water

Different types of plants have different water needs. Some plants can tolerate drought during the summer but need winter rains in order to flourish. Other plants need

a consistent supply of moisture to grow well. Careful attention to a plant's need for supplemental water can help you to select plants that need a minimum of irrigation to perform well in your garden. If you have poorly drained, chronically wet soil, you can select lovely garden plants that naturally grow in bogs, marshlands, and other wet places.

7. Soil pH

A plant root's ability to take up certain nutrients depends on the pH—a measure of the acidity or alkalinity—of your soil. Most plants grow best in soils that have a pH between 6.0 and 7.0. Most ericaceous plants, such as azaleas and blueberries, need acidic soils with a pH below 6.0 to grow well. Lime can be used to raise the soil's pH, and materials containing sulfates, such as aluminum sulfate and iron sulfate, can be used to lower the pH. The solubility of many trace elements is controlled by pH, and plants can only use the soluble forms of these important micronutrients.

Feeling the soil can give you a sense of how nutrient-rich it is. Dark, crumbly, soft soil is usually full of nutrients. However, determining the pH requires a soil test (see page 9).

A Basic Plant Glossary

Here is some terminology commonly used in reference to plants and gardening:

annual—a plant that completes its life cycle in one year or season.

arboretum—a landscaped space where trees, shrubs, and herbaceous plants are cultivated for scientific study or educational purposes, and to foster appreciation of plants.

axil—the area between a leaf and the stem from which the leaf arises.

bract—a leaflike structure that grows below a flower or cluster of flowers and is often colorful. Colored bracts attract pollinators, and are often mistaken for petals. Poinsettia and flowering dogwood are examples of plants with prominent bracts.

cold hardy—capable of withstanding cold weather conditions.

conifers—plants that predate true, flowering plants in evolution; conifers lack true flowers and produce separate male and female strobili, or cones. Some conifers, such as yews, have fruits enclosed in a fleshy seed covering.

cultivar—a cultivated variety of a plant selected for a feature that distinguishes it from the species from which it was selected.

deciduous—having leaves that fall off or are shed seasonally to avoid adverse weather conditions, such as cold or drought.

herbaceous—having little or no woody tissue. Most perennials or annuals are herbaceous.

hybrid—a plant, or group of plants, that results from the interbreeding of two distinct cultivars, varieties, species, or genera.

inflorescence—a floral axis that contains many individual flowers in a specific arrangement; also known as a flower cluster.

native plant—a plant that lives or grows naturally in a particular region without direct or indirect human intervention.

panicle—a pyramidal, loosely branched flower cluster; a panicle is a type of inflorescence.

perennial—a plant that persists for several years, usually dying back to a perennial crown during the winter and initiating new growth each spring

shrub—a low-growing, woody plant, usually less than 15 feet tall, that often has multiple stems and may have a suckering growth habit (the tendency to sprout from the root system).

taxonomy—the study of the general principles of scientific classification, especially the orderly classification of plants and animals according to their presumed natural relationships.

tree—a woody perennial plant having a single, usually elongated main stem, or trunk, with few or no branches on its lower part.

wildflower—a herbaceous plant that is native to a given area and is representative of unselected forms of its species.

woody plant—a plant with persistent woody parts that do not die back in adverse conditions. Most woody plants are trees or shrubs.

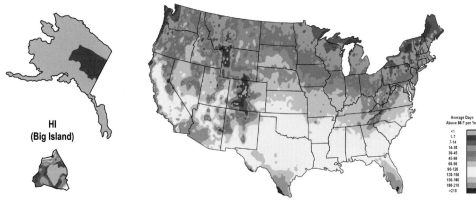

AK

HI
(Big Island)

Average Days
Above 86 F per Year
<1
1-7
7-14
14-30
30-45
45-60
60-90
90-120
120-150
150-180
180-210
>210

Parts of a Flower

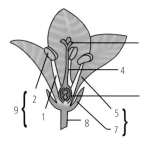

1—filament
2—anther
3—stigma
4—style
5—petal
6—ovary
7—sepal
8—pedicel
9—stamen
10—pistil
11—perianth

Selecting a Site for Your Garden

Selecting a site for your garden is the first step in growing the vegetables, fruits, and herbs that you want. You do not need a large space in order to grow a significant amount of vegetables, fruit, and herbs. Creating a garden that is about 25 feet square should be quite sufficient for a family. It is important that you don't start off with a space that is too large—it is better to start small and then work your way up if you find that gardening is something that you truly enjoy.

Five Factors to Consider When Choosing a Garden Site

1. Sunlight

Sunlight is crucial for the growth of vegetables and other plants. In order for your garden to grow, your plants will need at least six hours of direct sunlight per day. In order to make sure your garden receives an ample amount of sunlight, don't select a garden site that will be in the shade of trees, shrubs, houses, or other structures. Certain vegetables, such as broccoli and spinach, grow just fine in shadier spots, so if your garden does receive some shade, make sure to plant those types of vegetables in the shadier areas. However, on a whole, if your garden does not receive at least six hours of intense sunlight per day, it will not grow as efficiently or successfully.

2. Proximity

Another consideration is how close you place your garden to your home. If your garden is closer to your house and easy to reach, you will most likely use it more often—and to its fullest potential. Having a garden close to your home will help you to pick your vegetables and fruit at their peak ripeness, allowing you access to an abundance of fresh produce on a regular basis. Weeding, watering, and controlling pests are all more likely to be attended to if your garden is situated near your home. Overall, gardens placed closer to the home will receive more attention and thus be healthier and more productive.

3. Soil Quality

Contrary to some beliefs, you do not need high-quality soil to start and grow a productive garden. However, it is best to have soil that is fertile, is full of organic materials that provide nutrients to the plant roots, and is easy to dig and till. Loose, well-drained soil is ideal for

If you don't have enough space for a full garden, you can plant in flowerpots or other containers. Potted plants are especially convenient because you can move them around to get more light or to make watering easier.

A garden of about 25 feet square should be adequate to produce enough vegetables for a family of four to six to enjoy.

growing a good garden. If there is a section of your yard where water does not easily drain after a good, soaking rain, it is best not to plant your garden in that area, as the excess water will most likely drown your garden plants. Furthermore, soils that are of a clay or sandy consistency are not as effective in growing plants. To make these types of soils more nutrient-rich and fertile, add in organic materials (such as compost or manure) to improve their quality.

4. Water Availability

Water is vital to keeping your garden green, healthy, and productive. A successful garden needs around 1 inch of water per week to thrive. Rain and irrigation systems are effective in maintaining this 1-inch-per-week quota. Situating your garden near a spigot or hose is ideal, allowing you to keep the soil moist and your plants happy.

5. Elevation

It is essential to make sure your garden is not located in an area where air cannot circulate and where frost quickly forms. Placing your garden in a low-lying area, such as at the base of a slope, should be avoided, as these lower areas do not warm as quickly in the spring, and frost forms quickly during the spring and fall since the cold air collects in these areas. Your garden should, if at all possible, be elevated slightly, on ground that is higher up. This way, your garden plants will be less likely to be affected by frost and you'll be able to start your garden growing earlier in the spring and harvest well into the fall.

Some Other Things to Consider

When planning out your garden, it is useful to sketch a diagram of what you want your garden to look like. What sorts of plants to you want to grow? Do you want a garden purely for growing vegetables or do you want to mix in some fruits, herbs, and wildflowers? Choosing the appropriate plants to grow next to each other will help your garden grow well and will provide you with

Gloves, a trowel, and a watering can are some of the most basic tools you should have on hand for gardening.

ample produce throughout the growing season (see the charts on this page).

When planting a garden, be sure to have access to many types of tools. You'll need a spade or digging fork for digging holes for seeds or seedlings (or, if the soil is loose enough, you can just use your hands). You'll also need a trowel, rake, or hoe to smooth over the garden surface. A measuring stick is helpful when spacing your plants or seeds (if you don't have a measuring stick, you can use a precut string to measure). If you are planting seedlings or established plants, you may need stakes and string to tie them up (so they don't fall over in inclement weather or when they start producing fruit or vegetables). Finally, if you are interested in installing an irrigation system for your garden, you will need to buy the appropriate materials for this purpose.

Companion Planting

Plants have natural substances built into their structures that repel or attract certain insects and can have an effect on the growth rate and even the flavor of the other plants around them. Thus, some plants aid each other's growth when planted in close proximity and others inhibit each other. Smart companion planting will help your garden remain healthy, beautiful, and in harmony, while deterring certain insect pests and other factors that could be potentially detrimental to your garden plants.

These charts list various types of garden vegetables, herbs, and flowers and their respective companion and "enemy" plants.

Vegetables

Type	Companion plant(s)	Avoid
Asparagus	Tomatoes, parsley, basil	Onion, garlic, potatoes
Beans	Eggplant	Tomatoes, onion, kales
Beets	Mint	Runner beans
Broccoli	Onion, garlic, leeks	Tomatoes, peppers, mustard

Type	Companion plant(s)	Avoid
Cabbage	Onion, garlic, leeks	Tomatoes, peppers, beans
Carrot	Leeks, beans	Radish
Celery	Daisies, snapdragons	Corn, aster flower
Corn	Legumes, squash, cucumber	Tomatoes, celery
Cucumber	Radishes, beets, carrots	Tomatoes
Eggplant	Marigolds, mint	Runner beans
Leeks	Carrots	Legumes
Lettuce	Radish, carrots	Celery, cabbage, parsley
Melon	Pumpkin, squash	None
Peppers	Tomatoes	Beans, cabbage, kales
Onion	Carrots	Peas, beans
Peas	Beans, corn	Onion, garlic
Potato	Horseradish	Tomatoes, cucumber
Tomatoes	Carrots, celery, parsley	Corn, peas, potato, kales

Herbs

Type	Companion Plant(s)	Avoid
Basil	Chamomile, anise	Sage
Chamomile	Basil, cabbage	Other herbs (it will become oily)
Cilantro	Beans, peas	None
Chives	Carrots	Peas, beans
Dill	Cabbage, cucumber	Tomatoes, carrots
Fennel	Dill	Everything else
Garlic	Cucumber, peas, lettuce	None
Oregano	Basil, peppers	None
Peppermint	Broccoli, cabbage	None
Rosemary	Sage, beans, carrots	None
Sage	Rosemary, beans	None
Summer savory	Onion, green beans	None

Bee balm does well in partial shade. Its bright color and sweet nectar have a tendency to attract bees and humming birds.

Flowering plants that do well in partial and full shade:

- Bee balm
- Bellflower
- Bleeding heart
- Cardinal flower
- Coleus
- Columbine
- Daylily
- Dichondra
- Fern
- Forget-me-not
- Globe daisy
- Golden bleeding heart
- Impatiens
- Leopardbane
- Lily of the valley
- Meadow rue
- Pansy
- Periwinkle
- Persian violet
- Primrose
- Rue anemone
- Snapdragon
- Sweet alyssum
- Thyme

Vegetable plants that can grow in partial shade:

- Arugula
- Beans
- Beets
- Broccoli
- Brussels sprouts
- Cauliflower
- Endive
- Kale
- Leaf lettuce
- Peas
- Radish
- Spinach
- Swiss chard

Flowers

Type	Companion Plant(s)	Avoid
Geraniums	Roses, tomatoes	None
Marigolds	Tomatoes, peppers, most plants	None
Petunias	Squash, asparagus	None
Sunflowers	Corn, tomatoes	None
Tansies	Roses, cucumber, squash	None

Plants for the Shade

It is best to situate your garden in an area that receives at least six hours of direct sunlight per day—especially if you want to grow vegetables or fruits. However, if the only part of your yard suitable for gardening is blocked by partial or full shade (or part of your sunlit garden receives partial shade during the day), you can still grow plenty of things in these areas—you just need to select plants that grow best in these types of environments. It is a good idea, either when buying seedlings from your local nursery or planting your own seeds, to read the accompanying label or packet or do a little research before planting to make sure your plants will thrive in a shadier environment.

Beets like cool weather and do well in shady areas with rich soil. Plant beets at least 1 inch deep and 2 inches part. Weed regularly to ensure strong root development.

Improving Your Soil

When gardening, it is essential to have nutrient-rich, fertile soil in order to grow the best and healthiest plants—plants that will supply you with quality fruits, vegetables, and flowers. Sometimes, soil loses its fertility (or has minimum fertility based on the region in which you live), and so measures must be taken in order to improve your soil and, subsequently, your garden.

Soil Quality Indicators

Soil quality is an assessment of how well soil performs all of its functions now and how those functions are being preserved for future use. The quality of soil cannot just be determined by measuring row or garden yield, water quality, or any other single outcome, nor can it be measured directly. Thus, it is important to look at specific indicators to better understand the properties of soil. Plants can provide us with clues about how well the soil is functioning—whether a plant is growing and producing quality fruits and vegetables or failing to yield such things is a good indicator of the quality of the soil it's growing in.

Indicators are measurable properties of soil or plants that provide clues about how well the soil can function. Indicators can be physical, chemical, and biological properties, processes, or characteristics of soils. They can also be visual features of plants.

Useful indicators of soil quality:
- are easy to measure
- measure changes in soil functions
- encompass chemical, biological, and physical properties
- are accessible to many users
- are sensitive to variations in climate and management

Indicators can be assessed by qualitative or quantitative techniques, such as soil tests. After measurements are collected, they can be evaluated by looking for patterns and comparing results to measurements taken at a different time.

Good soil is usually dark, moist, and dense.

Spinach and other green, leafy vegetables tend to do well in shady areas. Just be sure they get enough water; trees or other shade-producing canopies can also block rainfall.

Examples of soil quality indicators:

1. Soil Organic Matter—promotes soil fertility, structure, stability, nutrient retention, and helps combat soil erosion.
2. Physical Indicators—these include soil structure, depth, infiltration and bulk density, and water hold capacity. Quality soil will retain and transport water and nutrients effectively; it will provide habitat for microbes; it will promote compaction and water movement; and, it will be porous and easy to work with.
3. Chemical Indicators—these include pH, electrical conductivity, and extractable nutrients. Quality soil will be at its threshold for plant, microbial, biological, and chemical activity; it will also have plant nutrients that are readily available.
4. Biological Indicators—these include microbial biomass, mineralizable nitrogen, and soil respiration. Quality soil is a good repository for nitrogen and other basic nutrients for prosperous plant growth; it has a high soil productivity and nitrogen supply; and there is a good amount of microbial activity.

Soil and Plant Nutrients

Nutrient Management

There are 20 nutrients that all plants require. Six of the most important nutrients, called macronutrients, are: calcium, magnesium, nitrogen, phosphorous, potassium, and sulfur. Of these, nitrogen, phosphorus, and potassium are essential to healthy plant growth and so are required in relatively large amounts. Nitrogen is associated with lush vegetative growth, phosphorus is required for flowering and fruiting, and potassium is necessary for durability and disease resistance. Calcium, sulfur, and magnesium are also required in comparatively large quantities and aid in the overall health of plants.

The other nutrients, referred to as micronutrients, are required in very small amounts. These include such elements as copper, zinc, iron, and boron. While both macro- and micronutrients are required for good plant growth, over-application of these nutrients can be as detrimental to the plant as a nutrient deficiency. Over-application of plant nutrients may not only impair plant growth, but may also contaminate groundwater by penetrating through the soil or may pollute surface waters.

Soil Testing

Testing your soil for nutrients and pH is important in order to provide your plants with the proper balance of nutrients (while avoiding over-application). If you are establishing a new lawn or garden, a soil test is strongly recommended. The cost of soil testing is minor in comparison to the cost of plant materials and labor. Correcting a problem before planting is much simpler and cheaper than afterwards.

Once your garden is established, continue to take periodic soil samples. While many people routinely lime their soil, this can raise the pH of the soil too high. Likewise, since many fertilizers tend to lower the soil's pH, it may drop below desirable levels after several years, depending on fertilization and other soil factors, so occasional testing is strongly encouraged.

Home tests for pH, nitrogen, phosphorus, and potassium are available from most garden centers. While these may give you a general idea of the nutrients in your soil, they are not as reliable as tests performed by the Cooperative Extension Service at land grant universities. University and other commercial testing services will provide more detail, and you can request special tests for micronutrients if you suspect a problem. In addition to the analysis of nutrients in your soil, these services often provide recommendations for the application of nutrients or how best to adjust the pH of your soil.

The test for soil pH is very simple. pH is a measure of how acidic or alkaline your soil is. A pH of 7 is considered neutral. Below 7 is acidic and above 7 is alkaline. Since pH greatly influences plant nutrients, adjusting the pH will often correct a nutrient problem. At a high pH, several of the micronutrients become less available for plant uptake. Iron deficiency is a common problem, even

This electronic soil tester runs on one AA battery and gives pH, nutrient, and moisture level readings within minutes.

To determine the various layers of your soil, called your "soil profile," a core sample can be taken. This requires a boring machine, which will insert a hollow core rod, or "probe" like these shown here, deep into the ground to extract soil. The layers will be distinguishable by the change in soil color. Several core samples can be mixed together for a more accurate soil test.

Steps for Taking a Soil Test

1. If you intend to send your sample to the land grant university in your state, contact the local Cooperative Extension Service for information and sample bags. If you intend to send your sample to a private testing lab, contact them for specific details about submitting a sample.
2. Follow the directions carefully for submitting the sample. The following are general guidelines for taking a soil sample:

   • Sample when the soil is moist but not wet.
   • Obtain a clean pail or similar container.
   • Clear away the surface litter or grass.
   • With a spade or soil auger, dig a small amount of soil to a depth of 6 inches.
   • Place the soil in the clean pail.
   • Repeat steps 3 through 5 until the required number of samples has been collected.
   • Mix the samples together thoroughly.
   • From the mixture, take the sample that will be sent for analysis.
   • Send immediately. Do not dry before sending.

3. If you are using a home soil testing kit, follow the above steps for taking your sample. Follow the directions in the test kit carefully so you receive the most accurate reading possible.

at a neutral pH, for such plants as rhododendrons and blueberries. At a very low soil pH, other micronutrients may be too available to the plant, resulting in toxicity.

Phosphorus and potassium are tested regularly by commercial testing labs. While there are soil tests for nitrogen, these may be less reliable. Nitrogen is present in the soil in several forms that can change rapidly. Therefore, a precise analysis of nitrogen is more difficult to obtain. Most university soil test labs do not routinely test for nitrogen. Home testing kits often contain a test for nitrogen that may give you a general, though not necessarily completely accurate, idea of the presence of nitrogen in your garden soil.

Organic matter is often part of a soil test. Organic matter has a large influence on soil structure and so is highly desirable for your garden soil. Good soil structure improves aeration, water movement, and retention. This encourages increased microbial activity and root growth, both of which influence the availability of nutrients for plant growth. Soils high in organic matter tend to have a greater supply of plant nutrients compared to many soils low in organic matter. Organic matter tends to bind up some soil pesticides, reducing their effectiveness, and so this should be taken into consideration if you are planning to apply pesticides to your garden.

Tests for micronutrients are usually not performed unless there is reason to suspect a problem. Certain plants have greater requirements for specific micronutrients and may show deficiency symptoms if those nutrients are not readily available. (See the chart listing nutrient deficiency symptoms on page 57.)

Enriching Your Soil

Organic and Commercial Fertilizers and Returning Nutrients to Your Soil

Once you have the results of the soil test, you can add nutrients or soil amendments as needed to alter the pH. If you need to raise the soil's pH, use lime. Lime is most effective when it is mixed into the soil; therefore, it is best to apply before planting (if you apply lime in the fall, it has a better chance of correcting any soil acidity problems for the next growing season). For large areas, rototilling is most effective. For small areas or around plants, working the lime into the soil with a spade or cultivator is preferable. When working around plants, be careful not to dig too deeply or roughly so that you damage plant roots. Depending on the form of lime and the soil conditions, the change in pH may be gradual. It may take several months before a significant change is noted. Soils high in organic matter and clay tend to take larger amounts of lime to change the pH than do sandy soils.

If you need to lower the pH significantly, especially for plants such as rhododendrons, you can use aluminum sulfate. In all cases, follow the soil test or manufacturer's recommended rates of application. Again, mixing well into the soil is recommended.

After rototilling or mixing in the fertilizer with a spade, you may wish to rake out the soil to make it smooth and well aerated.

There are numerous choices for providing nitrogen, phosphorus, and potassium, the nutrients your plants need to thrive. Nitrogen (N) is needed for healthy, green growth and regulation of other nutrients. Phosphorus (P) helps roots and seeds properly develop and resist disease. Potassium (K) is also important in root development and disease resistance. If your soil is of adequate fertility, applying compost may be the best method of introducing additional nutrients. While compost is relatively low in nutrients compared to commercial fertilizers, it is especially beneficial in improving the condition of the soil and is nontoxic. By keeping the soil loose, compost allows plant roots to grow well throughout the soil, helping them to extract nutrients from a larger area. A loose soil enriched with compost is also an excellent habitat for earthworms and other beneficial soil microorganisms that are essential for releasing nutrients for plant use. The nutrients from compost are also released slowly, so there is no concern about "burning" the plant with an over-application of synthetic fertilizer.

Manure is also an excellent source of plant nutrients and is an organic matter. Manure should be composted before applying, as fresh manure may be too strong and can injure plants. Be careful when composting manure. If left in the open, exposed to rain, nutrients may leach out of the manure and the runoff can contaminate nearby waterways. Make sure the manure is stored in a location away from wells and any waterways and that any runoff is confined or slowly released into a vegetated area. Improperly applied manure also can be a source of pollution. If you are not composting your own manure, you can purchase some at your local garden store. For best results, work composted manure into the soil around the plants or in your garden before planting.

If preparing a bed before planting, compost and manure may be worked into the soil to a depth of 8 to 12 inches. If adding to existing plants, work carefully around the plants so as not to harm the existing roots.

Green manures are another source of organic matter and plant nutrients. Green manures are crops that are grown and then tilled into the soil. As they break down, nitrogen and other plant nutrients become available. These manures may also provide additional benefits of reducing soil erosion. Green manures, such as rye and oats, are often planted in the fall after the crops have been harvested. In the spring, these are tilled under before planting.

With all organic sources of nitrogen, whether compost or manure, the nitrogen must be changed to an inorganic form before the plants can use it. Therefore, it is important to have well-drained, aerated soils that provide the favorable habitat for the soil microorganisms responsible for these conversions.

There are also numerous sources of commercial fertilizers that supply nitrogen, phosphorus, and potassium, though it is preferable to use organic fertilizers, such as compost and manures. However, if you choose to use a commercial fertilizer, it is important to know how to read the amount of nutrients contained in each bag. The first number on the fertilizer analysis is the percentage of nitrogen; the second number is phosphorus; and the third number is the potassium content. A fertilizer that has a 10-20-10 analysis contains twice as much of each of the nutrients as a 5-10-5. How much of each nutrient you need depends on your soil test results and the plants you are fertilizing.

As was mentioned before, nitrogen stimulates vegetative growth while phosphorus stimulates flowering.

Soil Test Reading	What to Do
High ph	Your soil is alkaline. To lower ph, add elemental sulfur, gypsum, or cottonseed meal. Sulfur can take several months to lower your soil's ph, as it must first convert to sulfuric acid with the help of the soil's bacteria.
Low ph	Your soil is too acidic. Add lime or wood ashes.
Low nitrogen	Add manure, horn or hoof meal, cottonseed meal, fish meal, or dried blood.
High nitrogen	Your soil may be over-fertilized. Water the soil frequently and don't add any fertilizer.
Low phosphorus	Add cottonseed meal, bonemeal, fish meal, rock phosphate, dried blood, or wood ashes.
High phosphorous	Your soil may be over-fertilized. Avoid adding phosphorous-rich materials and grow lots of plants to use up the excess.
Low potassium	Add potash, wood ashes, manure, dried seaweed, fish meal, or cottonseed meal.
High potassium	Continue to fertilize with nitrogen and phosphorous-rich soil additions, but avoid potassium-rich fertilizers for at least two years.
Poor drainage or too much drainage	If your soil is a heavy, clay-like consistency, it won't drain well. If it's too sandy, it won't absorb nutrients as it should. Mix in peat moss or compost to achieve a better texture.

For potted plants, you can apply fertilizer around the edge of the pot if needed, but try to avoid direct contact between the plant's roots, leaves, or stem, and the fertilizer.

Too much nitrogen can inhibit flowering and fruit production. For many flowers and vegetables, a fertilizer higher in phosphorus than nitrogen is preferred, such as a 5-10-5. For lawns, nitrogen is usually required in greater amounts, so a fertilizer with a greater amount of nitrogen is more beneficial.

Fertilizer Application

Commercial fertilizers are normally applied as a dry, granular material or mixed with water and poured onto the garden. If using granular materials, avoid spilling on sidewalks and driveways because these materials are water soluble and can cause pollution problems if rinsed into storm sewers. Granular fertilizers are a type of salt, and if applied too heavily, they have the capability of burning the plants. If using a liquid fertilizer, apply directly to or around the base of each plant and try to contain it within the garden only.

In order to decrease the potential for pollution and to gain the greatest benefits from fertilizer, whether it's a commercial variety, compost, or other organic materials, apply it when the plants have the greatest need for the nutrients. Plants that are not actively growing do not have a high requirement for nutrients; thus, nutrients applied to dormant plants, or plants growing slowly due to cool temperatures, are more likely to be wasted. While light applications of nitrogen may be recommended for lawns in the fall, generally, nitrogen fertilizers should not be applied to most plants in the fall in regions of the country that experience cold winters. Since nitrogen encourages vegetative growth, if it is applied in the fall it may reduce the plant's ability to harden properly for winter.

In some gardens, you can reduce fertilizer use by applying it around the individual plants rather than broadcasting it across the entire garden. Much of the phosphorus in fertilizer becomes unavailable to the plants once spread on the soil. For better plant uptake, apply the fertilizer in a band near the plant. Do not apply directly to the plant or in contact with the roots, as it may burn and damage the plant and its root system.

A Cheap Way to Fertilize

If you are looking to save money while still providing your lawn and garden with extra nutrients, you can do so by simply mowing your lawn on a regular basis and leaving the grass clippings to decompose on the lawn, or spreading them around your garden to decompose into the soil. Annually, this will provide nutrients equivalent to one or two fertilizer applications and it is a completely organic means of boosting a soil's nutrient content.

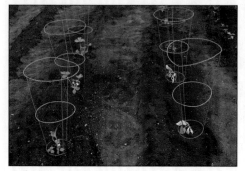

The fertilizer in this garden has only been applied to the garden rows.

Rules of Thumb for Proper Fertilizer Use

It is best to apply fertilizer before or at the time of planting. Fertilizers can either be spread over a large area or confined to garden rows, depending on the condition of your soil and the types of plants you will be growing. After spreading, till the fertilizer into the soil about 3 to 4 inches deep. Only spread about one half of the fertilizer this way and then dispatch the rest 3 inches to the sides of each row and also a little below each seed or established plant. This method, minus the spreader, is used when applying fertilizer to specific rows or plants by hand.

How to Properly Apply Fertilizer to Your Garden

- Apply fertilizer when the soil is moist, and then water lightly. This will help the fertilizer move into the root zone where its nutrients are available to the plants, rather than staying on top of the soil where it can be blown or washed away.
- Watch the weather. Avoid applying fertilizer immediately before a heavy rain system is predicted to arrive. Too much rain (or sprinkler water) will take the nutrients away from the lawn's root zone and could move the fertilizer into another water system, contaminating it.
- Use the minimum amount of fertilizer necessary and apply it in small, frequent applications. An application of two pounds of fertilizer, five times per year, is better than five pounds of fertilizer twice a year.
- If you are spreading the fertilizer by hand in your garden, wear gardening gloves and be sure not to damage the plant or roots around which you are fertilizing.

Composting in Your Backyard

Composting is nature's own way of recycling yard and household wastes by converting them into valuable fertilizer, soil organic matter, and a source of plant nutrients. The result of this controlled decomposition of organic matter—a dark, crumbly, earthy-smelling material—works wonders on all kinds of soil by providing vital nutrients and contributing to good aeration and moisture-holding capacity, to help plants grow and look better.

Composting can be as simple or as involved as you would like, depending on how much yard waste you have, how fast you want results, and the effort you are willing to invest. Since all organic matter eventually decomposes, composting speeds up the process by providing an ideal environment for bacteria and other decomposing microorganisms. The composting season coincides with the growing season, when conditions are favorable for plant growth, so those same conditions work well for biological activity in the compost pile. However, since compost generates heat, the process may continue later into the fall or winter. The final product—called humus or compost—looks and feels like fertile garden soil.

Compost Preparation

While a multitude of organisms, fungi, and bacteria is involved in the overall process, there are four basic ingredients for composting: nitrogen, carbon, water, and air.

A wide range of materials may be composted because anything that was once alive will naturally decompose. The starting materials for composting, commonly referred to as feed stocks, include leaves, grass clippings, straw, vegetable and fruit scraps, coffee grounds, livestock manure, sawdust, and shredded paper. However, some materials that should always be avoided include diseased plants, dead animals, noxious weeds, meat scraps that may attract animals, and dog or cat manure, which can carry disease. Since adding kitchen wastes to compost may attract flies and insects, make a hole in the center of your pile and bury the waste.

Most of your household food waste can be composted. Avoid composting meat scraps, dairy products, grains, or very greasy foods.

Common Composting Materials

Cardboard	Vegetable scraps
Coffee grounds	Weeds without seed heads
Corn cobs	Wood chips
Corn stalks	Woody brush
Food scraps	
Grass clippings	**Avoid using:**
Hedge trimmings	Bread and grains
Livestock manure	Cooking oil
Newspapers	Dairy products
Plant stalks	Dead animals
Pine needles	Diseased plant material
Old potting soil	Dog or cat manure
Sawdust	Grease or oily foods
Seaweed	Meat or fish scraps
Shredded paper	Noxious or invasive
Straw	weeds
Tea bags	Weeds with seed heads
Telephone books	
Tree leaves and twigs	

The calcium in eggshells encourages cell growth in plants. You can even mix crushed eggshells directly into the soil around tomatoes, zucchini, squash, and peppers to prevent blossom end rot. Eggshells also help deter slugs, snails, and cutworm.

For best results, you will want an even ratio of green, or wet, material, which is high in nitrogen, and brown, or dry, material, which is high in carbon. Simply layer or mix landscape trimmings and grass clippings, for example, with dried leaves and twigs in a pile or enclosure. If there is not a good supply of nitrogen-rich material, a handful of general lawn fertilizer or barnyard manure will help even out the ratio.

Though rain provides the moisture, you may need to water the pile in dry weather or cover it in extremely wet weather. The microorganisms in the compost pile function best when the materials are as damp as a wrung-out sponge—not saturated with water. A moisture content of 40 to 60 percent is preferable. To test for adequate moisture, reach into your compost pile, grab a handful of material, and squeeze it. If a few drops of water come out, it probably has enough moisture. If it doesn't, add water by putting a hose into the pile so that you aren't just wetting the top, or, better yet, water the pile as you turn it.

Air is the only part that cannot be added in excess. For proper aeration, you'll need to punch holes in the pile so it has many air passages. The air in the pile is usually used up faster than the moisture, and extremes of sun or rain can adversely affect this balance, so the materials must be turned or mixed up often with a pitchfork, rake, or other garden tool to add air that will sustain high temperatures, control odor, and yield faster decomposition.

Over time, you'll see that the microorganisms, which are small forms of plant and animal life, will break down the organic material. Bacteria are the first to break down plant tissue and are the most numerous and effective compost makers in your compost pile. Fungi and protozoans soon join the bacteria and, later in the cycle, centipedes, millipedes, beetles, sow bugs, nematodes, worms, and numerous others complete the composting process. With the right ingredients and favorable weather conditions, you can have a finished compost pile in a few weeks.

How to Make Your Own Backyard Composting Heap

1. Choose a level, well-drained site, preferably near your garden.
2. Decide whether you will be using a bin after checking on any local or state regulations for composting in urban areas, as some communities require rodent-proof bins. There are numerous styles of compost bins available, depending on your needs, ranging from a moveable bin formed by wire mesh to a more substantial wooden structure consisting of several compartments. You can also easily make your own bin using chicken wire or scrap wood. While a bin will help contain the pile, it is not absolutely necessary, as you can build your pile directly on the ground. To help with aeration, you may want to place some woody material on the ground where you will build your pile.
3. Ensure that your pile will have a minimum dimension of 3 feet all around, but is no taller than 5 feet, as not enough air will reach the microorganisms at the center if it is too tall. If you don't have this amount at one time, simply stockpile your materials until a sufficient quantity is available for proper mixing. When composting is completed, the total volume of the original materials is usually reduced by 30 to 50 percent.
4. Build your pile by using either alternating equal layers of high-carbon and high-nitrogen material or by mixing equal parts of both together and then heaping it into a pile. If you choose to alternate layers, make each layer 2 to 4 inches thick. Some composters find that mixing the two together is more effective than layering. Adding a few shovels of soil will also help get the pile off to a good start because soil adds commonly found, decomposing organisms to your compost.

As your compost begins to break down, you may notice gases escaping from the pile.

Any large bucket can be turned into a compost barrel. You can cut out a piece of the barrel for easy access to the compost, as shown here, or simply access the compost through the lid. Drilling holes in the sides and lids of the bucket will increase air circulation and speed up the process. Leave your bucket in the sun and shake it, roll it, or stir the contents regularly.

5. Keep the pile moist but not wet. Soggy piles encourage the growth of organisms that can live without oxygen and cause unpleasant odors.

6. Punch holes in the sides of the pile for aeration. The pile will heat up and then begin to cool. The most efficient decomposing bacteria thrive in temperatures between 110 and 160°F. You can track this with a compost thermometer, or you can simply reach into the pile to determine if it is uncomfortably hot to the touch. At these temperatures, the pile kills most weed seeds and plant diseases. However, studies have shown that compost produced at these temperatures has less ability to suppress diseases in the soil, since these temperatures may kill some of the beneficial bacteria necessary to suppress disease.

8. Check your bin regularly during the composting season to assure optimum moisture and aeration are present in the material being composted.

9. Move materials from the center to the outside of the pile and vice versa. Turn every day or two and you should get compost in less than four weeks. Turning every other week will make compost in one to three months. Finished compost will smell sweet and be cool and crumbly to the touch.

Other Types of Composting

Cold or Slow Composting

Cold composting allows you to just pile organic material on the ground or in a bin. This method requires no maintenance, but it will take several months to a year or more for the pile to decompose, though the process is faster in warmer climates than in cooler areas. Cold

Grass clippings, weeds, and other plant debris can all be added to your compost pile.

composting works well if you are short on time needed to tend to the compost pile at least every other day, have little yard waste, and are not in a hurry to use the compost.

For this method, add yard waste as it accumulates. To speed up the process, shred or chop the materials by running over small piles of trimmings with your lawn mower, because the more surface area the microorganisms have to feed on, the faster the materials will break down.

Cold composting has been shown to be better at suppressing soil-borne diseases than hot composting and also leaves more non-decomposed bits of material, which can be screened out if desired. However, because of the low temperatures achieved during decomposition, weed seeds and disease-causing organisms may not be destroyed.

Vermicomposting

Vermicomposting uses worms to compost. This takes up very little space and can be done year-round in a basement or garage. It is an excellent way to dispose of kitchen wastes.

Here's how to make your own vermicomposting pile:

1. Obtain a plastic storage bin. One bin measuring 1 foot by 2 feet by 3½ feet will be enough to meet the needs of a family of six.

2. Drill 8 to 10 holes about ¼ inch in diameter in the bottom of the bin for drainage.

3. Line the bottom of the bin with a fine nylon mesh to keep the worms from escaping.

4. Put a tray underneath to catch the drainage.

5. Rip newspaper into pieces to use as bedding and pour water over the strips until they are thoroughly moist. Place these shredded bits on one side of your bin. Do not let them dry out.

6. Add worms to your bin. It's best to have about two pounds of worms (roughly 2,000 worms) per one pound of food waste. You may want to start with less food waste and increase the amount as your

Worms will filter your organic waste through their systems and turn it into nutrient-rich humus.

worm population grows. Redworms are recommended for best composting, but other species can be used. Redworms are the common, small worms found in most gardens and lawns. You can collect them from under a pile of mulch or order them from a garden catalog.

7. Provide worms with food wastes such as vegetable peelings. Do not add fat or meat products. Limit their feed, as too much at once may cause the material to rot.

8. Keep the bin in a dark location away from extreme temperatures.

9. Wait about three months and you'll see that the worms have changed the bedding and food wastes into compost. At this time, open your bin in a bright light and the worms will burrow into the bedding. Add fresh bedding and more food to the other side of the bin. The worms should migrate to the new food supply.

10. Scoop out the finished compost and apply to your plants or save to use in the spring.

Uses for Compost

Compost contains nutrients, but it is not a substitute for fertilizers. Compost holds nutrients in the soil until plants can use them, loosens and aerates clay soils, and retains water in sandy soils.

To use as a soil amendment, mix 2 to 5 inches of compost into vegetable and flower gardens each year before planting. In a potting mixture, add one part compost to two parts commercial potting soil, or make your own mixture by using equal parts of compost and sand, or Perlite.

As a mulch, spread an inch or two of compost around annual flowers and vegetables, and up to 6 inches around trees and shrubs. Studies have shown that compost used as mulch, or mixed with the top 1-inch layer of soil, can help prevent some plant diseases, including some of those that cause damping of seedlings.

As a top dressing, mix finely sifted compost with sand and sprinkle evenly over lawns.

Common Problems

Composting is not an exact science. Experience will tell you what works best for you. If you notice that nothing is happening, you may need to add more nitrogen, water, or air, chip or grind the materials, or adjust the size of the pile.

If the pile is too hot, you probably have too much nitrogen and need to add additional carbon materials to reduce the heating.

A bad smell may indicate not enough air or too much moisture. Simply turn the pile or add dry materials to the wet pile to get rid of the odor.

Planting Your Garden

Once you've chosen a spot for your garden (as well as the size you want to make your garden bed), and prepared the soil with compost or other fertilizer, it's time to start planting. Seeds are very inexpensive at your local garden center, or you can browse through seed catalogs and order seeds that will do well in your area. Alternately, you can start with bedding plants (or seedlings) available at nurseries and garden centers.

Read the instructions on the back of the seed package or on the plastic tag in your plant pot. You may have to ask experts when to plant the seeds if this information is not stated on the back of the package. Some seeds (such as tomatoes) should be started indoors, in small pots or seed trays, before the last frost, and only transplanted outdoors when the weather warms up. For established plants or seedlings, be sure to plant as directed on the plant tag or consult your local nursery about the best planting times.

Some plugs are biodegradable so that you can insert them directly into the garden bed, rather than having to transplant them.

Seedlings

If you live in a cooler region with a shorter growing period, you will want to start some of your plants indoors. To do this, obtain plug flats (trays separated into many small cups or "cells") or make your own small planters by poking holes in the bottom of paper cups. Fill the cups two-thirds full with potting soil or composted soil. Bury the seed at the recommended depth, according to the instructions on the package. Tamp down the soil lightly and water. Keep the seedlings in a warm, well-lit place, such as the kitchen, to encourage germination.

Once the weather begins to warm up and you are fairly certain you won't be getting any more frosts (you can contact your local extension office to find out the last "frost free" date for your area) you can begin to acclimate your seedlings to the great outdoors. First place them in a partially shady spot outdoors that is protected from strong wind. After a couple of days, move them into direct sunlight, and then finally transplant them to the garden.

Recommended plants to start as seedlings

Crop [s] small seed [l] large seed (planting cell size)	Weeks before transplanting	Seed planting depth (inches)	Transplant spacing	
			Within row	between row
Broccoli [s]	(1)	4-6	1/4-1/2	8-10" 18-24"
Cabbage [s]	(1)	4-6	1/4-1/2	18-24" 30"
Cucumber [l]	(2)	4-5	1/2	2' 5-6'
Eggplant [s]	(2)	8	1/4	18" 18-24"
Herbs [s]	(1)	4	1/4	4-6" 12-18"
Lettuce [s]	(2)	4-5	1/4	12" 12"
Melon [l]	(3)	4-5	1/4	2-3' 6'
Onion [s]	(*)	8	1/4	4" 12"
Pepper [s]	(2)	8	1/4	12-18" 2-3'
Pumpkin [l]	(3)	2-4	1	5-6' 5-6'
Summer squash [l]	(3)	2-4	3/4-1	18" 2-3'
Tomato [s]	(3)	8	1/4	18"-24" 3'
Watermelon [l]	(3)	4-5	1/2-3/4	3-4' 3-4'
Winter squash [l]	(3)	2-4	1	3-4' 4-5'

Seeds can be sprouted and eaten on sandwiches, salads, or stirfries any time of the year. They are delicious and full of vitamins and proteins. Mung bean, soybean, alfalfa, wheat, corn, barley, mustard, clover, chickpeas, radish, and lentils all make good sprouts. Find seeds for sprouting from your local health food store or use dried peas, beans, or lentils from the grocery store. Never use seeds intended for planting unless you've harvested the seeds yourself—commercially available planting seeds are often treated with a poisonous chemical fungicide.

To grow sprouts, thoroughly rinse and strain the seeds, then soak overnight in cool water. You'll need about four times as much water as you have seeds. Drain the seeds and place them in a wide-mouthed bowl or on a cookie sheet with a lip. Sprinkle with water to keep the seeds slightly damp. You may wish to place the seeds on a damp paper towel to better hold in the moisture. Keep the seeds at 60 to 80°F and rinse twice a day, returning them to their bowl or tray after. Once sprouts are 1 to 1 ½ inches long (generally after 3 to 5 days), they are ready to eat.

Radish sprouts are delicious on their own or in sandwiches or salads

You can grow seedlings in any wood, metal, or plastic container that is at least 3 inches deep. Egg cartons work very well if you don't have access to regular plug flats. Just punch holes in the bottom for drainage.

How to Best Water Your Soil

After your seeds or seedlings are planted, the next step is to water your soil. Different soil types have different watering needs. You don't need to be a soil scientist to know how to water your soil properly. Here are some tips that can help to make your soil moist and primed for gardening:

1. Loosen the soil around plants so water and nutrients can be quickly absorbed.

2. Use a 1- to 2-inch protective layer of mulch on the soil surface above the root area. Cultivating and mulching help reduce evaporation and soil erosion.

3. Water your plants at the appropriate time of day. Early morning or night is the best time for watering, as evaporation is less likely to occur at these times. Do not water your plants when it is extremely windy outside. Wind will prevent the water from reaching the soil where you want it to go.

A gentle spray will soak into the soil without damaging the plants. The thin layer of mulch will help to keep the water from evaporating too quickly.

Types of Soil and Their Water Retention

Knowing the type of soil you are planting in will help you best understand how to properly water and grow your garden plants. Three common types of soil and their various abilities to absorb water are listed below:

Clay soil: In order to make this type of soil more loamy, add organic materials, such as compost, peat moss, and well-rotted leaves, in the spring before growing and also in the fall after harvesting your vegetables and fruits. Adding these organic materials allows this type of soil to hold more nutrients for healthy plant growth. Till or spade to help loosen the soil.

Since clay soil absorbs water very slowly, water only as fast as the soil can absorb the water.

Sandy soil: As with clay soil, adding organic materials in the spring and fall will help supplement the sandy soil and promote better plant growth and water absorption.

Left on its own (with no added organic matter) the water will run through sandy soil so quickly that plants won't be able to absorb it through their roots and will fail to grow and thrive.

Loam soil: This is the best kind of soil for gardening. It's a combination of sand, silt, and clay. Loamy soil is fertile, deep, easily crumbles, and is made up of organic matter. It will help promote the growth of quality fruits and vegetables, as well as flowers and other plants.

Loam absorbs water readily and stores it for plants to use. Water as frequently as the soil needs to maintain its moisture and to promote plant growth.

Sandy soil is usually lighter in color and won't easily clump together in your hands. It needs organic matter and plenty of water to be suitable for growing.

A good old-fashioned watering can is great for small gardens and potted plants.

Conserving Water

Wise use of water for hydrating your garden and lawn not only helps protect the environment, but saves money and also provides optimum growing conditions for your plants. There are simple ways of reducing the amount of water used for irrigation, such as growing xeriphytic species (plants that are adapted to dry conditions), mulching, adding water-retaining organic matter to the soil, and installing windbreaks and fences to slow winds and reduce evapotranspiration.

You can conserve water by watering your plants and lawn in the early morning, before the sun is too intense. This helps reduce the amount of water lost due to evaporation. Furthermore, installing rain gutters and collecting water from downspouts—in collection bins such as rain barrels—also helps reduce water use.

How Plants Use Water

Water is a critical component of photosynthesis, the process by which plants manufacture their own food from carbon dioxide and water in the presence of light. Water is one of the many factors that can limit plant growth. Other important factors include nutrients, temperature, and amount and duration of sunlight.

Plants take in carbon dioxide through their stomata—microscopic openings on the undersides of the leaves. The stomata are also the place where water is lost, in a process called transpiration. Transpiration, along with evaporation from the soil's surface, accounts for most of the moisture lost from the soil and subsequently from the plants.

When there is a lack of water in the plant tissue, the stomata close to try to limit excessive water loss. If the tissues lose too much water, the plant will wilt. Plants adapted to dry conditions have developed certain characteristics that support numerous mechanisms for reducing water loss—they typically have narrow, hairy leaves and thick, fleshy stems and leaves. Pines, hemlocks, and junipers are also well-adapted to survive extended periods of dry conditions—an environmental factor they encounter each winter when the frozen soil prevents the uptake of water. Cacti, which have thick stems and leaves reduced to spines, are the best example of plants well-adapted to extremely dry environments.

Even very dry areas can be made attractive with tasteful placement of grasses, yarrow, and similar plants.

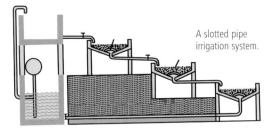

A slotted pipe irrigation system.

Heath flowers are well-adapted to dry environments and make a very attractive ground cover.

Choosing Plants for Low Water Use

You are not limited to cacti, succulents, or narrow-leafed evergreens when selecting plants adapted to low water requirements. Many plants growing in humid environments are well-adapted to low levels of soil moisture. Numerous plants found growing in coastal or mountainous regions have developed mechanisms for dealing with extremely sandy, excessively well-drained soils or rocky, cold soils in which moisture is limited for months at a time. Try alfalfa, aloe, artichokes, asparagus, blue hibiscus, chives, columbine, eucalyptus, garlic, germander, lamb's ear, lavender, ornamental grasses, prairie turnip, rosemary, sage, sedum, shrub roses, thyme, yarrow, yucca, and verbena.

Installing Irrigation Systems

An irrigation system can be easy to install, and there are many different products available for home irrigation systems. The simplest system consists of a soaker hose that is laid out around the plants and connected to an outdoor spigot. No installation is required, and the hose can be moved as needed to water the entire garden.

A slightly more sophisticated system is a slotted pipe system. Here are the steps needed in order to install this type of irrigation system in your garden:

1. Sketch the layout of your garden so you know what materials you will need. If you intend to water a vegetable garden, you may want one pipe next to every row or one pipe between every two rows.
2. Depending on the layout and type of garden, purchase the required lengths of pipe. You will need a length of solid pipe for the width of your garden, and perforated pipes that are the length of your lateral rows (and remember to buy one pipe for each row or two).
3. Measure the distances between rows and cut the solid pipe to the proper lengths.
4. Place T-connectors between the pieces of solid pipe.
5. In the approximate center of the solid pipe, place a T-connector to which a hose connector will be fitted.

Trickle Irrigation Systems

Trickle irrigation and drip irrigation systems help reduce water use and successfully meet the needs of most plants. With these systems, very small amounts of water are supplied to the bases of the plants. Since the water is applied directly to the soil—rather than onto the plant—evaporation from the leaf surfaces is reduced, thus allowing more water to effectively reach the roots. In these types of systems, the water is not wasted by being spread all over the garden; rather, it is applied directly to the appropriate source.

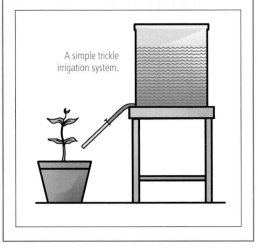

A simple trickle irrigation system.

6. Cut the perforated pipe to the length of the rows.
7. Attach the perforated pipes to the T-connectors so that the perforations are facing downward. Cap the end of the pipe.
8. Connect a garden hose to the hose connector on the solid pipe. Adjust the pressure of the water flowing from the spigot until the water slowly emerges from each of the perforated pipes.

Rain Barrels

Another very efficient and easy way to conserve water—and save money—is to buy or make your own rain barrel. A rain barrel is a large bin that is placed beneath a downspout and that collects rainwater runoff from a roof. The water collected in the rain barrel can then be routed through a garden hose and used to water your garden and lawn.

Rain barrels can be purchased from specialty home and garden stores, but a simple rain barrel is also quite easy to make. Here are simple instructions on how to make your own rain barrel.

Instructions

1. Obtain a suitable plastic barrel, a large plastic trashcan with a lid, or a wooden barrel (e.g., a wine barrel) that has not been stored dry for too many seasons, since it can start to leak. Good places to find plastic barrels include suppliers of dairy products, metal plating companies, and bulk food suppliers. Just be sure that nothing toxic or harmful to plants and animals (including you!) was stored in the barrel. A wine barrel can be obtained through a winery. Barrels that allow less light to penetrate through will eliminate the risk of algae growth and the establishment of other microorganisms.

2. Once you have your barrel, find a location for it under or near one of your home's downspouts. In order for the barrel to fit, you will probably need to shorten the downspout by a few feet. You can do this by removing the screws or rivets located at a joint of the downspout, or by simply cutting off the last few feet with a hacksaw or other cutter. If your barrel will not be able to fit underneath the downspout, you can purchase a flexible downspout at your local home improvement store. These flexible tubes will direct the water from the downspout into the barrel. An alternative, and aesthetically appealing, option is to use a rain chain—a large, metal chain that water can run down.

3. Create a level, stable platform for your rain barrel to sit on by raking the dirt under the spout, adding gravel to smooth out lawn bumps, or using bricks or concrete blocks to make a low platform. Keep in mind that a barrel full of water is very heavy, so if you decide to build a platform, make sure it is sturdy enough to hold such heavy weight.

4. If your barrel has a solid top, you'll need to make a good-sized hole in it for the downspout to pour into. You can do this using a hole-cutting attachment on a power drill or by drilling a series of smaller holes close together and then cutting out the remaining material with a hacksaw blade or a scroll saw.

5. Mosquitoes are drawn to standing water, so to reduce the risk of breeding these insects, and to also keep debris from entering the barrel, fasten a piece of window screen to the underside of the top so it covers the entire hole.

6. Next, drill a hole so the hose bib you'll attach to the side of the barrel fits snugly. Place the hose bib as close to the bottom of the barrel as possible, so you'll be able to gain access to the maximum amount of water in the barrel. Attach the hose bib using screws driven into the barrel. You'll probably need to apply some caulking, plumber's putty, or silicon sealant around the joint between the barrel and the hose bib to prevent leaks, depending on the type of hardware you're using and how snug it fits in the hole you drilled.

7. Attach a second hose bib to the side of the barrel near the top, to act as an overflow drain. Attach a short piece of garden hose to this hose bib and route it to a flowerbed, lawn, or another nearby area that won't be damaged by some running water if your barrel gets too full (or, if you want to have a second rain barrel for excess water, you can attach it to another hose bib on a second barrel. If you are chaining multiple barrels together, one of them should have a hose attached to drain off the overflow.

8. Attach a garden hose to the lower hose bib and open the valve to allow collected rain water to flow to your plants. The lower bib can also be used to connect multiple rain barrels together for a larger water reservoir.

9. Consider using a drip irrigation system in conjunction with the rain barrels. Rain barrels don't achieve anything near the pressure of city water supplies, so you won't be able to use microsprinkler attachments, and you will need to use button attachments that are intended to deliver four times the amount of city-supplied water you need.

10. Now, wait for a heavy downpour and start enjoying your rain barrel!

Rain barrels can be made from any large bucket. It is especially convenient to have a spigot coming from the bottom of the bucket so you can fill smaller containers with water as needed.

Mary Maddox and her husband and children maintain a full vegetable garden and raise chickens, ducks, turkeys, and a goose on less than half an acre of land. They describe their experiences and share tips on their blog, "The Yardstead," www.yardstead.com.

My husband, children, and I live in a small town in North Florida. Like most of our neighbors we live on a little less than ½ acre lot. We dream of becoming homesteaders on 10 to 15 acres but until that dream becomes reality, we do what we can on our small plot. We currently maintain a 30 ft. x 30 ft. vegetable garden, and keep chickens, ducks, turkeys, and a goose. These birds only require 3-4 sq. ft. per bird and are easy to care for in an appropriate size pen.

We keep between 10 and 20 chickens most of the time in a 72 sq. ft. pen, with an adjoining 200 sq. ft. pen for a few ducks, turkeys, and a goose. We supply our family, friends, and neighbors with fresh eggs year round and put a few chickens in the freezer as well. We recently were given a rooster by one of our neighbors and our hens have hatched their first babies this spring.

We try to keep something growing in the garden all year round. Each year we are able to grow enough squash and zucchini to eat fresh all spring and summer and put enough up in the freezer to last through the winter. We also grow enough onions and garlic most years to meet all our needs and share with our friends and family. We dabble in other vegetables and grow a variety of gourds on our fence line each year.

We have landscaped the yard with mostly edible plants and trees. Our backyard shade is provided by a pecan, mulberry, persimmon, and other trees. We have chosen some native shrubs, like the pineapple guava, that also produces edible flowers and fruit. We keep several dwarf citrus as potted plants that can be moved in and out of the house depending on our winter temperatures each year. Last fall we planted a few small canes of sugar cane. These clumps of sugar cane will be mostly for our children to enjoy in late summer each year.

We try to garden and care for our animals and yard with an emphasis on permaculture and we follow organic practices as much as possible. All of the yard waste and food waste we produce go first to the chickens and other birds who love to eat table scraps as well as grass

How to Make a Simple Rain Barrel

Things You'll Need

- A clean, plastic barrel, tall trash can with lid, or a wooden barrel that does not leak—a 55 gallon plastic drum or barrel does a very good job at holding rainwater
- Two hose bibs (a valve with a fitting for a garden hose on one end and a flange with a short pipe sticking out of it at the other end)
- Garden hose
- Plywood and paint (if your barrel doesn't already have a top)
- Window screen
- Wood screws
- Vegetable oil
- A drill
- A hacksaw
- A screwdriver

clippings and the like. They eat what they like and the leftovers along with the rich droppings are raked out occasionally and added to the compost pile. This provides us a constant supply of rich compost, which is the fertilizer we use in the garden. We also let some chickens roam the garden after the plants have grown to an 8-10 in. height. They do an excellent job of keeping the garden pest free by eating every bug they can find.

We love teaching our children about gardening and caring for animals and we all enjoy a healthy sense of self-reliance. We share our produce as much as possible and also try to share as much knowledge as possible with anyone who is interested.

Things to Consider

- Put some water in the barrel from a garden hose once everything is in place and any sealants have had time to thoroughly dry. The first good downpour is *not* the time to find out there's a leak in your barrel.
- If you don't own the property on which you are thinking of installing a rain barrel, be sure to get permission before altering the downspouts.
- If your barrel doesn't already have a solid top, cover it securely with a circle of painted plywood, an old trashcan lid screwed to the walls of the barrel, or a heavy tarp secured over the top of the barrel with bungee cords. This will protect children and small animals from falling into the barrel and drowning.
- As stated before, stagnant water is an excellent breeding ground for mosquitoes, so it would be a good idea to take additional steps to keep them out of your barrel by sealing all the openings into the barrel with caulk or putty. You might also consider adding enough non-toxic oil (such as vegetable cooking oil) to the barrel to form a film on top of the water that will prevent mosquito larvae from hatching.

Always double check to make sure the barrel you're using (particularly if it is from a food distribution center or other recycled source) did not contain pesticides, industrial chemicals, weed killers, or other toxins or biological materials that could be harmful to you, your plants, or the environment. If you are concerned about this, it is best to purchase a new barrel or trashcan so there is no doubt about its safety.

Mulching in Your Garden and Yard

Mulching is one of the simplest and most beneficial practices you can use in your garden. Mulch is simply a protective layer of material that is spread on top of the soil to enrich the soil, prevent weed growth, and help provide a better growing environment for your garden plants and flowers.

Mulches can either be organic—such as grass clippings, bark chips, compost, ground corncobs, chopped cornstalks, leaves, manure, newspaper, peanut shells, peat moss, pine needles, sawdust, straw, and wood shavings—or inorganic—such as stones, brick chips, and plastic. Both organic and inorganic mulches have numerous benefits, including:

1. Protecting the soil from erosion
2. Reducing compaction from the impact of heavy rains
3. Conserving moisture, thus reducing the need for frequent watering
4. Maintaining a more even soil temperature
5. Preventing weed growth
6. Keeping fruits and vegetables clean
7. Keeping feet clean and allowing access to the garden even when it's damp
8. Providing a "finished" look to the garden

Organic mulches also have the benefit of improving the condition of the soil. As these mulches slowly decompose, they provide organic matter to help keep the soil loose. This improves root growth, increases the infiltration of water, improves the water-holding capacity of the soil, provides a source of plant nutrients, and establishes an ideal environment for earthworms and other beneficial soil organisms.

While inorganic mulches have their place in certain landscapes, they lack the soil-improving properties of organic mulches. Inorganic mulches, because of their permanence, may be difficult to remove if you decide to change your garden plans at a later date.

Wood chips or shavings are some of the most common forms of mulch.

Where to Find Mulch Materials

You can find mulch materials right in your own backyard. They include:

1. Lawn clippings. They make an excellent mulch in the vegetable garden if spread immediately to avoid heating and rotting. The fine texture allows them to be spread easily, even around small plants.
2. Newspaper. As a mulch, newspaper works especially well to control weeds. Save your own newspapers and only use the text pages, or those with black ink, as color dyes may be harmful to soil microflora and fauna if composted and used. Use three or four sheets together, anchored with grass clippings or other mulch material to prevent them from blowing away.
3. Leaves. Leaf mold, or the decomposed remains of leaves, gives the forest floor its absorbent, spongy structure. Collect leaves in the fall and chop with a lawnmower or shredder. Compost leaves over winter, as some studies have indicated that freshly chopped leaves may inhibit the growth of certain crops.
4. Compost. The mixture makes wonderful mulch—if you have a large supply—as it not only improves the soil structure but also provides an excellent source of plant nutrients.
5. Bark chips and composted bark mulch. These materials are available at garden centers and are

A trowel and hand fork are helpful for mulching small areas around and between plants.

sometimes used with landscape fabric or plastic that is spread atop the soil and beneath the mulch to provide additional protection against weeds. However, the barrier between the soil and the mulch also prevents any improvement in the soil condition and makes planting additional plants more difficult. Without the barrier, bark mulch makes a neat finish to the garden bed and will eventually improve the condition of the soil. It may last for one to three years or more, depending on the size of the chips or how well-composted the bark mulch is. Smaller chips are easier to spread, especially around small plants.

6. Hay and straw. These work well in the vegetable garden, although they may harbor weed seeds.
7. Seaweed mulch, ground corncobs, and pine needles. Depending on where you live, these materials may be readily available and can also be used as mulch. However, pine needles tend to increase the acidity of the soil, so they work best around acid-loving plants, such as rhododendrons and blueberries.

When choosing a mulch material, think of your primary objective. Newspaper and grass clippings are great for weed control, while bark mulch gives a perfect, finishing touch to a front-yard perennial garden. If you're looking for a cheap solution, consider using materials found in your own yard or see if your community offers chipped wood or compost to its residents.

If you want the mulch to stay in place for several years around shrubs, for example, you might want to consider using inorganic mulches. While they will not provide organic matter to the soil, they will be more or less permanent.

Mulch can be neat and attractive, especially if kept from spilling into your yard with a row or circle of stones.

Common Organic Mulching Materials

Bark chips	Chopped cornstalks
Compost	Grass clippings
Ground corncobs	Hay
Leaves	Manure
Newspaper	Peanut shells
Peat moss	Pine needles
Sawdust	Straw
Wood shavings	

Hay and straw make excellent, inexpensive mulch.

General Mulching Guidelines

Mulch is measured in cubic feet, so, for example, if you have an area measuring 10 feet by 10 feet, and you wish to apply 3 inches (1/4 foot) of mulch, you would need 25 cubic feet to do the job correctly.

While some mulch can come from recycled material in your own yard, it can also be purchased bagged or in bulk from a garden center. Buying in bulk may be cheaper if you need a large volume and have a way to haul it. Bagged mulch is often easier to handle, especially for smaller projects, as most bagged mulch comes in 3-cubic-foot bags.

To start, remove any weeds. Begin mulching by spreading the materials in your garden, being careful not to apply mulch to the plants themselves. Leave an inch or so of space next to the plants to help prevent diseases from flourishing in times of excess humidity.

When to Apply Mulch

Time of application depends on what you hope to achieve by mulching. Mulches, by providing an insulating barrier between the soil and the air, moderate the soil temperature. This means that a mulched soil in the summer will be cooler than an adjacent, unmulched soil; while in the winter, the mulched soil may not freeze as deeply. However, since mulch acts as an insulating layer, mulched soils tend to warm up more slowly in the spring and cool down more slowly in the fall than unmulched soils.

If you are using mulches in your vegetable or flower garden, it is best to apply or add additional mulch after the soil has warmed up in the spring. Organic mulches reduce the soil temperature by 8 to 10°F during the summer, so if they are applied to cold garden soils, the soil will warm up more slowly and plant maturity will be delayed.

Mulches used to help moderate winter temperatures can be applied late in the fall after the ground has frozen, but before the coldest temperatures arrive. Applying mulches before the ground has frozen may attract rodents looking for a warm over-wintering site. Delayed applications of mulch should prevent this problem.

Mulches used to protect plants over the winter should be composed of loose material, such as straw, hay, or pine boughs that will help insulate the plants without compacting under the weight of snow and ice. One of the benefits from winter applications of mulch is the reduction in the freezing and thawing of the soil in the late winter and early spring. These repeated cycles of freezing at night and then thawing in the warmth of the sun cause many small or shallow-rooted plants to be heaved out

of the soil. This leaves their root systems exposed and results in injury, or death, of the plant. Mulching helps prevent these rapid fluctuations in soil temperature and reduces the chances of heaving.

How Much Do I Apply?

The amount of mulch to apply to your garden depends on the mulching material used. Spread bark mulch and wood chips 2 to 4 inches deep, keeping it an inch or two away from tree trunks.

Scatter chopped and composted leaves 3 to 4 inches deep. If using dry leaves, apply about 6 inches.

Grass clippings, if spread too thick, tend to compact and rot, becoming quite slimy and smelly. They should be applied 2 to 3 inches deep, and additional layers should be added as clippings decompose. Make sure not to use clippings from lawns treated with herbicides.

Sheets of newspaper should only be ¼ inch thick and covered lightly with grass clippings or other mulch material to anchor them. If other mulch materials are not available, cover the edges of the newspaper with soil.

If using compost, apply 3 to 4 inches deep, as it's an excellent material for enriching the soil.

Gather fallen leaves in the fall and compost them or use them in large plastic bags as extra house insulation over the winter. Come spring, the decomposed leaves will be ready for mulch.

Organic Gardening

"Organically grown" food is food grown and processed using no synthetic fertilizers or pesticides. Pesticides derived from natural sources (such as biological pesticides—compost and manure) may be used in producing organically grown food.

Organic gardeners grow the healthiest, highest quality foods and flowers—all without the addition of chemical fertilizers, pesticides, or herbicides. Organic gardening methods are healthier, environmentally friendly, safe for animals and humans, and are typically less expensive, since you are working with natural materials. It is easy to grow and harvest organic foods in your backyard garden and typically, organic gardens are easier to maintain than gardens that rely on chemical and unnatural components to help them grow effectively.

Organic production is not simply the avoidance of conventional chemical inputs, nor is it the substitution of natural inputs for synthetic ones. Organic farmers apply techniques first used thousands of years ago, such as crop rotations and the use of composted animal manures and green manure crops, in ways that are economically sustainable in today's world.

Organic farming entails:

- Use of cover crops, green manures, animal manures, and crop rotations to fertilize the soil, maximize biological activity, and maintain long-term soil health.
- Use of biological control, crop rotations, and other techniques to manage weeds, insects, and diseases.
- An emphasis on biodiversity of the agricultural system and the surrounding environment.
- Reduction of external and off-farm inputs and elimination of synthetic pesticides and fertilizers and other materials, such as hormones and antibiotics.
- A focus on renewable resources, soil and water conservation, and management practices that restore, maintain, and enhance ecological balance.

How to Start Your Own Organic Garden

Step One: Choose a Site for Your Garden

1. Think small, at least at first. A small garden takes less work and materials than a large one. If done well, a 4 x 4-foot garden will yield enough vegetables and fruit for you and your family to enjoy.

2. Be careful not to over-plant your garden. You do not want to end up with too many vegetables that will end up over-ripening or rotting in your garden.

3. You can even start a garden in a window box if you are unsure of your time and dedication to a larger bed.

Step Two: Make a Compost Pile

1. Compost is the main ingredient for creating and maintaining rich, fertile soil. You can use most organic materials to make compost that will provide your soil with essential nutrients. To start a compost pile, all you need are fallen leaves, weeds, grass clippings, and other vegetation that is in your yard. (See the Compost chapter for more details on how to make compost.)

Step Three: Add Soil

1. In order to have a thriving organic garden, you must have excellent soil. Adding organic material (such as that in your compost pile) to your existing soil will only make it better. Soil containing copious amounts of organic material is very good for your garden. Organically rich soil:

- Nourishes your plants without any chemicals, keeping them natural
- Is easy to use when planting seeds or seedlings, and it also allows for weeds to be more easily picked
- Is softer than chemically treated soil, so the roots of your plants can spread and grow deeper
- Helps water and air find the roots

Step Four: Weed Control

1. Weeds are invasive to your garden plants and thus must be removed in order for your organic garden to grow efficiently. Common weeds that can invade your garden are ivy, mint, and dandelions.

2. Using a sharp hoe, go over each area of exposed soil frequently to keep weeds from sprouting. Also, plucking off the green portions of weeds will deprive them of the nutrients they need to survive.

3. Gently pull out weeds by hand to remove their root systems and to stop continued growth. Be careful when weeding around established plants so you don't uproot them as well.

4. Mulch unplanted areas of your garden so that weeds will be less likely to grow. You can find organic mulches, such as wood chips and grass clippings, at your local garden store. These mulches will not only discourage weed growth but will also eventually break down and help enrich the soil. Mulching also helps regulate soil

Your garden can be as small or large as your space allows, but be sure to start with a size you can manage.

A row of lettuce thrives in the compost-fertilized soil.

temperatures and helps in conserving water by decreasing evaporation. (See the "Mulch" chapter for more on mulching.)

Step Five: Be Careful of Lawn Fertilizers

If you have a lawn and your organic garden is situated in it, be mindful that any chemicals you might place on your lawn may find their way into your organic garden. Therefore, refrain from fertilizing your lawn with chemicals and, if you wish to return nutrients to your grass, simply let your cut grass clippings remain in the yard to decompose naturally and enrich the soil beneath.

Things to Consider

- "Organic" means that you don't use any kinds of materials, such as paper or cardboard, that contain chemicals, and especially not fertilizer or pesticides. Make sure that these products do not find their way into your garden or compost pile.
- If you are adding grass clippings to your compost pile, make sure they don't come from a lawn that has been treated with chemical fertilizer.
- If you don't want to start a compost pile, simply add leaves and grass clippings directly to your garden bed. This will act like a mulch, deter weeds from growing, and will eventually break down to help return nutrients to your soil.
- If you find insects attacking your plants, the best way to control them is by picking them off by hand. Also practice crop rotation (planting different types of plants in a given area from year to year), which might reduce your pest problem. For some insects, just a strong stream of water is effective in removing them from your plants.
- Shy away from using bark mulch. It robs nitrogen from the soil as it decomposes and can also attract termites.

A hand fork can be useful in digging up tough roots of pesky weeds.

Terracing

Terraces can create several mini-gardens in your backyard. On steep slopes, terracing can make planting a garden possible. Terraces also prevent erosion by shortening a long slope into a series of shorter, more level steps. This allows heavy rains to soak into the soil rather than to run off and cause erosion and poor plant growth.

Materials Needed for Terraces

Numerous materials are available for building terraces. Treated wood is often used in terrace building and has several advantages: It is easy to work with, it blends well with plants and the surrounding environment, and it is often less expensive than other materials. There are many types of treated wood available for terracing—railroad ties and landscaping timbers are just two examples. These materials will last for years, which is crucial if you are hoping to keep your terraced garden intact for any length of time. There has been some concern about using these treated materials around plants, but studies by Texas A&M University and the Southwest Research Institute concluded that these materials are not harmful to gardens or people when used as recommended.

Other materials for terraces include bricks, rocks, concrete blocks, and similar masonry materials. Some masonry materials are made specifically for walls and terraces and can be more easily installed by a homeowner than other materials. These include fieldstone and brick. One drawback is that most stone or masonry products tend to be more expensive than wood, so if you are looking to save money, treated wood will make a sufficient terrace wall.

Terraces help prevent erosion and encourage vegetation on sloped ground.

How High Should the Terrace Walls Be?

The steepness of the slope on which you wish to garden often dictates the appropriate height of the terrace wall. Make the terraces in your yard high enough so the land between them is fairly level. Be sure the terrace material is strong enough and anchored well to stay in place through freezing and thawing, and during heavy rainstorms. Do not underestimate the pressure of waterlogged soil behind a wall—it can be enormous and will cause improperly constructed walls to bulge or collapse.

Many communities have building codes for walls and terraces. Large projects will most likely need the expertise of a professional landscaper to make sure the walls can stand up to water pressure in the soil. Large terraces also need to be built with adequate drainage and tied back into the slope properly. Because of the expertise and equipment required to do this correctly, you will probably want to restrict terraces you build on your own to no more than a foot or two high.

Building Your Own Terrace

The safest way to build a terrace is by using the cut and fill method. With this method, little soil is disturbed, giving you protection from erosion should a sudden storm occur while the work is in progress. This method will also require little, if any, additional soil. Here are the steps needed to build your own terrace:

1. Contact your utility companies to identify the location of any buried utility lines and pipes before starting to dig.
2. Determine the rise and run of your slope. The rise is the vertical distance from the bottom of the slope to the top. The run is the horizontal distance between the top and the bottom. This will allow you to determine how many terraces you will need. For example, if your run is 20 feet and the rise is 8 feet, and you want each bed to be 5 feet wide, you will need four beds. The rise of each bed will be 2 feet.
3. Start building the beds at the bottom of your slope. You will need to dig a trench in which to place your first tier. The depth and width of the trench will vary depending on how tall the terrace will be and the specific building materials you are using. Follow the manufacturer's instructions carefully when using masonry products, as many of these have limits on the number of tiers or the height that can be safely built. If you are using landscape timbers and your terrace is low (less than 2 feet), you only need to bury the timber to about half its thickness or less. The width of the trench should be slightly wider than your timber. Make sure the bottom of the trench is firmly packed and completely level, and then place your timbers into the trench.
4. For the sides of your terrace, dig a trench into the slope. The bottom of this trench must be level with the bottom of the first trench. When the depth of the trench is one inch greater than the thickness of your timber, you have reached the back of the terrace and can stop digging.
5. Cut a piece of timber to the correct length and place it into the trench.
6. Drill holes through your timbers and pound long spikes, or pipes, through the holes and into the ground. A minimum of 18 inches of pipe length is recommended, and longer pipes may be needed in higher terraces for added stability.
7. Place the next tier of timbers on top of the first, overlapping the corners and joints. Pound a spike through both tiers to fuse them together.
8. Move the soil from the back of the bed to the front of the bed until the surface is level. Add another tier as needed.

Neat rows of green plants line this terraced hill, which would otherwise likely be barren.

Heather grows wild in many areas but can also be planted on your hillsides to help prevent erosion.

9. Repeat, starting with step 2, to create the remaining terraces. In continuously connected terrace systems, the first timber of the second tier will also be the back wall of your first terrace.
10. The back wall of the last bed will be level with its front wall.
11. When finished, you can start to plant and mulch your terraced garden.

Other Ways to Make Use of Slopes in Your Yard

If terraces are beyond the limits of your time or money, you may want to consider other options for backyard slopes. If you have a slope that is hard to mow, consider using groundcovers on the slope rather than grass. There are many plants adapted to a wide range of light and moisture conditions that require little care (and do not need mowing) and provide soil erosion protection. These include:

- Juniper
- Wintercreeper
- Periwinkle
- Cotoneaster
- Potentilla
- Heathers and heaths

Strip-cropping is another way to deal with long slopes in your yard. Rather than terracing to make garden beds level, plant perennial beds and strips of grass across the slope. Once established, many perennials are effective in reducing erosion. Adding mulch also helps reduce erosion. If erosion does occur, it will be basically limited to the gardened area. The grass strips will act as filters to catch much of the soil that may run off the beds. Grass strips should be wide enough to mow easily, as well as wide enough to reduce erosion effectively.

Periwinkles require little maintenance, spread quickly, and will grow easily on a slope in your yard.

Start Your Own Vegetable Garden

If you want to start your own vegetable garden, just follow these simple steps and you'll be on your way to growing your own yummy vegetables—right in your own backyard.

Steps to Making Your Own Vegetable Garden

1 Select a site for your garden.
   - Vegetables grow best in well-drained, fertile soil (loamy soils are the best).
   - Some vegetables can cope with shady conditions, but most prefer a site with a good amount of sunshine—at least six hours a day of direct sunlight.
2. Remove all weeds in your selected spot and dispose of them. If you are using compost to supplement your garden soil, do not put the weeds on the compost heap, as they may germinate once again and cause more weed growth among your vegetable plants.
3. Prepare the soil by tilling it. This will break up large soil clumps and allow you to see and remove pesky weed roots. This would also be the appropriate time to add organic materials (such as compost) to the existing soil to help make it more fertile. The tools used for tilling will depend on the size of your garden. Some examples are:
   - Shovel and turning fork—using these tools is hard work, requiring strong upper body strength.
   - Rotary tiller—this will help cut up weed roots and mix the soil.
4. After the soil has been tilled, you are ready to begin planting. If you would like straight rows in your garden, a guide can be made from two wooden stakes and a bit of rope.

After soil is tilled it should be loose and free from weeds or root systems.

Tomato plants will grow best if begun as seedlings indoors and then transplanted into your garden well after the last frost.

You can often grow two crops of cabbage or other green leafy vegetables in one growing season if you start the garden early enough.

5. Vegetables can be grown from seeds or transplanted.
   - If your garden has problems with pests such as slugs, it's best to transplant older plants, as they are more likely to survive attacks from these organisms.
   - Transplanting works well for vegetables like tomatoes and onions, which usually need a head start to mature within a shorter growing season. These can be germinated indoors on seed trays on a windowsill before the growing season begins.
6. Follow these basic steps to grow vegetables from seeds:
   - Information on when and how deep to plant vegetable seeds is usually printed on seed packages or on various websites. You can also contact your local nursery or garden center to inquire after this information.
   - Measure the width of the seed to determine how deep it should be planted. Take the width and multiply by 2. That is how deep the seed should be placed in the hole. As a general rule, the larger the seed, the deeper it should be planted.
7. Water the plants and seeds well to ensure a good start. Make sure they receive water at least every other day, especially if there is no rain in the forecast.

A shovel is perfectly adequate for turning over soil in a small garden.

Things to Consider

- In the early days of a vegetable garden, all your plants are vulnerable to attack by insects and animals. It is best to plant multiples of the same plant to ensure that some survive. Placing netting and fences around your garden can help keep out certain animal pests. Coffee grains or slug traps filled with beer will also help protect your plants against insect pests.
- If sowing seed straight onto your bed, be sure to obtain a photograph of what your seedlings will look like so you don't mistake the growing plant for a weed.
- Weeding early on is very important to the overall success of your garden. Weeds steal water, nutrients, and light from your vegetables, which will stunt their growth and make it more difficult for them to thrive.

Seeds should be planted at a depth of twice their width. If the seed is ¼ inch wide, it should be planted ½ inch below the surface.

For very small seeds, such as carrot seeds, you can sprinkle 15 to 20 seeds per inch in a shallow channel. To make the row straight, tie a string to two small sticks and drive each stick into the ground on either side of your garden so that the string is taut. Use a hoe to dig a shallow channel in the string's shadow.

Start Your Own Flower Garden

If you are looking to grow a beautiful garden full of flowers, just follow these simple steps to achieve the perfect beginner's flower garden.

Step One: Start with a Small Garden

Gardening takes a lot of work, and so for the beginner gardener, tackling a large garden can be overwhelming. Start with a small flowerbed around 25 square feet. This will provide you with room for about 20 to 30 plants—enough room for three types of annuals and two types of perennials. As your gardening experience grows, so can the size of your garden!

If you are looking to start even smaller, you can always begin your first flower garden in a container, or create a border from treated wood or bricks and stones around your existing bed. That way, when you are ready to expand your garden, all you need to do is remove the temporary border and you'll be all set. Even a small container filled with a few different types of plants can be a wonderful addition to any yard.

Step Two: Plan Your Flower Garden

Draw up a plan of how you'd like your garden to look, and then dig a flowerbed to fit that plan. Planning your garden before gathering the seeds or plants and beginning the digging can give you a clearer sense of how your garden will be organized and can facilitate the planting process.

Step Three: Choose a Spot for Your Garden

It is important, when choosing where your flower garden will be located, that you consider an area that receives at least six hours of direct sunlight per day, as this will be adequate for a large variety of garden plants. Be careful that you will not be digging into utility lines or pipes, and that you place your garden at least a short distance away from fences or other structures.

If you live in a part of the country that is quite hot, it might be beneficial for your flowers to be placed in an area that gets some shade during the hot afternoon sun. Placing your garden on the east side of your home will help your flowers flourish. If your garden will get more than six hours of sunlight per day, it would be wise to choose flowers that thrive in hot, sunny spaces, and make sure to water them frequently.

It is also important to choose a spot that has good, fertile soil in which your flowers can grow. Try to avoid any areas with rocky, shallow soil or where water collects and pools. Make sure your garden is away from large trees and shrubs, as these plants will compete with your flowers for water and nutrients. If you are concerned that your soil may not contain enough nutrients for your flowers to grow properly, you can have a soil test done, which will tell you the pH of the soil. Depending on the results,

Flower gardens do not need to be as carefully organized as vegetable gardens. Experiment with different color combinations and flower varieties. In general, it's best to put taller plants toward the center or back of your garden so that the shorter flowers will still be visible.

Some flowers, like lilies, do best if started in pots and then transplanted into your garden.

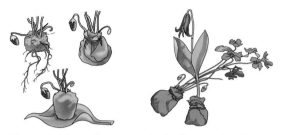

To transplant flowers from one growing location to another, dig up the plant, being careful not to damage the root system. Wrap the root ball in a large leaf or a cloth and tie at the top around the stems to keep the roots from drying out. Leaf wrappings do not need to be removed before replanting. Be sure to water the plant thoroughly after planting it in its new location.

you can then adjust the types of nutrients needed in your soil by adding organic materials or certain types of fertilizers.

Step Four: Start Digging

Now that you have a site picked out, mark out the boundaries with a hose or string. Remove the sod and any weed roots that may re-grow. Use your spade or garden fork to dig up the bed at least 8 to 12 inches deep, removing any rocks or debris you come across.

Once your bed is dug, level it and break up the soil with a rake. Add compost or manure if the soil is not fertile. If your soil is sandy, adding peat moss or grass clippings will help it hold more water. Work any additions into the top 6 inches of soil.

Step Five: Purchase Your Seeds or Plants

Once you've chosen which types of flowers you'd like to grow in your garden, visit your local garden store or nursery and pick out already-established plants or packaged seeds. Follow the planting instructions on the plant tabs or seed packets. The smaller plants should be situated in the front of the bed. Once your plants or seeds are in their holes, pack in the soil around them. Make sure to leave ample space between your seeds or plants for them to grow and spread out (most labels and packets will alert you to how large your flower should be expected to grow, so you can adjust the spacing as needed).

Step Six: Water Your Flower Garden

After your plants or seeds are first put into the ground, be sure they get a thorough watering. Continue to check your garden to see whether or not the soil is drying out. If so, give your garden a good soaking with the garden hose or watering can. The amount of water your garden needs is dependant on the climate you live in, the exposure to the sun, and how much rain your area has received.

Step Seven: Cutting Your Flowers

Once your flowers begin to bloom, feel free to cut them and display the beautiful blooms in your home. Pruning your flower garden (cutting the dead or dying blooms off the plant) will help certain plants to re-bloom. Also, if you have plants that are becoming top heavy, support them with a stake and some string so you can enjoy their blossoms to the fullest.

Things to Consider

- Annuals are plants that you need to replant every year. They are often inexpensive, and many have brightly colored flowers. Annuals can be rewarding for beginner gardeners, as they take little effort and provide lovely color to your garden. The following season, you'll need to replant or start over from seed.

Echinacea is beautiful as well as useful for medicinal purposes. It grows best in sunny areas. Plant in early spring for summer blooming, or about two months before the first frost for flowers the next year.

Bright, fragrant flowers will attract butterflies to your garden.

Barrel Plant Holder

If you have some perennials you want to display in your yard away from your flower garden, you can create a planter out of an old barrel. This plant holder is made by sawing an old barrel (wooden or metal) into two pieces and mounting it on short or tall legs—whichever design fits better in your yard. You can choose to either paint it or leave it natural. Filling the planter with good quality soil and compost and planting an array of multi-colored flowers into the barrel planter will brighten up your yard all summer long. If you do not want to mount the barrel on legs, it can be placed on the ground on a smooth and level surface where it won't easily tip over.

- Perennials last from one year to the next. They, too, will require annual maintenance but not yearly replanting. Perennials may require division, support, and extra care during winter months. Perennials may also need their old blooms and stems pruned and cut back every so often.

- Healthy, happy plants tend not to be as susceptible to pests and diseases. It is easier to practice prevention rather than curing existing problems. Do your best to give your plants good soil, nutrients, and appropriate moisture, and choose plants that are well-suited to your climate. This way, your garden will be more likely to grow to its maximum potential and your plants will be strong and healthy.

Garden centers or farm stands often sell flowers that are started in flats or plugs. Because the root systems are already established, they are easier to grow and create an instantly attractive garden.

Rustic Plant Stand

If you'd like to incorporate a rustic, natural-looking plant stand in your garden or on your patio or deck, one can easily be made from a preexisting wooden box or by nailing boards together. This box should be mounted on legs (see picture below). To make the legs, saw the piece of wood meant for the leg in half to a length from the top equal to the depth of the box. Then, cross-cut and remove one half. The corner of the box can then be inserted in the middle of the crosscut and the leg nailed to the side of the box.

The plant stand can be decorated to suit your needs and preference. You can nail smaller, alternating twigs or cut branches around the stand to give it a more natural feel or you can simply paint it a soothing, natural color and place it in your yard.

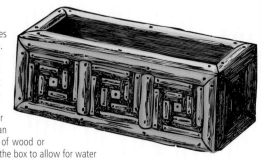

A fence can be set up around your garden to keep out deer and other wild animals. See page 181 for fence construction ideas.

Wooden Window Box

Planting perennial flowers and cascading plants in window boxes is the perfect way to brighten up the front exterior of your home. Making a simple wooden window box to hold your flowers and plants is quite easy. These boxes can be made from preexisting wooden boxes (such as fruit crates) or you can make your own out of simple boards. Whatever method you choose, make sure the boards are stout enough to hold the brads firmly.

The size of your window will ultimately determine the size of your box, but this plan calls for a box roughly 21 x 7 x 7 inches. You can decorate your boxes with waterproof paint or you can nail strips of wood or sticks to the panels. Make sure to cut a few holes in the bottom of the box to allow for water drainage.

Planting Trees

Trees in your yard can become home to many different types of wildlife. Trees also reduce your cooling costs by providing shade, help clean the air, add beauty and color, provide shelter from the wind and the sun, and add value to your home.

Choosing a Tree

Choosing a tree should be a well-thought-out decision. Tree planting can be a significant investment, both in money and time. Selecting the proper tree for your yard can provide you with years of enjoyment, as well as significantly increase the value of your property. However, a tree that is inappropriate for your property can be a constant maintenance problem, or even a danger to your and others' safety. Before you decide to purchase a tree, take advantage of the many references on gardening at local libraries, universities, arboretums, native plant and gardening clubs, and nurseries. Some questions to consider in selecting a tree include:

1. What purpose will this tree serve?

Trees can serve numerous landscape functions, including beautification, screening of sights and sounds, shade and energy conservation, and wildlife habitat.

2. Is the species appropriate for your area?

Reliable nurseries will not sell plants that are not suitable for your area. However, some mass marketers have trees and shrubs that are not fitted for the environment in which they are sold. Even if a tree is hardy, it may not flower consistently from year to year if the environmental factors are not conducive for it to do so. If you are buying a tree for its spring flowers and fall fruits, consider climate when deciding which species of tree to plant.

- Be aware of microclimates. Microclimates are localized areas where weather conditions may vary from the norm. A very sheltered yard may support vegetation not normally adapted to the region. On the other hand, a north-facing slope may be significantly cooler or windier than surrounding areas, and survival of normally adapted plants may be limited.
- Select trees native to your area. These trees will be more tolerant of local weather and soil conditions, enhance natural biodiversity in your neighborhood, and be more beneficial to wildlife than many non-native trees. Avoid exotic trees that can invade other areas, crowd out native plants, and harm natural ecosystems.

3. How big will it get?

When planting a small tree, it is often difficult to imagine that in 20 years it will most likely be shading your entire yard. Unfortunately, many trees are planted and later removed when the tree grows beyond the dimensions of the property.

4. What is the average life expectancy of the tree?

Some trees can live for hundreds of years. Others are considered "short-lived" and may live for only 20 to 30 years. Many short-lived trees tend to be smaller, ornamental species. Short-lived species should not necessarily be ruled out when considering plantings, as they may have other desirable characteristics, such as size, shape, tolerance of

Fruit trees provide sweet-smelling flowers in the spring and fruit in the fall.

Full-grown trees create a shade-producing canopy of branches and leaves. Shade can be a good addition to your property, but be sure you don't plant trees in an area where you want a garden that requires full sun.

shade, or fruit, that would be useful in the landscape. These species may also fill a void in a young landscape and can be removed as other larger, longer-lived species mature.

5. Does it have any particular ornamental value, such as leaf color or flowers and fruits?

Some species provide beautiful displays of color for short periods in the spring or fall. Other species may have foliage that is reddish or variegated and can add color in your yard year-round. Trees bearing fruits or nuts can provide an excellent source of food for many species of wildlife.

6. Does it have any particular insect, disease, or other problem that may reduce its usefulness in the future?

Certain insects and diseases can cause serious problems for some desirable species in certain regions. Depending on the pest, control of the problem may be difficult and the pest may significantly reduce the attractiveness, if not the life expectancy, of the tree. Other species, such as the silver maple, are known to have weak wood that is susceptible to damage in ice storms or heavy winds. All these factors should be kept in mind, as controlling pests or dealing with tree limbs that have snapped in foul weather can be expensive and potentially damaging.

7. How common is this species in your neighborhood or town?

Some species are over-planted. Increasing the natural diversity in your area will provide habitat for wildlife and help limit the opportunity for a single pest to destroy large numbers of trees.

8. Is the tree evergreen or deciduous?

Evergreen trees will provide cover and shade year-round. They may also be more effective as wind and noise barriers. On the other hand, deciduous trees will give you summer shade but allow the winter sun to shine in. If planting a deciduous tree, keep these heating and cooling factors in mind when placing the tree in your yard.

Placement of Trees

Proper placement of trees is critical for your enjoyment and for their long-term survival. Check with local authorities about regulations pertaining to placement of trees in your area. Some communities have ordinances restricting placement of trees within a specified distance from a street, sidewalk, streetlight, or other city utilities.

Before planting your tree, consider the tree's potential maximum size. Ask yourself these simple questions:

1. When the tree nears maturity, will it be too close to your or a neighbor's house? An evergreen tree planted on your north side may block the winter sun from your next-door neighbor.
2. Will it provide too much shade for your vegetable and flower gardens? Most vegetables and many flowers require considerable amounts of sun. If you intend to grow these plants in your yard, consider how the placement of trees will affect these gardens.
3. Will the tree obstruct any driveways or sidewalks?
4. Will it cause problems for buried or overhead power lines and utility pipes?

Once you have taken these questions into consideration and have bought the perfect tree for your yard, it is time to start digging!

Planting a Tree

A properly planted and maintained tree will grow faster and live longer than one that is incorrectly planted. Trees can be planted almost any time of the year, as long as the ground is not frozen. Late summer or early fall is the optimum time to plant trees in many areas. By planting during these times, the tree has a chance to establish new roots before winter arrives and the ground freezes. When spring comes, the tree is then ready to grow. Another feasible time for planting trees is late winter or early spring. Planting in hot summer weather should be avoided if possible as the heat may cause the young tree to wilt. Planting in frozen soil during the winter is very difficult and is tough on tree roots. When the tree is dormant and the ground is frozen, there is no opportunity for the new roots to begin growing.

Trees can be purchased as container-grown, balled and burlapped (B&B), or bare root. Generally, container-grown are the easiest to plant and successfully establish in any season, including summer. With container-grown stock, the plant has been growing in a container for a period of time. When planting container-grown trees, little damage is done to the roots as the plant is transferred to the soil. Container-grown trees range in size from very small plants in gallon pots up to large trees in huge pots.

Bare root trees are usually extremely small plants. Because there is no soil around the roots, they must be planted when they are dormant to avoid drying out, and the roots must be kept moist until planted. Frequently, bare root trees are offered by seed and nursery mail order catalogs, or in the wholesale trade. Many state-operated nurseries and local conservation districts also sell bare root stock in bulk quantities for only a few cents per plant. Bare root plants are usually offered in the early spring and should be planted as soon as possible.

B&B trees are dug from a nursery, wrapped in burlap, and kept in the nursery for an additional period of time, giving the roots opportunity to regenerate. B&B plants can be quite large.

Be sure to carefully follow the planting instructions that come with your tree. If specific instructions are not available, here are some general tree-planting guidelines:

1. Before starting any digging, call your local utility companies to identify the location of any underground wires or lines. In the U.S., you can call 811 to have your utility lines marked for free.

2. Dig a hole twice as wide as, and slightly shallower than, the root ball. Roughen the sides and bottom of the hole with a pick or shovel so that the roots can easily penetrate the soil.

3. With a potted tree, gently remove the tree from the container. To do this, lay the tree on its side with the container end near the planting hole. Hit the bottom and sides of the container until the root ball is loosened. If roots are growing in a circular pattern around the root ball, slice through the roots on a couple of sides of the root ball. With trees wrapped in burlap, remove the string or wire that holds the burlap to the root crown; it is not necessary to remove the burlap completely. Plastic wraps must be completely removed. Gently separate circling roots on the root ball. Shorten exceptionally long roots and guide the shortened roots downward and outward. Root tips die quickly when exposed to light and air, so complete this step as quickly as possible.

4. Place the root ball in the hole. Leave the top of the root ball (where the roots end and the trunk begins) ½ to 1 inch above the surrounding soil, making sure not to cover it unless the roots are exposed. For bare root plants, make a mound of soil in the middle of the hole and spread plant roots out evenly over the mound. Do not set the tree too deep into the hole.

5. As you add soil to fill in around the tree, lightly tap the soil to collapse air pockets, or add water to help settle the soil. Form a temporary water basin

Burlap wraps do not need to be removed before planting your tree. They will decompose in the soil with time.

Pruning

Usually, pruning is not needed on newly planted trees. As the tree grows, lower branches may be pruned to provide clearance above the ground, or to remove dead or damaged limbs or suckers that sprout from the trunk. Sometimes larger trees need pruning to allow more light to enter the canopy. Small branches can be removed easily with pruners. Large branches should be removed with a pruning saw. All cuts should be vertical. This will allow the tree to heal quickly without the use of any artificial sealants. Major pruning should be done in late winter or early spring. At this time, the tree is more likely to "bleed," as sap is rising through the plant. This is actually healthy and will help prevent invasion by many disease-carrying organisms.

Under no circumstance should trees be topped (topping is chopping off large top tree branches). Not only does this practice ruin the natural shape of the tree, but it also increases its susceptibility to diseases and results in very narrow crotch angles (the angle between the trunk and the side branch). Narrow crotch angles are weaker than wide ones and more susceptible to damage from wind and ice. If a large tree requires major reduction in height or size, contact a professionally trained arborist.

around the base of the tree to encourage water penetration, and be sure to water the tree thoroughly after planting. A tree with a dry root ball cannot absorb water; if the root ball is extremely dry, allow water to trickle into the soil by placing the hose at the trunk of the tree.

6. Place mulch around the tree. A circle of mulch, 3-foot in diameter, is common.

7. Depending on the size of the tree and the site condiions, staking the tree in place may be beneficial. Staking supports the tree until the roots are well established to properly anchor it. Staking should allow for some movement of the tree on windy days. After trees are established, remove all supporting wires. If these are not removed, they can girdle the tree, cut into the trunk, and eventually kill the tree.

Maintenance

For the first year or two, especially after a week or so of especially hot or dry weather, watch your tree closely for signs of moisture stress. If you see any leaf wilting or hard, caked soil, water the tree well and slowly enough to allow the water to soak in. This will encourage deep root growth. Keep the area under the tree mulched.

Some species of evergreen trees may need protection against winter sun and wind. A thorough watering in the fall before the ground freezes is recommended.

Fertilization is usually not needed for newly planted trees. Depending on the soil and growing conditions, fertilizer may be beneficial at a later time.

Things You'll Need

- Tree
- Shovel
- Watering can or garden hose
- Measuring stick
- Mulch
- Optional: scissors or knife to cut the burlap or container, stakes, and supporting wires

Young trees need protection against rodents, frost cracks, sunscald, lawn mowers, and weed whackers. In the winter months, mice and rabbits frequently girdle small trees by chewing away the bark at the snow level. Since the tissues that transport nutrients in the tree are located just under the bark, a girdled tree often dies in the spring when growth resumes. Weed whackers are also a common cause of girdling. In order to prevent girdling from occurring, use plastic guards, which are inexpensive and easy to control.

Frost cracking is caused by the sunny side of the tree expanding at a different rate than the colder, shaded side. This can cause large splits in the trunk. To prevent this, wrap young trees with paper tree wrap, starting from the base and wrapping up to the bottom branches. Sunscald can occur when a young tree is suddenly moved from a shady spot into direct sunlight. Light-colored tree wraps can be used to protect the trunk from sunscald.

Final Thoughts

Trees are natural windbreaks, slowing the wind and providing shelter and food for wildlife. Trees can help protect livestock, gardens, and larger crops. They also help prevent dust particles from adding to smog over urban areas. Tree plantings are key components of an effective conservation system and can provide your yard with beauty, shade, and rich, natural resources.

Container Gardening

An alternative to growing vegetables, flowers, and herbs in a traditional garden is to grow them in containers. While the amount that can be grown in a container is certainly limited, container gardens work well for tomatoes, peppers, cucumbers, herbs, salad greens, and many flowering annuals. Choose vegetable varieties that have been specifically bred for container growing. You can obtain this information online or at your garden center. Container gardening also brings birds and butterflies right to your doorstep. Hanging baskets of fuchsia or pots of snapdragons are frequently visited by hummingbirds, allowing for up-close observation.

Container gardening is an excellent method of growing vegetables, herbs, and flowers, especially if you do not have adequate outdoor space for a full garden bed. A container garden can be placed anywhere—on the patio, balcony, rooftop, or windowsill. Vegetables such as leaf lettuce, radishes, small tomatoes, and baby carrots can all be grown successfully in pots.

How to Grow Vegetables in a Container Garden

Here are some simple steps to follow for growing vegetables in containers.

1. Choose a sunny area for your container plants. Your plants will need at least five to six hours of sunlight a day. Some plants, such as cucumbers, may need more. Select plants that are suitable for container growing. Usually their name will have words such as "patio," "bush," "dwarf," "toy," or "miniature" in them. Peppers, onions, and carrots are also good choices.
2. Choose a planter that is at least 5 gallons, unless the plant is very small. Poke holes in the bottom if they don't already exist; the soil must be able to drain in order to prevent the roots from rotting. Avoid terracotta or dark colored pots as they tend to dry out quickly.

You only need a few simple tools for container gardening.

3. Fill your container with potting soil. Good potting soil will have a mixture of peat moss and vermiculite. You can make your own potting soil using composted soil (see page 13). Read the directions on the seed packet or label to determine how deep to plant your seeds.

4. Check the moisture of the soil frequently. You don't want the soil to become muddy, but the soil should always feel damp to the touch. Do not wait until the plant is wilting to water it—at that point, it may be too late.

Things to Consider

- Follow normal planting schedules for your climate when determining when to plant your container garden.
- You may wish to line your container with porous materials such as shredded newspaper or rags to keep the soil from washing out. Be sure the water can still drain easily.

How to Grow Herbs in a Container

Herbs will thrive in containers if cared for properly. And if you keep them near your kitchen, you can easily snip off pieces to use in cooking. Here's how to start your own herb container garden:

1. If your container doesn't already have holes in the bottom, poke several to allow the soil to drain. Pour gravel into the container until it is about a quarter of the way full. This will help the water drain and help to keep the soil from washing out.

2. Fill your container three-quarters of the way with potting soil or a soil-based compost.

3. It's best to use seedlings when planting herbs in containers. Tease the roots slightly, gently spreading them apart with your fingertips. This will encourage them to spread once planted. Place each herb into the pot and cover the root base with soil. Place herbs that will grow taller in the center of your container, and the smaller ones around the edges. Leave about four square inches of space between each seedling.

4. As you gently press in soil between the plants, leave an inch or so between the container's top and the soil. You don't want the container to overflow when you water the herbs.

5. Cut the tops off the taller herb plants to encourage them to grow faster and to produce more leaves.

6. Pour water into the container until it begins to leak out the bottom. Most herbs like to dry out between watering, and over-watering can cause some herbs to rot and die, so only water every few days unless the plants are in a very hot place.

It's easiest to grow herbs from seedlings like these, though you can certainly grow them from seeds, too.

Things to Consider

- Growing several kinds of herbs together helps the plants to thrive. A few exceptions to this rule are oregano, lemon balm, and tea balm. These herbs should be planted on their own because they will overtake the other herbs in your container.
- You may wish to choose your herbs according to color to create attractive arrangements for your home. Any of the following herbs will grow well in containers:
- Silver herbs: artemsias, curry plans, santolinas
- Golden herbs: lemon thyme, calendula, nasturtium, sage, lemon balm
- Blue herbs: borage, hyssop, rosemary, catnip
- Green herbs: basil, mint, marjoram, thyme, parsley, chives, tarragon
- Pink and purple herbs: oregano (the flowers) are pink, lavender
- If you decide to transplant your herbs in the summer months, they will grow quite well outdoors and will give you a larger harvest.

How to Grow Flowers from Seeds in a Container

1. Cover the drainage hole in the bottom of the pot with a flat stone. This will keep the soil from trickling out when the plant is watered.
2. Fill the container with soil. The container should be filled almost to the top and for the best results, use potting soil from your local nursery or garden center.

3. Make holes for the seeds. Refer to the seed packet to see how deep to make the holes. Always save the seed packet for future reference—it most likely has helpful directions about thinning young plants.
4. Place a seed in each hole. Pat the soil gently on top of each seed.
5. Use a light mist to water your seeds, making sure that the soil is only moist and not soaked.
6. Make sure your seeds get the correct amount of sunlight. Refer to the seed packet for the adequate amount of sunlight each seedling needs.
7. Watch your seeds grow. Most seeds take 3 to 17 days to sprout. Once the plants start sprouting, be sure to pull out plants that are too close together so the remaining plants will have enough space to establish good root systems.
8. Remember to water and feed your container plants. Keep the soil moist so your plants can grow. And in no time at all, you should have wonderful flowers growing in your container garden.

Preserving Your Container Plants

As fall approaches, frost will soon descend on your container plants and can ultimately destroy your garden. Container plants are particularly susceptible to frost damage, especially if you are growing tropical plants, perennials, and hardy woody plants in a single container garden. There are many ways that you can preserve and maintain your container garden plants throughout the winter season.

Preservation techniques will vary depending on the plants in your container garden. Tropical plants can be over-wintered using methods replicating a dry season, forcing the plant into dormancy; hardy perennials and woody shrubs need a cold dormancy to grow in the spring, so they must stay outside; cacti and succulents

Cinder blocks or simple wooden planters made of scrap wood can make inexpensive container gardens.

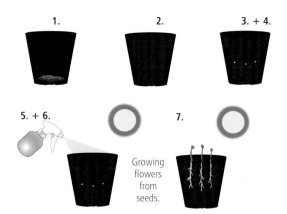

1.   2.   3. + 4.

5. + 6.   7.

Growing flowers from seeds.

prefer their winters warm and dry and must be brought inside, while many annuals can be propagated by stem cuttings or can just be repotted and maintained inside.

Preserving Tropical Bulbs and Tubers

Many tropical plants, such as cannas, elephant ears, and angel's trumpets can be saved from an untimely death by over-wintering them in a dark corner or sunny window of your home, depending on the type of plant. A lot of bulbous and tuberous tropical plants have a natural dry season (analogous to our winter) when their leafy parts die off, leaving the bulb behind. Don't throw the bulbs away. After heavy frosts turn the aboveground plant parts to mush, cut the damaged foliage off about 4 inches above the thickened bulb. Then, dig them up and remove all excess soil from the roots. At this point, you can determine if the clump needs dividing. If it needs dividing, be sure to dust all cut surfaces with a sulfur-based fungicide made for bulbs to prevent the wounds from rotting. Cut the roots back to 1 inch from the bulb and leave to dry out evenly. Rotten bulbs or roots need to be thrown away so infection doesn't spread to the healthy bulbs.

A bulb's or tuber's drying time can last up to two weeks if it is sitting on something absorbent like newspaper and located somewhere shaded and dry—preferably around 50°F—such as a garage or basement. Once clean and dry, bulbs should be stored all winter in damp (not soggy) milled peat moss. This prevents the bulbs from drying out any further, which could cause them to die. Many gardeners don't have a perfectly cool basement or garage to keep bulbs dormant. Alternative methods for dry storage include a dark closet with the door cracked for circulation, a cabinet, or underneath a bed in a cardboard box with a few holes punched for airflow. The important thing to keep in mind is that the bulb needs to be kept on the dry side, in the dark, and moderately warm.

If a bulb was grown as a single specimen in its own pot, the entire pot can be placed in a garage that stays above 50°F or a cool basement and allowed to dry out completely. Cut all aboveground plant parts flush with the soil and don't water until the outside temperatures stabilize above 60°F. Often, bulbs break dormancy unexpectedly in this dry pot method. If this happens, pots can be moved to a sunny location near a window and watered sparingly until they can be placed outside. The emerging leaves will be stunted, but once outside, the plant will replace any spindly leaves with lush, new ones.

Annuals

Many herbaceous annuals can also be saved for the following year. By rooting stem cuttings in water on a sunny windowsill, plants like impatiens, coleus, sweet potato vine cultivars, and purple heart can be held over winter until needed in the spring. Otherwise, the plants can be cut back by half, potted in a peat-based, soilless mix, and placed on a sunny windowsill. With a wide assortment of "annuals" available on the market, some research is required to determine which annuals can be over-wintered successfully. True annuals (such as basils, cockscomb, and zinnias)—regardless of any treatment given—will go to seed and die when brought inside.

Cacti and Succulents

If you planted a mixed dry container this year and want to retain any of the plants for next year, they should be removed from the main container and repotted into a high-sand-content soil mix for cacti and succulents. Keep them near a sunny window and water when dry. Many succulents and cacti do well indoors, either in a heated garage or a moderately sunny corner of a living room.

You can make container gardens out of almost anything.

ers. Crack-resistant, four-season containers can house perennials and woody shrubs year-round. Below is a list of specific perennials and woody plants that do well in both hot and cold weather, indoors and out:

- Shade perennials, like coral bells, lenten rose, assorted hardy ferns, and Japanese forest grass are great for all weather containers.
- Sun-loving perennials, such as sedges, some salvias, purple coneflower, daylily, spiderwort, and bee blossom are also very hardy and do well in year-round containers. Interplant them with cool growing plants, like kale, pansies, and Swiss chard, for fall and spring interest.
- Woody shrubs and vines—many of which have great foliage interest with four-season appeal—are ideal for container gardens. Red-twigged dogwood cultivars, clematis vine cultivars, and dwarf crape myrtle cultivars are great container additions that can stay outdoors year-round.

If the container has to be removed, hardy perennials and woody shrubs can be temporarily planted in the ground and mulched. Dig them from the garden in the spring, if you wish, and replant into a container. Or, leave them in their garden spot and start over with fresh ideas and new plant material for your container garden.

Sustainable Plants and Money in Your Pocket

Over-wintering is a great form of sustainable plant conservation achieved simply and effectively by adhering to each plant's cultural and environmental needs. With careful planning and storage techniques, you'll save money as well as plant material. The beauty and interest you've created in this season's well-grown container garden can also provide enjoyment for years to come.

As with other tropical plants, succulents also need time to adjust to sunnier conditions in the spring. Move them to a shady spot outside when temperatures have stabilized above 60°F and then gradually introduce them to brighter conditions.

Hardy Perennials, Shrubs, and Vines

Hardy perennials, woody shrubs, and vines needn't be thrown away when it's time to get rid of accent contain-

Rooftop Gardens

If you live in an urban area and don't have a lawn, that does not mean that you cannot have a garden. Whether you live in an apartment building or own your own home without yard space, you can grow your very own garden, right on your roof!

Is Your Roof Suitable for a Rooftop Garden?

Theoretically, any roof surface can be greened—even sloped or curved roofs can support a layer of sod or wildflowers. However, if the angle of your roof is over 30 degrees you should consult with a specialist. Very slanted roofs make it difficult to keep the soil in place until the plant's roots take hold. Certainly, a flat roof, approximating level ground conditions is the easiest on which to grow a garden, though a slight slant can be helpful in allowing drainage.

Also consider how much weight your roof can bear. A simple, lightweight rooftop garden will weigh between 13 and 30 pounds per square foot. Add to this your own weight—or that of anyone who will be tending or enjoying the garden—gardening tools, and, if you live in a colder climate, the additional weight of snow in the winter.

Will a Rooftop Garden Cause Water Leakage or Other Damage?

No. In fact, planting beds or surfaces are often used to protect and insulate roofs. However, you should take some precautions to protect your roof:

1. Cover your roof with a layer of waterproof material, such as a heavy-duty pond liner. You may want to place an old rug on top of the waterproof material to help it stay in place and to give additional support to the materials on top.

Rooftop gardens are becoming more popular in urban areas around the world.

You can use container plants on your rooftop rather than laying a garden directly on the roof. However, still be sure that your roof is sturdy enough to hold the pots and the people who will be tending them.

Benefits of Rooftop Gardening

- Create more outdoor green space within your urban environment.
- Grow your own fresh vegetables—even in the city.
- Improve air quality and reduce CO_2 emissions.
- Help delay storm water runoff.
- Give additional insulation to building roofs.
- Reduce noise.

2. Place a protective drainage layer on top of the waterproof material. Otherwise, shovels, shoe heels, or dropped tools could puncture the roof. Use a coarse material such as gravel, pumice, or expanded shale.
3. Place a filter layer on top of the drainage layer to keep soil in place so that it won't clog up your drainage. A lightweight polyester geotextile (an inexpensive, non-woven fabric found at most home improvement stores) is ideal for this. Note that if your roof has an angle of over 10 degrees, only install the filter layer around the edges of the roof as it can increase slippage.
4. Using moveable planters or containers, modular walkways and surfacing treatment, and compartmentalized planting beds will make it easier to fix leaks should they appear.

Things to Consider

1. If you live in a very hot area, you may want to build small wooden platforms to elevate your plants above the hot rooftop. This will help increase the ventilation around the plants.
2. When determining whether or not your roof is strong enough to support a garden, remember that large pots full of water and soil will be very heavy, and if the roof is not strong enough, your garden could cause structural damage.
3. You can use pots or other containers on your rooftop rather than making a full garden bed. You should still first find out how much weight your roof can hold and choose lightweight containers.
4. Consider adding a fence or railing around your roof, especially if children will be helping in the garden.

How to Make a Rooftop Garden

Preparation

1. Before you begin, find out if it is possible and legal to create a garden on your roof. You don't want to spend lots of time and money preparing for a garden and then find out that it is prohibited.
2. Make sure that the roof is able to hold the weight of a rooftop garden. If so, figure out how much weight it can hold. Remember this when making the garden and use lighter containers and soil as needed.

Setting Up the Garden

1. Install your waterproof, protective drainage, and filter layers, as described earlier. If your roof is angled, you may want to place a wooden frame around the edges of the roof to keep the layers from sliding off. Be sure to use rot-resistant wood and cut outlets into the frame to allow excess water to drain away. Layer pebbles around the outlets to aid drainage and to keep vegetation from clogging them.
2. Add soil to your garden. It should be 1–4 inches thick and will be best if it's a mix of ¾ inorganic soil (crushed brick or a similar granular material) and ¼ organic compost.

Planting and Maintaining the Garden

1. Start planting. You can plant seeds, seedlings, or transplant mature plants. Choose plants that are wind-resistant and won't need a great deal of maintenance. Sedums make excellent rooftop plants as they require very little attention once planted, are hardy, and are attractive throughout most of the year. Most vegetables can be grown in-season on rooftops, though the wind will make taller vegetables (like corn or beans) difficult to grow. If your roof is slanted, plant drought-resistant plant varieties near the peak, as they'll get less water.
2. Water your garden immediately after planting, and then regularly throughout the growing season, unless rain does the work for you.

Raised Beds

If you live in an area where the soil is wet (preventing a good vegetable garden from growing in the spring), find it difficult to bend over to plant and cultivate your vegetables or flowers, or if you just want a different look to your backyard garden, consider building a raised bed.

A raised bed is an interesting and affordable way to garden. It creates an ideal environment for growing vegetables, since the soil concentration can be closely monitored and, as it is raised above the ground, it reduces the compaction of plants from people walking on the soil.

Raised beds are typically 2 to 6 feet wide and as long as needed. In most cases, a raised bed consists of a "frame" that is filled in with nutrient-rich soil (including compost or organic fertilizers) and is then planted with a variety of vegetables or flowers, depending on the gardener's preference. By controlling the bed's construction and the soil mixture that goes into the bed, a gardener can effectively reduce the amount of weeds that will grow in the garden.

When planting seeds or young sprouts in a raised bed, it is best to space the plants equally from each other on all sides. This will ensure that the leaves will be touching once the plant is mature, thus saving space and reducing the soil's moisture loss.

How to Make a Raised Bed

Step One: Plan Out Your Raised Bed

1. Think about how you'd like your raised bed to look, and then design the shape. A raised bed is not extremely complicated, and all you need to do is build an open-top and open-bottom box (if you are ambitious, you can create a raised bed in the shape of a circle, hexagon, or star). The main purpose of this box is to hold soil.
2. Make a drawing of your raised bed, measure your available garden space, and add those measurements to your drawing. This will allow you to determine how much material is needed. Generally, your bed should be at least 24 inches in height.

Raised beds make neat, attractive gardens and make it easy to monitor the condition of the soil.

Follow the package instructions for how best to mix it in.
3. Decide what you want to plant. Some people like to grow flowers in their raised beds; others prefer to grow vegetables. If you do want to grow food, raised beds are excellent choices for salad greens, carrots, onions, radishes, beets, and other root crops.

Things to Consider

1. To save money, try to dig up and use soil from your yard. Potting soil can be expensive, and yard soil is just as effective when mixed with compost.
2. Be creative when building your raised planting bed. You can construct a great raised bed out of recycled goods or old lumber.
3. You can convert your raised bed into a greenhouse. Just add hoops to your bed by bending and connecting PVC pipe over the bed. Then clip greenhouse plastic to the PVC pipes, and you have your own greenhouse.
4. Make sure to water your raised bed often. Because it is above ground, your raised bed will not retain water as well as the soil in the ground. If you keep your bed narrow, it will help conserve water.
5. Decorate or illuminate your raised bed to make it a focal point in your yard.
6. If you use lumber to construct your raised bed, keep a watch out for termites.
7. Beware of old, pressure-treated lumber, as it may contain arsenic and could potentially leak into the root systems of any vegetables you might grow in your raised bed. Newer pressure-treated lumber should not contain these toxic chemicals.

3. Decide what kind of material you want to use for your raised bed. You can use lumber, plastic, synthetic wood, railroad ties, bricks, rocks, or a number of other items to hold the dirt. Using lumber is the easiest and most efficient method.
4. Gather your supplies.

Step Two: Build Your Raised Bed

1. Make sure your bed will be situated in a place that gets plenty of sunlight. Carefully assess your placement, as your raised bed will be fairly permanent.
2. Connect the sides of your bed together (with either screws or nails) to form the desired shape of your bed. If you are using lumber, you can use 4 x 4-inch posts to serve as the corners of your bed, and then nail or screw the sides to these corner posts. By doing so, you will increase the strength of the structure and ensure that the dirt will stay inside.
3. Cut a piece of gardening plastic to fit inside your raised bed, and lay it out in the appropriate location. This will significantly reduce the amount of weeds growing in your garden.
4. Place your frame over the gardening plastic (this might take two people).

Step Three: Start Planting

1. Add some compost into the bottom of the bed and then layer potting soil on top of the compost. If you have soil from other parts of your yard, feel free to use that in addition to the compost and potting soil. Plan on filling at least $\frac{1}{3}$ of your raised bed with compost or composted manure (available from nurseries or garden centers in 40-pound bags).
2. Mix in dry organic fertilizers (like wood ash, bone meal, and blood meal) while building your bed.

Things You'll Need

- Forms for your raised bed (consider using 4 x 4-inch posts cut to 24 inches in height for corners, and 2 x 12-inch boards for the sides)
- Nails or screws
- Hammer or screwdriver
- Plastic liner (to act as a weed barrier at the bottom of your bed)
- Shovel
- Compost, or composting manure
- Soil (either potting soil or soil from another part of your yard)
- Rake (to smooth out the soil once in the bed)
- Seeds or young plants
- Optional: PVC piping and greenhouse plastic (to convert your raised bed to a greenhouse)

Growing Plants without Soil

Plants grown in soilless cultures still need the basic requirements of plant growth, such as temperature, light (if indoors, use a heat-lamp and set the container near or on a windowsill), water, oxygen (you can produce good airflow by using a small, rotating fan indoors), carbon dioxide, and mineral nutrients (derived from solutions). But palnts grown without soil have their roots either free-floating in a nutrient-rich solution or bedded in a soil-like medium, such as sand, gravel, brick shards, Perlite, or rockwool. These plants do not have to exert as much energy to gather nutrients from the soil and thus they grow more quickly and, usually, more productively.

Types of Soilless Systems

There are two main types of soilless cultures that can be used in order to grow plants and vegetables. The first is a water culture, in which plants are supplied with mineral nutrients directly from the water solution. The second, called aggregate culture or "sand culture," uses an aggregate (such as sand, gravel, or Perlite) as soil to provide an anchoring support for the plant roots. Both types of hydroponics are effective in growing soilless plants and in providing essential nutrients for healthy and productive plant growth.

The Benefits and Drawbacks of Growing Plants in a Hydroponics System

Hydroponics is the method of growing plants in a container filled with a nutrient-rich bath (water with special fertilizer) and no soil.

Lettuce is especially well-suited to hydroponics systems.

In this type of hydroponics system, a dripper releases the nutrient solution into the top layer of piping. It then flows in a steady stream down through the other layers of piping.

Benefits:

- Plants can be grown in areas where normal plant agriculture is difficult (such as deserts and other arid places, or cities).
- Most terrestrial plants will grow in a hydroponics system.
- There is minimal weed growth.
- The system takes up less space than soil system.
- It conserves water.
- No fear of contaminated runoff from garden fertilizers.
- There is less labor and cost involved.
- Certain seasonal plants can be raised during any season.
- The quality of produce is generally consistent.
- Old nutrient solution can be used to water houseplants.

Drawbacks:

- Can cause salmonella to grow due to the wet and confined conditions.
- More difficult to grow root vegetables, such as carrots and potatoes.
- If nutrient solution is not regularly changed, plants can become nutrient deficient and thus not grow or produce.

Water Culture

The main advantage of using a water culture system is that a significant part of the nutrient solution is always in contact with the plants' roots. This provides an adequate amount of water and nutrients. The main challenges of this system are providing sufficient air supply for the roots and providing the roots with proper support and anchorage.

Water culture systems are not extremely expensive, though the cost does depend on the price of the chemicals and water used in the preparation of the nutrient solutions, the size of your container, and whether or not your are using mechanized objects, such as pumps and filters. You can decrease the cost by starting small and using readily available materials.

Materials Needed to Make Your Own Water Culture

A large water culture system will need either a wood or concrete tank 6 to 18 inches deep and 2 to 3 feet wide. If you use a wooden container, be sure there are no knots in the wood and seal the tank with non-creosote or tar asphalt.

For small water culture systems, which are recommended for beginners, glass jars, earthenware crocks, or plastic buckets will suffice as your holding tanks. If your container is transparent, be sure to paint the outside of the container with black paint to keep the light out (and to keep algae from growing inside your system). Keep a narrow, vertical strip unpainted in order to see the level of the nutrient solution inside your container.

The plant bed should be 3 or more inches deep and large enough to cover the container or tank. In order to support the weight of the litter (where your seeds or seedlings are placed), cover the bottom of the bed with chicken wire and then fill the bed with litter (wood shavings, sphagnum moss, peat, or other organic materials that do not easily decay). If you are starting your plants from seeds, germinate the seeds in a bed of sand and then transplant to the water culture bed, keeping the bed moist until the plants get their roots down into the nutrient solution.

In a water culture system, the roots are always in contact with the nutrient solution.

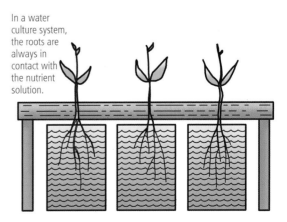

Aeration

A difficulty in using water culture is keeping the solution properly aerated. It is important to keep enough space between the seed bed and the nutrient solution so the plant's roots can receive proper oxygen. In order to make sure that air can easily flow into the container, either prop up the seed bed slightly to allow air flow or drill a hole in your container just above the highest solution level.

To make sure there is sufficient oxygen reaching the plant roots, you can install an aquarium pump in your water culture system. Just make sure that the water is not agitated too much or the roots may be damaged. You can also use an air stone or perforated pipe to gently introduce air flow into your container.

Water Supply

Your hydroponics system needs an adequate supply of fresh water to maintain healthy plant life. Make sure that the natural minerals in your water are not going to adversely affect your hydroponics plants. If there is too much sodium in your water (usually an effect of softened water), it could become toxic to your plants. In general, the minerals in water are not harmful to the growth of your plants.

Nutrient Solution

You may add nutrient solution by hand, by a gravity-feed system, or mechanically. In smaller water culture systems, mixing the nutrient solution in a small container and adding it by hand, as needed, is typically adequate.

If you are using a larger setup, a gravity-feed system will work quite well. In this type of system, the nutrient solution is mixed in a vat and then tapped from the vat into your container as needed. You can use a plastic container or larger earthenware jar as the vat.

A pump can also be used to supply your system with adequate nutrient solution. You can insert the pump into the vat and then transfer the solution to your hydroponics system.

When your plants are young, it is important to keep the space between your seed bed and the nutrient solution small (that way, the young plant roots can reach the nutrients). As your plants grow, the amount of space between the bed and solution should increase (but do this slowly and keep the level rather consistent).

If the temperature is rather high and there is increased evaporation, it is important to keep the roots at the correct level in the water and change the nutrient solution every day, if needed.

Drain your container every two weeks and then renew the nutrient solution from your vat or by hand. This must be done in a short amount of time so the roots do not dry out.

Transplanting

When transplanting your seedlings, it's important that you are careful with the tiny root systems. Gently work

---

Things You'll Need

- External pump
- Air line or tubing
- Air stones
- Waterproof bin, bucket, or fish tank to use as a reserve
- Styrofoam
- Net pots
- Type of growing medium, such as rockwool or grow rocks
- Hydroponics nutrients, such as grow formula, bloom formula, supplements, and pH
- Black spray paint (this is only required if the reservoir is transparent)
- Knife, box cutter, or scissors
- Tape measure

---

the roots through the support netting and down into the nutrient solution. Then fill in the support netting with litter to help the plant remain upright.

How to Build a Simple, Homemade Hydroponics System

Steps to Building Your Hydroponics System:

1. Find a container to use as a reservoir, such as a fish tank, a bin, or a bucket of some sort. The reservoir should be painted black if it is not lightproof (or covered with a thick, black trash bag if you want to reuse the tank at some point), and allowed to dry before moving on to the next step. Allowing light to enter the reservoir will promote the growth of algae. It is a good idea to use a reservoir that is the same dimensions (length and width) from top to bottom.

2. Using a knife or sharp object, score a line on the tank (scratch off some paint in a straight line from top to bottom). This will be your water level meter, which will allow you to see how much water is in the reservoir and will give you a more accurate and convenient view of the nutrient solution level in your tank.

3. Use a tape measure to determine the length and width of your reservoir. Measure the inside of the reservoir from one end to the other. Once you have the dimensions, cut the Styrofoam ¼ inch smaller than the size of the reservoir. For example, if your dimensions are 36 x 20 inches, you should cut the Styrofoam to 35¾ x 19¾ inches. The Styrofoam should fit nicely in the reservoir, with just enough room to adjust to any water level changes. If the reservoir tapers off at the bottom (the bottom is smaller in dimension than the top) the floater (Styrofoam) should be 2 to 4 inches smaller than the reservoir, or more if necessary.

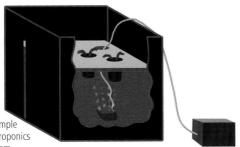

A simple hydroponics system.

4. Do not place the Styrofoam in the reservoir yet. First, you need to cut holes for the net pots. Put the net pots on the Styrofoam where you want to place each plant. Using a pen or pencil, trace around the bottom of each net pot. Use a knife or box cutter to follow the trace lines and cut the holes for pots. On one end of the Styrofoam, cut a small hole for the air line to run into the reservoir.

5. The number of plants you can grow will depend on the size of the garden you build and the types of crops you want to grow. Remember to space plants appropriately so that each receives ample amounts of light.

6. The pump you choose must be strong enough to provide enough oxygen to sustain plant life. Ask for advice choosing a pump at your local hydroponics supply store or garden center.

7. Connect the air line to the pump and attach the air stone to the free end. The air line should be long enough to travel from the pump into the bottom of the reservoir, or at least float in the middle of the tank so the oxygen bubbles can get to the plant roots. It also must be the right size for the pump you choose. Most pumps will come with the correct size air line. To determine the tank's capacity, use a one-gallon bucket or bottle and fill the reservoir. Remember to count how many gallons it takes to fill the reservoir and you will know the correct capacity of your tank.

Setting Up Your Hydroponics System

1. Fill the reservoir with the nutrient solution.
2. Place the Styrofoam into the reservoir.
3. Run the air line through the designated hole or notch.

Things to Consider

- A homemade hydroponics system like this is not ideal for large-scale production of plants or for commercial usage. This particular system does not offer a way to conveniently change the nutrient solution. An extra container would be required to hold the floater while you change the solution.
- Lettuce, watercress, tomatoes, cucumbers, and herbs grow especially well hydroponically.

4. Fill the net pots with growing medium and place one plant in each pot.

5. Put the net pots into the designated holes in the Styrofoam.

6. Plug in the pump, turn it on, and start growing with your fully functional, homemade hydroponics system.

Aggregate Culture

Aggregate culture systems utilize different mediums that act in place of soil to stabilize the plant and its roots. The aggregate in the container is flooded with the nutrient solution. The advantage of this type of system is that there is not as much trouble with aerating the roots. Also, aggregate culture systems allow for the easy transplantation of seedlings into the aggregate medium and it is less expensive.

Materials Needed for an Aggregate Culture System

The container should be watertight to help conserve the nutrient solution. Large tanks can be made of concrete or wood, and smaller operations can effectively be done in glass jars, earthenware containers, or plastic buckets. Make sure to paint transparent containers black.

Aggregate materials may differ greatly, depending on what type you choose to use. Silica sand (well washed) is one of the best materials that can be used. Any other type of coarse-textured sand is also effective, but make sure it does not contain lime. Sand holds moisture quite well and it allows for easy transplantation. A mixture of sand and gravel together is also an effective aggregate. Other materials, such as peat moss, vermiculite, wood shavings, and coco peat, are also good aggregates. You can find aggregate materials at your local garden center, home center, or garden-supply house.

Aeration

Aggregate culture systems allow much easier aeration than water culture systems. Draining and refilling the container with nutrient solution helps the air to move in and out of the aggregate material. This brings a fresh supply of oxygen to the plant roots.

Water Supply

The same water requirements are needed for this type of hydroponics system as for a water culture system. Minerals in the water tend to collect in the aggregate material, so it's a good idea to flush the material with fresh water every few weeks.

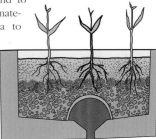

Nutrient Solution

The simplest way of adding the nutrient solution to aggregate cultures is to pour it over the aggregates by hand. You may also use a manual gravity-feed system with buckets or vats. Attach the vat to the bottom of the container with a flexible hose, raise the vat to flood the container, and lower it to drain it. Cover the vat to prevent evaporation and replenish it with new nutrient solution once every two weeks.

A gravity drip-feed system also works well and helps reduce the amount of work you do. Place the vat higher than the container, and then control the solution drip so it is just fast enough to keep the aggregate moist.

It is important that the nutrient solution is added and drained or raised and lowered at least once a day. In hotter weather, the aggregate material may need more wetting with the solution. Make sure that the material is not drying out the roots. Drenching the aggregate with solution often will not harm the plants but letting the roots dry out could have detrimental effects.

Always replace your nutrient solution after two weeks. Not replacing the solution will cause salts and harmful fertilizer residues to build up, which may ultimately damage your plants.

Planting

You may use either seedlings or rooted cuttings in an aggregate culture system. The aggregate should be flooded and solution drained before planting to create a moist, compacted seed bed. Seeds may also be planted directly into the aggregate material. Do not plant the seeds too deep, and flood the container frequently with water to keep the aggregate moist. Once the seedlings have germinated, you may start using the nutrient solution.

If you are transplanting seedlings from a germination bed, make sure they have germinated in soilless material, as any soil left on the roots may cause them to rot and may hamper them in obtaining nutrients from the solution.

Pre-mixed Chemicals

Many of the essential nutrients needed for hydroponic plant growth are now available already mixed in their correct proportions. You may find these solutions in catalogs or from garden-supply stores. They are typically inexpensive and only small quantities are needed to help your plants grow strong and healthy. Always follow the directions on the container when using pre-mixed chemicals.

Making Your Own Solution

In the event that you want to make your own nutrient solution, here is a formula for a solution that will provide all the major elements required for your plants to grow.

You can obtain all of these chemicals from garden-supply stores or drugstores.

Making Nutrient Solutions

For plants to grow properly, they must receive nitrogen, phosphorous, potassium, calcium, magnesium, sulfur, iron, manganese, boron, zinc, copper, molybdenum, and chlorine. There is a wide range of nutrient solutions that can be used. If your plants are receiving inadequate amounts of nutrients, they will show this in different ways. This means that you must proceed with caution when selecting and adding the minerals that will be present in your nutrient solution.

It is important to have pure nutrient materials when preparing the solution. Using fertilizer-grade chemicals is always the best route to go, as it is cheapest. Make sure the containers are closed and not exposed to air. Evaporated solutions increase the amount of salt which could harm your plants.

Salt	Grade	Nutrients	Amt. for 25 gallons of solution
Potassium phosphate	Technical	Potassium, phosphorus	½ ounce (1 Tbsp)
Potassium nitrate	Fertilizer	Potassium, nitrogen	2 ounces (4 Tbsp of powdered salt)
Calcium nitrate	Fertilizer	Calcium, nitrogen	3 ounces (7 Tbsp)
Magnesium sulfate	Fertilizer	Magnesium, sulfur	1½ ounces (4 Tbsp)

After all the chemicals have been mixed into the solution, check the pH of the solution. A pH of 7.0 is neutral; anything below 7.0 is acidic and anything above is alkaline. Certain plants grow best in certain pHs. Plants that grow well at a lower pH (between 4.5 and 5.5) are azaleas, buttercups, gardenias, and roses; plants that grow well at a neutral pH are potatoes, zinnias, and pumpkins; most plants grow best in a slightly acidic pH (between 5.5 and 6.5).

To determine the pH of your solution, use a pH indicator (these are usually paper strips). The strip will change color when placed in different levels of pH. If you find your pH level to be above your desired range, you can bring it down by adding dilute sulfuric acid in small quantities using an eyedropper. Keep retesting until you reach your desired pH level.

Plant Nutrient Deficiencies

When plants are lacking nutrients, they typically display these deficiencies outwardly. Following is a list of symptoms that might occur if a plant is lacking a certain type of nutrient. If your plants display any of these symptoms, it is imperative that the level of that particular nutrient be increased.

Deficient Nutrient	Symptoms
Boron	Tip of the shoot dies; stems and petioles are brittle
Calcium	Tip of the shoot dies; tips of the young leaves die; tips of the leaves are hooked
Iron	New upper leaves turn yellow between the veins; edges and tips of leaves may die
Magnesium	Lower leaves are yellow between the veins; leaf margins curl up or down; leaves die
Manganese	New upper leaves have dead spots; leaf might appear netted
Nitrogen	Leaves are small and light green; lower leaves are lighter than upper leaves; weak stalks
Phosphorous	Dark-green foliage; lower leaves are yellow between the veins; purplish color on leaves
Potassium	Lower leaves might be mottled; dead areas near tips of leaves; yellowing at leaf margins and toward the center
Sulfur	Light-green upper leaves; leaf veins are lighter than surrounding area

Aggregate culture is especially useful in urban areas where quality soil is not readily available. If the only spot you have for a garden is outside your window, you should still be able to grow a variety of flowers, vegetables, or herbs.

Pest and Disease Management

Pest management can be one of the greatest challenges to the home gardener. Yard pests include weeds, insects, diseases, and some species of wildlife. Weeds are plants that are growing out of place. Insect pests include an enormous number of species, from tiny thrips that are nearly invisible to the naked eye, to the large larvae of the tomato hornworm. Plant diseases are caused by fungi, bacteria, viruses, and other organisms—some of which are only now being classified. Poor plant nutrition and misuse of pesticides also can cause injury to plants. Slugs, mites, and many species of wildlife, such as rabbits, deer, and crows can be extremely destructive as well.

Identify the Problem

Careful identification of the problem is essential before taking measures to control the issue in your garden. Some insect damage may at first appear to be a disease, especially if no visible insects are present. Nutrient problems may also mimic diseases. Herbicide damage, resulting from misapplication of chemicals, can also be mistaken for other problems. Learning about different types of garden pests is the first step in keeping your plants healthy and productive.

Insects and Mites

All insects have six legs, but other than that they are extremely different depending on the species. Some insects include such organisms as beetles, flies, bees, ants, moths, and butterflies. Mites and spiders have eight legs—they are not, in fact, insects but will be treated as such for the purposes of this section.

Insects damage plants in several ways. The most visible damage caused by insects is chewed plant leaves and flowers. Many pests are visible and

Leaf damage from Japanese beetles

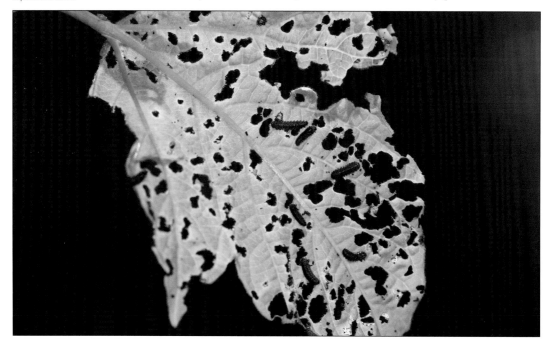

A Japanese beetles eats holes in a leaf

Other insects cause damage to plants by boring into stems, fruits, and leaves, possibly disrupting the plant's ability to transport water. They also create opportunities for disease organisms to attack the plants. You may suspect the presence of boring insects if you see small accumulations of sawdust-like material on plant stems or fruits. Common examples of boring insects include squash vine borers and corn borers.

Integrated Pest Management (IPM)

It is difficult, if not impossible, to prevent all pest problems in your garden every year. If your best prevention efforts have not been entirely successful, you may need to use some control methods. Integrated pest management (IPM) relies on several techniques to keep pests at acceptable population levels without excessive use of chemical controls. The basic principles of IPM include monitoring (scouting), determining tolerable injury levels (thresholds), and applying appropriate strategies and tactics to solve the pest issue. Unlike other methods of pest control where pesticides are applied on a rigid schedule, IPM applies only those controls that are needed, when they are needed, to control pests that will cause more than a tolerable level of damage to the plant.

Monitoring

Monitoring is essential for a successful IPM program. Check your plants regularly. Look for signs of damage from insects and diseases as well as indications of ade-

can be readily identified, including the Japanese beetle, Colorado potato beetle, and numerous species of caterpillars such as tent caterpillars and tomato hornworms. Other chewing insects, however, such as cutworms (which are caterpillars), come out at night to eat, and burrow into the soil during the day. These are much harder to identify but should be considered likely culprits if young plants seem to disappear overnight or are found cut off at ground level.

Sucking insects are extremely common in gardens and can be very damaging to your vegetable plants and flowers. The most known of these insects are leafhoppers, aphids, mealy bugs, thrips, and mites. These insects insert their mouthparts into the plant tissues and suck out the plant juices. They also may carry diseases that they spread from plant to plant as they move about the yard. You may suspect that these insects are present if you notice misshapen plant leaves or flower petals. Often the younger leaves will appear curled or puckered. Flowers developing from the buds may only partially develop if they've been sucked by these bugs. Look on the undersides of the leaves—that is where many insects tend to gather.

Certain kinds of worms and beetles will leave damaging holes in your plants.

Aphids

quate fertility and moisture. Early identification of potential problems is essential.

There are thousands of insects in a garden, many of which are harmless or even beneficial to the plants. Proper identification is needed before control strategies can be adopted. It is important to recognize the different stages of insect development for several reasons. The caterpillar eating your plants may be the larvae of the butterfly you were trying to attract. Any small larvae with six spots on its back is probably a young ladybug, a very beneficial insect.

Thresholds

It is not necessary to kill every insect, weed, or disease organism invading your garden in order to maintain the plants' health. When dealing with garden pests, an economic threshold comes into play and is the point where the damage caused by the pest exceeds the cost of control. In a home garden, this can be difficult to determine. What you are growing and how you intend to use it will determine how much damage you are willing to tolerate. Remember that larger plants, especially those close to harvest, can tolerate more damage than a tiny seedling. A few flea beetles on a radish seedling may warrant control, whereas numerous Japanese beetles eating the leaves of beans close to harvest may not.

If the threshold level for control has been exceeded, you may need to employ control strategies. Effective and safe strategies can be discussed with your local Cooperative Extension Service, garden centers, or nurseries.

Mechanical/Physical Control Strategies

Many insects can simply be removed by hand. This method is definitely preferable if only a few, large insects are causing the problem. Simply remove the insect from the plant and drop it into a container of soapy water or vegetable oil. Be aware that some insects have prickly

Beneficial Insects that Help Control Pest Populations

Insect	Pest Controlled
Green lacewings	Aphids, mealy bugs, thrips, and spider mites
Ladybugs	Aphids and Colorado potato beetles
Praying mantises	Almost any insect
Ground beetles	Caterpillars that attack trees and shrubs
Seedhead weevils and other beetles	Weeds

spines or excrete oily substances that can cause injury to humans. Use caution when handling unfamiliar insects. Wear gloves or remove insects with tweezers.

Many insects can be removed from plants by spraying water from a hose or sprayer. Small vacuums can also be used to suck up insects. Traps can be used effectively for some insects as well. These come in a variety of styles depending on the insect to be caught. Many traps rely on the use of pheromones—naturally occurring chemicals produced by the insects and used to attract the opposite sex during mating. They are extremely specific for each species and, therefore, will not harm beneficial species. One caution with traps is that they may actually draw more insects into your yard, so don't place them directly into your garden. Other traps (such as yellow and blue sticky cards) are more generic and will attract numerous species. Different insects are attracted to different colors of these traps. Sticky cards also can be used effectively to monitor insect pests.

Other Pest Controls

Diatomaceous earth, a powder-like dust made of tiny marine organisms called diatoms, can be used to reduce damage from soft-bodied insects and slugs. Spread this material on the soil—it is sharp and cuts or irritates these soft organisms. It is harmless to other organisms. In order to trap slugs, put out shallow dishes of beer.

Biological Controls

Biological controls are nature's way of regulating pest populations. Biological controls rely on predators and parasites to keep organisms under control. Many of our present pest problems result from the loss of predator species and other biological control factors.

Some biological controls include birds and bats that eat insects. A single bat can eat up to 600 mosquitoes an hour. Many bird species eat insect pests on trees and in the garden.

Chemical Controls

When using biological controls, be very careful with pesticides. Most common pesticides are broad spectrum,

Cutworms

stream of water from a hose all work to dislodge insects from your garden plants.

Another solution is to also consider using plants that naturally repel insects. These plants have their own chemical defense systems, and when planted among flowers and vegetables, they help keep unwanted insects away.

Plant Diseases

Plant disease identification is extremely difficult. In some cases, only laboratory analysis can conclusively identify some diseases. Disease organisms injure plants in several ways: Some attack leaf surfaces and limit the plant's ability to carry on photosynthesis; others produce substances that clog plant tissues that transport water and nutrients; still other disease organisms produce toxins that kill the plant or replace plant tissue with their own.

Natural Pest Repellants

Pest	Repellant
Ant	Mint, tansy, or pennyroyal
Aphids	Mint, garlic, chives, coriander, or anise
Bean leaf beetle	Potato, onion, or turnip
Codling moth	Common oleander
Colorado potato bug	Green beans, coriander, or nasturtium
Cucumber beetle	Radish or tansy
Flea beetle	Garlic, onion, or mint
Imported cabbage worm	Mint, sage, rosemary, or hyssop
Japanese beetle	Garlic, larkspur, tansy, rue, or geranium
Leaf hopper	Geranium or petunia
Mice	Onion
Root knot nematodes	French marigolds
Slugs	Prostrate rosemary or wormwood
Spider mites	Onion, garlic, cloves, or chives
Squash bug	Radish, marigolds, tansy, or nasturtium
Stink bug	Radish
Thrips	Marigolds
Tomato hornworm	Marigolds, sage, or borage
Whitefly	Marigolds or nasturtium

which means that they kill a wide variety of organisms. Spray applications of insecticides are likely to kill numerous beneficial insects as well as the pests. Herbicides applied to weed species may drift in the wind or vaporize in the heat of the day and injure non-targeted plants. Runoff of pesticides can pollute water. Many pesticides are toxic to humans as well as pets and small animals that may enter your yard. Try to avoid using these types of pesticides at all costs—and if you do use them, read the labels carefully and avoid spraying them on windy days.

Some common, non-toxic household substances are as effective as many toxic pesticides. A few drops of dishwashing detergent mixed with water and sprayed on plants is extremely effective in controlling many soft-bodied insects, such as aphids and whiteflies. Crushed garlic mixed with water may control certain insects. A baking soda solution has been shown to help control some fungal diseases on roses.

Alternatives to Pesticides and Chemicals

When used incorrectly, pesticides can pollute water. They also kill beneficial as well as harmful insects. Natural alternatives prevent both of these events from occurring and save you money. Consider using natural alternatives for chemical pesticides: Non-detergent insecticidal soaps, garlic, hot pepper spray, 1 teaspoon of liquid soap in a gallon of water, used dishwater, or a forceful

Symptoms that are associated with plant diseases may include the presence of mushroom-like growths on trunks of trees; leaves with a grayish, mildewed appearance; spots on leaves, flowers, and fruits; sudden wilting or death of a plant or branch; sap exuding from branches or trunks of trees; and stunted growth.

Misapplication of pesticides and nutrients, air pollutants, and other environmental conditions—such as flooding and freezing—can also mimic some disease problems. Yellowing or reddening of leaves and stunted growth may indicate a nutritional problem. Leaf curling or misshapen growth may be a result of herbicide application.

Pest and Disease Management Practices

Preventing pests should be your first goal when growing a garden, although it is unlikely that you will be able to avoid all pest problems because some plant seeds and disease organisms may lay dormant in the soil for years.

Diseases need three elements to become established in plants: the disease organism, a susceptible species, and the proper environmental conditions. Some disease organisms can live in the soil for years; other organisms are carried in infected plant material that falls to the ground. Some disease organisms are carried by insects. Good sanitation will help limit some problems with disease. Choosing resistant varieties of plants also prevents many diseases from occurring. Rotating annual plants in a garden can also prevent some diseases.

Plants that have adequate, but not excessive, nutrients are better able to resist attacks from both diseases and insects. Excessive rates of nitrogen often result in extremely succulent vegetative growth and can make plants more susceptible to insect and disease problems, as well as decreasing their winter hardiness. Proper watering and spacing of plants limits the spread of some diseases and provides good aeration around plants, so diseases that fester in standing water cannot multiply. Trickle irrigation, where water is applied to the soil and not the plant leaves, may be helpful.

Removal of diseased material certainly limits the spread of some diseases. It is important to clean up litter

Powdery mildew leaf disease

dropped from diseased plants. Prune diseased branches on trees and shrubs to allow for more air circulation. When pruning diseased trees and shrubs, disinfect your pruners between cuts with a solution of chlorine bleach to avoid spreading the disease from plant to plant. Also try to control insects that may carry diseases to your plants.

You can make your own natural fungicide by combining 5 teaspoons each of baking soda and hydrogen peroxide with a gallon of water. Spray on your infected plants. Milk diluted with water is also an effective fungicide, due to the potassium phosphate in it, which boosts a plant's immune system. The more diluted the solution, the more frequently you'll need to spray the plant.

Harvesting Your Garden

It is essential, in order to get the best freshness, flavor, and nutritional benefits from your garden vegetables and fruits, to harvest them at the appropriate time. The vegetable's stage of maturity and the time of day at which it is harvested are essential for good-tasting and nutritious produce. Overripe vegetables and fruits will be stringy and coarse. When possible, harvest your vegetables during the cool part of the morning. If you are going to can and preserve your vegetables and fruits, do so as soon as possible. Or, if this process must be delayed, cool the vegetables in ice water or crushed ice and store them in the refrigerator. Here are some brief guidelines for harvesting various types of common garden produce:

Asparagus—Harvest the spears when they are at least 6 to 8 inches tall by snapping or cutting them at ground level. A few spears may be harvested the second year after crowns are set out. A full harvest season will last four to six weeks during the third growing season.

Beans, snap—Harvest before the seeds develop in the pod. Beans are ready to pick if they snap easily when bent in half.

Beans, lima—Harvest when the pods first start to bulge with the enlarged seeds. Pods must still be green, not yellowish.

Broccoli—Harvest the dark green, compact cluster, or head, while the buds are shut tight, before any yellow flowers appear. Smaller side shoots will develop later, providing a continuous harvest.

Brussels sprouts—Harvest the lower sprouts (small heads) when they are about 1 to 1 ½ inches in diameter by twisting them off. Removing the lower leaves along the stem will help to hasten the plant's maturity.

Cabbage—Harvest when the heads feel hard and solid.

Cantaloupe—Harvest when the stem slips easily from the fruit with a gentle tug. Another indicator of ripeness is when the netting on the skin becomes rounded and the flesh between the netting turns from a green to a tan color.

Carrots—Harvest when the roots are ¾ to 1 inch in diameter. The largest roots generally have darker tops.

Cauliflower—When preparing to harvest, exclude sunlight when the curds (heads) are 1 to 2 inches in diameter by loosely tying the outer leaves

Dried corn can be made into cornmeal by removing the kernels from the husk and grinding them in a food processor.

If you have an over-abundance of snap peas, blanche them for 1 to 2 minutes, drain, dunk them in ice water, drain again, and freeze in airtight plastic bags.

together above the curd with a string or rubber band. This process is known as blanching. Harvest the curds when they are 4 to 6 inches in diameter but still compact, white, and smooth. The head should be ready 10 to 15 days after tying the leaves.

Collards—Harvest older, lower leaves when they reach a length of 8 to 12 inches. New leaves will grow as long as the central growing point remains, providing a continuous harvest. Whole plants may be harvested and cooked if desired.

Corn, sweet—The silks begin to turn brown and dry out as the ears mature. Check a few ears for maturity by opening the top of the ear and pressing a few kernels with your thumbnail. If the exuded liquid is milky rather than clear, the ear is ready for harvesting. Cooking a few ears is also a good way to test for maturity.

Cucumbers—Harvest when the fruits are 6 to 8 inches in length. Harvest when the color is deep green and before yellow color appears. Pick four to five times per week to encourage continuous production. Leaving mature cucumbers on the vine will stop the production of the entire plant.

Eggplant—Harvest when the fruits are 4 to 5 inches in diameter and their color is a glossy, purplish black. The fruit is getting too ripe when the color starts to dull or become bronzed. Because the stem is woody, cut—do not pull—the fruit from the plant. A short stem should remain on each fruit.

Kale—Harvest by twisting off the outer, older leaves when they reach a length of 8 to 10 inches and are medium green in color. Heavy, dark green leaves are overripe and are likely to be tough and bitter. New leaves will grow, providing a continuous harvest.

Lettuce—Harvest the older, outer leaves from leaf lettuce as soon as they are 4 to 6 inches long. Harvest heading types when the heads are moderately firm and before seed stalks form.

Mustard—Harvest the leaves and leaf stems when they are 6 to 8 inches long; new leaves will provide a continuous harvest until they become too strong in flavor and tough in texture, due to temperature extremes.

Okra—Harvest young, tender pods when they are 2 to 3 inches long. Pick the okra at least every other day during the peak growing season. Overripe pods become woody and are too tough to eat.

Onions—Harvest when the tops fall over and begin to turn yellow. Dig up the onions and allow them to dry out in the open sun for a few days to toughen the skin. Then remove the dried soil by brushing the onions lightly. Cut the stem, leaving 2 to 3 inches attached, and store in a net-type bag in a cool, dry place.

Peas—Harvest regular peas when the pods are well rounded; edible-pod varieties should be harvested when the seeds are fully developed but still fresh and bright green. Pods are getting too old when they lose their brightness and turn light or yellowish green.

Peppers—Harvest sweet peppers with a sharp knife when the fruits are firm, crisp, and full size. Green peppers will turn red if left on the plant. Allow hot peppers to attain their bright red color and full flavor while attached to the vine; then cut them and hang them to dry.

Potatoes (Irish)—Harvest the tubers when the plants begin to dry and die down. Store the tubers in a cool, high-humidity location with good ventilation, such as the basement or crawl space of your house. Avoid exposing the tubers to light, as greening, which denotes the presence of dangerous alkaloids, will occur even with small amounts of light.

Pumpkins—Harvest pumpkins and winter squash before the first frost. After the vines dry up, the fruit color darkens and the skin surface resists puncture from your thumbnail. Avoid bruising or scratching the fruit while handling it. Leave a 3- to 4-inch portion of the stem

Don't cut asparagus below the soil as it could damage other buds on the crown that would otherwise send up new spears.

attached to the fruit and store it in a cool, dry location with good ventilation.

Radishes—Harvest when the roots are ½ to 1½ inches in diameter. The shoulders of radish roots often appear through the soil surface when they are mature. If left in the ground too long, the radishes will become tough and woody.

Rutabagas—Harvest when the roots are about 3 inches in diameter. The roots may be stored in the ground and used as needed, if properly mulched.

Spinach—Harvest by cutting all the leaves off at the base of the plant when they are 4 to 6 inches long. New leaves will grow, providing additional harvests.

Squash, summer—Harvest when the fruit is soft, tender, and 6 to 8 inches long. The skin color often changes to a dark, glossy green or yellow, depending on the variety. Pick every two to three days to encourage continued production.

Sweet potatoes—Harvest the roots when they are large enough for use before the first frost. Avoid bruising or scratching the potatoes during handling. Ideal storage conditions are at a temperature of 55°F and a relative humidity of 85 percent. The basement or crawl space of a house may suffice.

Swiss chard—Harvest by breaking off the developed outer leaves 1 inch above the soil. New leaves will grow, providing a continuous harvest.

Tomatoes—Harvest the fruits at the most appealing stage of ripeness, when they are bright red. The flavor is best at room temperature, but ripe fruit may be held in the refrigerator at 45 to 50°F for 7 to 10 days.

Turnips—Harvest the roots when they are 2 to 3 inches in diameter but before heavy fall frosts occur. The tops may be used as salad greens when the leaves are 3 to 5 inches long.

Watermelons—Harvest when the watermelon produces a dull thud rather than a sharp, metallic sound when thumped—this means the fruit is ripe. Other ripeness indicators are a deep yellow rather than a white color where the melon touches the ground, brown tendrils on the stem near the fruit, and a rough, slightly ridged feel to the skin surface.

PART TWO   # The Pantry

One of the greatest pleasures of self-sufficiency is preparing, preserving, and eating your own food. After the hard work of planting and tending your gardens, or raising animals for eggs, milk, or meat, your kitchen will become a joyful laboratory where you can create wonderful foods from the fruits of your labor to enjoy or to share. With a little preparation, your pantry can become a treasure trove of canned and dried foods, ready to draw from all winter long. There is something distinctly rewarding about running out to the garden to pick salad makings in the summer, or reaching into the cupboard for a new jar of strawberry jam in the middle of the winter. It's a gift more and more people are finding time to accept, as the quality of super-market offerings seems to plummet and a new awareness of the benefits of locally grown food sweeps across rural and urban areas alike. If you don't have the space or time to grow or produce your own food, there are farmers' markets springing up all over where you can find fresh, delicious produce, meats, baked goods, and dairy products to enjoy on your own or to inspire a festive dinner party. Whether you go to the garden, the pantry, or the market for your food, remember the work that went into its growth and preparation and you will begin to see food not only as a necessity and a pleasure, but as a great gift.

Canning

Introduction to Canning

On the next few pages, you will find descriptions of proper canning methods, with details on how canning works and why it is both safe and economical. Much of the information here is from the USDA, which has done extensive research on home canning and preserving. If you are new to home canning, read this section carefully as it will help to ensure success with the recipes that follow.

Whether you are a seasoned home canner or this is your first foray into food preservation, it is important to follow directions carefully. With some recipes it is okay to experiment with varied proportions or added ingredients, and with others it is important to stick to what's written. In many instances it is noted whether creative liberty is a good idea for a particular recipe, but if you are not sure, play it safe—otherwise you may end up with a jam that is too runny, a vegetable that is mushy, or a product that is spoiled. Take time to read the directions and prepare your foods and equipment adequately, and you will find that home canning is safe, economical, tremendously satisfying, and a great deal of fun!

Why Can Foods?

Canning is fun and a good way to preserve your precious produce. As more and more farmers' markets make their way into urban centers, city dwellers are also discovering how rewarding it is to make seasonal treats last all year round. Besides the value of your labor, canning home-grown or locally grown food may save you half the cost of buying commercially canned food. And what makes a nicer, more thoughtful gift than a jar of homemade jam, tailored to match the recipient's favorite fruits and flavors?

The nutritional value of home canning is an added benefit. Many vegetables begin to lose their vitamins as soon as they are harvested. Nearly half

Canned jams and nut butters.

the vitamins may be lost within a few days unless the fresh produce is kept cool or preserved. Within one to two weeks, even refrigerated produce loses half or more of certain vitamins. The heating process during canning destroys from one-third to one-half of vitamins A and C, thiamin, and riboflavin. Once canned, foods may lose from 5 percent to 20 percent of these sensitive vitamins each year. The amounts of other vitamins, however, are only slightly lower in canned compared with fresh food. If vegetables are handled properly and canned promptly after harvest, they can be more nutritious than fresh produce sold in local stores.

The advantages of home canning are lost when you start with poor quality foods; when jars fail to seal properly; when food spoils; and when flavors, texture, color, and nutrients deteriorate during prolonged storage. The tips that follow explain many of these problems and recommend ways to minimize them.

How Canning Preserves Foods

The high percentage of water in most fresh foods makes them very perishable. They spoil or lose their quality for several reasons:

- Growth of undesirable microorganisms—bacteria, molds, and yeasts
- Activity of food enzymes
- Reactions with oxygen
- Moisture loss

Microorganisms live and multiply quickly on the surfaces of fresh food and on the inside of bruised, insect-damaged, and diseased food. Oxygen and enzymes are present throughout fresh food tissues.

Proper canning practices include:

- Carefully selecting and washing fresh food
- Peeling some fresh foods
- Hot packing many foods
- Adding acids (lemon juice, citric acid, or vinegar) to some foods
- Using acceptable jars and self-sealing lids
- Processing jars in a boiling-water or pressure canner for the correct amount of time

Collectively, these practices remove oxygen; destroy enzymes; prevent the growth of undesirable bacteria, yeasts, and molds; and help form a high vacuum in jars. High vacuums form tight seals, which keep liquid in and air and microorganisms out.

CANNING began in France, at the turn of the nineteenth century, when Napoleon Bonaparte was desperate for a way to keep his troops well-fed while on the march. In 1800, he decided to hold a contest, offering 12,000 francs to anyone who could devise a suitable method of food preservation. Nicolas François Appert, a French confectioner, rose to the challenge, considering that if wine could be preserved in bottles, perhaps food could be as well. He experimented until he was able to prove that heating food to boiling after it had been sealed in airtight glass bottles prevented the food from deteriorating. Interestingly, this all took place about 100 years before Louis Pasteur found that heat could destroy bacteria. Nearly ten years after the contest began, Napoleon personally presented Nicolas with the cash reward.

Canned applesauce and peaches line this pantry's shelves.

Canning Glossary

Acid foods—Foods that contain enough acid to result in a pH of 4.6 or lower. Includes most tomatoes; fermented and pickled vegetables; relishes; jams, jellies, and marmalades; and all fruits except figs. Acid foods may be processed in boiling water.

Ascorbic acid—The chemical name for vitamin C. Commonly used to prevent browning of peeled, light-colored fruits and vegetables.

Blancher—A 6- to 8-quart lidded pot designed with a fitted, perforated basket to hold food in boiling water or with a fitted rack to steam foods. Useful for loosening skins on fruits to be peeled or for heating foods to be hot packed.

Boiling-water canner—A large, standard-sized, lidded kettle with jar rack designed for heat-processing seven quarts or eight to nine pints in boiling water.

Botulism—An illness caused by eating a toxin produced by growth of *Clostridium botulinum* bacteria in moist, low-acid food containing less than 2 percent oxygen and stored between 40°F and 120°F. Proper heat processing destroys this bacterium in canned food. Freezer temperatures inhibit its growth in frozen food. Low moisture controls its growth in dried food. High oxygen controls its growth in fresh foods.

Canning—A method of preserving food that employs heat processing in airtight, vacuum-sealed containers so that food can be safely stored at normal home temperatures.

Canning salt—Also called pickling salt. It is regular table salt without the anti-caking or iodine additives.

Citric acid—A form of acid that can be added to canned foods. It increases the acidity of low-acid foods and may improve their flavor.

Cold pack—Canning procedure in which jars are filled with raw food. "Raw pack" is the preferred term for describing this practice. "Cold pack" is often used incorrectly to refer to foods that are open-kettle canned or jars that are heat-processed in boiling water.

Enzymes—Proteins in food that accelerate many flavor, color, texture, and nutritional changes, especially when food is cut, sliced, crushed, bruised, or exposed

Green beans should be chopped into small pieces before canning.

to air. Proper blanching or hot-packing practices destroy enzymes and improve food quality.

Exhausting—Removing air from within and around food and from jars and canners. Exhausting or venting of pressure canners is necessary to prevent botulism in low-acid canned foods.

Headspace—The unfilled space above food or liquid in jars that allows for food expansion as jars are heated and for forming vacuums as jars cool.

Heat processing—Treatment of jars with sufficient heat to enable storing food at normal home temperatures.

Hermetic seal—An absolutely airtight container seal that prevents reentry of air or microorganisms into packaged foods.

Hot pack—Heating of raw food in boiling water or steam and filling it hot into jars.

Low-acid foods—Foods that contain very little acid and have a pH above 4.6. The acidity in these foods is insufficient to prevent the growth of botulism bacteria. Vegetables, some varieties of tomatoes, figs, all meats, fish, seafood, and some dairy products are low-acid foods. To control all risks of botulism, jars of these foods must be either heat processed in a pressure canner or acidified to a pH of 4.6 or lower before being processed in boiling water.

Microorganisms—Independent organisms of microscopic size, including bacteria, yeast, and mold. In a suitable environment, they grow rapidly and may divide or reproduce every 10 to 30 minutes. Therefore, they reach high populations very quickly. Microorganisms are sometimes intentionally added to ferment foods, make antibiotics, and for other reasons. Undesirable microorganisms cause disease and food spoilage.

Mold—A fungus-type microorganism whose growth on food is usually visible and colorful. Molds may grow on many foods, including acid foods like jams and jellies and canned fruits. Recommended heat processing and sealing practices prevent their growth on these foods.

Mycotoxins—Toxins produced by the growth of some molds on foods.

Open-kettle canning—A non-recommended canning method. Food is heat-processed in a covered kettle, filled while hot into sterile jars, and then sealed. Foods canned this way have low vacuums or too much air, which permits rapid loss of quality in foods. Also, these foods often spoil because they become recontaminated while the jars are being filled.

Pasteurization—Heating food to temperatures high enough to destroy disease-causing microorganisms.

pH—A measure of acidity or alkalinity. Values range from 0 to 14. A food is neutral when its pH is 7.0. Lower values are increasingly more acidic; higher values are increasingly more alkaline.

PSIG—Pounds per square inch of pressure as measured by a gauge.

Pressure canner—A specifically designed metal kettle with a lockable lid used for heat-processing low-acid food. These canners have jar racks, one or more safety devices, systems for exhausting air, and a way to measure or control pressure. Canners with 20- to 21-quart capacity are common. The minimum size of canner that should be used has a 16-quart capacity and can hold seven one-quart jars. Use of pressure saucepans with a capacity of less than 16 quarts is not recommended.

Raw pack—The practice of filling jars with raw, unheated food. Acceptable for canning low-acid foods, but allows more rapid quality losses in acid foods that are heat-processed in boiling water. Also called "cold pack."

Style of pack—Form of canned food, such as whole, sliced, piece, juice, or sauce. The term may also be used to specify whether food is filled raw or hot into jars.

Vacuum—A state of negative pressure that reflects how thoroughly air is removed from within a jar of processed food; the higher the vacuum, the less air left in the jar.

Peel potatoes before canning them.

A large stockpot with a lid can be used in place of a boiling-water canner for high-acid foods like tomatoes, pickles, apples, peaches, and jams. Simply place a rack inside the pot so that the jars do not rest directly on the bottom of the pot.

Proper Canning Practices

Growth of the bacterium *Clostridium botulinum* in canned food may cause botulism—a deadly form of food poisoning. These bacteria exist either as spores or as vegetative cells. The spores, which are comparable to plant seeds, can survive harmlessly in soil and water for many years. When ideal conditions exist for growth, the spores produce vegetative cells, which multiply rapidly and may produce a deadly toxin within three to four days in an environment consisting of:

- A moist, low-acid food
- A temperature between 40°F and 120°F, and
- Less than 2 percent oxygen.

Botulinum spores are on most fresh food surfaces. Because they grow only in the absence of air, they are harmless on fresh foods. Most bacteria, yeasts, and molds are difficult to remove from food surfaces. Washing fresh food reduces their numbers only slightly. Peeling root crops, underground stem crops, and tomatoes reduces their numbers greatly. Blanching also helps, but the vital controls are the method of canning and use of the recommended research-based processing times. These processing times ensure destruction of the largest expected number of heat-resistant microorganisms in home-canned foods.

Properly sterilized canned food will be free of spoilage if lids seal and jars are stored below 95°F. Storing jars at 50 to 70°F enhances retention of quality.

Food Acidity and Processing Methods

Whether food should be processed in a pressure canner or boiling-water canner to control botulism bacteria depends on the acidity in the food. Acidity may be natural, as in most fruits, or added, as in pickled food. Low-acid canned foods contain too little acidity to prevent the growth of these bacteria. Other foods may contain enough acidity to block their growth or to destroy them rapidly when heated. The term "pH" is a measure of acidity: the lower its value, the more acidic the food. The acidity level in foods can be increased by adding lemon juice, citric acid, or vinegar.

Low-acid foods have pH values higher than 4.6. They include red meats, seafood, poultry, milk, and all fresh vegetables except for most tomatoes. Most products that are mixtures of low-acid and acid foods also have pH values above 4.6 unless their ingredients include enough lemon juice, citric acid, or vinegar to make them acid foods. Acid foods have a pH of 4.6 or lower. They include fruits, pickles, sauerkraut, jams, jellies, marmalade, and fruit butters.

Although tomatoes usually are considered an acid food, some are now known to have pH values slightly above 4.6. Figs also have pH values slightly above 4.6. Therefore, if they are to be canned as acid foods, these products must be acidified to a pH of 4.6 or lower with lemon juice or citric acid. Properly acidified tomatoes and figs are acid foods and can be safely processed in a boiling-water canner.

Botulinum spores are very hard to destroy at boiling-water temperatures; the higher the canner temperature, the more easily they are destroyed. Therefore, all low-acid foods should be sterilized at temperatures of 240 to 250°F, attainable with pressure canners operated at 10 to 15 PSIG. (PSIG means pounds per square inch of pressure as measured by a gauge.) At these temperatures, the time needed to destroy bacteria in low-acid canned foods ranges from 20 to 100 minutes. The exact time depends on the kind of food being canned, the way it is packed into jars, and the size of jars. The time needed to safely process low-acid foods in boiling water ranges from 7 to 11 hours; the time needed to process acid foods in boiling water varies from 5 to 85 minutes.

Know Your Altitude

It is important to know your approximate elevation or altitude above sea level in order to determine a safe processing time for canned foods. Since the boiling temperature of liquid is lower at higher elevations, it is critical that additional time be given for the safe processing of foods at altitudes above sea level.

What Not to Do

Open-kettle canning and the processing of freshly filled jars in conventional ovens, microwave ovens, and dishwashers are not recommended because these practices do not prevent all risks of spoilage. Steam canners are not recommended because processing times for use with current models have not been adequately researched. Because steam canners may not heat foods in the same manner as boiling-water canners, their use with boiling-water processing times may result in spoilage. So-called canning powders are useless as preservatives and do not replace the need for proper heat processing.

Label your jars after processing with the contents and the date.

It is not recommended that pressures in excess of 15 PSIG be applied when using new pressure-canning equipment.

Ensuring High-Quality Canned Foods

Examine food carefully for freshness and wholesomeness. Discard diseased and moldy food. Trim small diseased lesions or spots from food.

Can fruits and vegetables picked from your garden or purchased from nearby producers when the products are at their peak of quality—within 6 to 12 hours after harvest for most vegetables. However, apricots, nectarines, peaches, pears, and plums should be ripened one or more days between harvest and canning. If you must delay the canning of other fresh produce, keep it in a shady, cool place.

Fresh, home-slaughtered red meats and poultry should be chilled and canned without delay. Do not can meat from sickly or diseased animals. Put fish and seafood on ice after harvest, eviscerate immediately, and can them within two days.

Maintaining Color and Flavor in Canned Food

To maintain good natural color and flavor in stored canned food, you must:

- Remove oxygen from food tissues and jars,
- Quickly destroy the food enzymes, and
- Obtain high jar vacuums and airtight jar seals.

Follow these guidelines to ensure that your canned foods retain optimal colors and flavors during processing and storage:

- Use only high-quality foods that are at the proper maturity and are free of diseases and bruises.
- Use the hot-pack method, especially with acid foods to be processed in boiling water.
- Don't unnecessarily expose prepared foods to air; can them as soon as possible.
- While preparing a canner load of jars, keep peeled, halved, quartered, sliced or diced apples, apricots, nectarines, peaches, and pears in a solution of 3 grams (3,000 milligrams) ascorbic acid to 1 gallon of cold water. This procedure is also useful in maintaining the natural color of mushrooms and potatoes and for preventing stem-end discoloration in cherries and grapes. You can get ascorbic acid in several forms:

Pure powdered form—Seasonally available among canning supplies in supermarkets. One level teaspoon of pure powder weighs about 3 grams. Use 1 teaspoon per gallon of water as a treatment solution.

Vitamin C tablets—Economical and available year-round in many stores. Buy 500-milligram tablets; crush and dissolve six tablets per gallon of water as a treatment solution.

Commercially prepared mixes of ascorbic and citric acid—Seasonally available among canning supplies in supermarkets. Sometimes citric acid powder is sold

in supermarkets, but it is less effective in controlling discoloration. If you choose to use these products, follow the manufacturer's directions.

- Fill hot foods into jars and adjust headspace as specified in recipes.
- Tighten screw bands securely, but if you are especially strong, not as tightly as possible.
- Process and cool jars.
- Store the jars in a relatively cool, dark place, preferably between 50 and 70°F.
- Can no more food than you will use within a year.

Advantages of Hot Packing

Many fresh foods contain from 10 percent to more than 30 percent air. The length of time that food will last at premium quality depends on how much air is removed from the food before jars are sealed. The more air that is removed, the higher the quality of the canned product.

Raw packing is the practice of filling jars tightly with freshly prepared but unheated food. Such foods, especially fruit, will float in the jars. The entrapped air in and around the food may cause discoloration within two to three months of storage. Raw packing is more suitable for vegetables processed in a pressure canner.

Hot packing is the practice of heating freshly prepared food to boiling, simmering it three to five minutes, and promptly filling jars loosely with the boiled food.

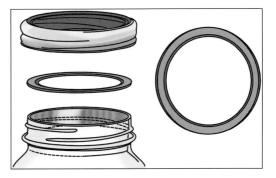

Hot packing is the best way to remove air and is the preferred pack style for foods processed in a boiling-water canner. At first, the color of hot-packed foods may appear no better than that of raw-packed foods, but within a short storage period, both color and flavor of hot-packed foods will be superior.

Whether food has been hot packed or raw packed, the juice, syrup, or water to be added to the foods should be heated to boiling before it is added to the jars. This practice helps to remove air from food tissues, shrinks food, helps keep the food from floating in the jars, increases vacuum in sealed jars, and improves shelf life. Preshrinking food allows you to add more food to each jar.

Controlling Headspace

The unfilled space above the food in a jar and below its lid is termed headspace. It is best to leave a ¼-inch headspace for jams and jellies, ½-inch for fruits and tomatoes to be processed in boiling water, and from 1 to 1¼ inches in low-acid foods to be processed in a pressure canner.

This space is needed for expansion of food as jars are processed and for forming vacuums in cooled jars. The extent of expansion is determined by the air content in the food and by the processing temperature. Air expands greatly when heated to high temperatures—the higher the temperature, the greater the expansion. Foods expand less than air when heated.

Jars and Lids

Food may be canned in glass jars or metal containers. Metal containers can be used only once. They require special sealing equipment and are much more costly than jars.

Mason-type jars designed for home canning are ideal for preserving food by pressure or boiling-water canning. Regular and wide-mouthed threaded mason jars with self-sealing lids are the best choices. They are available in half-pint, pint, 1½-pint, and quart sizes. The standard jar mouth opening is about 2⅜ inches. Wide-mouthed jars have openings of about 3 inches, making them more easily filled and emptied. Regular-mouthed decorative jelly jars are available in 8-ounce and 12-ounce sizes.

With careful use and handling, mason jars may be reused many times, requiring only new lids each time. When lids are used properly, jar seals and vacuums are excellent.

Jar Cleaning

Before reuse, wash empty jars in hot water with detergent and rinse well by hand, or wash in a dishwasher. Rinse thoroughly, as detergent residue may cause unnatural flavors and colors. Scale or hard-water films on jars are easily removed by soaking jars for several hours in a solution containing 1 cup of vinegar (5 percent acid) per gallon of water.

Sterilization of Empty Jars

Use sterile jars for all jams, jellies, and pickled products processed less than 10 minutes. To sterilize empty jars, put them right side up on the rack in a boiling-water canner. Fill the canner and jars with hot (not boiling) water to 1 inch above the tops of the jars. Boil for 10 minutes. Remove and drain hot, sterilized jars one at a time. Save the hot water for processing filled jars. Fill jars with food, add lids, and tighten screw bands.

Empty jars used for vegetables, meats, and fruits to be processed in a pressure canner need not be sterilized beforehand. It is also unnecessary to sterilize jars for fruits, tomatoes, and pickled or fermented foods that will be processed 10 minutes or longer in a boiling-water canner.

Lid Selection, Preparation, and Use

The common self-sealing lid consists of a flat metal lid held in place by a metal screw band during processing. The flat lid is crimped around its bottom edge to form a trough, which is filled with a colored gasket material. When jars are processed, the lid gasket softens and flows slightly to cover the jar-sealing surface, yet allows air to escape from the jar. The gasket then forms an airtight seal as the jar cools. Gaskets in unused lids work well for at least five years from date of manufacture. The gasket material in older, unused lids may fail to seal on jars.

It is best to buy only the quantity of lids you will use in a year. To ensure a good seal, carefully follow the manufacturer's directions in preparing lids for use. Examine all metal lids carefully. Do not use old, dented, or deformed lids or lids with gaps or other defects in the sealing gasket.

After filling jars with food, release air bubbles by inserting a flat, plastic (not metal) spatula between the food and the jar. Slowly turn the jar and move the spatula up and down to allow air bubbles to escape. Adjust the headspace and then clean the jar rim (sealing surface) with a dampened paper towel. Place the lid, gasket down, onto the cleaned jar-sealing surface. Uncleaned jar-sealing surfaces may cause seal failures.

Then fit the metal screw band over the flat lid. Follow the manufacturer's guidelines enclosed with or on the box for tightening the jar lids properly.

- If screw bands are too tight, air cannot vent during processing, and food will discolor during storage. Overtightening also may cause lids to buckle and jars to break, especially with raw-packed, pressure-processed food.
- If screw bands are too loose, liquid may escape from jars during processing, seals may fail, and the food will need to be reprocessed.

Do not retighten lids after processing jars. As jars cool, the contents in the jar contract, pulling the self-sealing lid firmly against the jar to form a high vacuum. Screw bands are not needed on stored jars. They can be removed easily after jars are cooled. When removed, washed, dried, and stored in a dry area, screw bands may be used many times. If left on stored jars, they become difficult to remove, often rust, and may not work properly again.

Selecting the Correct Processing Time

When food is canned in boiling water, more processing time is needed for most raw-packed foods and for quart jars than is needed for hot-packed foods and pint jars.

To destroy microorganisms in acid foods processed in a boiling-water canner, you must:

- Process jars for the correct number of minutes in boiling water.
- Cool the jars at room temperature.

To destroy microorganisms in low-acid foods processed with a pressure canner, you must:

- Process the jars for the correct number of minutes at 240°F (10 PSIG) or 250°F (15 PSIG).
- Allow canner to cool at room temperature until it is completely depressurized.

The food may spoil if you fail to use the proper processing times, fail to vent steam from canners properly, process at lower pressure than specified, process for fewer minutes than specified, or cool the canner with water.

Processing times for half-pint and pint jars are the same, as are times for 1½-pint and quart jars. For some products, you have a choice of processing at 5, 10, or 15 PSIG. In these cases, choose the canner pressure (PSIG) you wish to use and match it with your pack style (raw or hot) and jar size to find the correct processing time.

Recommended Canners

There are two main types of canners for heat-processing home-canned food: boiling-water canners and pressure canners. Most are designed to hold seven one-quart jars or eight to nine one-pint jars. Small pressure canners hold four one-quart jars; some large pressure canners hold eighteen one-pint jars in two layers but hold only seven quart jars. Pressure saucepans with smaller volume capacities are not recommended for use in canning. Treat small pressure canners the same as standard larger canners; they should be vented using the typical venting procedures.

A boiling water canner

Low-acid foods must be processed in a pressure canner to be free of botulism risks. Although pressure canners also may be used for processing acid foods, boiling-water canners are recommended because they are faster. A pressure canner would require from 55 to 100 minutes to can a load of jars; the total time for canning most acid foods in boiling water varies from 25 to 60 minutes.

A boiling-water canner loaded with filled jars requires about 20 to 30 minutes of heating before its water begins to boil. A loaded pressure canner requires about 12 to 15 minutes of heating before it begins to vent, another 10 minutes to vent the canner, another 5 minutes to pressurize the canner, another 8 to 10 minutes to process the acid food, and, finally, another 20 to 60 minutes to cool the canner before removing jars.

Boiling-Water Canners

These canners are made of aluminum or porcelain-covered steel. They have removable perforated racks and fitted lids. The canner must be deep enough so that at least 1 inch of briskly boiling water will cover the tops of jars during processing. Some boiling-water canners do not have flat bottoms. A flat bottom must be used on an electric range. Either a flat or ridged bottom can be used on a gas burner. To ensure uniform processing of all jars with an electric range, the canner should be no more than 4 inches wider in diameter than the element on which it is heated.

Using a Boiling-Water Canner

Follow these steps for successful boiling-water canning:

1. Fill the canner halfway with water.
2. Preheat water to 140°F for raw-packed foods and to 180°F for hot-packed foods.
3. Load filled jars, fitted with lids, into the canner rack and use the handles to lower the rack into

the water; or fill the canner, one jar at a time, with a jar lifter.

4. Add more boiling water, if needed, so the water level is at least 1 inch above jar tops.

5. Turn heat to its highest position until water boils vigorously.

6. Set a timer for the minutes required for processing the food.

7. Cover with the canner lid and lower the heat setting to maintain a gentle boil throughout the processing time.

8. Add more boiling water, if needed, to keep the water level above the jars.

9. When jars have been boiled for the recommended time, turn off the heat and remove the canner lid.

10. Using a jar lifter, remove the jars and place them on a towel, leaving at least 1 inch of space between the jars during cooling.

Pressure Canners

Pressure canners for use in the home have been extensively redesigned in recent years. Models made before the 1970s were heavy-walled kettles with clamp-on lids. They were fitted with a dial gauge, a vent port in the form of a petcock or counterweight, and a safety fuse. Modern pressure canners are lightweight, thin-walled kettles; most have turn-on lids. They have a jar rack, gasket, dial or weighted gauge, an automatic vent or cover lock, a vent port (steam vent) that is closed with a counterweight or weighted gauge, and a safety fuse.

Pressure does not destroy microorganisms, but high temperatures applied for a certain period of time do. The success of destroying all microorganisms capable of growing in canned food is based on the temperature obtained in pure steam, free of air, at sea level. At sea level, a canner operated at a gauge pressure of 10 pounds provides an internal temperature of 240°F.

Air trapped in a canner lowers the inside temperature and results in under-processing. The highest volume of

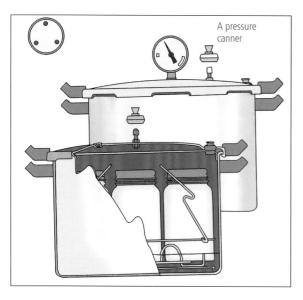

A pressure canner

air trapped in a canner occurs in processing raw-packed foods in dial-gauge canners. These canners do not vent air during processing. To be safe, all types of pressure canners must be vented 10 minutes before they are pressurized.

To vent a canner, leave the vent port uncovered on newer models or manually open petcocks on some older models. Heating the filled canner with its lid locked into place boils water and generates steam that escapes through the petcock or vent port. When steam first escapes, set a timer for 10 minutes. After venting 10 minutes, close the petcock or place the counterweight or weighted gauge over the vent port to pressurize the canner.

Weighted-gauge models exhaust tiny amounts of air and steam each time their gauge rocks or jiggles during processing. The sound of the weight rocking or jiggling indicates that the canner is maintaining the recommended pressure and needs no further attention until the load has been processed for the set time. Weighted-gauge canners cannot correct precisely for higher altitudes, and at altitudes above 1,000 feet must be operated at a pressure of 15.

Check dial gauges for accuracy before use each year and replace if they read high by more than 1 pound at 5, 10, or 15 pounds of pressure. Low readings cause over-processing and may indicate that the accuracy of the gauge is unpredictable. If a gauge is consistently low, you may adjust the processing pressure. For example, if the directions call for 12 pounds of pressure and your dial gauge has tested 1 pound low, you can safely process at 11 pounds of pressure. If the gauge is more than 2 pounds low, it is unpredictable, and it is best to replace it. Gauges may be checked at most USDA county extension offices, which are located in every state across the country. To find one near you, visit www.csrees.usda.gov.

Handle gaskets of canner lids carefully and clean them according to the manufacturer's directions. Nicked or dried gaskets will allow steam leaks during pressurization of canners. Gaskets of older canners may need to be lightly coated with vegetable oil once per year, but newer models are pre-lubricated. Check your canner's instructions.

Lid safety fuses are thin, metal inserts or rubber plugs designed to relieve excessive pressure from the canner. Do not pick at or scratch fuses while cleaning lids. Use only canners that have Underwriter's Laboratory (UL) approval to ensure their safety.

Replacement gauges and other parts for canners are often available at stores offering canner equipment or from canner manufacturers. To order parts, list canner model number and describe the parts needed.

Using a Pressure Canner

Follow these steps for successful pressure canning:

1. Put 2 to 3 inches of hot water in the canner. Place filled jars on the rack, using a jar lifter. Fasten canner lid securely.

2. Open petcock or leave weight off vent port. Heat at the highest setting until steam flows from the petcock or vent port.

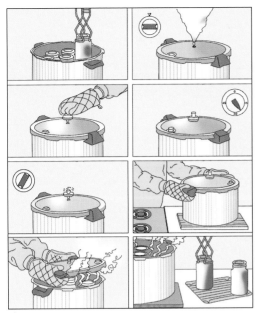
Using a pressure canner

Cooling Jars

Cool the jars at room temperature for 12 to 24 hours. Jars may be cooled on racks or towels to minimize heat damage to counters. The food level and liquid volume of raw-packed jars will be noticeably lower after cooling because air is exhausted during processing, and food shrinks. If a jar loses excessive liquid during processing, do not open it to add more liquid. As long as the seal is good, the product is still usable.

Testing Jar Seals

After cooling jars for 12 to 24 hours, remove the screw bands and test seals with one of the following methods:

Method 1: Press the middle of the lid with a finger or thumb. If the lid springs up when you release your finger, the lid is unsealed and reprocessing will be necessary.

Method 2: Tap the lid with the bottom of a teaspoon. If it makes a dull sound, the lid is not sealed. If food is in contact with the underside of the lid, it will also cause a dull sound. If the jar lid is sealed correctly, it will make a ringing, high-pitched sound.

Method 3: Hold the jar at eye level and look across the lid. The lid should be concave (curved down slightly in the center). If center of the lid is either flat or bulging, it may not be sealed.

Reprocessing Unsealed Jars

If a jar fails to seal, remove the lid and check the jar-sealing surface for tiny nicks. If necessary, change the jar, add a new, properly prepared lid, and reprocess within 24 hours using the same processing time.

Another option is to adjust headspace in unsealed jars to 1½ inches and freeze jars and contents instead of reprocessing. However, make sure jars have straight sides. Freezing may crack jars with "shoulders."

Foods in single, unsealed jars could be stored in the refrigerator and consumed within several days.

Storing Canned Foods

If lids are tightly vacuum-sealed on cooled jars, remove screw bands, wash the lid and jar to remove food residue, then rinse and dry jars. Label and date the jars and store them in a clean, cool, dark, dry place. Do not store jars at temperatures above 95°F or near hot pipes, a range, a furnace, in an uninsulated attic, or in direct sunlight. Under these conditions, food will lose quality

Testing jar seals

3. Maintain high heat setting, exhaust steam 10 minutes, and then place weight on vent port or close petcock. The canner will pressurize during the next three to five minutes.

4. Start timing the process when the pressure reading on the dial gauge indicates that the recommended pressure has been reached or when the weighted gauge begins to jiggle or rock.

5. Regulate heat under the canner to maintain a steady pressure at or slightly above the correct gauge pressure. Quick and large pressure variations during processing may cause unnecessary liquid losses from jars. Weighted gauges on Mirro canners should jiggle about two or three times per minute. On Presto canners, they should rock slowly throughout the process.

When processing time is completed, turn off the heat, remove the canner from heat if possible, and let the canner depressurize. Do not force-cool the canner. If you cool it with cold running water in a sink or open the vent port before the canner depressurizes by itself, liquid will spurt from the jars, causing low liquid levels and jar seal failures. Force-cooling also may warp the canner lid of older model canners, causing steam leaks.

Depressurization of older models should be timed. Standard size heavy-walled canners require about 30 minutes when loaded with pints and 45 minutes with quarts. Newer thin-walled canners cool more rapidly and are equipped with vent locks. These canners are depressurized when their vent lock piston drops to a normal position.

1. After the vent port or petcock has been open for two minutes, unfasten the lid and carefully remove it. Lift the lid away from you so that the steam does not burn your face.

2. Remove jars with a lifter, and place on towel or cooling rack, if desired.

in a few weeks or months and may spoil. Dampness may corrode metal lids, break seals, and allow recontamination and spoilage.

Accidental freezing of canned foods will not cause spoilage unless jars become unsealed and re-contaminated. However, freezing and thawing may soften food. If jars must be stored where they may freeze, wrap them in newspapers, place them in heavy cartons, and cover them with more newspapers and blankets.

Identifying and Handling Spoiled Canned Food

Growth of spoilage bacteria and yeast produces gas, which pressurizes the food, swells lids, and breaks jar seals. As each stored jar is selected for use, examine its lid for tightness and vacuum. Lids with concave centers have good seals.

Next, while holding the jar upright at eye level, rotate the jar and examine its outside surface for streaks of dried food originating at the top of the jar. Look at the contents for rising air bubbles and unnatural color.

While opening the jar, smell for unnatural odors and look for spurting liquid and cotton-like mold growth (white, blue, black, or green) on the top food surface and underside of lid. Do not taste food from a stored jar you discover to have an unsealed lid or that otherwise shows signs of spoilage.

All suspect containers of spoiled, low-acid foods should be treated as having produced botulinum toxin and should be handled carefully as follows:

- If the suspect glass jars are unsealed, open, or leaking, they should be detoxified before disposal.
- If the suspect glass jars are sealed, remove lids and detoxify the entire jar, contents, and lids.

Detoxification Process

Carefully place the suspect containers and lids on their sides in an eight-quart-volume or larger stockpot, pan, or boiling-water canner. Wash your hands thoroughly. Carefully add water to the pot. The water should completely cover the containers with a minimum of 1 inch of water above the containers. Avoid splashing the water. Place a lid on the pot and heat the water to boiling. Boil 30 minutes to ensure detoxifying the food and all container components. Cool and discard lids and food in the trash or bury in soil.

Thoroughly clean all counters, containers, and equipment including can opener, clothing, and hands that may have come in contact with the food or the containers. Discard any sponges or washcloths that were used in the cleanup. Place them in a plastic bag and discard in the trash.

Canned Foods for Special Diets

The cost of commercially canned, special diet food often prompts interest in preparing these products at home. Some low-sugar and low-salt foods may be easily and safely canned at home. However, it may take some experimentation to create a product with the desired color, flavor, and texture. Start with a small batch and then make appropriate adjustments before producing large quantities.

Canning without Sugar

In canning regular fruits without sugar, it is very important to select fully ripe but firm fruits of the best quality. It is generally best to can fruit in its own juice, but blends of unsweetened apple, pineapple, and white grape juice are also good for pouring over solid fruit pieces. Adjust headspaces and lids and use the processing recommendations for regular fruits. Add sugar substitutes, if desired, when serving.

Fruit

There's nothing quite like opening a jar of home-preserved strawberries in the middle of a winter snowstorm. It takes you right back to the warm, early-summer sunshine, the smell of the strawberry patch's damp earth, and the feel of the firm berries as you snipped them from the vines. Best of all, you get to indulge in the sweet, summery flavor even as the snow swirls outside the windows.

Preserving fruit is simple, safe, and it allows you to enjoy the fruits of your summer's labor all year-round. On the next pages, you will find reference charts for processing various fruits and fruit products in a dial-gauge pressure canner or a weighted-gauge pressure canner. The same information is also included with each recipe's directions. In some cases, a boiling-water canner will serve better; for these instances, directions for its use are offered instead.

Adding syrup to canned fruit helps to retain its flavor, color, and shape, although it does not prevent spoilage. To maintain the most natural flavor, use the Very Light Syrup listed in the table found on page 78. Many fruits that are typically packed in heavy syrup are just as good—and a lot better for you—when packed in lighter syrups. However, if you're preserving fruit that's on the sour side, like cherries or tart apples, you might want to splurge on one of the sweeter versions.

Syrups

Adding syrup to canned fruit helps to retain its flavor, color, and shape, although jars still need to be processed to prevent spoilage. Follow the chart into the right for syrups of varying sweetness. Light corn syrups or mild-flavored honey may be used to replace up to half the table sugar called for in syrups.

Directions
1. Bring water and sugar to a boil in a medium saucepan.
2. Pour over raw fruits in jars.

Process Times for Fruits and Fruit Products in a Dial-Gauge Pressure Canner*

				Canner Pressure (PSI) at Altitudes of:			
Type of Fruit	Style of Pack	Jar Size	Process Time	0– 2,000 ft	2,001–4,000 ft	4,001–6,000 ft	6,001–8,000 ft
Applesauce	Hot	Pints	8 minutes	6 lbs	7 lbs	8 lbs	9 lbs
	Hot	Quarts	10 minutes	6 lbs	7 lbs	8 lbs	9 lbs
Apples, sliced	Hot	Pints or Quarts	8 minutes	6 lbs	7 lbs	8 lbs	9 lbs
Berries, whole	Hot	Pints or Quarts	8 minutes	6 lbs	7 lbs	8 lbs	9 lbs
	Raw	Pints	8 minutes	6 lbs	7 lbs	8 lbs	9 lbs
	Raw	Quarts	10 minutes	6 lbs	7 lbs	8 lbs	9 lbs
Cherries, sour or sweet	Hot	Pints	8 minutes	6 lbs	7 lbs	8 lbs	9 lbs
	Hot	Quarts	10 minutes	6 lbs	7 lbs	8 lbs	9 lbs
	Raw	Pints or Quarts	10 minutes	6 lbs	7 lbs	8 lbs	9 lbs
Fruit purées	Hot	Pints or Quarts	8 minutes	6 lbs	7 lbs	8 lbs	9 lbs
Grapefruit or orange sections	Hot	Pints or Quarts	8 minutes	6 lbs	7 lbs	8 lbs	9 lbs
	Raw	Pints	8 minutes	6 lbs	7 lbs	8 lbs	9 lbs
	Raw	Quarts	10 minutes	6 lbs	7 lbs	8 lbs	9 lbs
Peaches, apricots, or nectarines	Hot or Raw	Pints or Quarts	10 minutes	6 lbs	7 lbs	8 lbs	9 lbs
Pears	Hot	Pints or Quarts	10 minutes	6 lbs	7 lbs	8 lbs	9 lbs
Plums	Hot or Raw	Pints or Quarts	10 minutes	6 lbs	7 lbs	8 lbs	9 lbs
Rhubarb	Hot	Pints or Quarts	8 minutes	6 lbs	7 lbs	8 lbs	9 lbs

*After the process is complete, turn off the heat and remove the canner lid. Wait 5 to 10 minutes before removing jars.

Process Times for Fruits and Fruit Products in a Weighted-Gauge Pressure Canner*

				Canner Pressure (PSI) at Altitudes of:	
Type of Fruit	Style of Pack	Jar Size	Process Time	0–1,000 ft	Above 1,000 ft
Applesauce	Hot	Pints	8 minutes	5 lbs	10 lbs
	Hot	Quarts	10 minutes	5 lbs	10 lbs
Apples, sliced	Hot	Pints or Quarts	8 minutes	5 lbs	10 lbs
Berries, whole	Hot	Pints or Quarts	8 minutes	5 lbs	10 lbs
	Raw	Pints	8 minutes	5 lbs	10 lbs
	Raw	Quarts	10 minutes	5 lbs	10 lbs
Cherries, sour or sweet	Hot	Pints	8 minutes	5 lbs	10 lbs
	Hot	Quarts	10 minutes	5 lbs	10 lbs
	Raw	Pints or Quarts	10 minutes	5 lbs	10 lbs
Fruit purées	Hot	Pints or Quarts	8 minutes	5 lbs	10 lbs
Grapefruit or orange sections	Hot	Pints or Quarts	8 minutes	5 lbs	10 lbs
	Raw	Pints	8 minutes	5 lbs	10 lbs
	Raw	Quarts	10 minutes	5 lbs	10 lbs
Peaches, apricots, or nectarines	Hot or Raw	Pints or Quarts	10 minutes	5 lbs	10 lbs
Pears	Hot	Pints or Quarts	10 minutes	5 lbs	10 lbs
Plums	Hot or Raw	Pints or Quarts	10 minutes	5 lbs	10 lbs
Rhubarb	Hot	Pints or Quarts	8 minutes	5 lbs	10 lbs

*After the process is complete, turn off the heat and remove the canner lid. Wait 5 to 10 minutes before removing jars.

Sugar and Water in Syrup

Syrup Type	Approx. % Sugar	Measures of Water and Sugar				Fruits Commonly Packed in Syrup
		For 9-Pt Load*		For 7-Qt Load		
		Cups Water	Cups Sugar	Cups Water	Cups Sugar	
Very Light	10	6½	¾	10½	1¼	Approximates natural sugar levels in most fruits and adds the fewest calories.
Light	20	5¾	1½	9	2¼	Very sweet fruit. Try a small amount the first time to see if your family likes it.
Medium	30	5¼	2¼	8¼	3¾	Sweet apples, sweet cherries, berries, grapes.
Heavy	40	5	3¼	7¾	5¼	Tart apples, apricots, sour cherries, gooseberries, nectarines, peaches, pears, plums.
Very Heavy	50	4¼	4¼	6½	6¾	Very sour fruit. Try a small amount the first time to see if your family likes it.

*This amount is also adequate for a four-quart load.

Apple Juice

The best apple juice is made from a blend of varieties. If you don't have your own apple press, try to buy fresh juice from a local cider maker within 24 hours after it has been pressed.

Directions

1. Refrigerate juice for 24 to 48 hours.
2. Without mixing, carefully pour off clear liquid and discard sediment. Strain the clear liquid through a paper coffee filter or double layers of damp cheesecloth.
3. Heat quickly in a saucepan, stirring occasionally, until juice begins to boil.
4. Fill immediately into sterile pint or quart jars or into clean, half-gallon jars, leaving ¼-inch headspace.
5. Adjust lids and process. See below for recommended times for a boiling-water canner.

Process Times for Apple Juice in a Boiling-Water Canner*

Style of Pack	Jar Size	Process Time at Altitudes of:		
		0–1,000 ft	1,001–6,000 ft	Above 6,000 ft
Hot	Pints or Quarts	5 min	10	15
	Half-gallons	10	15	20

*After the process is complete, turn off the heat and remove the canner lid. Wait five minutes before removing jars.

Apple Butter

The best apple varieties to use for apple butter include Jonathan, Winesap, Stayman, Golden Delicious, and Macintosh apples, but any of your favorite varieties will work. Don't bother to peel the apples, as you will strain the fruit before cooking it anyway. This recipe will yield eight to nine pints.

Ingredients

8 lbs apples
2 cups vinegar
2¼ cups packed brown sugar
2 cups cider
2¼ cups white sugar
2 tbsp ground cinnamon
1 tbsp ground cloves

Directions

1. Wash, stem, quarter, and core apples.
2. Cook slowly in cider and vinegar until soft. Press fruit through a colander, food mill, or strainer.
3. Cook fruit pulp with sugar and spices, stirring frequently. To test for doneness, remove a spoonful and hold it away from steam for 2 minutes. If the butter remains mounded on the spoon, it is done. If you're still not sure, spoon a small quantity onto a plate. When a rim of liquid does not separate around the edge of the butter, it is ready for canning.
4. Fill while hot into sterile half-pint or pint jars, leaving ¼-inch headspace. Quart jars need not be pre-sterilized.

Process Times for Apple Butter in a Boiling-Water Canner*

Style of Pack	Jar Size	Process Time at Altitudes of:		
		0–1,000 ft	1,001–6,000 ft	Above 6,000 ft
Hot	Half-pints or Pints	5 minutes	10 minutes	15 minutes
	Quarts	10 minutes	15 minutes	20 minutes

*After the process is complete, turn off the heat and remove the canner lid. Wait five minutes before removing jars.

Applesauce

Besides being delicious on its own or paired with dishes like pork chops or latkes, applesauce can be used as a butter substitute in many baked goods. Select apples that are sweet, juicy, and crisp. For a tart flavor, add one to two pounds of tart apples to each three pounds of sweeter fruit.

Quantity

1. An average of 21 pounds of apples is needed per canner load of seven quarts.
2. An average of 13½ pounds of apples is needed per canner load of nine pints.
3. A bushel weighs 48 pounds and yields 14 to 19 quarts of sauce—an average of three pounds per quart.

Directions
1. Wash, peel, and core apples. Slice apples into water containing a little lemon juice to prevent browning.
2. Place drained slices in an 8- to 10-quart pot. Add ½ cup water. Stirring occasionally to prevent burning, heat quickly until tender (5 to 20 minutes, depending on maturity and variety).
3. Press through a sieve or food mill, or skip the pressing step if you prefer chunky-style sauce. Sauce may be packed without sugar, but if desired, sweeten to taste (start with ⅛ cup sugar per quart of sauce).
4. Reheat sauce to boiling. Fill jars with hot sauce, leaving ½-inch headspace. Adjust lids and process.

Process Times for Applesauce in a Boiling-Water Canner*

Style of Pack	Jar Size	Process Time at Altitudes of:			
		0–1,000 ft	1,001–3,000 ft	3,001–6,000 ft	Above 6,000 ft
Hot	Pints	15 minutes	20 minutes	20 minutes	25 minutes
	Quarts	20 minutes	25 minutes	30 minutes	35 minutes

*After the process is complete, turn off the heat and remove the canner lid. Wait five minutes before removing jars.

Process Times for Applesauce in a Dial-Gauge Pressure Canner*

Style of Pack	Jar Size	Process Time	Canner Pressure (PSI) at Altitudes of:			
			0–2,000 ft	2,001–4,000 ft	4,001–6,000 ft	6,001–8,000 ft
Hot	Pints	8 minutes	6 lbs	7 lbs	8 lbs	9 lbs
	Quarts	10 minutes	6 lbs	7 lbs	8 lbs	9 lbs

*After the canner is completely depressurized, remove the weight from the vent port or open the petcock. Wait 10 minutes; then unfasten the lid and remove it carefully. Lift the lid with the underside away from you so that the steam coming out of the canner does not burn your face.

Process Times for Applesauce in a Weighted-Gauge Pressure Canner*

Style of Pack	Jar Size	Process Time	Canner Pressure (PSI) at Altitudes of:	
			0–1,000 ft	Above 1,000 ft
Hot	Pints	8 minutes	5 lbs	10 lbs
	Quarts	10 minutes	5 lbs	10 lbs

*After the canner is completely depressurized, remove the weight from the vent port or open the petcock. Wait 10 minutes, then unfasten the lid and remove it carefully. Lift the lid with the underside away from you so that the steam coming out of the canner does not burn your face.

Apricots, Halved or Sliced

Apricots are excellent in baked goods, stuffing, chutney, or on their own. Choose firm, well-colored, mature fruit for best results.

Quantity

- An average of 16 pounds is needed per canner load of seven quarts.
- An average of 10 pounds is needed per canner load of nine pints.

- A bushel weighs 50 pounds and yields 20 to 25 quarts—an average of 2¼ pounds per quart.

Directions

1. Dip fruit in boiling water for 30 to 60 seconds until skins loosen. Dip quickly in cold water and slip off skins.
2. Cut in half, remove pits, and slice if desired. To prevent darkening, keep peeled fruit in water with a little lemon juice.
3. Prepare and boil a very light, light, or medium syrup (see page 78) or pack apricots in water, apple juice, or white grape juice.

Process Times for Halved or Sliced Apricots in a Dial-Gauge Pressure Canner*

Style of Pack	Jar Size	Process Time	Canner Pressure (PSI) at Altitudes of:			
			0–2,000 ft	2,001–4,000 ft	4,001–6,000 ft	6,001–8,000 ft
Hot or Raw	Pints or Quarts	10 minutes	6 lbs	7 lbs	8 lbs	9 lbs

*After the process is complete, turn off the heat and remove the canner lid. Wait five minutes before removing jars.

Process Times for Halved or Sliced Apricots in a Weighted-Gauge Pressure Canner*

Style of Pack	Jar Size	Process Time	Canner Pressure (PSI) at Altitudes of:	
			0–1,000 ft	Above 1,000 ft
Hot or Raw	Pints or Quarts	10 minutes	5 lbs	10 lbs

*After the process is complete, turn off the heat and remove the canner lid. Wait five minutes before removing jars.

Berries, Whole

Preserved berries are perfect for use in pies, muffins, pancakes, or in poultry or pork dressings. Nearly every berry preserves well, including blackberries, blueberries, currants, dewberries, elderberries, gooseberries, huckleberries, loganberries, mulberries, and raspberries. Choose ripe, sweet berries with uniform color.

Quantity

- An average of 12 pounds is needed per canner load of seven quarts.
- An average of 8 pounds is needed per canner load of nine pints.
- A 24-quart crate weighs 36 pounds and yields 18 to 24 quarts—an average of 1¾ pounds per quart.

Directions

1. Wash 1 or 2 quarts of berries at a time. Drain, cap, and stem if necessary. For gooseberries, snip off heads and tails with scissors.
2. Prepare and boil preferred syrup, if desired (see page 78). Add ½ cup syrup, juice, or water to each clean jar.

Hot pack—(Best for blueberries, currants, elderberries, gooseberries, and huckleberries) Heat berries in boiling water for 30 seconds and drain. Fill jars and cover with hot juice, leaving ½-inch headspace.

Raw pack—Fill jars with any of the raw berries, shaking down gently while filling. Cover with hot syrup, juice, or water, leaving ½-inch headspace.

Recommended Process Times for Whole Berries in a Boiling-Water Canner*

Style of Pack	Jar Size	Process Time at Altitudes of:			
		0–1,000 ft	1,001–3,000 ft	3,001–6,000 ft	Above 6,000 ft
Hot	Pints or Quarts	15 minutes	20 minutes	20 minutes	25 minutes
Raw	Pints	15 minutes	20 minutes	20 minutes	25 minutes
Raw	Quarts	20 minutes	25 minutes	30 minutes	35 minutes

*After the process is complete, turn off the heat and remove the canner lid. Wait five minutes before removing jars.

Process Times for Whole Berries in a Dial-Gauge Pressure Canner*

Style of Pack	Jar Size	Process Time	Canner Pressure (PSI) at Altitudes of:			
			0–2,000 ft	2,001–4,000 ft	4,001–6,000 ft	6,001–8,000 ft
Hot	Pints or Quarts	8 minutes	6 lbs	7 lbs	8 lbs	9 lbs
Raw	Pints	8 minutes	6 lbs	7 lbs	8 lbs	9 lbs
Raw	Quarts	10 minutes	6 lbs	7 lbs	8 lbs	9 lbs

*After the process is complete, turn off the heat and remove the canner lid. Wait five minutes before removing jars.

Process Times for Whole Berries in a Weighted-Gauge Pressure Canner*

Style of Pack	Jar Size	Process Time	Canner Pressure (PSI) at Altitudes of:	
			0–1,000 ft	Above 1,000 ft
Hot	Pints or Quarts	8 minutes	5 lbs	10 lbs
Raw	Pints	8 minutes	5 lbs	10 lbs
Raw	Quarts	10 minutes	5 lbs	10 lbs

*After the process is complete, turn off the heat and remove the canner lid. Wait five minutes before removing jars.

Berry Syrup

Juices from fresh or frozen blueberries, cherries, grapes, raspberries (black or red), and strawberries are easily made into toppings for use on ice cream and pastries. For an elegant finish to cheesecakes or pound cakes, drizzle a thin stream in a zigzag across the top just before serving. Berry syrups are also great additions to smoothies or milkshakes. This recipe makes about nine half-pints.

Directions

1. Select 6½ cups of fresh or frozen berries of your choice. Wash, cap, and stem berries and crush in a saucepan.
2. Heat to boiling and simmer until soft (5 to 10 minutes). Strain hot through a colander placed in a large pan and drain until cool enough to handle.

3. Strain the collected juice through a double layer of cheesecloth or jelly bag. Discard the dry pulp. The yield of the pressed juice should be about 4½ to 5 cups.
4. Combine the juice with 6¾ cups of sugar in a large saucepan, bring to a boil, and simmer 1 minute.
5. Fill into clean half-pint or pint jars, leaving ½-inch headspace. Adjust lids and process.

> To make syrup with whole berries, rather than crushed, save 1 or 2 cups of the fresh or frozen fruit, combine these with the sugar, and simmer until soft. Remove from heat, skim off foam, and fill into clean jars, following processing directions for regular berry syrup.

Process Times for Berry Syrup in a Boiling-Water Canner*

Style of Pack	Jar Size	Process Time at Altitudes of:		
		0–1,000 ft	1,001–6,000 ft	Above 6,000 ft
Hot	Half-pints or Pints	10 minutes	15 minutes	20 minutes

*After the process is complete, turn off the heat and remove the canner lid. Wait five minutes before removing jars.

Fruit Purées

Almost any fruit can be puréed for use as baby food, in sauces, or just as a nutritious snack. Puréed prunes and apples can be used as a butter replacement in many baked goods. Use this recipe for any fruit except figs and tomatoes.

Directions

1. Stem, wash, drain, peel, and remove pits if necessary. Measure fruit into large saucepan, crushing slightly if desired.
2. Add 1 cup hot water for each quart of fruit. Cook slowly until fruit is soft, stirring frequently. Press through sieve or food mill. If desired, add sugar to taste.
3. Reheat pulp to boil, or until sugar dissolves (if added). Fill hot into clean jars, leaving ¼-inch headspace. Adjust lids and process.

Process Times for Fruit Purées in a Boiling-Water Canner*

Style of Pack	Jar Size	Process Time at Altitudes of:		
		0–1,000 ft	1,001–6,000 ft	Above 6,000 ft
Hot	Pints or Quarts	15 minutes	20 minutes	25 minutes

*After the process is complete, turn off the heat and remove the canner lid. Wait five minutes before removing jars.

Process Times for Fruit Purées in a Dial-Gauge Pressure Canner*

Style of Pack	Jar Size	Process Time	Canner Pressure (PSI) at Altitudes of:			
			0–2,000 ft	2,001–4,000 ft	4,001–6,000 ft	6,001–8,000 ft
Hot	Pints or Quarts	8 minutes	6 lbs	7 lbs	8 lbs	9 lbs

*After the canner is completely depressurized, remove the weight from the vent port or open the petcock. Wait 10 minutes, then unfasten the lid and remove it carefully. Lift the lid with the underside away from you so that the steam coming out of the canner does not burn your face.

Process Times for Fruit Purées in a Weighted-Gauge Pressure Canner*

Style of Pack	Jar Size	Process Time (Min)	Canner Pressure (PSI) at Altitudes of:	
			0–1,000 ft	Above 1,000 ft
Hot	Pints or Quarts	8 minutes	5 lbs	10 lbs

*After the canner is completely depressurized, remove the weight from the vent port or open the petcock. Wait 10 minutes; then unfasten the lid and remove it carefully. Lift the lid with the underside away from you so that the steam coming out of the canner does not burn your face.

Grape Juice

Purple grapes are full of antioxidants and help to reduce the risk of heart disease, cancer, and Alzheimer's disease. For juice, select sweet, well-colored, firm, mature fruit.

Quantity

- An average of 24½ pounds is needed per canner load of seven quarts.
- An average of 16 pounds per canner load of nine pints.
- A lug weighs 26 pounds and yields seven to nine quarts of juice—an average of 3½ pounds per quart.

Directions

1. Wash and stem grapes. Place grapes in a saucepan and add boiling water to cover. Heat and simmer slowly until skin is soft.
2. Strain through a damp jelly bag or double layers of cheesecloth, and discard solids. Refrigerate juice for 24 to 48 hours.
3. Without mixing, carefully pour off clear liquid and save; discard sediment. If desired, strain through a paper coffee filter for a clearer juice.

4. Add juice to a saucepan and sweeten to taste. Heat and stir until sugar is dissolved. Continue heating with occasional stirring until juice begins to boil. Fill into jars immediately, leaving ¼-inch headspace. Adjust lids and process.

Process Times for Grape Juice in a Boiling-Water Canner*

Style of Pack	Jar Size	Process Time at Altitudes of:		
		0–1,000 ft	1,001–6,000 ft	Above 6,000 ft
Hot	Pints or Quarts	5 minutes	10 minutes	15 minutes
	Half-gallons	10 minutes	15 minutes	20 minutes

*After the process is complete, turn off the heat and remove the canner lid. Wait five minutes before removing jars.

Peaches, Halved or Sliced

Peaches are delicious in cobblers, crisps, and muffins, or grilled for a unique cake topping. Choose ripe, mature fruit with minimal bruising.

Quantity

- An average of 17½ pounds is needed per canner load of seven quarts.
- An average of 11 pounds is needed per canner load of nine pints.
- A bushel weighs 48 pounds and yields 16 to 24 quarts—an average of 2½ pounds per quart.

Directions

1. Dip fruit in boiling water for 30 to 60 seconds until skins loosen. Dip quickly in cold water and slip off skins. Cut in half, remove pits, and slice if desired. To prevent darkening, keep peeled fruit in ascorbic acid solution.
2. Prepare and boil a very light, light, or medium syrup or pack peaches in water, apple juice, or white grape juice. Raw packs make poor-quality peaches.

Hot pack—In a large saucepan, place drained fruit in syrup, water, or juice and bring to boil. Fill jars with hot fruit and cooking liquid, leaving ½-inch headspace. Place halves in layers, cut side down.

Raw pack—Fill jars with raw fruit, cut side down, and add hot water, juice, or syrup, leaving ½-inch headspace.

3. Adjust lids and process.

Process Times for Halved or Sliced Peaches in a Boiling-Water Canner*

Style of Pack	Jar Size	Process Time at Altitudes of:			
		0–1,000 ft	1,001–3,000 ft	3,001–6,000 ft	Above 6,000 ft
Hot	Pints	20 minutes	25 minutes	30 minutes	35 minutes
	Quarts	25 minutes	30 minutes	35 minutes	40 minutes
Raw	Pints	25 minutes	30 minutes	35 minutes	40 minutes
	Quarts	30 minutes	35 minutes	40 minutes	45 minutes

*After the process is complete, turn off the heat and remove the canner lid. Wait five minutes before removing jars.

Process Times for Halved or Sliced Peaches in a Dial-Gauge Pressure Canner*

Style of Pack	Jar Size	Process Time	Canner Pressure (PSI) at Altitudes of:			
			0–2,000 ft	2,001–4,000 ft	4,001–6,000 ft	6,001–8,000 ft
Hot or Raw	Pints or Quarts	10 minutes	6 lbs	7 lbs	8 lbs	9 lbs

*After the canner is completely depressurized, remove the weight from the vent port or open the petcock. Wait 10 minutes; then unfasten the lid and remove it carefully. Lift the lid with the underside away from you so that the steam coming out of the canner does not burn your face.

Process Times for Halved or Sliced Peaches in a Weighted-Gauge Pressure Canner*

Style of Pack	Jar Size	Process Time	Canner Pressure (PSI) at Altitudes of:	
			0–1,000 ft	Above 1,000 ft
Hot or Raw	Pints or Quarts	10 minutes	5 lbs	10 lbs

*After the canner is completely depressurized, remove the weight from the vent port or open the petcock. Wait 10 minutes; then unfasten the lid and remove it carefully. Lift the lid with the underside away from you so that the steam coming out of the canner does not burn your face.

Pears, Halved

Choose ripe, mature fruit for best results. For a special treat, filled halved pears with a mixture of chopped dried apricots, pecans, brown sugar, and butter; bake or microwave until warm and serve with vanilla ice cream.

Quantity

- An average of 17½ pounds is needed per canner load of seven quarts.
- An average of 11 pounds is needed per canner load of nine pints.
- A bushel weighs 50 pounds and yields 16 to 25 quarts—an average of 2½ pounds per quart.

Directions
1. Wash and peel pears. Cut lengthwise in halves and remove core. A melon baller or metal measuring spoon works well for coring pears. To prevent discoloration, keep pears in water with a little lemon juice.
2. Prepare a very light, light, or medium syrup (see page 78) or use apple juice, white grape juice, or water. Raw packs make poor quality pears. Boil drained pears for 5 minutes in syrup, juice, or water. Fill jars with hot fruit and cooking liquid, leaving ½-inch headspace. Adjust lids and process.

Process Times for Halved Pears in a Boiling-Water Canner*

Style of Pack	Jar Size	Process Time at Altitudes of:			
		0–1,000 ft	1,001–3,000 ft	3,001–6,000 ft	Above 6,000 ft
Hot	Pints	20 minutes	25 minutes	30 minutes	35 minutes
	Quarts	25 minutes	30 minutes	35 minutes	40 minutes

*After the process is complete, turn off the heat and remove the canner lid. Wait five minutes before removing jars.

Process Times for Halved Pears in a Dial-Gauge Pressure Canner*

Style of Pack	Jar Size	Process Time	Canner Pressure (PSI) at Altitudes of:			
			0–2,000 ft	2,001–4,000 ft	4,001–6,000 ft	6,001–8,000 ft
Hot or Raw	Pints or Quarts	10 minutes	6 lbs	7 lbs	8 lbs	9 lbs

*After the canner is completely depressurized, remove the weight from the vent port or open the petcock. Wait 10 minutes; then unfasten the lid and remove it carefully. Lift the lid with the underside away from you so that the steam coming out of the canner does not burn your face.

Process Times for Halved Pears in a Weighted-Gauge Pressure Canner*

Style of Pack	Jar Size	Process Time	Canner Pressure (PSI) at Altitudes of:	
			0–1,000 ft	Above 1,000 ft
Hot	Pints or Quarts	10 minutes	5 lbs	10 lbs

*After the canner is completely depressurized, remove the weight from the vent port or open the petcock. Wait 10 minutes; then unfasten the lid and remove it carefully. Lift the lid with the underside away from you so that the steam coming out of the canner does not burn your face.

Rhubarb, Stewed

Rhubarb in the garden is a sure sign that spring has sprung and summer is well on its way. But why not enjoy rhubarb all year-round? The brilliant red stalks make it as appropriate for a holiday table as for an early summer feast. Rhubarb is also delicious in crisps, cobblers, or served hot over ice cream. Select young, tender, well-colored stalks from the spring or, if available, late fall crop.

Quantity

- An average of 10½ pounds is needed per canner load of seven quarts.
- An average of 7 pounds is needed per canner load of nine pints.
- A lug weighs 28 pounds and yields 14 to 28 quarts—an average of 1½ pounds per quart.

Directions
1. Trim off leaves. Wash stalks and cut into ½-inch to 1-inch pieces.
2. Place rhubarb in a large saucepan, and add ½ cup sugar for each quart of fruit. Let stand until juice appears. Heat gently to boiling. Fill jars without delay, leaving ½-inch headspace. Adjust lids and process.

Process Times for Stewed Rhubarb in a Boiling-Water Canner*

Style of Pack	Jar Size	Process Time at Altitudes of:		
		0–1,000 ft	1,001–6,000 ft	Above 6,000 ft
Hot	Pints or Quarts	15 minutes	20 minutes	25 minutes

*After the process is complete, turn off the heat and remove the canner lid. Wait five minutes before removing jars.

Process Times for Stewed Rhubarb in a Dial-Gauge Pressure Canner*

Style of Pack	Jar Size	Process Time	Canner Pressure (PSI) at Altitudes of			
			0–2,000 ft	2,001–4,000 ft	4,001–6,000 ft	6,001–8,000 ft
Hot	Pints or Quarts	8 minutes	6 lbs	7 lbs	8 lbs	9 lbs

*After the canner is completely depressurized, remove the weight from the vent port or open the petcock. Wait 10 minutes; then unfasten the lid and remove it carefully. Lift the lid with the underside away from you so that the steam coming out of the canner does not burn your face.

Process Times for Stewed Rhubarb in a Weighted-Gauge Pressure Canner*

Style of Pack	Jar Size	Process Time	Canner Pressure (PSI) at Altitudes of:	
			0–1,000 ft	Above 1,000 ft
Hot	Pints or Quarts	8 minutes	5 lbs	10 lbs

*After the canner is completely depressurized, remove the weight from the vent port or open the petcock. Wait 10 minutes; then unfasten the lid and remove it carefully. Lift the lid with the underside away from you so that the steam coming out of the canner does not burn your face.

Canned Pie Fillings

Using a pre-made pie filling will cut your pie preparation time by more than half, but most commercially produced fillings are oozing with high fructose corn syrup and all manner of artificial coloring and flavoring. (Food coloring is not at all necessary, but if you're really concerned about how the inside of your pie will look, appropriate amounts are added to each recipe as an optional ingredient.) Making and preserving your own pie fillings means that you can use your own fresh ingredients and adjust the sweetness to your taste. Because some folks like their pies rich and sweet and others prefer a natural tart flavor, you might want to first make a single quart, make a pie with it, and see how you like it. Then you can adjust the sugar and spices in the recipe to suit your personal preferences before making a large batch. Experiment with combining fruits or adding different spices, but the amount of lemon juice should not be altered, as it aids in controlling the safety and storage stability of the fillings.

These recipes use Clear Jel (sometimes sold as Clear Jel A), a chemically modified cornstarch that produces excellent sauce consistency even after fillings are canned and baked. By using Clear Jel, you can lower the sugar content of your fillings without sacrificing safety, flavor, or texture. (Note: Instant Clear Jel is not meant to be cooked and should not be used for these recipes. Sure-Gel is a natural fruit pectin and is not a suitable substitute for Clear Jel. Cornstarch, tapioca starch, or arrowroot starch can be used in place of Clear Jel, but the finished product is likely to be runny.) One pound of Clear Jel costs less than five dollars and is enough to make fillings for about 14 pies. It will keep for at least a year if stored in a cool, dry place. Clear Jel is increasingly available among canning and freezing supplies in some stores. Alternately, you can order it by the pound at any of the following online stores:

- www.barryfarm.com
- www.kitchenkrafts.com
- www.theingredientstore.com

> When using frozen cherries and blueberries, select unsweetened fruit. If sugar has been added, rinse it off while fruit is frozen. Thaw fruit, then collect, measure, and use juice from fruit to partially replace the water specified in the recipe.

Apple Pie Filling

Use firm, crisp apples, such as Stayman, Golden Delicious, or Rome varieties for the best results. If apples lack tartness, use an additional ¼ cup of lemon juice for each six quarts of slices. Ingredients are included for a one-quart (enough for one 8-inch pie) or a seven-quart recipe.

Ingredients

	1 Quart	7 Quarts
Blanched, sliced fresh apples	3½ cups	6 quarts
Granulated sugar	¾ cup + 2 tbsp	5½ cups
Clear Jel®	¼ cup	1½ cup
Cinnamon	¼ tsp	1 tbsp
Cold water	½ cup	2½ cups
Apple juice	¾ cup	5 cups
Bottled lemon juice	2 tbsp	¾ cup
Nutmeg (optional)	⅛ tsp	1 tsp

Directions

1. Wash, peel, and core apples. Prepare slices ½ inch wide and place in water containing a little lemon juice to prevent browning.
2. For fresh fruit, place 6 cups at a time in 1 gallon of boiling water. Boil each batch 1 minute after the water returns to a boil. Drain, but keep heated fruit in a covered bowl or pot.
3. Combine sugar, Clear Jel, and cinnamon in a large kettle with water and apple juice. Add nutmeg, if desired. Stir and cook on medium-high heat until mixture thickens and begins to bubble.
4. Add lemon juice and boil 1 minute, stirring constantly. Fold in drained apple slices immediately and fill jars with mixture without delay, leaving 1-inch headspace. Adjust lids and process immediately.

Process Times for Apple Pie Filling in a Boiling-Water Canner*

Style of Pack	Jar Size	Process Time at Altitudes of:			
		0–1,000 ft	1,001–3,000 ft	3,001–6,000 ft	Above 6,000 ft
Hot	Pints or Quarts	25 minutes	30 minutes	35 minutes	40 minutes

*After the process is complete, turn off the heat and remove the canner lid. Wait five minutes before removing jars.

Blueberry Pie Filling

Select fresh, ripe, and firm blueberries. Unsweetened frozen blueberries may be used. If sugar has been added, rinse it off while fruit is still frozen. Thaw fruit, then collect, measure, and use juice from fruit to partially replace the water specified in the recipe. Ingredients are included for a one-quart (enough for one 8-inch pie) or seven-quart recipe.

Ingredients

	1 Quart	7 Quarts
Fresh or thawed blueberries	3½ cups	6 quarts
Granulated sugar	¾ cup + 2 tbsp	6 cups
Clear Jel®	¼ cup + 1 tbsp	2¼ cup
Cold water	1 cup	7 cups
Bottled lemon juice	3½ cups	½ cup
Blue food coloring (optional)	3 drops	20 drops
Red food coloring (optional)	1 drop	7 drops

Directions

1. Wash and drain blueberries. Place 6 cups at a time in 1 gallon boiling water. Allow water to return to a boil and cook each batch for 1 minute. Drain but keep heated fruit in a covered bowl or pot.
2. Combine sugar and Clear Jel in a large kettle. Stir. Add water and food coloring if desired. Cook on medium-high heat until mixture thickens and begins to bubble.
3. Add lemon juice and boil 1 minute, stirring constantly. Fold in drained berries immediately and fill jars with mixture without delay, leaving 1-inch headspace. Adjust lids and process immediately.

Process Times for Blueberry Pie Filling in a Boiling-Water Canner*

Style of Pack	Jar Size	Process Time at Altitudes of:			
		0–1,000 ft	1,001–3,000 ft	3,001–6,000 ft	Above 6,000 ft
Hot	Pints or Quarts	30 minutes	35 minutes	40 minutes	45 minutes

*After the process is complete, turn off the heat and remove the canner lid. Wait five minutes before removing jars.

Cherry Pie Filling

Select fresh, very ripe, and firm cherries. Unsweetened frozen cherries may be used. If sugar has been added, rinse it off while the fruit is still frozen. Thaw fruit, then collect, measure, and use juice from fruit to partially replace the water specified in the recipe. Ingredients are included for a one-quart (enough for one 8-inch pie) or seven-quart recipe.

Ingredients

	1 Quart	7 Quarts
Fresh or thawed sour cherries	3⅓ cups	6 quarts
Granulated sugar	1 cup	7 cups
Clear Jel®	¼ cup + 1 tbsp	1-¾ cups
Cold water	1⅓ cups	9⅓ cups
Bottled lemon juice	1 tbsp + 1 tsp	½ cup
Cinnamon (optional)	⅛ tsp	1 tsp
Almond extract (optional)	¼ tsp	2 tsp
Red food coloring (optional)	6 drops	¼ tsp

Directions

1. Rinse and pit fresh cherries, and hold in cold water. To prevent stem end from browning, use water with a little lemon juice. Place 6 cups at a time in 1 gallon boiling water. Boil each batch 1 minute after the water returns to a boil. Drain but keep heated fruit in a covered bowl or pot.
2. Combine sugar and Clear Jel in a large saucepan and add water. If desired, add cinnamon, almond extract, and food coloring. Stir mixture and cook over medium-high heat until mixture thickens and begins to bubble.
3. Add lemon juice and boil 1 minute, stirring constantly. Fold in drained cherries immediately and fill jars with mixture without delay, leaving 1-inch headspace. Adjust lids and process immediately.

Process Times for Cherry Pie Filling in a Boiling-Water Canner*

Style of Pack	Jar Size	Process Time at Altitudes of:			
		0–1,000 ft	1,001–3,000 ft	3,001–6,000 ft	Above 6,000 ft
Hot	Pints or Quarts	30 minutes	35 minutes	40 minutes	45 minutes

*After the process is complete, turn off the heat and remove the canner lid. Wait five minutes before removing jars.

Festive Mincemeat Pie Filling

Mincemeat pie originated as "Christmas Pie" in the eleventh century, when the English crusaders returned from the Holy Land bearing oriental spices. They added three of these spices—cinnamon, cloves, and nutmeg—to their meat pies to represent the three gifts that the magi brought to the Christ child. Mincemeat pies are traditionally small and are perfect paired with a mug of hot buttered rum. Walnuts or pecans can be used in place of meat if preferred. This recipe yields about seven quarts.

Ingredients

2 cups finely chopped suet

4 lbs ground beef or 4 lbs ground venison and 1 lb
sausage

5 qts chopped apples

2 lbs dark, seedless raisins

1 lb white raisins

2 qts apple cider

2 tbsp ground cinnamon

2 tsp ground nutmeg

½ tsp cloves

5 cups sugar

2 tbsp salt

Directions

1. Cook suet and meat in water to avoid browning.
   Peel, core, and quarter apples. Put suet, meat, and
   apples through food grinder using a medium blade.
2. Combine all ingredients in a large saucepan and simmer 1 hour or until slightly thickened. Stir often.
3. Fill jars with mixture without delay, leaving 1-inch
   headspace. Adjust lids and process.

Process Times for Festive Mincemeat Pie Filling in a Dial-Gauge Pressure Canner*

Style of Pack	Jar Size	Process Time	Canner Pressure (PSI) at Altitudes of:			
			0–2,000 ft	2,001–4,000 ft	4,001–6,000 ft	6,000–8,000 ft
Hot	Quarts	90 minutes	11 lbs	12 lbs	13 lbs	14 lbs

*After the canner is completely depressurized, remove the weight from the vent port or open the petcock. Wait 10 minutes, then unfasten the lid and remove it carefully. Lift the lid with the underside away from you so that the steam coming out of the canner does not burn your face.

Making Jams and Jellies without Added Pectin

If you are not sure if a fruit has enough of its own pectin, combine 1 tablespoon of rubbing alcohol with 1 tablespoon of extracted fruit juice in a small glass. Let stand 2 minutes. If the mixture forms into one solid mass, there's plenty of pectin. If you see several weak blobs, you need to add pectin or combine with another high-pectin fruit.

Process Times for Festive Mincemeat Pie Filling in a Weighted-Gauge Pressure Canner*

Style of Pack	Jar Size	Process Time	Canner Pressure (PSI) at Altitudes of:	
			0–1,000 ft	Above 1,000 ft
Hot	Quarts	90 minutes	10 lbs	15 lbs

*After the canner is completely depressurized, remove the weight from the vent port or open the petcock. Wait 10 minutes, then unfasten the lid and remove it carefully. Lift the lid with the underside away from you so that the steam coming out of the canner does not burn your face.

Jams, Jellies, and Other Fruit Spreads

Homemade jams and jellies have lots more flavor than store-bought, over-processed varieties. The combina-tions of fruits and spices are limitless, so have fun exper-imenting with these recipes. If you can bear to part with your creations when you're all done, they make wonder-ful gifts for any occasion.

Pectin is what makes jams and jellies thicken and gel. Many fruits, such as crab apples, citrus fruits, sour plums, currants, quinces, green apples, or Concord grapes, have plenty of their own natural pectin, so there's no need to add more pectin to your recipes. You can use less sugar when you don't add pectin, but you will have to boil the fruit for longer. Still, the process is relatively simple and you don't have to worry about having store-bought pectin on hand.

To use fresh fruits with a low-pectin content or canned or frozen fruit juice, powdered or liquid pec-tin must be added for your jams and jellies to thicken and set properly. Jelly or jam made with added pectin requires less cooking and generally gives a larger yield. These products have more natural fruit flavors, too. In addition, using added pectin eliminates the need to test hot jellies and jams for proper gelling.

Beginning this section are descriptions of the dif-ferences between methods, and tips for success with whichever you use.

Jelly Without Added Pectin

Making jelly without added pectin is not an exact sci-ence. You can add a little more or less sugar accord-ing to your taste, substitute honey for up to ½ of the sugar, or experiment with combining small amounts of low-pectin fruits with other high-pectin fruits. The Ingre-dients table below shows you the basics for common high-pectin fruits. Use it as a guideline as you experi-ment with other fruits.

As fruit ripens, its pectin content decreases, so use fruit that has recently been picked, and mix ¾ ripe fruit with ¼ under-ripe. Cooking cores and peels along with the fruit will also increase the pectin level. Avoid using canned or frozen fruit as they contain very little pectin.

Be sure to wash all fruit thoroughly before cooking. One pound of fruit should yield at least 1 cup of clear juice.

Ingredients

| Fruit | Water to be Added per Pound of Fruit | Minutes to Simmer Fruit before Extracting Juice | Ingredients Added to Each Cup of Strained Juice | | Yield from 4 Cups of Juice (Half-pints) |
			Sugar (Cups)	Lemon Juice (Tsp)	
Apples	1 cup	20 to 25	¾	1½ (opt)	4 to 5
Blackberries	None or ¼ cup	5 to 10	¾ to 1	None	7 to 8
Crab apples	1 cup	20 to 25	1	None	4 to 5
Grapes	None or ¼ cup	5 to 10	¾ to 1	None	8 to 9
Plums	½ cup	15 to 20	¾	None	8 to 9

Directions

1. Crush soft fruits or berries; cut firmer fruits into small pieces (there is no need to peel or core the fruits, as cooking all the parts adds pectin).
2. Add water to fruits that require it, as listed in the Ingredients table above. Put fruit and water in large saucepan and bring to a boil. Then simmer according to the times in the chart until fruit is soft, while stirring to prevent scorching.
3. When fruit is tender, strain through a colander, then strain through a double layer of cheesecloth or a jelly bag. Allow juice to drip through, using a stand or colander to hold the bag. Avoid pressing or squeezing the bag or cloth as it will cause cloudy jelly.
4. Using no more than 6 to 8 cups of extracted fruit juice at a time, measure fruit juice, sugar, and lemon juice according to the Ingredients table, and heat to boiling.
5. Stir until the sugar is dissolved. Boil over high heat to the jelling point. To test jelly for doneness, use one of the following methods:

Temperature test—Use a jelly or candy thermometer and boil until mixture reaches the following temperatures:

Sea Level	1,000 ft	2,000 ft	3,000 ft	4,000 ft	5,000 ft	6,000 ft	7,000 ft	8,000 ft
220°F	218°F	216°F	214°F	212°F	211°F	209°F	207°F	205°F

Sheet or spoon test—Dip a cool, metal spoon into the boiling jelly mixture. Raise the spoon about 12 inches above the pan (out of steam). Turn the spoon so the liquid runs off the side. The jelly is done when the syrup forms two drops that flow together and sheet or hang off the edge of the spoon.

6. Remove from heat and quickly skim off foam. Fill sterile jars with jelly. Use a measuring cup or ladle the jelly through a wide-mouthed funnel, leaving ¼-inch headspace. Adjust lids and process.

Process Times for Jelly without Added Pectin in a Boiling Water Canner*

| | | Process Time at Altitudes of: | | |
Style of Pack	Jar Size	0–1,000 ft	1,001– 6,000 ft	Above 6,000 ft
Hot	Half-pints or pints	5 minutes	10 minutes	15 minutes

*After the process is complete, turn off the heat and remove the canner lid. Wait five minutes before removing jars.

Lemon Curd

Lemon curd is a rich, creamy spread that can be used on (or in) a variety of teatime treats—crumpets, scones, cake fillings, tartlets, or meringues are all enhanced by its tangy-sweet flavor. Follow the recipe carefully, as variances in ingredients, order, and temperatures may lead to a poor texture or flavor. For Lime Curd, use the same recipe but substitute 1 cup bottled lime juice and ¼ cup fresh lime zest for the lemon juice and zest. This recipe yields about three to four half-pints.

Ingredients
2½ cups superfine sugar*

_____

* If superfine sugar is not available, run granulated sugar through a grinder or food processor for 1 minute, let settle, and use in place of superfine sugar. Do not use powdered sugar.

½ cup lemon zest (freshly zested), optional

1 cup bottled lemon juice**

¾ cup unsalted butter, chilled, cut into approximately ¾-inch pieces

7 large egg yolks

4 large whole eggs

Directions

1. Wash 4 half-pint canning jars with warm, soapy water. Rinse well; keep hot until ready to fill. Prepare canning lids according to manufacturer's directions.

2. Fill boiling water canner with enough water to cover the filled jars by 1 to 2 inches. Use a thermometer to preheat the water to 180°F by the time filled jars are ready to be added. **Caution:** Do not heat the water in the canner to more than 180°F before jars are added. If the water in the canner is too hot when jars are added, the process time will not be long enough. The time it takes for the canner to reach boiling after the jars are added is expected to be 25 to 30 minutes for this product. Process time starts after the water in the canner comes to a full boil over the tops of the jars.

3. Combine the sugar and lemon zest in a small bowl, stir to mix, and set aside about 30 minutes. Pre-measure the lemon juice and prepare the chilled butter pieces.

4. Heat water in the bottom pan of a double boiler*** until it boils gently. The water should not boil vigorously or touch the bottom of the top double boiler pan or bowl in which the curd is to be cooked. Steam produced will be sufficient for the cooking process to occur.

5. In the top of the double boiler, on the countertop or table, whisk the egg yolks and whole eggs together until thoroughly mixed. Slowly whisk in the sugar and zest, blending until well-mixed and smooth. Blend in the lemon juice and then add the butter pieces to the mixture.

6. Place the top of the double boiler over boiling water in the bottom pan. Stir gently but continuously with a silicone spatula or cooking spoon, to prevent the mixture from sticking to the bottom of the pan. Continue cooking until the mixture reaches a temperature of 170°F. Use a food thermometer to monitor the temperature.

7. Remove the double boiler pan from the stove and place on a protected surface, such as a dishcloth or towel on the countertop. Continue to stir gently until the curd thickens (about 5 minutes). Strain

curd through a mesh strainer into a glass or stainless steel bowl; discard collected zest.

8. Fill hot, strained curd into the clean, hot half-pint jars, leaving ½-inch headspace. Remove air bubbles and adjust headspace if needed. Wipe rims of jars with a dampened, clean paper towel; apply two-piece metal canning lids. Process. Let cool, undisturbed, for 12 to 24 hours and check for seals.

Process Times for Lemon Curd in a Boiling-Water Canner*

Style of Pack	Jar Size	Process Time at Altitudes of:		
		0–1,000 ft	1,001–6,000 ft	Above 6,000 ft
Hot	Half-pints	15 minutes	20 minutes	25 minutes

*After the process is complete, turn off the heat and remove the canner lid. Wait five minutes before removing jars.

Jam Without Added Pectin

Making jam is even easier than making jelly, as you don't have to strain the fruit. However, you'll want to be sure to remove all stems, skins, and pits. Be sure to wash and rinse all fruits thoroughly before cooking, but don't let them soak. For best flavor, use fully ripe fruit. Use the Ingredients table below as a guideline as you experiment with less common fruits.

Ingredients

Fruit	Quantity (Crushed)	Sugar	Lemon Juice	Yield (Half-pints)
Apricots	4 to 4 ½ cups	4 cups	2 tbsp	5 to 6
Berries*	4 cups	4 cups	None	3 to 4
Peaches	5 ½ to 6 cups	4 to 5 cups	2 tbsp	6 to 7

*Includes blackberries, boysenberries, dewberries, gooseberries, loganberries, raspberries, and strawberries.

1. Remove stems, skins, seeds, and pits; cut into pieces and crush. For berries, remove stems and blossoms and crush. Seedy berries may be put through a sieve or food mill. Measure crushed fruit into large saucepan using the ingredient quantities specified above.

2. Add sugar and bring to a boil while stirring rapidly and constantly. Continue to boil until mixture thickens. Use one of the following tests to determine when jams and jellies are ready to fill. Remember that the jam will thicken as it cools.

** Bottled lemon juice is used to standardize acidity. Fresh lemon juice can vary in acidity and is not recommended.

*** If a double boiler is not available, a substitute can be made with a large bowl or saucepan that can fit partway down into a saucepan of a smaller diameter. If the bottom pan has a larger diameter, the top bowl or pan should have a handle or handles that can rest on the rim of the lower pan.

Temperature test—Use a jelly or candy thermometer and boil until mixture reaches the temperature for your altitude.

Sea Level	1,000 ft	2,000 ft	3,000 ft	4,000 ft	5,000 ft	6,000 ft	7,000 ft	8,000 ft
220°F	218°F	216°F	214°F	212°F	211°F	209°F	207°F	205°F

Refrigerator test—Remove the jam mixture from the heat. Pour a small amount of boiling jam on a cold plate and put it in the freezer compartment of a refrigerator for a few minutes. If the mixture gels, it is ready to fill.

3. Remove from heat and skim off foam quickly. Fill sterile jars with jam. Use a measuring cup or ladle the jam through a wide-mouthed funnel, leaving ¼-inch headspace. Adjust lids and process.

Process Times for Jams without Added Pectin in a Boiling-Water Canner*

Style of Pack	Jar Size	Process Time at Altitudes of:		
		0–1,000 ft	1,001–6,000 ft	Above 6,000 ft
Hot	Half-pints	5 minutes	10 minutes	15 minutes

*After the process is complete, turn off the heat and remove the canner lid. Wait five minutes before removing jars.

Jams and Jellies With Added Pectin

To use fresh fruits with a low-pectin content or canned or frozen fruit juice, powdered or liquid pectin must be added for your jams and jellies to thicken and set properly. Jelly or jam made with added pectin requires less cooking and generally gives a larger yield. These products have more natural fruit flavors, too. In addition, using added pectin eliminates the need to test hot jellies and jams for proper gelling.

Commercially produced pectin is a natural ingredient, usually made from apples and available at most grocery stores. There are several types of pectin now commonly available; liquid, powder, low-sugar, and no-sugar pectins each have their own advantages and downsides. Pomona's Universal Pectin® is a citrus pectin that allows you to make jams and jellies with little or no sugar. Because the order of combining ingredients depends on the type of pectin used, it is best to follow the common jam and jelly recipes that are included right on most pectin packages. However, if you want to try something a little different, follow one of the following recipes for mixed fruit and spiced fruit jams and jellies.

Tips

- Adding ½ teaspoon of butter or margarine with the juice and pectin will reduce foaming. However, these may cause off-flavor in a long-term storage of jellies and jams.
- Purchase fresh fruit pectin each year. Old pectin may result in poor gels.
- Be sure to use mason canning jars, self-sealing two-piece lids, and a five-minute process (corrected for altitude, as necessary) in boiling water.

Process Times for Jams and Jellies with Added Pectin in a Boiling-Water Canner*

Style of Pack	Jar Size	Process Time at Altitudes of:		
		0–1,000 ft	1,001–6,000 ft	Above 6,000 ft
Hot	Half-pints	5 minutes	10 minutes	15 minutes

*After the process is complete, turn off the heat and remove the canner lid. Wait five minutes before removing jars.

Pear-Apple Jam

This is a delicious jam perfect for making at the end of autumn, just before the frost gets the last apples. For a warming, spicy twist, add a teaspoon of fresh, grated ginger along with the cinnamon. This recipe yields seven to eight half-pints.

Ingredients

2 cups peeled, cored, and finely chopped pears (about 2 lbs)

1 cup peeled, cored, and finely chopped apples

¼ tsp ground cinnamon

6½ cups sugar

⅓ cup bottled lemon juice

6 oz liquid pectin

Directions

1. Peel, core, and slice apples and pears into a large saucepan and stir in cinnamon. Thoroughly mix sugar and lemon juice with fruits and bring to a boil over high heat, stirring constantly and crushing fruit with a potato masher as it softens.
2. Once boiling, immediately stir in pectin. Bring to a full rolling boil and boil hard 1 minute, stirring constantly.
3. Remove from heat, quickly skim off foam, and fill sterile jars, leaving ¼-inch headspace. Adjust lids and process.

Process Times for Pear-Apple Jam in a Boiling Water Canner*

Style of Pack	Jar Size	Process Time at Altitudes of:		
		0–1,000 ft	1,001–6,000 ft	Above 6,000 ft
Hot	Half-pints	5 minutes	10 minutes	15 minutes

*After the process is complete, turn off the heat and remove the canner lid. Wait five minutes before removing jars.

Strawberry-Rhubarb Jelly

Strawberry-rhubarb jelly will turn any ordinary piece of bread into a delightful treat. You can also spread it on shortcake or pound cake for a simple and unique dessert. This recipe yields about seven half-pints.

Ingredients

1½ lbs red stalks of rhubarb

1½ qts ripe strawberries

½ tsp butter or margarine to reduce foaming (optional)

6 cups sugar

6 oz liquid pectin

Directions

1. Wash and cut rhubarb into 1-inch pieces and blend or grind. Wash, stem, and crush strawberries, one layer at a time, in a saucepan. Place both fruits in a jelly bag or double layer of cheesecloth and gently squeeze juice into a large measuring cup or bowl.
2. Measure 3½ cups of juice into a large saucepan. Add butter and sugar, thoroughly mixing into juice. Bring to a boil over high heat, stirring constantly.
3. As soon as mixture begins to boil, stir in pectin. Bring to a full, rolling boil and boil hard 1 minute, stirring constantly. Remove from heat, quickly skim off foam, and fill sterile jars, leaving ¼-inch headspace. Adjust lids and process.

Process Times for Strawberry-Rhubarb Jelly in a Boiling-Water Canner*

Style of Pack	Jar Size	Process Time at Altitudes of:		
		0–1,000 ft	1,001–6,000 ft	Above 6,000 ft
Hot	Half-pints or pints	5 minutes	10 minutes	15 minutes

*After the process is complete, turn off the heat and remove the canner lid. Wait five minutes before removing jars.

Blueberry-Spice Jam

This is a summery treat that is delicious spread over waffles with a little butter. Using wild blueberries results in a stronger flavor, but cultivated blueberries also work well. This recipe yields about five half-pints.

Ingredients

2½ pints ripe blueberries

1 tbsp lemon juice

½ tsp ground nutmeg or cinnamon

¾ cup water

5½ cups sugar

1 box (1¾ oz) powdered pectin

Directions

1. Wash and thoroughly crush blueberries, adding one layer at a time, in a saucepan. Add lemon juice, spice, and water. Stir pectin and bring to a full, rolling boil over high heat, stirring frequently.
2. Add the sugar and return to a full, rolling boil. Boil hard for 1 minute, stirring constantly. Remove from heat, quickly skim off foam, and fill sterile jars, leaving ¼-inch headspace. Adjust lids and process.

Process Times for Blueberry-Spice Jam in a Boiling-Water Canner*

Style of Pack	Jar Size	Process Time at Altitudes of:		
		0–1,000 ft	1,001–6,000 ft	Above 6,000 ft
Hot	Half-pints or pints	5 minutes	10 minutes	15 minutes

*After the process is complete, turn off the heat and remove the canner lid. Wait five minutes before removing jars.

Grape-Plum Jelly

If you think peanut butter and jelly sandwiches are only for kids, try grape-plum jelly spread with a natural nut butter over a thick slice of whole wheat bread. You'll change your mind. This recipe yields about 10 half-pints.

Ingredients
3½ lbs ripe plums
3 lbs ripe Concord grapes
8½ cups sugar
1 cup water
½ tsp butter or margarine to reduce foaming (optional)
1 box (1¾ oz) powdered pectin

Directions
1. Wash and pit plums; do not peel. Thoroughly crush the plums and grapes, adding one layer at a time, in a saucepan with water. Bring to a boil, cover, and simmer 10 minutes.
2. Strain juice through a jelly bag or double layer of cheesecloth. Measure sugar and set aside. Combine 6½ cups of juice with butter and pectin in large saucepan. Bring to a hard boil over high heat, stirring constantly.
3. Add the sugar and return to a full, rolling boil. Boil hard for 1 minute, stirring constantly. Remove from heat, quickly skim off foam, and fill sterile jars, leaving ¼-inch headspace. Adjust lids and process.

Process Times for Grape-Plum Jelly in a Boiling-Water Canner*

Style of Pack	Jar Size	Process Time at Altitudes of:		
		0–1,000 ft	1,001–6,000 ft	Above 6,000 ft
Hot	Half-pints or pints	5 minutes	10 minutes	15 minutes

*After the process is complete, turn off the heat and remove the canner lid. Wait five minutes before removing jars.

Making Reduced-Sugar Fruit Spreads

A variety of fruit spreads may be made that are tasteful, yet lower in sugars and calories than regular jams and jellies. The most straightforward method is probably to buy low-sugar pectin and follow the directions on the package, but the following recipes show alternate methods of using gelatin or fruit pulp as thickening agents. Gelatin recipes should not be processed and should be refrigerated and used within four weeks.

Peach-Pineapple Spread

This recipe may be made with any combination of peaches, nectarines, apricots, and plums. You can use no sugar, up to two cups of sugar, or a combination of sugar and another sweetener (such as honey, Splenda, or agave nectar). Note that if you use aspartame, the spread may lose its sweetness within three to four weeks. Add cinnamon or star anise if desired. This recipe yields five to six half-pints.

Ingredients
4 cups drained peach pulp (follow directions below)
2 cups drained unsweetened crushed pineapple
¼ cup bottled lemon juice
2 cups sugar (optional)

Directions
1. Thoroughly wash 4 to 6 pounds of firm, ripe peaches. Drain well. Peel and remove pits. Grind fruit flesh with a medium or coarse blade, or crush with a fork (do not use a blender).
2. Place ground or crushed peach pulp in a 2-quart saucepan. Heat slowly to release juice, stirring constantly, until fruit is tender. Place cooked fruit in a jelly bag or strainer lined with four layers of cheesecloth. Allow juice to drip about 15 minutes. Save the juice for jelly or other uses.
3. Measure 4 cups of drained peach pulp for making spread. Combine the 4 cups of pulp, pineapple, and lemon juice in a 4-quart saucepan. Add up to 2 cups of sugar or other sweetener, if desired, and mix well.
4. Heat and boil gently for 10 to 15 minutes, stirring enough to prevent sticking. Fill jars quickly, leaving ¼-inch headspace. Adjust lids and process.

Process Times for Peach-Pineapple Spread in a Boiling-Water Canner*

Style of Pack	Jar Size	Process Time at Altitudes of:			
		0–1,000 ft	1,001–3,000 ft	3,001–6,000 ft	Above 6,000 ft
Hot	Half-pints	15 minutes	20 minutes	20 minutes	25 minutes
	Pints	20 minutes	25 minutes	30 minutes	35 minutes

*After the process is complete, turn off the heat and remove the canner lid. Wait five minutes before removing jars.

Refrigerated Apple Spread

This recipe uses gelatin as a thickener, so it does not require processing but it should be refrigerated and used within four weeks. For spiced apple jelly, add two sticks of cinnamon and four whole cloves to mixture before boiling. Remove both spices before adding the sweetener and food coloring (if desired). This recipe yields four half-pints.

Ingredients
2 tbsp unflavored gelatin powder
1 qt bottle unsweetened apple juice
2 tbsp bottled lemon juice
2 tbsp liquid low-calorie sweetener (e.g., sucralose, honey, or 1–2 tsp liquid stevia)

Directions
1. In a saucepan, soften the gelatin in the apple and lemon juices. To dissolve gelatin, bring to a full,

rolling boil and boil 2 minutes. Remove from heat.

2. Stir in sweetener and food coloring (if desired). Fill jars, leaving ¼-inch headspace. Adjust lids. Refrigerate (do not process or freeze).

Refrigerated Grape Spread

This is a simple, tasty recipe that doesn't require processing. Be sure to refrigerate and use within four weeks. This recipe makes three half-pints.

Ingredients

2 tbsp unflavored gelatin powder
1 bottle (24 oz) unsweetened grape juice
2 tbsp bottled lemon juice
2 tbsp liquid low-calorie sweetener (e.g., sucralose, honey, or 1–2 tsp liquid stevia)

Directions

1. In a saucepan, heat the gelatin in the grape and lemon juices until mixture is soft. Bring to a full, rolling boil to dissolve gelatin. Boil 1 minute and remove from heat. Stir in sweetener.
2. Fill jars quickly, leaving ¼-inch headspace. Adjust lids. Refrigerate (do not process or freeze).

Remaking Soft Jellies

Sometimes jelly just doesn't turn out right the first time. Jelly that is too soft can be used as a sweet sauce to drizzle over ice cream, cheesecake, or angel food cake, but it can also be re-cooked into the proper consistency.

To Remake with Powdered Pectin

1. Measure jelly to be re-cooked. Work with no more than 4 to 6 cups at a time. For each quart (4 cups) of jelly, mix ¼ cup sugar, ½ cup water, 2 tablespoons bottled lemon juice, and 4 teaspoons powdered pectin. Bring to a boil while stirring.
2. Add jelly and bring to a rolling boil over high heat, stirring constantly. Boil hard for ½ minute. Remove from heat, quickly skim foam off jelly, and fill sterile

jars, leaving ¼-inch headspace. Adjust new lids and process as recommended.

To Remake With Liquid Pectin

1. Measure jelly to be re-cooked. Work with no more than 4 to 6 cups at a time. For each quart (4 cups) of jelly, measure into a bowl ¾ cup sugar, 2 tablespoons bottled lemon juice, and 2 tablespoons liquid pectin.
2. Bring jelly only to boil over high heat, while stirring. Remove from heat and quickly add the sugar, lemon juice, and pectin. Bring to a full, rolling boil, stirring constantly. Boil hard for 1 minute. Quickly skim off foam and fill sterile jars, leaving ¼-inch headspace. Adjust new lids and process as recommended.

To Remake without Added Pectin

1. For each quart of jelly, add 2 tablespoons bottled lemon juice. Heat to boiling and continue to boil for 3 to 4 minutes.
2. To test jelly for doneness, use one of the following methods:

Temperature test—Use a jelly or candy thermometer and boil until mixture reaches the following temperatures at the altitudes below:

Sea Level	1,000 ft	2,000 ft	3,000 ft	4,000 ft	5,000 ft	6,000 ft	7,000 ft	8,000 ft
220°F	218°F	216°F	214°F	212°F	211°F	209°F	207°F	205°F

Sheet or spoon test—Dip a cool metal spoon into the boiling jelly mixture. Raise the spoon about 12 inches above the pan (out of steam). Turn the spoon so the liquid runs off the side. The jelly is done when the syrup forms two drops that flow together and sheet or hang off the edge of the spoon.

3. Remove from heat, quickly skim off foam, and fill sterile jars, leaving ¼-inch headspace. Adjust new lids and process.

Process Times for Remade Soft Jellies in a Boiling-Water Canner

Style of Pack	Jar Size	Process Time at Altitudes of:		
		0–1,000 ft	1,001–6,000 ft	Above 6,000 ft
Hot	Half-pints or pints	5 minutes	10 minutes	15 minutes

*After the process is complete, turn off the heat and remove the canner lid. Wait five minutes before removing jars.

Vegetables, Pickles, and Tomatoes

Beans or Peas, Shelled or Dried (All Varieties)

Shelled or dried beans and peas are inexpensive and easy to buy or store in bulk, but they are not very convenient when it comes to preparing them to eat. Hydrating and canning beans or peas enable you to simply open a can and use them rather than waiting for them to soak. Sort and discard discolored seeds before rehydrating.

Quantity

- An average of five pounds is needed per canner load of seven quarts.
- An average of 3¼ pounds is needed per canner load of nine pints—an average of ¾ pounds per quart.

Directions

1. Place dried beans or peas in a large pot and cover with water. Soak 12 to 18 hours in a cool place. Drain water. To quickly hydrate beans, you may cover sorted and washed beans with boiling water in a saucepan. Boil 2 minutes, remove from heat, soak 1 hour, and drain.

2. Cover beans soaked by either method with fresh water and boil 30 minutes. Add ½ teaspoon of salt per pint or 1 teaspoon per quart to each jar, if desired. Fill jars with beans or peas and cooking water, leaving 1-inch headspace. Adjust lids and process.

Process Times for Beans or Peas in a Dial-Gauge Pressure Canner*

Style of Pack	Jar Size	Process Time	Canner Pressure (PSI) at Altitudes of:			
			0–2,000 ft	2,001–4,000 ft	4,001–6,000 ft	6,001–8,000 ft
Hot	Pints	75 minutes	11 lbs	12 lbs	13 lbs	14 lbs
	Quarts	90 minutes	11 lbs	12 lbs	13 lbs	14 lbs

*After the canner is completely depressurized, remove the weight from the vent port or open the petcock. Wait 10 minutes; then unfasten the lid and remove it carefully. Lift the lid with the underside away from you so that the steam coming out of the canner does not burn your face.

Process Times for Beans or Peas in a Weighted-Gauge Pressure Canner*

Style of pack	Jar Size	Process Time	Canner Pressure (PSI) at Altitudes of:	
			0–1,000 ft	Above 1,000 ft
Hot	Pints	75 minutes	10 lbs	15 lbs
	Quarts	90 minutes	10 lbs	15 lbs

*After the canner is completely depressurized, remove the weight from the vent port or open the petcock. Wait 10 minutes, then unfasten the lid and remove it carefully. Lift the lid with the underside away from you so that the steam coming out of the canner does not burn your face.

Baked Beans

Baked beans are an old New England favorite, but every cook has his or her favorite variation. Two recipes are included here, but feel free to alter them to your own taste.

Quantity

- An average of five pounds of beans is needed per canner load of seven quarts.
- An average of 3¼ pounds is needed per canner load of nine pints—an average of ¾ pounds per quart.

Directions

1. Sort and wash dry beans. Add 3 cups of water for each cup of dried beans. Boil 2 minutes, remove from heat, soak 1 hour, and drain.

2. Heat to boiling in fresh water, and save liquid for making sauce. Make your choice of the following sauces:

Tomato Sauce—Mix 1 quart tomato juice, 3 tablespoons sugar, 2 teaspoons salt, 1 tablespoon chopped onion, and ¼ teaspoon each of ground cloves, allspice, mace, and cayenne pepper. Heat to boiling. Add 3 quarts cooking liquid from beans and bring back to boiling.

Molasses Sauce—Mix 4 cups water or cooking liquid from beans, 3 tablespoons dark molasses, 1 tablespoon vinegar, 2 teaspoons salt, and ¾ teaspoon powdered dry mustard. Heat to boiling.

3. Place seven ¾-inch pieces of pork, ham, or bacon in an earthenware crock, a large casserole, or a pan. Add beans and enough molasses sauce to cover beans.

4. Cover and bake 4 to 5 hours at 350°F. Add water as needed—about every hour. Fill jars, leaving 1-inch headspace. Adjust lids and process.

Process Times for Baked Beans in a Dial-Gauge Pressure Canner*

Style of Pack	Jar Size	Process Time	Canner Pressure (PSI) at Altitudes of:			
			0–2,000 ft	2,001–4,000 ft	4,001–6,000 ft	6,001–8,000 ft
Hot	Pints	65 minutes	11 lbs	12 lbs	13 lbs	14 lbs
	Quarts	75 minutes	11 lbs	12 lbs	13 lbs	14 lbs

*After the canner is completely depressurized, remove the weight from the vent port or open the petcock. Wait 10 minutes, then unfasten the lid and remove it carefully. Lift the lid with the underside away from you so that the steam coming out of the canner does not burn your face.

Process Times for Baked Beans in a Weighted-Gauge Pressure Canner*

Style of pack	Jar Size	Process Time	Canner Pressure (PSI) at Altitudes of:	
			0–1,000 ft	Above 1,000 ft
Hot	Pints	65 minutes	10 lbs	15 lbs
	Quarts	75 minutes	10 lbs	15 lbs

*After the canner is completely depressurized, remove the weight from the vent port or open the petcock. Wait 10 minutes, then unfasten the lid and remove it carefully. Lift the lid with the underside away from you so that the steam coming out of the canner does not burn your face.

Green Beans

This process will work equally well for snap, Italian, or wax beans. Select filled but tender, crisp pods, removing any diseased or rusty pods.

Quantity

- An average of 14 pounds is needed per canner load of seven quarts.
- An average of nine pounds is needed per canner load of nine pints.
- A bushel weighs 30 pounds and yields 12 to 20 quarts—an average of 2 pounds per quart.

Directions

1. Wash beans and trim ends. Leave whole, or cut or break into 1-inch pieces.

Hot pack—Cover with boiling water; boil 5 minutes. Fill jars loosely, leaving 1-inch headspace.

Raw pack—Fill jars tightly with raw beans, leaving 1-inch headspace. Add 1 teaspoon of salt per quart to each jar, if desired. Add boiling water, leaving 1-inch headspace.

2. Adjust lids and process.

Process Times for Green Beans in a Dial-Gauge Pressure Canner*

Style of Pack	Jar Size	Process Time	Canner Pressure (PSI) at Altitudes of:			
			0–2,000 ft	2,001–4,000 ft	4,001–6,000 ft	6,001–8,000 ft
Hot or Raw	Pints	20 minutes	11 lb	12 lb	13 lb	14 lb
	Quarts	25 minutes	11 lb	12 lb	13 lb	14 lb

*After the canner is completely depressurized, remove the weight from the vent port or open the petcock. Wait 10 minutes, then unfasten the lid and remove it carefully. Lift the lid with the underside away from you so that the steam coming out of the canner does not burn your face.

Process Times for Green Beans in a Weighted-Gauge Pressure Canner*

Style of Pack	Jar Size	Process Time	Canner Pressure (PSI) at Altitudes of:	
			0–1,000 ft	Above 1,000 ft
Hot or Raw	Pints	20 minutes	10 lbs	15 lbs
	Quarts	25 minutes	10 lbs	15 lbs

*After the canner is completely depressurized, remove the weight from the vent port or open the petcock. Wait 10 minutes; then unfasten the lid and remove it carefully. Lift the lid with the underside away from you so that the steam coming out of the canner does not burn your face.

Beets

You can preserve beets whole, cubed, or sliced, according to your preference. Beets that are 1 to 2 inches in diameter are the best, as larger ones tend to be too fibrous.

Quantity

- An average of 21 pounds (without tops) is needed per canner load of seven quarts.
- An average of 13½ pounds is needed per canner load of nine pints.
- A bushel (without tops) weighs 52 pounds and yields 15 to 20 quarts—an average of three pounds per quart.

Directions

1. Trim off beet tops, leaving an inch of stem and roots to reduce bleeding of color. Scrub well. Cover with boiling water. Boil until skins slip off easily, about 15 to 25 minutes depending on size.
2. Cool, remove skins, and trim off stems and roots. Leave baby beets whole. Cut medium or large beets into ½-inch cubes or slices. Halve or quarter very large slices. Add 1 teaspoon of salt per quart to each jar, if desired.
3. Fill jars with hot beets and fresh hot water, leaving 1-inch headspace. Adjust lids and process.

Process Times for Beets in a Dial-Gauge Pressure Canner*

Style of Pack	Jar Size	Process Time	Canner Pressure (PSI) at Altitudes of:			
			0–2,000 ft	2,001–4,000 ft	4,001–6,000 ft	6,001–8,000 ft
Hot	Pints	30 minutes	11 lbs	12 lbs	13 lbs	14 lbs
	Quarts	35 minutes	11 lbs	12 lbs	13 lbs	14 lbs

*After the canner is completely depressurized, remove the weight from the vent port or open the petcock. Wait 10 minutes, then unfasten the lid and remove it carefully. Lift the lid with the underside away from you so that the steam coming out of the canner does not burn your face.

Process Times for Beets in a Weighted-Gauge Pressure Canner*

Style of Pack	Jar Size	Process Time	Canner Pressure (PSI) at Altitudes of:	
			0–1,000 ft	Above 1,000 ft
Hot or Raw	Pints	30 minutes	10 lbs	15 lbs
	Quarts	35 minutes	10 lbs	15 lbs

*After the canner is completely depressurized, remove the weight from the vent port or open the petcock. Wait 10 minutes; then unfasten the lid and remove it carefully. Lift the lid with the underside away from you so that the steam coming out of the canner does not burn your face.

Carrots

Carrots can be preserved sliced or diced according to your preference. Choose small carrots, preferably 1 to 1¼ inches in diameter, as larger ones are often too fibrous.

Quantity

- An average of 17½ pounds (without tops) is needed per canner load of seven quarts.
- An average of 11 pounds is needed per canner load of nine pints.
- A bushel (without tops) weighs 50 pounds and yields 17 to 25 quarts—an average of 2½ pounds per quart.

Directions

1. Wash, peel, and rewash carrots. Slice or dice.

Hot pack—Cover with boiling water; bring to boil and simmer for 5 minutes. Fill jars with carrots, leaving 1-inch headspace.

Raw pack—Fill jars tightly with raw carrots, leaving 1-inch headspace.

2. Add 1 teaspoon of salt per quart to the jar, if desired. Add hot cooking liquid or water, leaving 1-inch headspace. Adjust lids and process.

Process Times for Carrots in a Dial-Gauge pressure Canner*

Style of Pack	Jar Size	Process Time	Canner Pressure (PSI) at Altitudes of:			
			0–2,000 ft	2,001–4,000 ft	4,001–6,000 ft	6,001–8,000 ft
Hot or Raw	Pints	25 minutes	11 lbs	12 lbs	13 lbs	14 lbs
	Quarts	30 minutes	11 lbs	12 lbs	13 lbs	14 lbs

*After the canner is completely depressurized, remove the weight from the vent port or open the petcock. Wait 10 minutes; then unfasten the lid and remove it carefully. Lift the lid with the underside away from you so that the steam coming out of the canner does not burn your face.

Process Times for Carrots in a Weighted-Gauge Pressure Canner*

Style of Pack	Jar Size	Process Time	Canner Pressure (PSI) at Altitudes of:	
			0–1,000 ft	Above 1,000 ft
Hot or Raw	Pints	25 minutes	10 lb	15 lb
	Quarts	30 minutes	10 lb	15 lb

*After the canner is completely depressurized, remove the weight from the vent port or open the petcock. Wait 10 minutes; then unfasten the lid and remove it carefully. Lift the lid with the underside away from you so that the steam coming out of the canner does not burn your face.

Corn, Cream Style

The creamy texture comes from scraping the corncobs thoroughly and including the juices and corn pieces with the kernels. If you want to add milk or cream, butter, or other ingredients, do so just before serving (do not add dairy products before canning). Select ears containing slightly immature kernels for this recipe.

Quantity

- An average of 20 pounds (in husks) of sweet corn is needed per canner load of nine pints.
- A bushel weighs 35 pounds and yields 12 to 20 pints—an average of 2¼ pounds per pint.

Directions

1. Husk corn, remove silk, and wash ears. Cut corn from cob at about the center of kernel. Scrape remaining corn from cobs with a table knife.

Hot pack—To each quart of corn and scrapings in a saucepan, add 2 cups of boiling water. Heat to boiling. Add ½ teaspoon salt to each jar, if desired. Fill pint jars with hot corn mixture, leaving 1-inch headspace.

Raw pack—Fill pint jars with raw corn, leaving 1-inch headspace. Do not shake or press down. Add ½ teaspoon salt to each jar, if desired. Add fresh boiling water, leaving 1-inch headspace.

2. Adjust lids and process.

Process Times for Cream-Style Corn in a Dial-Gauge Pressure Canner

Style of pack	Jar Size	Process Time	Canner Pressure (PSI) at Altitudes of:			
			0–2,000 ft	2,001–4,000 ft	4,001–6,000 ft	6,001–8,000 ft
Hot	Pints	85 minutes	11 lbs	12 lbs	13 lbs	14 lbs
Raw	Pints	95 minutes	11 lbs	12 lbs	13 lbs	14 lbs

*After the canner is completely depressurized, remove the weight from the vent port or open the petcock. Wait 10 minutes; then unfasten the lid and remove it carefully. Lift the lid with the underside away from you so that the steam coming out of the canner does not burn your face.

Process Times for Cream-Style Corn in a Weighted-Gauge Pressure Canner*

			Canner Pressure (PSI) at Altitudes of:	
Style of Pack	Jar Size	Process Time	0–1,000 ft	Above 1,000 ft
Hot	Pints	85 minutes	10 lb	15 lb
Raw	Pints	95 minutes	10 lb	15 lb

*After the canner is completely depressurized, remove the weight from the vent port or open the petcock. Wait 10 minutes; then unfasten the lid and remove it carefully. Lift the lid with the underside away from you so that the steam coming out of the canner does not burn your face.

Corn, Whole Kernel

Select ears containing slightly immature kernels. Canning of some sweeter varieties or kernels that are too immature may cause browning. Try canning a small amount to test color and flavor before canning large quantities.

Quantity

- An average of 31½ pounds (in husks) of sweet corn is needed per canner load of seven quarts.
- An average of 20 pounds is needed per canner load of nine pints.
- A bushel weighs 35 pounds and yields 6 to 11 quarts—an average of 4½ pounds per quart.

Directions

1. Husk corn, remove silk, and wash. Blanch 3 minutes in boiling water. Cut corn from cob at about three-fourths the depth of kernel. Do not scrape cob, as it will create a creamy texture.

Hot pack—To each quart of kernels in a saucepan, add 1 cup of hot water, heat to boiling, and simmer 5 minutes. Add 1 teaspoon of salt per quart to each jar, if desired. Fill jars with corn and cooking liquid, leaving 1-inch headspace.

Raw pack—Fill jars with raw kernels, leaving 1-inch headspace. Do not shake or press down. Add 1 teaspoon of salt per quart to the jar, if desired.

2. Add fresh boiling water, leaving 1-inch headspace. Adjust lids and process.

Process Times for Whole Kernel Corn in a Dial-Gauge Pressure Canner*

			Canner Pressure (PSI) at Altitudes of:			
Style of Pack	Jar Size	Process Time	0–2,000 ft	2,001–4,000 ft	4,001–6,000 ft	6,001–8,000 ft
Hot or Raw	Pints	55 minutes	11 lbs	12 lbs	13 lbs	14 lbs
	Quarts	85 minutes	11 lbs	12 lbs	13 lbs	14 lbs

*After the canner is completely depressurized, remove the weight from the vent port or open the petcock. Wait 10 minutes; then unfasten the lid and remove it carefully. Lift the lid with the underside away from you so that the steam coming out of the canner does not burn your face.

Process Times for Whole Kernel Corn in a Weighted-Gauge Pressure Canner*

			Canner Pressure (PSI) at Altitudes of:	
Style of Pack	Jar Size	Process Time	0–1,000 ft	Above 1,000 ft
Hot or Raw	Pints	55 minutes	10 lbs	15 lbs
	Quarts	85 minutes	10 lbs	15 lbs

*After the canner is completely depressurized, remove the weight from the vent port or open the petcock. Wait 10 minutes; then unfasten the lid and remove it carefully. Lift the lid with the underside away from you so that the steam coming out of the canner does not burn your face.

Mixed Vegetables

Use mixed vegetables in soups, casseroles, pot pies, or as a quick side dish. You can change the suggested proportions or substitute other favorite vegetables, but avoid leafy greens, dried beans, cream-style corn, winter squash, and sweet potatoes as they will ruin the consistency of the other vegetables. This recipe yields about seven quarts.

Ingredients

6 cups sliced carrots
6 cups cut, whole-kernel sweet corn
6 cups cut green beans
6 cups shelled lima beans
4 cups diced or crushed tomatoes
4 cups diced zucchini

Directions

1. Carefully wash, peel, de-shell, and cut vegetables as necessary. Combine all vegetables in a large pot or kettle, and add enough water to cover pieces.

2. Add 1 teaspoon salt per quart to each jar, if desired. Boil 5 minutes and fill jars with hot pieces and liquid, leaving 1-inch headspace. Adjust lids and process.

Process Times for Mixed Vegetables in a Dial-Gauge Pressure Canner*

| Style of Pack | Jar Size | Process Time | Canner Pressure (PSI) at Altitudes of: | | | |
			0–2,000 ft	2,001–4,000 ft	4,001–6,000 ft	6,001–8,000 ft
Hot	Pints	75 minutes	11 lbs	12 lbs	13 lbs	14 lbs
	Quarts	90 minutes	11 lbs	12 lbs	13 lbs	14 lbs

*After the canner is completely depressurized, remove the weight from the vent port or open the petcock. Wait 10 minutes; then unfasten the lid and remove it carefully. Lift the lid with the underside away from you so that the steam coming out of the canner does not burn your face.

Process Times for Mixed Vegetables in a Weighted-Gauge Pressure Canner*

| Style of Pack | Jar Size | Process Time | Canner Pressure (PSI) at Altitudes of: | |
			0–1,000 ft	Above 1,000 ft
Hot	Pints	75 minutes	10 lbs	15 lbs
	Quarts	90 minutes	10 lbs	15 lbs

*After the canner is completely depressurized, remove the weight from the vent port or open the petcock. Wait 10 minutes; then unfasten the lid and remove it carefully. Lift the lid with the underside away from you so that the steam coming out of the canner does not burn your face.

Peas, Green or English, Shelled

Green and English peas preserve well when canned, but sugar snap and Chinese edible pods are better frozen. Select filled pods containing young, tender, sweet seeds, and discard any diseased pods.

Quantity

- An average of 31½ pounds (in pods) is needed per canner load of seven quarts.
- An average of 20 pounds is needed per canner load of nine pints.
- A bushel weighs 30 pounds and yields 5 to 10 quarts—an average of 4½ pounds per quart.

Directions

1. Shell and wash peas. Add 1 teaspoon of salt per quart to each jar, if desired.

Hot pack—Cover with boiling water. Bring to a boil in a saucepan, and boil 2 minutes. Fill jars loosely with hot peas, and add cooking liquid, leaving 1-inch headspace.

Raw pack—Fill jars with raw peas, and add boiling water, leaving 1-inch headspace. Do not shake or press down on peas.

2. Adjust lids and process.

Process Times for Peas in a Dial-Gauge Pressure Canner*

| Style of Pack | Jar Size | Process Time | Canner Pressure (PSI) at Altitudes of: | | | |
			0–2,000 ft	2,001–4,000 ft	4,001–6,000 ft	6,001–8,000 ft
Hot or Raw	Pints or Quarts	40 minutes	11 lbs	12 lbs	13 lbs	14 lbs

*After the canner is completely depressurized, remove the weight from the vent port or open the petcock. Wait 10 minutes; then unfasten the lid and remove it carefully. Lift the lid with the underside away from you so that the steam coming out of the canner does not burn your face.

Process Times for Peas in a Weighted-Gauge Pressure Canner*

			Canner Pressure (PSI) at Altitudes of:	
Style of Pack	Jar Size	Process Time	0–1,000 ft	Above 1,000 ft
Hot or Raw	Pints or Quarts	40 minutes	10 lbs	15 lbs

*After the canner is completely depressurized, remove the weight from the vent port or open the petcock. Wait 10 minutes; then unfasten the lid and remove it carefully. Lift the lid with the underside away from you so that the steam coming out of the canner does not burn your face.

Potatoes, Sweet

Sweet potatoes can be preserved whole, in chunks, or in slices, according to your preference. Choose small to medium-sized potatoes that are mature and not too fibrous. Can within one to two months after harvest.

Quantity

- An average of 17½ pounds is needed per canner load of seven quarts.
- An average of 11 pounds is needed per canner load of nine pints.
- A bushel weighs 50 pounds and yields 17 to 25 quarts—an average of 2½ pounds per quart.

Directions
1. Wash potatoes and boil or steam until partially soft (15 to 20 minutes). Remove skins. Cut medium potatoes, if needed, so that pieces are uniform in size. Do not mash or purée pieces.
2. Fill jars, leaving 1-inch headspace. Add 1 teaspoon salt per quart to each jar, if desired. Cover with your choice of fresh boiling water or syrup, leaving 1-inch headspace. Adjust lids and process.

Process Times for Sweet Potatoes in a Dial-Gauge Pressure Canner*

			Canner Pressure (PSI) at Altitudes of:			
Style of Pack	Jar Size	Process Time	0–2,000 ft	2,001–4,000 ft	4,001–6,000 ft	6,001–8,000 ft
Hot	Pints	65 minutes	11 lbs	12 lbs	13 lbs	14 lbs
	Quarts	90 minutes	11 lbs	12 lbs	13 lbs	14 lbs

*After the canner is completely depressurized, remove the weight from the vent port or open the petcock. Wait 10 minutes; then unfasten the lid and remove it carefully. Lift the lid with the underside away from you so that the steam coming out of the canner does not burn your face.

Process Times for Sweet Potatoes in a Weighted-Gauge Pressure Canner*

			Canner Pressure (PSI) at Altitudes of:	
Style of Pack	Jar Size	Process Time	0–1,000 ft	Above 1,000 ft
Hot	Pints	65 minutes	10 lbs	15 lbs
	Quarts	90 minutes	10 lbs	15 lbs

*After the canner is completely depressurized, remove the weight from the vent port or open the petcock. Wait 10 minutes; then unfasten the lid and remove it carefully. Lift the lid with the underside away from you so that the steam coming out of the canner does not burn your face.

Pumpkin and Winter Squash

Pumpkin and squash are great to have on hand for use in pies, soups, quick breads, or as side dishes. They should have a hard rind and stringless, mature pulp. Small pumpkins (sugar or pie varieties) are best. Before using for pies, drain jars and strain or sieve pumpkin or squash cubes.

Quantity

- An average of 16 pounds is needed per canner load of seven quarts.
- An average of 10 pounds is needed per canner load of nine pints—an average of 2¼ pounds per quart.

Directions
1. Wash, remove seeds, cut into 1-inch-wide slices, and peel. Cut flesh into 1-inch cubes. Boil 2 minutes in water. Do not mash or purée.
2. Fill jars with cubes and cooking liquid, leaving 1-inch headspace. Adjust lids and process.

Process Times for Pumpkin and Winter Squash in a Dial-Gauge Pressure Canner*

Style of Pack	Jar Size	Process Time	Canner Pressure (PSI) at Altitudes of:			
			0–2,000 ft	2,001–4,000 ft	4,001–6,000 ft	6,001–8,000 ft
Hot	Pints	55 minutes	11 lbs	12 lbs	13 lbs	14 lbs
	Quarts	90 minutes	11 lbs	12 lbs	13 lbs	14 lbs

*After the canner is completely depressurized, remove the weight from the vent port or open the petcock. Wait 10 minutes; then unfasten the lid and remove it carefully. Lift the lid with the underside away from you so that the steam coming out of the canner does not burn your face.

Process Times for Pumpkin and Winter Squash in a Weighted-Gauge Pressure Canner*

Style of Pack	Jar Size	Process Time	Canner Pressure (PSI) at Altitudes of:	
			0–1,000 ft	Above 1,000 ft
Hot	Pints	55 minutes	10 lbs	15 lbs
	Quarts	90 minutes	10 lbs	15 lbs

*After the canner is completely depressurized, remove the weight from the vent port or open the petcock. Wait 10 minutes; then unfasten the lid and remove it carefully. Lift the lid with the underside away from you so that the steam coming out of the canner does not burn your face.

Succotash

To spice up this simple, satisfying dish, add a little paprika and celery salt before serving. It is also delicious made into a pot pie, with or without added chicken, turkey, or beef. This recipe yields seven quarts.

Ingredients
1 lb unhusked sweet corn or 3 qts cut whole kernels
14 lbs mature green podded lima beans or 4 qts shelled lima beans
2 qts crushed or whole tomatoes (optional)

Directions
1. Husk corn, remove silk, and wash. Blanch 3 minutes in boiling water. Cut corn from cob at about three-fourths the depth of kernel. Do not scrape cob, as it will create a creamy texture. Shell lima beans and wash thoroughly.

Hot pack—Combine all prepared vegetables in a large kettle with enough water to cover the pieces. Add 1 teaspoon salt to each quart jar, if desired. Boil gently 5 minutes and fill jars with pieces and cooking liquid, leaving 1-inch headspace.

Raw pack—Fill jars with equal parts of all prepared vegetables, leaving 1-inch headspace. Do not shake or press down pieces. Add 1 teaspoon salt to each quart jar, if desired. Add fresh boiling water, leaving 1-inch headspace.

2. Adjust lids and process.

Process Times for Succotash in a Dial-Gauge Pressure Canner*

Style of Pack	Jar Size	Process Time	Canner Pressure (PSI) at Altitudes of:			
			0–2,000 ft	2,001–4,000 ft	4,001–6,000 ft	6,001–8,000 ft
Hot or Raw	Pints	60 minutes	11 lbs	12 lbs	13 lbs	14 lbs
	Quarts	85 minutes	11 lbs	12 lbs	13 lbs	14 lbs

*After the canner is completely depressurized, remove the weight from the vent port or open the petcock. Wait 10 minutes; then unfasten the lid and remove it carefully. Lift the lid with the underside away from you so that the steam coming out of the canner does not burn your face.

Process Times for Succotash in a Weighted-Gauge Pressure Canner*

Style of Pack	Jar Size	Process Time	Canner Pressure (PSI) at Altitudes of:	
			0–1,000 ft	Above 1,000 ft
Hot or Raw	Pints	60 minutes	10 lbs	15 lbs
	Quarts	85 minutes	10 lbs	15 lbs

*After the canner is completely depressurized, remove the weight from the vent port or open the petcock. Wait 10 minutes; then unfasten the lid and remove it carefully. Lift the lid with the underside away from you so that the steam coming out of the canner does not burn your face.

Soups

Vegetable, dried bean or pea, meat, poultry, or seafood soups can all be canned. Add pasta, rice, or other grains to soup just prior to serving, as grains tend to get soggy when canned. If dried beans or peas are used, they *must* be fully rehydrated first. Dairy products should also be avoided in the canning process.

Directions
1. Select, wash, and prepare vegetables.
2. Cook vegetables. For each cup of dried beans or peas, add 3 cups of water, boil 2 minutes, remove from heat, soak 1 hour, and heat to boil. Drain and combine with meat broth, tomatoes, or water to cover. Boil 5 minutes.
3. Salt to taste, if desired. Fill jars halfway with solid mixture. Add remaining liquid, leaving 1-inch headspace. Adjust lids and process.

Process Times for Soups in a Dial-Gauge Pressure Canner*

Style of Pack	Jar Size	Process Time	Canner Pressure (PSI) at Altitudes of:			
			0– 2,000 ft	2,001–4,000 ft	4,001–6,000 ft	6,001– 8,000 ft
Hot	Pints	60** minutes	11 lbs	12 lbs	13 lbs	14 lbs
	Quarts	75** minutes	11 lbs	12 lbs	13 lbs	14 lbs

**Caution: Process 100 minutes if soup contains seafood.

*After the canner is completely depressurized, remove the weight from the vent port or open the petcock. Wait 10 minutes; then unfasten the lid and remove it carefully. Lift the lid with the underside away from you so that the steam coming out of the canner does not burn your face.

Process Times for Soups in a Weighted-Gauge Pressure Canner*

Style of Pack	Jar Size	Process Time	Canner Pressure (PSI) at Altitudes of:	
			0–1,000 ft	Above 1,000 ft
Hot	Pints	60** minutes	10 lbs	15 lbs
	Quarts	75** minutes	10 lbs	15 lbs

**Caution: Process 100 minutes if soup contains seafood.

*After the canner is completely depressurized, remove the weight from the vent port or open the petcock. Wait 10 minutes; then unfasten the lid and remove it carefully. Lift the lid with the underside away from you so that the steam coming out of the canner does not burn your face.

Meat Stock (Broth)

"Good broth will resurrect the dead," says a South American proverb. Bones contain calcium, magnesium, phosphorus, and other trace minerals, while cartilage and tendons hold glucosamine, which is important for joints and muscle health. When simmered for extended periods, these nutrients are released into the water and broken down into a form that our bodies can absorb. Not to mention that good broth is the secret to delicious risotto, reduction sauces, gravies, and dozens of other gourmet dishes.

Beef
1. Saw or crack fresh, trimmed beef bones to enhance extraction of flavor. Rinse bones and place in a large stockpot or kettle, cover bones with water, add pot cover, and simmer 3 to 4 hours.
2. Remove bones, cool broth, and pick off meat. Skim off fat, add meat removed from bones to broth, and reheat to boiling. Fill jars, leaving 1-inch headspace. Adjust lids and process.

Chicken or Turkey
1. Place large carcass bones in a large stockpot, add enough water to cover bones, cover pot, and simmer 30 to 45 minutes or until meat can be easily stripped from bones.
2. Remove bones and pieces, cool broth, strip meat, discard excess fat, and return meat to broth. Reheat to boiling and fill jars, leaving 1-inch headspace. Adjust lids and process.

Process Times for Meat Stock in a Dial-Gauge Pressure Canner*

Style of Pack	Jar Size	Process Time	Canner Pressure (PSI) at Altitudes of:			
			0–2,000 ft	2,001–4,000 ft	4,001–6,000 ft	6,001–8,000 ft
Hot	Pints	20 minutes	11 lbs	12 lbs	13 lbs	14 lbs
	Quarts	25 minutes	11 lbs	12 lbs	13 lbs	14 lbs

*After the canner is completely depressurized, remove the weight from the vent port or open the petcock. Wait 10 minutes; then unfasten the lid and remove it carefully. Lift the lid with the underside away from you so that the steam coming out of the canner does not burn your face.

Process Times for Meat Stock in a Weighted-Gauge Pressure Canner*

Style of Pack	Jar Size	Process Time	Canner Pressure (PSI) at Altitudes of:	
			0–1,000 ft	Above 1,000 ft
Hot	Pints	20 minutes	10 lbs	15 lbs
	Quarts	25 minutes	10 lbs	15 lbs

*After the canner is completely depressurized, remove the weight from the vent port or open the petcock. Wait 10 minutes; then unfasten the lid and remove it carefully. Lift the lid with the underside away from you so that the steam coming out of the canner does not burn your face.

Fermented Foods and Pickled Vegetables

Pickled vegetables play a vital role in Italian antipasto dishes, Chinese stir-fries, British piccalilli, and much of Russian and Finnish cuisine. And, of course, the Germans love their sauerkraut, kimchee is found on nearly every Korean dinner table, and many an American won't eat a sandwich without a good, strong dill pickle on the side.

Fermenting vegetables is not complicated, but you'll want to have the proper containers, covers, and weights ready before you begin. For containers, keep the following in mind:

- A once-gallon container is needed for each five pounds of fresh vegetables. Therefore, a five-gallon stone crock is of ideal size for fermenting about 25 pounds of fresh cabbage or cucumbers.
- Food-grade plastic and glass containers are excellent substitutes for stone crocks. Other one- to three-gallon non-food-grade plastic containers may be used if lined inside with a clean food-grade plastic bag. **Caution: Be certain that foods contact only food-grade plastics. Do not use garbage bags or trash liners.**
- Fermenting sauerkraut in quart and half-gallon mason jars is an acceptable practice, but may result in more spoilage losses.

Some vegetables, like cabbage and cucumbers, need to be kept 1 to 2 inches under brine while fermenting. If you find them floating to top of the container, here are some suggestions:

- After adding prepared vegetables and brine, insert a suitably sized dinner plate or glass pie plate inside the fermentation container. The plate must be slightly smaller than the container opening, yet large enough to cover most of the shredded cabbage or cucumbers.
- To keep the plate under the brine, weight it down with two to three sealed quart jars filled with water. Covering the container opening with a clean, heavy bath towel helps to prevent contamination from insects and molds while the vegetables are fermenting.
- Fine quality fermented vegetables are also obtained when the plate is weighted down with a very large, clean, plastic bag filled with three quarts of water containing 4½ tablespoons of salt. Be sure to seal the plastic bag. Freezer bags sold for packaging turkeys are suitable for use with five-gallon containers.

Be sure to wash the fermentation container, plate, and jars in hot, sudsy water, and rinse well with very hot water before use.

Dill Pickles

Feel free to alter the spices in this recipe, but stick to the same proportion of cucumbers, vinegar, and water. Check the label of your vinegar to be sure it contains 5 percent acetic acid. Fully fermented pickles may be stored in the original container for about four to six months, provided they are refrigerated and surface scum and molds are removed regularly, but canning is a better way to store fully fermented pickles.

Ingredients

Use the following quantities for each gallon capacity of your container:

4 lbs of 4-inch pickling cucumbers

2 tbsp dill seed or 4 to 5 heads fresh or dry dill weed

½ cup salt

¼ cup vinegar (5 percent acetic acid)

8 cups water and one or more of the following ingredients:

2 cloves garlic (optional)

2 dried red peppers (optional)

2 tsp whole mixed pickling spices (optional)

Directions

1. Wash cucumbers. Cut 1/16-inch slice off blossom end and discard. Leave ¼ inch of stem attached. Place half of dill and spices on bottom of a clean, suitable container.

2. Add cucumbers, remaining dill, and spices. Dissolve salt in vinegar and water and pour over cucumbers. Add suitable cover and weight. Store where temperature is between 70°F and 75°F for about 3 to 4 weeks while fermenting. Temperatures of 55°F to 65°F are acceptable, but the fermentation will take 5 to 6 weeks. Avoid temperatures above 80°F, or pickles will become too soft during fermentation. Fermenting pickles cure slowly. Check the container several times a week and promptly remove surface scum or mold. **Caution: If the pickles become soft, slimy, or develop a disagreeable odor, discard them.**

3. Once fully fermented, pour the brine into a pan, heat slowly to a boil, and simmer 5 minutes. Filter brine through paper coffee filters to reduce cloudi-

ness, if desired. Fill jars with pickles and hot brine, leaving ½-inch headspace. Adjust lids and process in a boiling water canner, or use the low-temperature pasteurization treatment described here:

Low-Temperature Pasteurization Treatment

The following treatment results in a better product texture but must be carefully managed to avoid possible spoilage.

1. Place jars in a canner filled halfway with warm (120°F to 140°F) water. Then, add hot water to a level 1 inch above jars.
2. Heat the water enough to maintain 180°F to 185°F water temperature for 30 minutes. Check with a candy or jelly thermometer to be certain that the water temperature is at least 180°F during the entire 30 minutes. Temperatures higher than 185°F may cause unnecessary softening of pickles.

Process Times for Dill Pickles in a Boiling-Water Canner*

Style of Pack	Jar Size	Process Time at Altitudes of:		
		0–1,000 ft	1,001–6,000 ft	Above 6,000 ft
Raw	Pints	10 minutes	15 minutes	20 minutes
	Quarts	15 minutes	20 minutes	25 minutes

*After the process is complete, turn off the heat and remove the canner lid. Wait five minutes before removing jars.

Sauerkraut

For the best sauerkraut, use firm heads of fresh cabbage. Shred cabbage and start kraut between 24 and 48 hours after harvest. This recipe yields about nine quarts.

Ingredients

25 lbs cabbage
¾ cup canning or pickling salt

Directions

1. Work with about 5 pounds of cabbage at a time. Discard outer leaves. Rinse heads under cold running water and drain. Cut heads in quarters and remove cores. Shred or slice to the thickness of a quarter.
2. Put cabbage in a suitable fermentation container (see page 103 for suggestions on containers, lids, and weights), and add 3 tablespoons of salt. Mix thoroughly, using clean hands. Pack firmly until salt draws juices from cabbage.
3. Repeat shredding, salting, and packing until all cabbage is in the container. Be sure it is deep enough so that its rim is at least 4 or 5 inches above the cabbage. If juice does not cover cabbage, add boiled and cooled brine (1½ tablespoons of salt per quart of water).
4. Add plate and weights; cover container with a clean bath towel. Store at 70°F to 75°F while fermenting. At temperatures between 70°F and 75°F, kraut will be fully fermented in about 3 to 4 weeks; at 60°F to 65°F, fermentation may take 5 to 6 weeks. At tem-

peratures lower than 60°F, kraut may not ferment. Above 75°F, kraut may become soft.

Note: If you weigh the cabbage down with a brine-filled bag, do not disturb the crock until normal fermentation is completed (when bubbling ceases). If you use jars as weight, you will have to check the kraut 2 to 3 times each week and remove scum if it forms. Fully fermented kraut may be kept tightly covered in the refrigerator for several months or it may be canned as follows:

Hot pack—Bring kraut and liquid slowly to a boil in a large kettle, stirring frequently. Remove from heat and fill jars rather firmly with kraut and juices, leaving ½-inch headspace.

Raw pack—Fill jars firmly with kraut and cover with juices, leaving ½-inch headspace.

5. Adjust lids and process.

Process Times for Sauerkraut in a Boiling-Water Canner*

Style of Pack	Jar Size	Process Time at Altitudes of:			
		0–1,000 ft	1,001–3,000 ft	3,001–6,000 ft	Above 6,000 ft
Hot	Pints	10 minutes	15 minutes	15 minutes	20 minutes
	Quarts	15 minutes	20 minutes	20 minutes	25 minutes
Raw	Pints	20 minutes	25 minutes	30 minutes	35 minutes
	Quarts	25 minutes	30 minutes	35 minutes	40 minutes

*After the process is complete, turn off the heat and remove the canner lid. Wait five minutes before removing jars.

Pickled Three-Bean Salad

This is a great side dish to bring to a summer picnic or potluck. Feel free to add or adjust spices to your taste. This recipe yields about five to six half-pints.

Ingredients

1½ cups cut and blanched green or yellow beans (prepared as below)
1½ cups canned, drained red kidney beans
1 cup canned, drained garbanzo beans
½ cup peeled and thinly sliced onion (about 1 medium onion)
½ cup trimmed and thinly sliced celery (1½ medium stalks)
½ cup sliced green peppers (½ medium pepper)
½ cup white vinegar (5 percent acetic acid)
¼ cup bottled lemon juice
¾ cup sugar
1¼ cups water
¼ cup oil
½ tsp canning or pickling salt

Directions

1. Wash and snap off ends of fresh beans. Cut or snap into 1- to 2-inch pieces. Blanch 3 minutes and cool immediately. Rinse kidney beans with tap water and drain again. Prepare and measure all other vegetables.
2. Combine vinegar, lemon juice, sugar, and water and bring to a boil. Remove from heat. Add oil and salt and mix well. Add beans, onions, celery, and green pepper to solution and bring to a simmer.
3. Marinate 12 to 14 hours in refrigerator, then heat entire mixture to a boil. Fill clean jars with solids. Add hot liquid, leaving ½-inch headspace. Adjust lids and process.

Process Times for Pickled Three-Bean Salad in a Boiling Water Canner*

Style of Pack	Jar Size	Process Time at Altitudes of:		
		0–1,000 ft	1,001–6,000 ft	Above 6,000 ft
Hot	Half-pints or Pints	15 minutes	20 minutes	25 minutes

Pickled Horseradish Sauce

Select horseradish roots that are firm and have no mold, soft spots, or green spots. Avoid roots that have begun to sprout. The pungency of fresh horseradish fades within one to two months, even when refrigerated, so make only small quantities at a time. This recipe yields about two half-pints.

Ingredients

2 cups (¾ lb) freshly grated horseradish
1 cup white vinegar (5 percent acetic acid)
½ tsp canning or pickling salt
¼ tsp powdered ascorbic acid

Directions

1. Wash horseradish roots thoroughly and peel off brown outer skin. Grate the peeled roots in a food processor or cut them into small cubes and put through a food grinder.
2. Combine ingredients and fill into sterile jars, leaving ¼-inch headspace. Seal jars tightly and store in a refrigerator.

Marinated Peppers

Any combination of bell, Hungarian, banana, or jalapeño peppers can be used in this recipe. Use more jalapeño peppers if you want your mix to be hot, but remember to wear rubber or plastic gloves while handling them or wash hands thoroughly with soap and water before touching your face. This recipe yields about nine half-pints.

Ingredients

4 lbs firm peppers
1 cup bottled lemon juice
2 cups white vinegar (5 percent acetic acid)
1 tbsp oregano leaves

1 cup olive or salad oil
½ cup chopped onions
2 tbsp prepared horseradish (optional)
2 cloves garlic, quartered (optional)
2¼ tsp salt (optional)

Directions

1. Select your favorite pepper. Peppers may be left whole or quartered. Wash, slash two to four slits in each pepper, and blanch in boiling water or blister to peel tough-skinned hot peppers. Blister peppers using one of the following methods:

   Oven or broiler method—Place peppers in a hot oven (400°F) or broiler for 6 to 8 minutes or until skins blister.

   Range-top method—Cover hot burner, either gas or electric, with heavy wire mesh. Place peppers on burner for several minutes until skins blister.
2. Allow peppers to cool. Place in pan and cover with a damp cloth. This will make peeling the peppers easier. After several minutes of cooling, peel each pepper. Flatten whole peppers.
3. Mix all remaining ingredients except garlic and salt in a saucepan and heat to boiling. Place ¼ garlic clove (optional) and ¼ teaspoon salt in each half-pint or ½ teaspoon per pint. Fill jars with peppers, and add hot, well-mixed oil/pickling solution over peppers, leaving ½-inch headspace. Adjust lids and process.

Process Times for Marinated Peppers in a Boiling-Water Canner*

Style of Pack	Jar Size	Process Time at Altitudes of:			
		0–1,000 ft	1,001–3,000 ft	3,001–6,000 ft	Above 6,000 ft
Raw	Half-pints and Pints	15 minutes	20 minutes	20 minutes	25 minutes

*After the process is complete, turn off the heat and remove the canner lid. Wait five minutes before removing jars.

Piccalilli

Piccalilli is a nice accompaniment to roasted or braised meats and is common in British and Indian meals. It can also be mixed with mayonnaise or crème fraîche as the basis of a French remoulade. This recipe yields nine half-pints.

Ingredients

6 cups chopped green tomatoes
1½ cups chopped sweet red peppers
1½ cups chopped green peppers
2¼ cups chopped onions
7½ cups chopped cabbage
½ cup canning or pickling salt
3 tbsp whole mixed pickling spice
4½ cups vinegar (5 percent acetic acid)
3 cups brown sugar

Directions

1. Wash, chop, and combine vegetables with salt. Cover with hot water and let stand 12 hours. Drain and press in a clean, white cloth to remove all possible liquid.
2. Tie spices loosely in a spice bag and add to combined vinegar and brown sugar and heat to a boil in a saucepan. Add vegetables and boil gently 30 minutes or until the volume of the mixture is reduced by one-half. Remove spice bag.
3. Fill hot sterile jars with hot mixture, leaving ½-inch headspace. Adjust lids and process.

Process Times for Piccalilli in a Boiling-Water Canner

Style of Pack	Jar Size	Process Time at Altitudes of:		
		0–1,000 ft	1,001–6,000 ft	Above 6,000 ft
Hot	Half-pints or Pints	5 minutes	10 minutes	15 minutes

*After the process is complete, turn off the heat and remove the canner lid. Wait five minutes before removing jars.

Bread-and-Butter Pickles

These slightly sweet, spiced pickles will add flavor and crunch to any sandwich. If desired, slender (1 to 1½ inches in diameter) zucchini or yellow summer squash can be substituted for cucumbers. After processing and cooling, jars should be stored four to five weeks to develop ideal flavor. This recipe yields about eight pints.

Ingredients

6 lbs of 4- to 5-inch pickling cucumbers
8 cups thinly sliced onions (about 3 pounds)
½ cup canning or pickling salt
4 cups vinegar (5 percent acetic acid)
4½ cups sugar
2 tbsp mustard seed
1½ tbsp celery seed
1 tbsp ground turmeric
1 cup pickling lime (optional—for use in variation below for making firmer pickles)

Directions

1. Wash cucumbers. Cut ¹⁄₁₆ inch off blossom end and discard. Cut into ³⁄₁₆-inch slices. Combine cucumbers and onions in a large bowl. Add salt. Cover with 2 inches crushed or cubed ice. Refrigerate 3 to 4 hours, adding more ice as needed.
2. Combine remaining ingredients in a large pot. Boil 10 minutes. Drain cucumbers and onions, add to pot, and slowly reheat to boiling. Fill jars with slices and cooking syrup, leaving ½-inch headspace.
3. Adjust lids and process in boiling-water canner, or use the low-temperature pasteurization treatment described below.

Low-Temperature Pasteurization Treatment

The following treatment results in a better product texture but must be carefully managed to avoid possible spoilage.

1. Place jars in a canner filled halfway with warm (120°F to 140°F) water. Then, add hot water to a level 1 inch above jars.
2. Heat the water enough to maintain 180°F to 185°F water temperature for 30 minutes. Check with a candy or jelly thermometer to be certain that the water temperature is at least 180°F during the entire 30 minutes. Temperatures higher than 185°F may cause unnecessary softening of pickles.

Variation for firmer pickles: Wash cucumbers. Cut ¹⁄₁₆ inch off blossom end and discard. Cut into ³⁄₁₆-inch slices. Mix 1 cup pickling lime and ½ cup salt to 1 gallon water in a 2- to 3-gallon crock or enamelware container. Avoid inhaling lime dust while mixing the lime-water solution. Soak cucumber slices in lime water for 12 to 24 hours, stirring occasionally. Remove from lime solution, rinse, and resoak 1 hour in fresh cold water. Repeat the rinsing and soaking steps two more times. Handle carefully, as slices will be brittle. Drain well.

Process Times for Bread-and-Butter Pickles in a Boiling-Water Canner*

Style of Pack	Jar Size	Process Time at Altitudes of:		
		0–1,000 ft	1,001–6,000 ft	Above 6,000 ft
Hot	Pints or Quarts	10 minutes	15 minutes	20 minutes

*After the process is complete, turn off the heat and remove the canner lid. Wait five minutes before removing jars.

Quick Fresh-Pack Dill Pickles

For best results, pickle cucumbers within twenty-four hours of harvesting, or immediately after purchasing. This recipe yields seven to nine pints.

Ingredients

8 lbs of 3- to 5-inch pickling cucumbers
2 gallons water
1¼ to 1½ cups canning or pickling salt
1½ qts vinegar (5 percent acetic acid)

¼ cup sugar

2 to 2¼ quarts water

2 tbsp whole mixed pickling spice

3 to 5 tbsp whole mustard seed (2 tsp to 1 tsp per pint jar)

14 to 21 heads of fresh dill (1½ to 3 heads per pint jar) *or*

4½ to 7 tbsp dill seed (1-½ tsp to 1 tbsp per pint jar)

Directions

1. Wash cucumbers. Cut ¹⁄₁₆-inch slice off blossom end and discard, but leave ¼-inch of stem attached. Dissolve ¾ cup salt in 2 gallons water. Pour over cucumbers and let stand 12 hours. Drain.
2. Combine vinegar, ½ cup salt, sugar and 2 quarts water. Add mixed pickling spices tied in a clean white cloth. Heat to boiling. Fill jars with cucumbers. Add 1 tsp mustard seed and 1½ heads fresh dill per pint.
3. Cover with boiling pickling solution, leaving ½-inch headspace. Adjust lids and process.

Process Times for Quick Fresh-Pack Dill Pickles in a Boiling-Water Canner*

Style of Pack	Jar Size	Process Time at Altitudes of:		
		0–1,000 ft	1,001–6,000 ft	Above 6,000 ft
Raw	Pints	10 minutes	15 minutes	20 minutes
	Quarts	15 minutes	20 minutes	25 minutes

*After the process is complete, turn off the heat and remove the canner lid. Wait five minutes before removing jars.

Pickle Relish

A food processor will make quick work of chopping the vegetables in this recipe. Yields about nine pints.

Ingredients

3 qts chopped cucumbers

3 cups each of chopped sweet green and red peppers

1 cup chopped onions

¾ cup canning or pickling salt

4 cups ice

8 cups water

4 tsp each of mustard seed, turmeric, whole allspice, and whole cloves

2 cups sugar

6 cups white vinegar (5 percent acetic acid)

Directions

1. Add cucumbers, peppers, onions, salt, and ice to water and let stand 4 hours. Drain and re-cover vegetables with fresh ice water for another hour. Drain again.
2. Combine spices in a spice or cheesecloth bag. Add spices to sugar and vinegar. Heat to boiling and pour mixture over vegetables. Cover and refrigerate 24 hours.
3. Heat mixture to boiling and fill hot into clean jars, leaving ½-inch headspace. Adjust lids and process.

Process Times for Pickle Relish in a Boiling-Water Canner*

Style of Pack	Jar Size	Process Time at Altitudes of:		
		0–1,000 ft	1,001–6,000 ft	Above 6,000 ft
Hot	Half-pints or Pints	10 minutes	15 minutes	20 minutes

*After the process is complete, turn off the heat and remove the canner lid. Wait five minutes before removing jars.

Quick Sweet Pickles

Quick and simple to prepare, these are the sweet pickles to make when you're short on time. After processing and cooling, jars should be stored four to five weeks to develop ideal flavor. If desired, add two slices of raw whole onion to each jar before filling with cucumbers. This recipe yields about seven to nine pints.

Ingredients

8 lbs of 3- to 4-inch pickling cucumbers

⅓ cup canning or pickling salt

4½ cups sugar

3½ cups vinegar (5 percent acetic acid)

2 tsp celery seed

1 tbsp whole allspice
2 tbsp mustard seed
1 cup pickling lime (optional)

Directions

1. Wash cucumbers. Cut ¹⁄16 inch off blossom end and discard, but leave ¼ inch of stem attached. Slice or cut in strips, if desired.
2. Place in bowl and sprinkle with salt. Cover with 2 inches of crushed or cubed ice. Refrigerate 3 to 4 hours. Add more ice as needed. Drain well.
3. Combine sugar, vinegar, celery seed, allspice, and mustard seed in 6-quart kettle. Heat to boiling.

Hot pack—Add cucumbers and heat slowly until vinegar solution returns to boil. Stir occasionally to make sure mixture heats evenly. Fill sterile jars, leaving ½-inch headspace.

Raw pack—Fill jars, leaving ½-inch headspace.

4. Add hot pickling syrup, leaving ½-inch headspace. Adjust lids and process.

Variation for firmer pickles: Wash cucumbers. Cut ¹⁄16 inch off blossom end and discard, but leave ¼ inch of stem attached. Slice or strip cucumbers. Mix 1 cup pickling lime and ¹⁄3 cup salt with 1 gallon water in a 2- to 3-gallon crock or enamelware container. **Caution: Avoid inhaling lime dust while mixing the lime-water solution.** Soak cucumber slices or strips in lime-water solution for 12 to 24 hours, stirring occasionally. Remove from lime solution, rinse, and soak 1 hour in fresh cold water. Repeat the rinsing and soaking two more times. Handle carefully, because slices or strips will be brittle. Drain well.

Process Times for Quick Sweet Pickles in a Boiling-Water Canner*

Style of Pack	Jar Size	Process Time at Altitudes of:		
		0–1,000 ft	1,001–6,000 ft	Above 6,000 ft
Hot	Pints or Quarts	5 minutes	10 minutes	15 minutes
Raw	Pints	10 minutes	15 minutes	20 minutes
	Quarts	15 minutes	20 minutes	25 minutes

*After the process is complete, turn off the heat and remove the canner lid. Wait five minutes before removing jars.

Reduced-Sodium Sliced Sweet Pickles

Whole allspice can be tricky to find. If it's not available at your local grocery store, it can be ordered at www.spicebarn.com or at www.gourmetsleuth .com. This recipe yields about four to five pints.

Ingredients

4 lbs (3- to 4-inch) pickling cucumbers

Canning syrup: 1²⁄3 cups distilled white vinegar (5 percent acetic acid)

3 cups sugar

1 tbsp whole allspice

2¼ tsp celery seed

Brining solution: 1 qt distilled white vinegar (5 percent acetic acid)

1 tbsp canning or pickling salt

1 tbsp mustard seed

½ cup sugar

Directions

1. Wash cucumbers and cut ¹⁄16-inch off blossom end, and discard. Cut cucumbers into ¼-inch slices. Combine all ingredients for canning syrup in a saucepan and bring to boiling. Keep syrup hot until used.
2. In a large kettle, mix the ingredients for the brining solution. Add the cut cucumbers, cover, and simmer until the cucumbers change color from bright to dull green (about 5 to 7 minutes). Drain the cucumber slices.
3. Fill jars, and cover with hot canning syrup leaving ½-inch headspace. Adjust lids and process.

Process Times for Reduced-Sodium Sliced Sweet Pickles in a Boiling-Water Canner*

Style of Pack	Jar Size	Process Time at Altitudes of:		
		0–1,000 ft	1,001–6,000 ft	Above 6,000 ft
Hot	Pints	10 minutes	15 minutes	20 minutes

*After the process is complete, turn off the heat and remove the canner lid. Wait five minutes before removing jars.

Tomatoes

Canned tomatoes should be a staple in every cook's pantry. They are easy to prepare and, when made with garden-fresh produce, make ordinary soups, pizza, or pastas into five-star meals. Be sure to select only dis-

ease-free, preferably vine-ripened, firm fruit. Do not can tomatoes from dead or frost-killed vines.

Green tomatoes are more acidic than ripened fruit and can be canned safely with the following recommendations.

- To ensure safe acidity in whole, crushed, or juiced tomatoes, add two tablespoons of bottled lemon juice or ½ teaspoon of citric acid per quart of tomatoes. For pints, use one tablespoon bottled lemon juice or ¼ teaspoon citric acid.
- Acid can be added directly to the jars before filling with product. Add sugar to offset acid taste, if desired. Four tablespoons of 5 percent acidity vinegar per quart may be used instead of lemon juice or citric acid. However, vinegar may cause undesirable flavor changes.
- Using a pressure canner will result in higher quality and more nutritious canned tomato products. If your pressure canner cannot be operated above 15 PSI, select a process time at a lower pressure.

Tomato Juice

Tomato juice is a good source of vitamin A and C and is tasty on its own or in a cocktail. It's also the secret ingredient in some very delicious cakes. If desired, add carrots, celery, and onions, or toss in a few jalapeños for a little kick.

Quantity

- An average of 23 pounds is needed per canner load of seven quarts, or an average of 14 pounds per canner load of nine pints.

- A bushel weighs 53 pounds and yields 15 to 18 quarts of juice—an average of 3¼ pounds per quart.

Directions

1. Wash tomatoes, remove stems, and trim off bruised or discolored portions. To prevent juice from separating, quickly cut about 1 pound of fruit into quarters and put directly into saucepan. Heat immediately to boiling while crushing.
2. Continue to slowly add and crush freshly cut tomato quarters to the boiling mixture. Make sure the mixture boils constantly and vigorously while you add the remaining tomatoes. Simmer 5 minutes after you add all pieces.
3. Press heated juice through a sieve or food mill to remove skins and seeds. Add bottled lemon juice or citric acid to jars. Heat juice again to boiling.
4. Add 1 teaspoon of salt per quart to the jars, if desired. Fill jars with hot tomato juice, leaving ½-inch headspace. Adjust lids and process.

Process Times for Tomato Juice in a Boiling-Water Canner*

Style of Pack	Jar Size	Process Time at Altitudes of:			
		0–1,000 ft	1,001–3,000 ft	3,001–6,000 ft	Above 6,000 ft
Hot	Pints	35 minutes	40 minutes	45 minutes	50 minutes
	Quarts	40 minutes	45 minutes	50 minutes	55 minutes

*After the process is complete, turn off the heat and remove the canner lid. Wait five minutes before removing jars.

Process Times for Tomato Juice in a Dial-Gauge Pressure Canner*

Style of Pack	Jar Size	Process Time	Canner Gauge Pressure (PSI) at Altitudes of:			
			0–2,000 ft	2,001–4,000 ft	4,001–6,000 ft	6,001–8,000 ft
Hot	Pints or Quarts	20 minutes	6 lbs	7 lbs	8 lbs	9 lbs
		15 minutes	11 lbs	12 lbs	13 lbs	14 lbs

*After the canner is completely depressurized, remove the weight from the vent port or open the petcock. Wait 10 minutes; then unfasten the lid and remove it carefully. Lift the lid with the underside away from you so that the steam coming out of the canner does not burn your face.

Process Times for Tomato Juice in a Weighted-Gauge Pressure Canner*

Style of Pack	Jar Size	Process Time	Canner Gauge Pressure (PSI) at Altitudes of:	
			0–1,000 ft	Above 1,000 ft
Hot	Pints or Quarts	20 minutes	5 lbs	10 lbs
		15 minutes	10 lbs	15 lbs

Crushed Tomatoes with No Added Liquid

Crushed tomatoes are great for use in soups, stews, thick sauces, and casseroles. Simmer crushed tomatoes with kidney beans, chili powder, sautéed onions, and garlic to make an easy pot of chili.

Quantity

- An average of 22 pounds is needed per canner load of seven quarts.

- An average of 14 fresh pounds is needed per canner load of nine pints.
- A bushel weighs 53 pounds and yields 17 to 20 quarts of crushed tomatoes—an average of 2¾ pounds per quart.

Directions

1. Wash tomatoes and dip in boiling water for 30 to 60 seconds or until skins split. Then dip in cold water, slip off skins, and remove cores. Trim off any bruised or discolored portions and quarter.
2. Heat ⅙ of the quarters quickly in a large pot, crushing them with a wooden mallet or spoon as they are added to the pot. This will exude juice. Continue heating the tomatoes, stirring to prevent burning.
3. Once the tomatoes are boiling, gradually add remaining quartered tomatoes, stirring constantly. These remaining tomatoes do not need to be crushed; they will soften with heating and stirring. Continue until all tomatoes are added. Then boil gently 5 minutes.
4. Add bottled lemon juice or citric acid to jars. Add 1 teaspoon of salt per quart to the jars, if desired. Fill jars immediately with hot tomatoes, leaving ½-inch headspace. Adjust lids and process.

Process Times for Crushed Tomatoes in a Dial-Gauge Pressure Canner*

Style of Pack	Jar Size	Process Time	Canner Gauge Pressure (PSI) at Altitudes of:			
			0–2,000 ft	2,001–4,000 ft	4,001–6,000 ft	6,001–8,000 ft
Hot	Pints or Quarts	20 minutes	6 lbs	7 lbs	8 lbs	9 lbs
		15 minutes	11 lbs	12 lbs	13 lbs	14 lbs

*After the canner is completely depressurized, remove the weight from the vent port or open the petcock. Wait 10 minutes; then unfasten the lid and remove it carefully. Lift the lid with the underside away from you so that the steam coming out of the canner does not burn your face.

Process Times for Crushed Tomatoes in a Weighted-Gauge Pressure Canner*

Style of Pack	Jar Size	Process Time	Canner Gauge Pressure (PSI) at Altitudes of:	
			0–1,000 ft	Above 1,000 ft
Hot	Pints or Quarts	20 minutes	5 lbs	10 lbs
		15 minutes	10 lbs	15 lbs

*After the canner is completely depressurized, remove the weight from the vent port or open the petcock. Wait 10 minutes; then unfasten the lid and remove it carefully. Lift the lid with the underside away from you so that the steam coming out of the canner does not burn your face.

Process Times for Crushed Tomatoes in a Boiling-Water Canner*

Style of Pack	Jar Size	Process Time at Altitudes of:			
		0–1,000 ft	1,001–3,000 ft	3,001–6,000 ft	Above 6,000 ft
Hot	Pints	35 minutes	40 minutes	45 minutes	50 minutes
	Quarts	45 minutes	50 minutes	55 minutes	60 minutes

*After the process is complete, turn off the heat and remove the canner lid. Wait five minutes before removing jars.

Tomato Sauce

This plain tomato sauce can be spiced up before using in soups or in pink or red sauces. The thicker you want your sauce, the more tomatoes you'll need.

Quantity

For thin sauce:
- An average of 35 pounds is needed per canner load of seven quarts.
- An average of 21 pounds is needed per canner load of nine pints.
- A bushel weighs 53 pounds and yields 10 to 12 quarts of sauce—an average of five pounds per quart.

For thick sauce:
- An average of 46 pounds is needed per canner load of seven quarts.
- An average of 28 pounds is needed per canner load of nine pints.
- A bushel weighs 53 pounds and yields seven to nine quarts of sauce—an average of 6½ pounds per quart.

Directions

1. Prepare and press as for making tomato juice (see page 109). Simmer in a large saucepan until sauce reaches desired consistency. Boil until volume is reduced by about one-third for thin sauce, or by one-half for thick sauce.
2. Add bottled lemon juice or citric acid to jars. Add 1 teaspoon of salt per quart to the jars, if desired. Fill jars, leaving ¼-inch headspace. Adjust lids and process.

Process Times for Tomato Sauce in a Boiling-Water Canner*

Style of Pack	Jar Size	Process Time at Altitudes of:			
		0–1,000 ft	1,001–3,000 ft	3,001–6,000 ft	Above 6,000 ft
Hot	Pints	35 minutes	40 minutes	45 minutes	50 minutes
	Quarts	40 minutes	45 minutes	50 minutes	55 minutes

*After the process is complete, turn off the heat and remove the canner lid. Wait five minutes before removing jars.

Process Times for Tomato Sauce in a Dial-Gauge Pressure Canner*

Style of Pack	Jar Size	Process Time	Canner Gauge Pressure (PSI) at Altitudes of:			
			0–2,000 ft	2,001–4,000 ft	4,001–6,000 ft	6,001–8,000 ft
Hot	Pints or Quarts	20 minutes	6 lbs	7 lbs	8 lbs	9 lbs
		15 minutes	11 lbs	12 lbs	13 lbs	14 lbs

*After the canner is completely depressurized, remove the weight from the vent port or open the petcock. Wait 10 minutes; then unfasten the lid and remove it carefully. Lift the lid with the underside away from you so that the steam coming out of the canner does not burn your face.

Process Times for Tomato Sauce in a Weighted-Gauge Pressure Canner*

Style of Pack	Jar Size	Process Time	Canner Gauge Pressure (PSI) at Altitudes of:	
			0–1,000 ft	Above 1,000 ft
Hot	Pints or Quarts	20 minutes	5 lbs	10 lbs
		15 minutes	10 lbs	15 lbs

*After the canner is completely depressurized, remove the weight from the vent port or open the petcock. Wait 10 minutes; then unfasten the lid and remove it carefully. Lift the lid with the underside away from you so that the steam coming out of the canner does not burn your face.

Tomatoes, Whole or Halved, Packed in Water

Whole or halved tomatoes are used for scalloped tomatoes, savory pies (baked in a pastry crust with parmesan cheese, mayonnaise, and seasonings), or stewed tomatoes.

Quantity

- An average of 21 pounds is needed per canner load of seven quarts.
- An average of 13 pounds is needed per canner load of nine pints.
- A bushel weighs 53 pounds and yields 15 to 21 quarts—an average of three pounds per quart.

Directions

1. Wash tomatoes. Dip in boiling water for 30 to 60 seconds or until skins split; then dip in cold water. Slip off skins and remove cores. Leave whole or halve.
2. Add bottled lemon juice or citric acid to jars. Add 1 teaspoon of salt per quart to the jars, if desired. For hot pack products, add enough water to cover the tomatoes and boil them gently for 5 minutes.
3. Fill jars with hot tomatoes or with raw peeled tomatoes. Add the hot cooking liquid to the hot pack, or hot water for raw pack to cover, leaving ½-inch headspace. Adjust lids and process.

Process Times for Water-Packed Whole Tomatoes in a Boiling-Water Canner*

Style of Pack	Jar Size	Process Time at Altitudes of:			
		0–1,000 ft	1,001–3,000 ft	3,001–6,000 ft	Above 6,000 ft
Hot or Raw	Pints	40 minutes	45 minutes	50 minutes	55 minutes
	Quarts	45 minutes	50 minutes	55 minutes	60 minutes

*After the process is complete, turn off the heat and remove the canner lid. Wait five minutes before removing jars.

Process Times for Water-Packed Whole Tomatoes in a Dial-Gauge Pressure Canner*

Style of Pack	Jar Size	Process Time	Canner Gauge Pressure (PSI) at Altitudes of:			
			0–2,000 ft	2,001–4,000 ft	4,001–6,000 ft	6,001–8,000 ft
Hot or Raw	Pints or Quarts	15 minutes	6 lbs	7 lbs	8 lbs	9 lbs
		10 minutes	11 lbs	12 lbs	13 lbs	14 lbs

*After the canner is completely depressurized, remove the weight from the vent port or open the petcock. Wait 10 minutes; then unfasten the lid and remove it carefully. Lift the lid with the underside away from you so that the steam coming out of the canner does not burn your face.

Process Times for Water-Packed Whole Tomatoes in a Weighted-Gauge Pressure Canner*

Style of Pack	Jar Size	Process Time	Canner Gauge Pressure (PSI) at Altitudes of:	
			0–1,000 ft	Above 1,000 ft
Hot or Raw	Pints or Quarts	15 minutes	5 lbs	10 lbs
		10 minutes	10 lbs	15 lbs

*After the canner is completely depressurized, remove the weight from the vent port or open the petcock. Wait 10 minutes; then unfasten the lid and remove it carefully. Lift the lid with the underside away from you so that the steam coming out of the canner does not burn your face.

Spaghetti Sauce without Meat

Homemade spaghetti sauce is like a completely different food than store-bought varieties—it tastes fresher, is more flavorful, and is far more nutritious. Adjust spices to taste, but do not increase proportions of onions, peppers, or mushrooms. This recipe yields about nine pints.

Ingredients
30 lbs tomatoes
1 cup chopped onions
5 cloves garlic, minced
1 cup chopped celery or green pepper
1 lb fresh mushrooms, sliced (optional)
4½ tsp salt
2 tbsp oregano
4 tbsp minced parsley
2 tsp black pepper
¼ cup brown sugar
¼ cup vegetable oil

Directions
1. Wash tomatoes and dip in boiling water for 30 to 60 seconds or until skins split. Dip in cold water and slip off skins. Remove cores and quarter tomatoes. Boil 20 minutes, uncovered, in large saucepan. Put through food mill or sieve.
2. Sauté onions, garlic, celery, or peppers, and mushrooms (if desired) in vegetable oil until tender. Combine sautéed vegetables and tomatoes and add spices, salt, and sugar. Bring to a boil.
3. Simmer uncovered, until thick enough for serving. Stir frequently to avoid burning. Fill jars, leaving 1-inch headspace. Adjust lids and process.

Process Times for Spaghetti Sauce without Meat in a Dial-Gauge Pressure Canner*

Style of Pack	Jar Size	Process Time	Canner Gauge Pressure (PSI) at Altitudes of:			
			0–2,000 ft	2,001–4,000 ft	4,001–6,000 ft	6,001–8,000 ft
Hot	Pints	20 minutes	11 lbs	12 lbs	13 lbs	14 lbs
	Quarts	25 minutes	11 lbs	12 lbs	13 lbs	14 lbs

*After the canner is completely depressurized, remove the weight from the vent port or open the petcock. Wait 10 minutes; then unfasten the lid and remove it carefully. Lift the lid with the underside away from you so that the steam coming out of the canner does not burn your face.

Process Times for Spaghetti Sauce without Meat in a Weighted-Gauge Pressure Canner*

Style of Pack	Jar Size	Process Time	Canner Gauge Pressure (PSI) at Altitudes of:	
			0–1,000 ft	Above 1,000 ft
Hot	Pints	20 minutes	10 lbs	15 lbs
	Quarts	25 minutes	10 lbs	15 lbs

*After the canner is completely depressurized, remove the weight from the vent port or open the petcock. Wait 10 minutes; then unfasten the lid and remove it carefully. Lift the lid with the underside away from you so that the steam coming out of the canner does not burn your face.

Tomato Ketchup

Ketchup forms the base of several condiments, including Thousand Island dressing, fry sauce, and barbecue sauce. And, of course, it's an American favorite in its own right. This recipe yields six to seven pints.

Ingredients
24 lbs ripe tomatoes
3 cups chopped onions
¾ tsp ground red pepper (cayenne)
4 tsp whole cloves
3 sticks cinnamon, crushed
1-½ tsp whole allspice
3 tbsp celery seeds
3 cups cider vinegar (5 percent acetic acid)
1-½ cups sugar
¼ cup salt

Directions
1. Wash tomatoes. Dip in boiling water for 30 to 60 seconds or until skins split. Dip in cold water. Slip off skins and remove cores. Quarter tomatoes into 4-gallon stockpot or a large kettle. Add onions and red pepper. Bring to boil and simmer 20 minutes, uncovered.
2. Combine remaining spices in a spice bag and add to vinegar in a 2-quart saucepan. Bring to boil. Turn off heat and let stand until tomato mixture has been cooked 20 minutes. Then, remove spice bag and combine vinegar and tomato mixture. Boil about 30 minutes.
3. Put boiled mixture through a food mill or sieve. Return to pot. Add sugar and salt, boil gently, and stir frequently until volume is reduced by one-half or until mixture rounds up on spoon without separation. Fill pint jars, leaving ⅛-inch headspace. Adjust lids and process.

Process Times for Tomato Ketchup in a Boiling-Water Canner*

		Process Time at Altitudes of:		
Style of Pack	Jar Size	0–1,000 ft	1,001–6,000 ft	Above 6,000 ft
Hot	Pints	15 minutes	20 minutes	25 minutes

*After the process is complete, turn off the heat and remove the canner lid. Wait five minutes before removing jars.

Chile Salsa (Hot Tomato-Pepper Sauce)

For fantastic nachos, cover corn chips with chile salsa, add shredded Monterey jack or cheddar cheese, bake under broiler for about five minutes, and serve with guacamole and sour cream. Be sure to wear rubber gloves while handling chiles or wash hands thoroughly with soap and water before touching your face. This recipe yields six to eight pints.

Ingredients
5 lbs tomatoes
2 lbs chile peppers
1 lb onions
1 cup vinegar (5 percent)
3 tsp salt
½ tsp pepper

Directions
1. Wash and dry chiles. Slit each pepper on its side to allow steam to escape. Peel peppers using one of the following methods:

Oven or broiler method:
Place chiles in oven (400°F) or broiler for 6 to 8 minutes until skins blister. Cool and slip off skins.

Range-top method:
Cover hot burner, either gas or electric, with heavy wire mesh. Place chiles on burner for several minutes until skins blister. Allow peppers to cool. Place in a pan and cover with a damp cloth. This will make peeling the peppers easier. After several minutes, peel each pepper.

2. Discard seeds and chop peppers. Wash tomatoes and dip in boiling water for 30 to 60 seconds or until skins split. Dip in cold water, slip off skins, and remove cores.
3. Coarsely chop tomatoes and combine chopped peppers, onions, and remaining ingredients in a large saucepan. Heat to boil, and simmer 10 minutes. Fill jars, leaving ½-inch headspace. Adjust lids and process.

Process Times for Chile Salsa in a Boiling-Water Canner*

		Process Time at Altitudes of:		
Style of Pack	Jar Size	0–1,000 ft	1,001–6,000 ft	Above 6,000 ft
Hot	Pints	15 minutes	20 minutes	25 minutes

*After the process is complete, turn off the heat and remove the canner lid. Wait five minutes before removing jars.

Drying and Freezing

Drying

Drying fruits, vegetables, herbs, and even meat is a great way to preserve foods for longer-term storage, especially if your pantry or freezer space is limited. Dried foods take up much less space than their fresh, frozen, or canned counterparts. Drying requires relatively little preparation time and is simple enough that kids will enjoy helping. Drying with a food dehydrator will ensure the fastest, safest, and best-quality results. However, you can also dry produce in the sunshine, in your oven, or strung up over a woodstove.

For more information on food drying, check out *So Easy to Preserve, 5th ed.* from the Cooperative Extension Service, the University of Georgia. Much of the information that follows is adapted from this excellent source.

Drying with a Food Dehydrator

Food dehydrators use electricity to produce heat and have a fan and vents for air circulation. Dehydrators are efficiently designed to dry foods fast at around 140°F. Look for food dehydrators in discount department stores, mail-order catalogs, the small appliance section of a department store, natural food stores, and seed or garden supply catalogs. Costs vary depending on features. Some models are expandable and additional trays can be purchased later. Twelve square feet of drying space dries about a half-bushel of produce.

Dehydrator Features to Look For

- Double-wall construction of metal or high-grade plastic. Wood is not recommended, because it is a fire hazard and is difficult to clean.
- Enclosed heating elements
- Countertop design
- An enclosed thermostat from 85 to 160°F
- Fan or blower

- Four to 10 open mesh trays made of sturdy, light-weight plastic for easy washing
- Underwriters Laboratory (UL) seal of approval
- A one-year guarantee
- Convenient service
- A dial for regulating temperature
- A timer. Often the completed drying time may occur during the night, and a timer turns the dehydrator off to prevent scorching.

Types of Dehydrators

There are two basic designs for dehydrators. One has horizontal air flow and the other has vertical air flow. In units with horizontal flow, the heating element and fan are located on the side of the unit. The major advantages of horizontal flow are: it reduces flavor mixture so several different foods can be dried at one time; all trays receive equal heat penetration; and juices or liquids do not drip down into the heating element. Vertical air flow dehydrators have the heating element and fan located at the base. If different foods are dried, flavors can mix and liquids can drip into the heating element.

Fruit Drying Procedures

Apples—Select mature, firm apples. Wash well. Pare, if desired, and core. Cut in rings or slices ⅛ to ¼ inch thick or cut in quarters or eighths. Soak in ascorbic acid, vinegar, or lemon juice for 10 minutes. Remove from solution and drain well. Arrange in single layer on trays, pit side up. Dry until soft, pliable, and leathery; there should be no moist area in center when cut.

Apricots—Select firm, fully ripe fruit. Wash well. Cut in half and remove pit. Do not peel. Soak in ascorbic acid, vinegar, or lemon juice for 10 minutes. Remove

from solution and drain well. Arrange in single layer on trays, pit side up with cavity popped up to expose more flesh to the air. Dry until soft, pliable, and leathery; there should be no moist area in center when cut.

Bananas—Select firm, ripe fruit. Peel. Cut in ⅛-inch slices. Soak in ascorbic acid, vinegar, or lemon juice for 10 minutes. Remove and drain well. Arrange in single layer on trays. Dry until tough and leathery.

Berries—Select firm, ripe fruit. Wash well. Leave whole or cut in half. Dip in boiling water 30 seconds to crack skins. Arrange on drying trays not more than two berries deep. Dry until hard and berries rattle when shaken on trays.

Cherries—Select fully ripe fruit. Wash well. Remove stems and pits. Dip whole cherries in boiling water 30 seconds to crack skins. Arrange in single layer on trays. Dry until tough, leathery, and slightly sticky.

Citrus peel—Select thick-skinned oranges with no signs of mold or decay and no color added to skin. Scrub oranges well with brush under cool running water. Thinly peel outer 1⁄16 to ⅛ inch of the peel; avoid white bitter part. Soak in ascorbic acid, vinegar, or lemon juice for 10 minutes. Remove from solution and drain well. Arrange in single layers on trays. Dry at 130°F for 1 to 2 hours, then at 120°F until crisp.

Figs—Select fully ripe fruit. Wash or clean well with damp towel. Peel dark-skinned varieties if desired. Leave whole if small or partly dried on tree; cut large figs in halves or slices. If drying whole figs, crack skins by dipping in boiling water for 30 seconds. For cut figs, soak in ascorbic acid, vinegar, or lemon juice for 10 minutes. Remove and drain well. Arrange in single layers on trays. Dry until leathery and pliable.

Grapes and black currants—Select seedless varieties. Wash, sort, and remove stems. Cut in half or leave whole. If drying whole, crack skins by dipping in boiling water for 30 seconds. If halved, dip in ascorbic acid or other antimicrobial solution for 10 minutes. Remove and drain well. Dry until pliable and leathery with no moist center.

Melons—Select mature, firm fruits that are heavy for their size; cantaloupe dries better than watermelon. Scrub outer surface well with brush under cool running water. Remove outer skin, any fibrous tissue, and seeds. Cut into ¼- to ½-inch-thick slices. Soak in ascorbic acid, vinegar, or lemon juice for 10 minutes. Remove and drain well. Arrange in single layer on trays. Dry until leathery and pliable with no pockets of moisture.

Nectarines and peaches—Select ripe, firm fruit. Wash and peel. Cut in half and remove pit. Cut in quarters or slices if desired. Soak in ascorbic acid, vinegar, or lemon juice for 10 minutes. Remove and drain well. Arrange in single layer on trays, pit side up. Turn halves over when visible juice disappears. Dry until leathery and somewhat pliable.

Pears—Select ripe, firm fruit. Bartlett variety is recommended. Wash fruit well. Pare, if desired. Cut in half lengthwise and core. Cut in quarters, eighths, or slices ⅛ to ¼ inch thick. Soak in ascorbic acid, vinegar, or lemon juice for 10 minutes. Remove and drain. Arrange in single layer on trays, pit side up. Dry until springy and suede-like with no pockets of moisture.

Plums and prunes—Wash well. Leave whole if small; cut large fruit into halves (pit removed) or slices. If left whole, crack skins in boiling water 1 to 2 minutes. If cut in half, dip in ascorbic acid or other antimicrobial solution for 10 minutes. Remove and drain. Arrange in single layer on trays, pit side up, cavity popped out. Dry until pliable and leathery; in whole prunes, pit should not slip when squeezed.

Fruit Leathers

Fruit leathers are a tasty and nutritious alternative to store-bought candies that are full of artificial sweeteners and preservatives. Blend the leftover fruit pulp from making jelly or use fresh, frozen, or drained canned fruit. Ripe or slightly overripe fruit works best.

Chances are the fruit leather will get eaten before it makes it into the cupboard, but it can keep up to one month at room temperature. For storage up to one year, place tightly wrapped rolls in the freezer.

Ingredients
2 cups fruit
2 tsp lemon juice or ⅛ tsp ascorbic acid (optional)
¼ to ½ cup sugar, corn syrup, or honey (optional)

Directions
1. Wash fresh fruit or berries in cool water. Remove peel, seeds, and stem.
2. Cut fruit into chunks. Use 2 cups of fruit for each 13 x 15-inch inch fruit leather. Purée fruit until smooth.
3. Add 2 teaspoons of lemon juice or ⅛ teaspoon ascorbic acid (375 mg) for each 2 cups light-colored fruit to prevent darkening.
4. Optional: To sweeten, add corn syrup, honey, or sugar. Corn syrup or honey is best for longer storage because these sweeteners prevent crystals. Sugar is fine for immediate use or short storage. Use ¼ to ½ cup sugar, corn syrup, or honey for each 2 cups of fruit. Avoid aspartame sweeteners as they may lose sweetness during drying.
5. Pour the leather. Fruit leathers can be poured into a single large sheet (13 x 15 inches) or into several smaller sizes. Spread purée evenly, about ⅛ inch thick, onto drying tray. Avoid pouring purée too close to the edge of the cookie sheet.
6. Dry the leather. Dry fruit leathers at 140°F. Leather dries from the outside edge toward the center.

Larger fruit leathers take longer to dry. Approximate drying times are 6 to 8 hours in a dehydrator, up to 18 hours in an oven, and 1 to 2 days in the sun. Test for dryness by touching center of leather; no indentation should be evident. While warm, peel from plastic and roll, allow to cool, and rewrap the roll in plastic. Cookie cutters can be used to cut out shapes that children will enjoy. Roll, and wrap in plastic.

Spices, Flavors, and Garnishes

To add interest to your fruit leathers, include spices, flavorings, or garnishes.

- **Spices to try**—Allspice, cinnamon, cloves, coriander, ginger, mace, mint, nutmeg, or pumpkin pie spice. Use sparingly; start with ⅛ teaspoon for each 2 cups of purée.
- **Flavorings to try**—Almond extract, lemon juice, lemon peel, lime juice, lime peel, orange extract, orange juice, orange peel, or vanilla extract. Use sparingly; try ⅛ to ¼ teaspoon for each 2 cups of purée.
- **Delicious additions to try**—Shredded coconut, chopped dates, other dried chopped fruits, granola, miniature marshmallows, chopped nuts, chopped raisins, poppy seeds, sesame seeds, or sunflower seeds.
- **Fillings to try**—Melted chocolate, softened cream cheese, cheese spreads, jam, preserves, marmalade, marshmallow cream, or peanut butter. Spread one or more of these on the leather after it is dried and then roll. Store in refrigerator.

Vegetable Leathers

Pumpkin, mixed vegetables, and tomatoes make great leathers. Just purée cooked vegetables, strain, spread on a tray lined with plastic wrap, and dry. Spices can be added for flavoring.

Mixed-Vegetable Leather

2 cups cored, cut-up tomatoes
1 small onion, chopped
¼ cup chopped celery
Salt to taste

Combine all ingredients in a covered saucepan and cook over low heat 15 to 20 minutes. Purée or force through a sieve or colander. Return to saucepan and cook until thickened. Spread on a cookie sheet or tray lined with plastic wrap. Dry at 140°F.

Pumpkin Leather

2 cups canned pumpkin or 2 cups fresh pumpkin, cooked and puréed
½ cup honey
¼ tsp cinnamon
⅛ tsp nutmeg
⅛ tsp powdered cloves

Blend ingredients well. Spread on tray or cookie sheet lined with plastic wrap. Dry at 140°F.

Tomato Leather

Core ripe tomatoes and cut into quarters. Cook over low heat in a covered saucepan, 15 to 20 minutes. Purée or force through a sieve or colander and pour into electric fry pan or shallow pan. Add salt to taste and cook over low heat until thickened. Spread on a cookie sheet or tray lined with plastic wrap. Dry at 140°F.

Vine Drying

One method of drying outdoors is vine drying. To dry beans (navy, kidney, butter, great northern, lima, lentils, and soybeans) leave bean pods on the vine in the garden until the beans inside rattle. When the vines and pods are dry and shriveled, pick the beans and shell them. No pretreatment is necessary. If beans are still moist, the drying process is not complete and the beans will mold if not more thoroughly dried. If needed, drying can be completed in the sun, an oven, or a dehydrator.

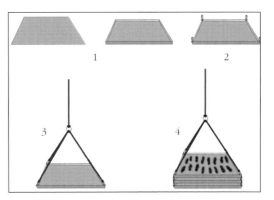

How to Make a Woodstove Food Dehydrator

1. Collect pliable wire mesh or screens (available at hardware stores) and use wire cutters to trim to squares 12 to 16 inches on each side. The trays should be of the same size and shape. Bend up the edges of each square to create a half-inch lip.
2. Attach one S hook from the hardware store or a large paperclip to each side of each square (four clips per tray) to attach the trays together.
3. Cut four equal lengths of chain or twine that will reach from the ceiling to the level of the top tray. Use a wire or metal loop to attach the four pieces together at the top and secure to a hook in the ceiling above the woodstove. Attach the chain or twine to the hooks on the top tray.
4. To use, fill trays with food to dry, starting with the top tray. Link trays together using the S hooks or strong paperclips. When the foods are dried, remove the entire stack and disassemble. Remove the dried food and store.

Herbs

Drying is the easiest method of preserving herbs. Simply expose the leaves, flowers, or seeds to warm, dry air. Leave the herbs in a well-ventilated area until the moisture evaporates. Sun drying is not recommended because the herbs can lose flavor and color.

The best time to harvest most herbs for drying is just before the flowers first open when they are in the bursting, bud stage. Gather the herbs in the early morning after the dew has evaporated to minimize wilting. Avoid bruising the leaves. They should not lie in the sun or unattended after harvesting. Rinse herbs in cool water and gently shake to remove excess moisture. Discard all bruised, soiled, or imperfect leaves and stems.

Dehydrator drying is another fast and easy way to dry high-quality herbs because temperature and air circulation can be controlled. Preheat dehydrator with the thermostat set to 95°F to 115°F. In areas with higher humidity, temperatures as high as 125°F may be needed. After rinsing under cool, running water and shaking to remove excess moisture, place the herbs in a single layer on dehydrator trays. Drying times may vary from one to four hours. Check periodically. Herbs are dry when they crumble, and stems break when bent. Check your dehydrator instruction booklet for specific details.

Less-tender herbs—The more sturdy herbs, such as rosemary, sage, thyme, summer savory, and parsley, are the easiest to dry without a dehydrator. Tie them into small bundles and hang them to air dry. Air drying outdoors is often possible; however, better color and flavor retention usually results from drying indoors.

Tender-leaf herbs—Basil, oregano, tarragon, lemon balm, and the mints have a high moisture content and will mold if not dried quickly. Try hanging the tender-leaf herbs or those with seeds inside paper bags to dry. Tear or punch holes in the sides of the bag. Suspend a small bunch (large amounts will mold) of herbs in a bag and close the top with a rubber band. Place where air currents will circulate through the bag. Any leaves and seeds that fall off will be caught in the bottom of the bag.

Another method, especially nice for mint, sage, or bay leaf, is to dry the leaves separately. In areas of high humidity, it will work better than air drying whole stems. Remove the best leaves from the stems. Lay the leaves on a paper towel, without allowing leaves to touch. Cover with another towel and layer of leaves. Five layers may

be dried at one time using this method. Dry in a very cool oven. The oven light of an electric range or the pilot light of a gas range furnishes enough heat for overnight drying. Leaves dry flat and retain a good color.

Microwave ovens are a fast way to dry herbs when only small quantities are to be prepared. Follow the directions that come with your microwave oven.

When the leaves are crispy, dry, and crumble easily between the fingers, they are ready to be packaged and stored. Dried leaves may be left whole and crumbled as used, or coarsely crumbled before storage. Husks can be removed from seeds by rubbing the seeds between the hands and blowing away the chaff. Place herbs in airtight containers and store in a cool, dry, dark area to protect color and fragrance.

Dried herbs are usually three to four times stronger than the fresh herbs. To substitute dried herbs in a recipe that calls for fresh herbs, use ¼ to ⅓ of the amount listed in the recipe.

Jerky

Jerky is great for hiking or camping because it supplies protein in a very lightweight form—not to mention the fact that it can be very tasty. A pound of meat or poultry weighs about four ounces after being made into jerky. In addition, because most of the moisture is removed, it can be stored for one to two months without refrigeration.

Jerky has been around since the ancient Egyptians began drying animal meat that was too big to eat all at once. Native Americans mixed ground dried meat with dried fruit or suet to make pemmican. *Biltong* is dried meat or game used in many African countries. The English word *jerky* came from the Spanish word *charque*, which means "dried, salted meat."

Drying is the world's oldest and most common method of food preservation. Enzymes require moisture in order to react with food. By removing the moisture, you prevent this biological action.

Jerky can be made from ground meat, which is often less expensive than strips of meat and allows you to combine different kinds of meat if desired. You can also make it into any shape you want! As with strips of meat, an internal temperature of 160°F is necessary to eliminate disease-causing bacteria such as *E. coli*, if present.

Food Safety

The USDA Meat and Poultry Hotline's current recommendation for making jerky safely is to heat meat to 160°F and poultry to 165°F before the dehydrating process.

This ensures that any bacteria present are destroyed by heat. If your food dehydrator doesn't heat up to 160°F, it's important to cook meat slightly in the oven or by steaming before drying. After heating, maintain a constant dehydrator temperature of 130°F to 140°F during the drying process.

According to the USDA, you should always:

- Wash hands thoroughly with soap and water before and after working with meat products.
- Use clean equipment and utensils.
- Keep meat and poultry refrigerated at 40°F or slightly below; use or freeze ground beef and poultry within two days, and whole red meats within three to five days.
- Defrost frozen meat in the refrigerator, not on the kitchen counter.
- Marinate meat in the refrigerator. Don't save marinade to re-use. Marinades are used to tenderize and flavor the jerky before dehydrating it.
- If your food dehydrator doesn't heat up to 160°F (or 165°F for poultry), steam or roast meat before dehydrating it.
- Dry meats in a food dehydrator that has an adjustable temperature dial and will maintain a temperature of at least 130°F to 140°F throughout the drying process.

Preparing the Meat

1. Partially freeze meat to make slicing easier. Slice meat across the grain ⅛ to ¼ inch thick. Trim and discard all fat, gristle, and membranes or connective tissue.
2. Marinate the meat in a combination of oil, salt, spices, vinegar, lemon juice, teriyaki, soy sauce, beer, or wine.

Marinated Jerky

¼ cup soy sauce
1 tbsp Worcestershire sauce
1 tsp brown sugar
¼ tsp black pepper
½ tsp fresh ginger, finely grated
1 tsp salt
1½ to 2 lbs of lean meat strips (beef, pork, or venison)

1. Combine all ingredients except the strips, and blend. Add meat, stir, cover, and refrigerate at least one hour.
2. If your food dehydrator doesn't heat up to 160°F, bring strips and marinade to a boil and cook for 5 minutes.

3. Drain meat in a colander and absorb extra moisture with clean, absorbent paper towels. Arrange strips in a single layer on dehydrator trays, or on cake racks placed on baking sheets for oven drying.
4. Place the racks in a dehydrator or oven preheated to 140°F, or 160°F if the meat wasn't precooked. Dry until a test piece cracks but does not break when it is bent (10 to 24 hours for samples not heated in marinade, 3 to 6 hours for preheated meat). Use a paper towel to pat off any excess oil from strips, and pack in sealed jars, plastic bags, or plastic containers.

Freezing Foods

Many foods preserve well in the freezer and can make preparing meals easy when you are short on time. If you make a big pot of soup, serve it for dinner, put a small container in the refrigerator for lunch the next day, and then stick the rest in the freezer. A few weeks later, you'll be ready to eat it again and it will only take a few minutes to thaw out and serve. Many fruits also freeze well and are perfect for use in smoothies and desserts, or served with yogurt for breakfast or dessert. Vegetables frozen shortly after harvesting keep many of the nutrients found in fresh vegetables and will taste delicious when cooked.

Containers for Freezing

The best packaging materials for freezing include rigid containers such as jars, bottles, or Tupperware, and freezer bags or aluminum foil. Sturdy containers with rigid sides are especially good for liquids such as soup or juice because they make the frozen contents much easier to get out. They are also generally reusable and make it easier to stack foods in the refrigerator. When using rigid containers, be sure to leave headspace so that the container won't explode when the contents expand with freezing. Covers for rigid containers should fit tightly. If they do not, reinforce the seal with freezer tape. Freezer tape is specially designed to stick at freezing temperatures. Freezer bags or aluminum foil are good for meats, breads and baked goods, or fruits and vegetables that don't contain much liquid. Be sure to remove as much air as possible from bags before closing.

Headspace to Allow Between Packed Food and Closure

Headspace is the amount of empty air left between the food and the lid. Headspace is necessary because foods expand when frozen.

Type of Pack	Container with Wide Opening		Container with Narrow Opening	
	Pint	Quart	Pint	Quart
Liquid pack*	½ inch	1 inch	3/4 inch	1½ inch
Dry pack**	½ inch	½ inch	½ inch	½ inch
Juices	½ inch	1 inch	1½ inch	1½ inch

*Fruit packed in juice, sugar syrup, or water; crushed or puréed fruit
**Fruit or vegetable packed without added sugar or liquid

Foods That Do Not Freeze Well

Food	Usual Use	Condition After Thawing
Cabbage*, celery, cress, cucumbers*, endive, lettuce, parsley, radishes	As raw salad	Limp, waterlogged; quickly develops oxidized color, aroma, and flavor
Irish potatoes, baked or boiled	In soups, salads, sauces or with butter	Soft, crumbly, waterlogged, mealy
Cooked macaroni, spaghetti, or rice	When frozen alone for later use	Mushy, tastes warmed over
Egg whites, cooked	In salads, creamed foods, sandwiches, sauces, gravy, or desserts	Soft, tough, rubbery, spongy
Meringue	In desserts	Soft, tough, rubbery, spongy
Icings made from egg whites	Cakes, cookies	Frothy, weeps
Cream or custard fillings	Pies, baked goods	Separates, watery, lumpy
Milk sauces	For casseroles or gravies	May curdle or separate
Sour cream	As topping, in salads	Separates, watery
Cheese or crumb toppings	On casseroles	Soggy
Mayonnaise or salad dressing	On sandwiches (not in salads)	Separates
Gelatin	In salads or desserts	Weeps
Fruit jelly	Sandwiches	May soak bread
Fried foods	All except French fried potatoes and onion rings	Lose crispness, become soggy

* Cucumbers and cabbage can be frozen as marinated products such as "freezer slaw" or "freezer pickles." These do not have the same texture as regular slaw or pickles.

Effect of Freezing on Spices and Seasonings

- Pepper, cloves, garlic, green pepper, imitation vanilla, and some herbs tend to get strong and bitter.
- Onion and paprika change flavor during freezing.
- Celery seasonings become stronger.
- Curry develops a musty off-flavor.
- Salt loses flavor and has the tendency to increase rancidity of any item containing fat.
- When using seasonings and spices, season lightly before freezing, and add additional seasonings when reheating or serving.

How to Freeze Vegetables

Because many vegetables contain enzymes that will cause them to lose color when frozen, you may want to blanche your vegetables before putting them in the freezer. To do this, first wash the vegetables thoroughly, peel if desired, and chop them into bite-size pieces. Then pour them into boiling water for a couple of minutes (or cook longer for very dense vegetables, such as beets), drain, and immediately dunk the vegetables in ice water to stop them from cooking further. Use a paper towel or cloth to absorb excess water from the vegetables, and then pack in resealable airtight bags or plastic containers.

Blanching Times for Vegetables

Artichokes	3–6 minutes
Asparagus	2–3 minutes
Beans	2–3 minutes
Beets	30-40 minutes
Broccoli	3 minutes
Brussels sprouts	4–5 minutes
Cabbage	3–4 minutes
Carrots	2–5 minutes
Cauliflower	6 minutes
Celery	3 minutes
Corn (off the cob)	2–3 minutes
Eggplant	4 minutes
Okra	3–4 minutes
Peas	1–2 minutes
Peppers	2–3 minutes
Squash	2–3 minutes
Turnips or Parsnips	2 minutes

How to Freeze Fruits

Many fruits freeze easily and are perfect for use in baking, smoothies, or sauces. Wash, peel, and core fruit before freezing. To easily peel peaches, nectarines, or apricots, dip them in boiling water for 15 to 20 seconds to loosen the skins. Then chill and remove the skins and stones.

Berries should be frozen immediately after harvesting and can be frozen in a single layer on a paper towel--lined tray or cookie sheet to keep them from clumping together. Allow them to freeze until hard (about 3 hours) and then pour them into a resealable plastic bag for long-term storage.

Some fruits have a tendency to turn brown when frozen. To prevent this, you can add ascorbic acid (crush a vitamin C in a little water), citrus juice, plain sugar, or a sweet syrup (1 part sugar and 2 parts water) to the fruit before freezing. Apples, pears, and bananas are best frozen with ascorbic acid or citrus juice, while berries, peaches, nectarines, apricots, pineapple, melons, and berries are better frozen with a sugary syrup.

How to Freeze Meat

Be sure your meat is fresh before freezing. Trim off excess fats and remove bones, if desired. Separate the meat into portions that will be easy to use when preparing meals and wrap in foil or place in resealable plastic bags or plastic containers. Refer to the chart to determine how long your meat will last at best quality in your freezer.

Meat	Months
Bacon and sausage	1 to 2
Ham, hotdogs, and lunchmeats	1 to 2
Meat, uncooked roasts	4 to 12
Meat, uncooked steaks or chops	4 to 12
Meat, uncooked ground	3 to 4
Meat, cooked	2 to 3
Poultry, uncooked whole	12
Poultry, uncooked parts	9
Poultry, uncooked giblets	3 to 4
Poultry, cooked	4
Wild game, uncooked	8 to 12

Edible Wild Plants and Mushrooms

Wild Vegetables, Fruits, and Nuts

Agave

Description: Agave plants have large clusters of thick leaves that grow around one stalk. They grow close to the ground and only flower once before dying.

Location: Agave like dry, open areas and are found in the deserts of the American west.

Edible Parts and Preparing: Only agave flowers and buds are edible. Boil these before consuming. The juice can be collected from the flower stalk for drinking.

Other Uses: Most agave plants have thick needles on the tips of their leaves that can be used for sewing.

Asparagus

Description: When first growing, asparagus looks like a collection of green fingers. Once mature, the plant has fernlike foliage and red berries (which are toxic if eaten). The flowers are small and green and several species have sharp, thornlike projections.

Location: It can be found growing wild in fields and along fences. Asparagus is found in temperate areas in the United States.

Edible Parts and Preparing: It is best to eat the young stems, before any leaves grow. Steam or boil them for 10 to 15 minutes before consuming. The roots are a good source of starch, but don't eat any part of the plant raw, as it could cause nausea or diarrhea.

Beech

Description: Beech trees are large forest trees. They have smooth, light gray bark, very dark leaves, and clusters of prickly seedpods.

Location: Beech trees prefer to grow in moist, forested areas. These trees are found in the Temperate Zone in the eastern United States.

Edible Parts and Preparing: Eat mature beechnuts by breaking the thin shells with your fingers and removing the sweet, white kernel found inside. These nuts can also be used as a substitute for coffee by roasting them until the kernel turns hard and golden brown. Mash up the kernel and boil or steep in hot water.

Blackberry and Raspberry

Description: These plants have prickly stems that grow upright and then arch back toward the ground. They have alternating leaves and grow red or black fruit.

Location: Blackberry and raspberry plants prefer to grow in wide, sunny areas near woods, lakes, and roads. They grow in temperate areas.

Edible Parts and Preparing: Both the fruits and peeled young shoots can be eaten. The leaves can be used to make tea.

Burdock

Description: Burdock has wavy-edged, arrow-shaped leaves. Its flowers grow in burrlike clusters and are purple or pink. The roots are large and fleshy.

Location: This plant prefers to grow in open waste areas during the spring and summer. It can be found in the Temperate Zone in the north.

Edible Parts and Preparing: The tender leaves growing on the stalks can be eaten raw or cooked. The roots can be boiled or baked.

Cattail

Description: These plants are grasslike and have leaves shaped like straps. The male flowers grow above the female flowers; have abundant, bright yellow pollen; and die off quickly. The female flowers become the brown cattails.

Location: Cattails like to grow in full-sun areas near lakes, streams, rivers, and brackish water. They can be found all over the country.

Edible Parts and Preparing: The tender, young shoots can be eaten either raw or cooked. The rhizome (rootstalk) can be pounded and made into flour. When the cattail is immature, the female flower can be harvested, boiled, and eaten like corn on the cob.

Other Uses: The cottony seeds of the cattail plant are great for stuffing pillows. Burning dried cattails helps repel insects.

Chicory

Description: This is quite a tall plant, with clusters of leaves at the base of the stem and very few leaves on the stem itself. The flowers are sky blue in color and open only on sunny days. It produces a milky juice.

Location: Chicory grows in fields, waste areas, and alongside roads. It grows primarily as a weed all throughout the country.

Edible Parts and Preparing: The entire plant is edible. The young leaves can be eaten in a salad. The leaves and roots may also be boiled as you would regular vegetables. Roast the roots until they are dark brown, mash them up, and use them as a substitute for coffee.

Cranberry

Description: The cranberry plant has tiny, alternating leaves. Its stems crawl along the ground and it produces red berry fruits.

Location: Cranberries only grow in open, sunny, wet areas. They thrive in the colder areas in the northern states.

Edible Parts and Preparing: The berries can be eaten raw, though they are best when cooked in a small amount of water, adding a little bit of sugar if desired.

Dandelion

Description: These plants have jagged leaves and grow close to the ground. They have bright yellow flowers.

Location: Dandelions grow in almost any open, sunny space in the United States.

Edible Parts and Preparing: All parts of this plant are edible. The leaves can be eaten raw or cooked and the roots boiled. Roasted and ground roots can make a good substitute for coffee.

Other Uses: The white juice in the flower stem can be used as glue.

Elderberry

Description: This shrub has many stems containing opposite, compound leaves. Its flower is white, fragrant, and grows in large clusters. Its fruits are berry-shaped and are typically dark blue or black.

Location: Found in open, wet areas near rivers, ditches, and lakes, the elderberry grows mainly in the eastern states.

Edible Parts and Preparing: The flowers can be soaked in water for eight hours and then the liquid can be drunk. The fruit is also edible but don't eat any other parts of the plant—they are poisonous.

Hazelnut

Description: The nuts grow on bushes in very bristly husks.

Location: Hazelnut grows in dense thickets near streambeds and in open areas and can be found all over the United States.

Edible Parts and Preparing: In the autumn, the hazelnut ripens and can be cracked open and the kernel eaten. Eating dried nuts is also tasty.

Juniper

Description: Also known as cedar, this shrub has very small, scaly leaves that are densely crowded on the branches. Berrylike cones on the plant are usually blue and are covered with a whitish wax.

Location: They grow in open, dry, sunny places throughout the country.

Edible Parts and Preparing: Both berries and twigs are edible. The berries can be consumed raw or the seeds may be roasted to make a substitute for coffee. Dried and crushed berries are good to season meat. Twigs can be made into tea.

Lotus

Description: This plant has large, yellow flowers and leaves that float on or above the surface of the water. The lotus fruit has a distinct, flattened shape and possesses around 20 hard seeds.

Location: Found on fresh water in quiet areas, the lotus plant is native to North America.

Edible Parts and Preparing: All parts of the lotus plant are edible, raw or cooked. Bake or boil the fleshy parts that grow underwater and boil young leaves. The seeds are quite nutritious and can be eaten raw or they can be ground into flour.

Marsh Marigold

Description: Marsh marigold has round, dark green leaves and a short stem. It also has bright yellow flowers.

Location: The plant can be found in bogs and lakes in the northeastern states.

Edible Parts and Preparing: All parts can be boiled and eaten. Do not consume any portion raw.

Mulberry

Description: The mulberry tree has alternate, lobed leaves with rough surfaces and blue or black seeded fruits.

Location: These trees are found in forested areas and near roadsides in temperate and tropical regions of the United States.

Edible Parts and Preparing: The fruit can be consumed either raw or cooked and it can also be dried. Make sure the fruit is ripe or it can cause hallucinations and extreme nausea.

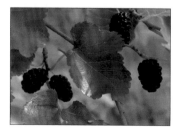

Nettle

Description: Nettle plants grow several feet high and have small flowers. The stems, leafstalks, and undersides of the leaves all contain fine, hairlike bristles that cause a stinging sensation on the skin.

Location: This plant grows in moist areas near streams or on the edges of forests. It can be found throughout the United States.

Edible Parts and Preparing: The young shoots and leaves are edible. To eat, boil the plant for 10 to 15 minutes.

Oak

Description: These trees have alternating leaves and acorns. Red oaks have bristly leaves and smooth bark on the upper part of the tree and their acorns need two years to reach maturity. White oaks have leaves with no bristles and rough bark on the upper part of the tree. Their acorns only take one year to mature.

Location: Found in various locations and habitats throughout the country.

Edible Parts and Preparing: All parts of the tree are edible, but most are very bitter. Shell the acorns and soak them in water for one or two days to remove their tannic acid. Boil the acorns to eat or grind them into flour for baking.

Palmetto Palm

Description: This is a tall tree with no branches and has a continual leaf base on the trunk. The leaves are large, simple, and lobed and it has dark blue or black fruits that contain a hard seed.

Location: This tree is found throughout the southeastern coast.

Edible Parts and Preparing: The palmetto palm fruit can be eaten raw. The seeds can also be ground into flour, and the heart of the palm is a nutritious source of food, but the top of the tree must be cut down in order to reach it.

Persimmon

Description: The persimmon tree has alternating, elliptical leaves that are dark green in color, and inconspicuous flowers. It has orange fruits that are very sticky and contain many seeds.

Location: Growing on the margins of forests, it resides in the eastern part of the country.

Edible Parts and Preparing: The leaves provide a good source of vitamin C and can be dried and soaked in hot water to make tea. The fruit can be consumed either baked or raw and the seeds may be eaten once roasted.

Pine

Description: Pine trees have needlelike leaves that are grouped into bundles of one to five needles. They have a very pungent, distinguishing odor.

Location: Pines grow best in sunny, open areas and are found all over the United States.

Edible Parts and Preparing: The seeds are completely edible and can be consumed either raw or cooked. Also, the young male cones can be boiled or baked and eaten. Peel the bark off of thin twigs and chew the juicy inner bark. The needles can be dried and brewed to make tea that's high in vitamin C.

Other Uses: Pine tree resin can be used to waterproof items. Collect the resin from the tree, put it in a container, heat it, and use it as glue or, when cool, rub it on items to waterproof them.

Plantain

Description: The broad-leafed plantain grows close to the ground and the flowers are situated on a spike that rises from the middle of the leaf cluster. The narrow-leaf species has leaves covered with hairs that form a rosette. The flowers are very small.

Location: Plantains grow in lawns and along the side of the road in the northern Temperate Zone.

Edible Parts and Preparing: Young, tender leaves can be eaten raw, and older leaves should be cooked before consumption. The seeds may also be eaten either raw or roasted. Tea can also be made by boiling 1 ounce of the plant leaves in a few cups of water.

Pokeweed

Description: A rather tall plant, pokeweed has elliptical leaves and produces many large clusters of purple fruits in the late spring.

Location: Pokeweed grows in open and sunny areas in fields and along roadsides in the eastern United States.

Edible Parts and Preparing: If cooked, the young leaves and stems are edible. Be sure to boil them twice and discard the water from the first boiling. The fruit is also edible if cooked. Never eat any part of this plant raw, as it is poisonous.

Prickly Pear Cactus

Description: This plant has flat, pad-like green stems and round, furry dots that contain sharp-pointed hairs.

Location: Found in arid regions and in dry, sandy areas in wetter regions, it can be found throughout the United States.

Edible Parts and Preparing: All parts of this plant are edible. To eat the fruit, peel it or crush it to make a juice. The seeds can be roasted and ground into flour.

Reindeer Moss

Description: This is a low plant that does not flower. However, it does produce bright red structures used for reproduction.

Location: It grows in dry, open areas in much of the country.

Edible Parts and Preparing: While having a crunchy, brittle texture, the whole plant can be eaten. To remove some of the bitterness, soak it in water and then dry and crush it, adding it to milk or other foods.

Sassafras

Description: This shrub has different leaves—some have one lobe, others two lobes, and others have none at all. The flowers are small and yellow and appear in the early spring. The plant has dark blue fruit.

Location: Sassafras grows near roads and forests in sunny, open areas. It is common throughout the eastern states.

Edible Parts and Preparing: The young twigs and leaves can be eaten either fresh or dried—add them to soups. Dig out the underground portion of the shrub, peel off the bark, and dry it. Boil it in water to make tea.

Other Uses: Shredding the tender twigs will make a handy toothbrush.

Spatterdock

Description: The leaves of this plant are quite long and have a triangular notch at the base. Spatterdock has yellow flowers that become bottle-shaped fruits, which are green when ripe.

Location: Found in fresh, shallow water throughout the country.

Edible Parts and Preparing: All parts of the plant are edible and the fruits have brown seeds that can be roasted and ground into flour. The rootstock can be dug out of the mud, peeled, and boiled.

Strawberry

Description: This is a small plant with a three-leaved pattern. Small, white flowers appear in the springtime and the fruit is red and very fleshy.

Location: These plants prefer sunny, open spaces, are commonly planted, and appear in the northern Temperate Zone.

Edible Parts and Preparing: The fruit can be eaten raw, cooked, or dried. The plant leaves may also be eaten or dried to make tea.

Thistle

Description: This plant may grow very high and has long-pointed, prickly leaves.

Location: Thistle grows in woods and fields all over the country.

Edible Parts and Preparing: Peel the stalks, cut them into smaller sections, and boil them to consume. The root may be eaten raw or cooked.

Walnut

Description: Walnuts grow on large trees and have divided leaves. The walnut has a thick, outer husk that needs to be removed before getting to the hard, inner shell.

Location: The black walnut tree is common in the eastern states.

Edible Parts and Preparing: Nut kernels become ripe in the fall and the meat can be obtained by cracking the shell.

Water Lily

Description: With large, triangular leaves that float on water, these plants have fragrant flowers that are white or red. They also have thick rhizomes that grow in the mud.

Location: Water lilies are found in many temperate areas.

Edible Parts and Preparing: The flowers, seeds, and rhizomes can be eaten either raw or cooked. Peel the corky rind off of the rhizome and eat it raw or slice it thinly, dry it, and grind into flour. The seeds can also be made into flour after drying, parching, and grinding.

Wild Grapevine

Description: This vine will climb on tendrils, and most of these plants produce deeply lobed leaves. The grapes grow in pyramidal bunches and are black-blue, amber, or white when ripe.

Location: Climbing over other vegetation on the edges of forested areas, they can be found in the eastern and southwestern parts of the United States.

Edible Parts and Preparing: Only the ripe grape can be eaten.

Wild Onion and Garlic

Description: These are recognized by their distinctive odors.

Location: They are found in open areas that get lots of sun throughout temperate areas.

Edible Parts and Preparing: The bulbs and young leaves are edible and can be consumed either raw or cooked.

Wild Rose

Description: This shrub has alternating leaves and sharp prickles. It has red, pink, or yellow flowers and fruit (rose hip) that remains on the shrub all year.

Location: These shrubs occur in dry fields throughout the country.

Edible Parts and Preparing: The flowers and buds are edible raw or boiled. Boil fresh, young leaves to make tea. The rose hips can be eaten once the flowers fall and they can be crushed once dried to make flour.

Violets

Violets can be candied and used to decorate cakes, cookies, or pastries. Pick the flowers with a tiny bit of stem, wash, and allow to dry thoroughly on a paper towel or a rack. Heat ½ cup water, 1 cup sugar, and ¼ teaspoon almond extract in a saucepan. Use tweezers to carefully dip each flower in the hot liquid. Set on wax paper and dust with sugar until every flower is thoroughly coated. If desired, snip off remaining stems with small scissors. Allow flowers to dry for a few hours in a warm, dry place.

Edible Wild Mushrooms

A walk through the woods will likely reveal several varieties of mushrooms, and chances are that some are the types that are edible. However, because some mushrooms are very poisonous, it is important never to try a mushroom of which you are unsure. Never eat a mushroom with gills, or, for that matter, any mushroom that you cannot positively identify as edible. Also, never eat mushrooms that appear wilted, damaged, or rotten.

Here are some common edible mushrooms that you can easily identify and enjoy.

Chanterelles

Chanterelles.

These trumpet-shaped mushrooms have wavy edges and interconnected blunt-ridged gills under the caps. They are varied shades of yellow and have a fruity fragrance. They grow in summer and fall on the ground of hardwood forests. Because chanterelles tend to be tough, they are best when slowly sautéed or added to stews or soups.

Notes: Beware of Jack O'Lantern mushrooms, which look and smell similarly to chanterelles. Jack O'Lanterns have sharp, knifelike gills instead of the blunt gills of chanterelles, and generally grow in large clusters at the base of trees or on decaying wood.

Coral Fungi

Corel fungi.

These fungi are aptly named for their bunches of upward-facing branching stems, which look strikingly like coral. They are whitish, tan, yellowish, or sometimes pinkish or purple. They may reach 8 inches in height. They grow in the summer and fall in shady, wooded areas.

Notes: Avoid coral fungi that are bitter, have soft, gelatinous bases, or turn brown when you poke or squeeze them. These may have a laxative effect, though are not life-threatening.

Morels

Morels are sometimes called sponge, pinecone, or honeycomb mushrooms because of the pattern of pits and ridges that appears on the caps. They can be anywhere from 2 to 12 inches tall. They may be yellow, brown, or black and grow in spring and early summer in wooded areas and on river bottoms. To cook, cut in half to check for insects, wash, and sauté, bake, or stew.

Notes: False morels can be poisonous and appear similar to morels because of their brainlike, irregularly shaped caps. However, they can be distinguished from true morels because false morel caps bulge inward instead of outward. The caps have lobes, folds, flaps, or wrinkles, but not pits and ridges like a true morel.

Puffballs

These round or pear-shaped mushrooms are often mistaken for golf balls or eggs. They are always whitish, tan, or gray and sometimes have a thick stem. Young puffballs tend to be white and older ones yellow or brown. Fully matured puffballs have dark spores scattered over the caps. Puffballs are generally found in late summer and fall on lawns, in the woods, or on old tree stumps. To eat, peel off the outer skin and eat raw or batter-fried.

Notes: Slice each puffball open before eating to be sure it is completely white inside. If there is any yellow, brown, or black, or **if there is a developing mushroom inside with a stalk, gills, and cap, do not eat!** Amanitas, which are very poisonous, can appear similar to puffballs when they are young. Do not eat if the mushroom gives off an unpleasant odor.

Shaggy Mane Mushrooms

This mushroom got its name from its cap, which is a white cylinder with shaggy, upturned, brownish scales. As the mushroom matures, the bottom outside circumference of the cap becomes black. Shaggy manes are generally 4 to 6 inches tall and grow in all the warm seasons in fields and on lawns.

Shaggy manes are tastiest eaten when young, but they're easiest to identify once the bottoms of the caps begin to turn black. They are delicious sautéed in butter or olive oil and lightly seasoned with salt, garlic, or nutmeg.

Morels

Puffballs

Poisonous amanita mushroom

Shaggy mane mushroom

Make Your Own Foods

Make Your Own Butter

Making butter the old-fashioned way is incredibly simple and very gratifying. It's a great project to do with kids, too. All you need is a jar, a marble, some fresh cream, and about 20 minutes.

1. Start with about twice as much heavy whipping cream as you'll want butter. Pour it into the jar, drop in the marble, close the lid tightly, and start shaking.
2. Check the consistency of the cream every three to four minutes. The liquid will turn into whipped cream, and then eventually you'll see little clumps of butter forming in the jar. Keep shaking for another few minutes and then begin to strain out the liquid into another jar. This is buttermilk, which is great for use in making pancakes, waffles, biscuits, and muffins.
3. The butter is now ready, but it will store better if you wash and work it. Add ½ cup of ice-cold water and continue to shake for two or three minutes. Strain out the water and repeat. When the strained water is clear, mash the butter to extract the last of the water, and strain.
4. Scoop the butter into a ramekin, mold, or wax paper.

If desired, add salt or chopped fresh herbs to your butter just before storing or serving. Butter can also be made in a food processor or blender to speed up the processing time.

Make Your Own Yogurt

Yogurt is simple to make and is delicious on its own, as a dessert, in baked goods, or in place of sour cream. Yogurt is basically fermented milk. You can make it by adding the active cultures *Streptococcus thermophilus* and *Lactobacillus bulgaricus* to heated milk, which will produce lactic acid, creating yogurt's tart flavor and thick consistency.

Yogurt is thought to have originated many centuries ago among the nomadic tribes of Eastern Europe and Western Asia. Milk stored in animal skins would acidify and coagulate. The acid helped preserve the milk from further spoilage and from the growth of pathogens (disease-causing microorganisms).

Ingredients
Makes 4 to 5 cups of yogurt

- **1 quart milk** (cream, whole, low-fat, or skim)—In general the higher the milk fat level in the yogurt, the creamier and smoother it will taste. **Note:** If you use home-produced milk it *must* be pasteurized before preparing yogurt. See the center box for tips on pasteurizing milk.
- **Nonfat dry milk powder**—Use ⅓ cup powder when using whole or low-fat milk, or use ⅔ cup powder when using skim milk. The higher the milk solids, the firmer the yogurt will be. For even more firmness add gelatin (directions below).
- **Commercial, unflavored, cultured yogurt**—Use ¼ cup. Be sure the product label indicates that it contains a live culture. Also note the content of the culture. *L. bulgaricus* and *S. thermophilus* are

required in yogurt, but some manufacturers may add *L. acidophilus* or *B. bifidum*. The latter two are used for slight variations in flavor, but more commonly for health reasons attributed to these organisms. All culture variations will make a successful yogurt.

- **2 to 4 tablespoons sugar or honey (optional)**
- **1 teaspoon unflavored gelatin (optional)**—For a thick, firm yogurt, swell 1 teaspoon gelatin in a little milk for 5 minutes. Add this to the milk and nonfat dry milk mixture before cooking.

Supplies
- **Double boiler or regular saucepan**—1 to 2 quarts in capacity larger than the volume of yogurt you wish to make.
- **Cooking or jelly thermometer**—A thermometer that can clip to the side of the saucepan and remain in the milk works best. Accurate temperatures are critical for successful processing.
- **Mixing spoon**
- **Yogurt containers**—cups with lids or canning jars with lids.
- **Incubator**—a yogurt-maker, oven, heating pad, or warm spot in your kitchen. To use your oven, place yogurt containers into deep pans of 110°F water. Water should come at least halfway up the containers. Set oven temperature at lowest point to maintain water temperature at 110°F. Monitor temperature throughout incubation, making adjustments as necessary.

Processing
1. Combine ingredients and heat. Heating the milk is necessary to change the milk proteins so that they set together rather than form curds and whey. Do not substitute this heating step for pasteurization. Place cold, pasteurized milk in a double boiler and stir in nonfat, dry milk powder. Adding nonfat, dry milk to heated milk will cause some milk proteins to coagulate and form strings. Add sugar or honey if a sweeter, less tart yogurt is desired. Heat milk to 200°F, stirring gently and hold

for 10 minutes for thinner yogurt, or hold 20 minutes for thicker yogurt. Do not boil. Be careful and stir constantly to avoid scorching if not using a double boiler.

2. Cool and inoculate. Place the top of the double boiler in cold water to cool milk rapidly to 112°F to 115°F. Remove one cup of the warm milk and blend it with the yogurt starter culture. Add this to the rest of the warm milk. The temperature of the mixture should now be 110°F to 112°F.

3. Incubate. Pour immediately into clean, warm containers; cover and place in prepared incubator. Close the incubator and incubate about 4 to 7 hours at 110°F, ± 5°F. Yogurt should set firm when the proper acid level is achieved (pH 4.6). Incubating yogurt for several hours past the time after the yogurt has set will produce more acidity. This will result in a more tart or acidic flavor and eventually cause the whey to separate.

4. Refrigerate. Rapid cooling stops the development of acid. Yogurt will keep for about 10 to 21 days if held in the refrigerator at 40°F or lower.

Yogurt Types

Set yogurt: A solid set where the yogurt firms in a container and is not disturbed.

Stirred yogurt: Yogurt made in a large container then spooned or otherwise dispensed into secondary serving containers. The consistency of the "set" is broken and the texture is less firm than set yogurt. This is the most popular form of commercial yogurt.

Drinking yogurt: Stirred yogurt into which additional milk and flavors are mixed. Add fruit or fruit syrups to taste. Mix in milk to achieve the desired thickness. The shelf life of this product is four to 10 days, since the pH is raised by the addition of fresh milk. Some whey separation will occur and is natural. Commercial products recommend a thorough shaking before consumption.

Fruit yogurt: Fruit, fruit syrups, or pie filling can be added to the yogurt. Place them on top, on bottom, or stir them into the yogurt.

Troubleshooting

- If milk forms some clumps or strings during the heating step, some milk proteins may have jelled. Take the solids out with a slotted spoon or, in difficult cases, after cooking pour the milk mixture through a clean colander or cheesecloth before inoculation.

How to Pasteurize Raw Milk

If you are using fresh milk that hasn't been processed, you can pasteurize it yourself. Heat water in the bottom section of a double boiler and pour milk into the top section. Cover the milk and heat to 165°F while stirring constantly for uniform heating. Cool immediately by setting the top section of the double boiler in ice water or cold running water. Store milk in the refrigerator in clean containers until ready for making yogurt.

- When yogurt fails to coagulate properly, it's because the pH is not low enough. Milk proteins will coagulate when the pH has dropped to 4.6. This is done by the culture growing and producing acids. Adding culture to very hot milk (+115°F) can kill bacteria. Use a thermometer to carefully control temperature.

- If yogurt takes too long to make, it may be because the temperature is off. Too hot or too cold of an incubation temperature can slow down culture growth. Use a thermometer to carefully control temperature.

- If yogurt just isn't working, it may be because the starter culture was of poor quality. Use a fresh, recently purchased culture from the grocery store each time you make yogurt.

- If yogurt tastes or smells bad, it's likely because the starter culture is contaminated. Obtain new culture for the next batch.

- If yogurt has over-set or incubated too long, refrigerate yogurt immediately after a firm coagulum has formed.

- If yogurt tastes a little odd, it could be due to overheating or boiling of the milk. Use a thermometer to carefully control temperature.

- When whey collects on the surface of the yogurt, it's called syneresis. Some syneresis is natural. Excessive separation of whey, however, can be caused by incubating yogurt too long or by agitating the yogurt while it is setting.

Storing Your Yogurt

- Always pasteurize milk or use commercially pasteurized milk to make yogurt.
- Discard batches that fail to set properly, especially those due to culture errors.
- Yogurt generally has a 10- to 21-day shelf life when made and stored properly in the refrigerator below 40°F.
- Always use clean and sanitized equipment and containers to ensure a long shelf life for your yogurt. Clean equipment and containers in hot water with detergent, then rinse well. Allow to air dry.

Make Your Own Cheese

There are endless varieties of cheese you can make, but they all fall into two main categories: soft and hard. Soft cheeses (like cream cheese) are easier to make because they don't require a cheese press. The curds in hard cheeses (like cheddar) are pressed together to form a solid block or wheel, which requires more time and effort, but hard cheeses will keep longer than soft cheeses, and generally have a much stronger flavor.

Cheese is basically curdled milk and is made by adding an enzyme (typically rennet) to milk, allowing curds to form, heating the mixture, straining out the whey, and finally pressing the curds together. Cheeses such as *queso fresco* or *queso blanco* (traditionally eaten in Latin American countries) and *paneer* (traditionally eaten in India), are made with an acid such as vinegar or lemon juice instead of bacterial cultures or rennet.

You can use any kind of milk to make cheese, including cow's milk, goat's milk, sheep's milk, and even buffalo's milk (used for traditional mozzarella). For the richest flavor, try to get raw milk from a local farmer. If you don't know of one near you, visit realmilk.com/where.html for a listing of raw milk suppliers in your state. You can use homogenized milk, but it will produce weaker curds and a milder flavor. If your milk is pasteurized, you'll need to "ripen" it by heating it in a double boiler until it reaches 86°F and then adding 1 cup of unpasteurized, preservative-free, cultured buttermilk per gallon of milk and letting it stand 30 minutes to three hours (the longer you leave it, the sharper the flavor will be). If you cannot find unpasteurized buttermilk, diluting ⅛ teaspoon calcium chloride (available from online cheesemaker suppliers) in ¼ cup of water and adding it to your milk will create a similar effect.

Rennet (also called rennin or chymosin) is sold online at cheesemaking sites in tablet or liquid form. You may also be able to find Junket rennet tablets near the pudding and gelatin in your grocery store. One teaspoon of liquid rennet is the equivalent of one rennet tablet, which is enough to turn 5 gallons of milk into cheese (estimate four drops of liquid rennet per gallon of milk). Microbial rennet is a vegetarian alternative that is available for purchase online.

Preparation

It's important to keep your hands clean and all equipment sterile when making cheese.

1. Wash hands and all equipment with soapy detergent before and after use.
2. Rinse all equipment with clean water, removing all soapy residue.
3. Boil all cheesemaking equipment between uses.
4. For best-quality cheese, use new cheesecloth each time you make cheese. (Sterilize cheesecloth by first washing, then boiling.)
5. Squeaky clean is clean. If you can feel a residue on the equipment, it is not clean.

Yogurt Cheese

This soft cheese has a flavor similar to sour cream and a texture like cream cheese. A pint of yogurt will yield approximately ¼ pound of cheese. The yogurt cheese has a shelf life of approximately seven to 14 days when wrapped and placed in the refrigerator and kept at less than 40°F.

Ingredients
Plain, whole-milk yogurt

Directions
1. Line a large strainer or colander with cheesecloth.
2. Place the lined strainer over a bowl and pour in the yogurt. Do not use yogurt made with the addition of gelatin, as gelatin will inhibit whey separation.
3. Let yogurt drain overnight, covered with plastic wrap. Empty the whey from the bowl.
4. Fill a strong, plastic storage bag with some water, seal, and place over the cheese to weigh it down. Let the cheese stand another 8 hours and then enjoy!

Queso Blanco

Queso blanco is a white, semi-hard cheese made without culture or rennet. It is eaten fresh and may be flavored with peppers, herbs, and spices. It is considered a "frying cheese," meaning it does not melt and may be deep-fried or grilled. *Queso blanco* is best eaten fresh, so try this small recipe the first time you make it. If it disappears quickly, next time double or triple the recipe. This recipe will yield about ½ cup of cheese.

Ingredients
2 cups milk
4 tsp white vinegar
Salt
Minced jalapeño, black pepper, chives, or other herbs to taste

Directions
1. Heat milk to 176°F for 20 minutes.
2. Add vinegar slowly to the hot milk until the whey is semi-clear and the curd particles begin to form stretchy clumps. Stir for 5 to 10 minutes. When it's ready, you should be able to stretch a piece of curd about ⅓ inch before it breaks.
3. Allow to cool, and strain off the whey by filtering through a cheesecloth-lined colander or a cloth bag.
4. Work in salt and spices to taste.
5. Press the curd in a mold or simply leave in a ball.
6. *Queso blanco* may keep for several weeks if stored in a refrigerator, but is best eaten fresh.

Ricotta Cheese

Making ricotta is very similar to making *queso blanco*, though it takes a bit longer. Start the cheese in the morning for use at dinner, or make a day ahead. Use it in lasagna, in desserts, or all on its own.

Ingredients
1 gallon milk
⅓ cup plus 1 tsp white vinegar
¼ tsp salt

Directions
1. Pour milk into a large pot, add salt, and heat slowly while stirring until the milk reaches 180°F.
2. Remove from heat and add vinegar. Stir for one minute as curds begin to form.
3. Cover and allow to sit undisturbed for two hours.
4. Pour mixture into a colander lined with cheesecloth, and allow to drain for two or more hours.
5. Store in a sealed container for up to a week.

Mozzarella

This mild cheese will make your homemade pizza especially delicious. Or slice it and eat with fresh tomatoes and basil from the garden. Fresh cheese can be stored in saltwater but must be eaten within two days.

Ingredients
1 gallon 2 percent milk
¼ cup fresh, plain yogurt (see recipe on page 130)
One tablet rennet or 1 tsp liquid rennet dissolved in ½ cup tap water
Brine: use 2 pounds of salt per gallon of water

Directions
1. Heat milk to 90°F and add yogurt. Stir slowly for 15 minutes while keeping the temperature constant.
2. Add rennet mixture and stir for 3 to 5 minutes.
3. Cover, remove from heat, and allow to stand until coagulated, about 30 minutes.
4. Cut curd into ½-inch cubes. Allow to stand for 15 minutes with occasional stirring.
5. Return to heat and slowly increase temperature to 118°F over a period of 45 minutes. Hold this temperature for an additional 15 minutes.
6. Drain off the whey by transferring the mixture to a cheesecloth-lined colander. Use a spoon to press the liquid out of the curds. Transfer the mat of curd to a flat pan that can be kept warm in a low oven. Do not cut mat, but turn it over every 15 minutes for a 2-hour period. Mat should be tight when finished.
7. Cut the mat into long strips 1 to 2 inches wide and place in hot water (180°F). Using wooden spoons, tumble and stretch it under water until it becomes elastic, about 15 minutes.
8. Remove curd from hot water and shape it by hand into a ball or a loaf, kneading in the salt. Place cheese in cold water (40°F) for approximately 1 hour.
9. Store in a solution of 2 teaspoons salt to 1 cup water.

Cheddar Cheese

Cheddar is a New England and Wisconsin favorite. The longer you age it, the sharper the flavor will be. Try a slice with a wedge of homemade apple pie.

Ingredients
1 gallon milk
¼ cup buttermilk
1 tablet rennet, or 1 tsp liquid rennet
1½ tsp salt

Directions
1. Combine milk and buttermilk and allow the mixture to ripen overnight.
2. The next day, heat milk to 90°F in a double boiler and add rennet.
3. After about 45 minutes, cut curds into small cubes and let sit 15 minutes.
4. Heat very slowly to 100°F and cook for about an hour or until a cooled piece of curd will keep its shape when squeezed.
5. Drain curds and rinse out the double boiler.

6. Place a rack lined with cheesecloth inside the double boiler and spread the curds on the cloth. Cover and reheat at about 98°F for 30 to 40 minutes. The curds will become one solid mass.
7. Remove the curds, cut them into 1-inch wide strips, and return them to the pan. Turn the strips every 15 to 20 minutes for one hour.
8. Cut the strips into cubes and mix in salt.
9. Let the curds stand for 10 minutes, place them in cheesecloth, and press in a cheese press with 15 pounds for 10 minutes, then with 30 pounds for an hour.
10. Remove the cheese from the press, unwrap it, dip in warm water, and fill in any cracks.
11. Wrap again in cheesecloth and press with 40 pounds for 24 hours.
12. Remove from the press and let the cheese dry about five days in a cool, well-ventilated area, turning the cheese twice a day and wiping it with a clean cloth. When a hard skin has formed, rub with oil or seal with wax. You can eat the cheese after six weeks, but for the strongest flavor, allow cheese to age for six months or more.

Make Your Own Simple Cheese Press

1. Remove both ends of a large coffee can or thoroughly cleaned paint can, saving one end. Use an awl or a hammer and long nail to pierce the sides in several places, piercing from the inside out.
2. Place the can on a cooling rack inside a larger basin. Leave the bottom of the can in place.
3. Use a saw to cut a ¾-inch-thick circle of wood to create a "cheese follower." It should be small enough in diameter to fit easily in the can.
4. Place cheese curds in the can, and top with the cheese follower. Place several bricks wrapped in cloth or foil on top of the cheese follower to weigh down curds.
5. Once the cheese is fully pressed, remove the bricks and bottom of the can. Use the cheese follower to push the cheese out of the can.

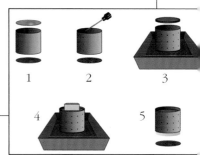

Make Your Own Ice Cream

Supplies
1-pound coffee can
3-pound coffee can
Duct tape
1 cup salt

Ingredients
2 cups half and half
½ cup sugar
1 tsp vanilla Ice

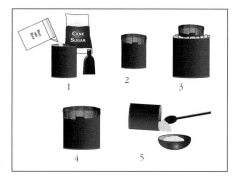

Directions

1. Mix all the ingredients in the 1-pound coffee can. Cover the lid with duct tape to ensure it is tightly sealed.
2. Place the smaller can inside the larger can and fill the space between the two with ice and salt.
3. Cover the large can and seal with duct tape. Roll the can back and forth for 15 minutes. To reduce noise, place a towel on your working surface, or work on a rug.
4. Dump out ice and water. Stir contents of small can. Store ice cream in a glass or plastic container (if you leave it in the can it may take on a metallic flavor).

If desired, add cocoa powder, coffee granules, crushed peppermint sticks or other candy, or fruit.

Brew Your Own Beer

Making your own brew is not difficult, but be sure to use water that is not heavily chlorinated or that has a strong mineral flavor. The sweetness of malt (from barley) and the bitterness of hops (the female flower of the hop vine) balance each other to create beer's rich flavor. The fermentation is caused by the yeast consuming the sugar, which produces carbon dioxide and alcohol.

Malt is barley that has begun to germinate, which creates enzymes necessary for converting starch to sugar. When you're first experimenting with brewing beer, use store-bought malt and hops, as they will have more predictable results. If you want to make your own malt, let the barley grains sprout. Once the shoots are the same length as the kernels, stop the growth by heating the barley to between 185°F and 230°F. At that point, the barley is malted and must be cracked and soaked in 150°F water for about six hours. Finally, strain the barley and use the liquid for your beer.

Supplies
10-gallon pail
Hydrometer
Siphon and clamp
12 2-liter bottles, sterilized

Ingredients
Water
40-oz can pre-hopped malt extract
6 to 7 cups white sugar or 8 to 9 cups corn sugar
1 tsp brewer's yeast
24 tsp white granulated sugar

Directions

1. Clean pail, hydrometer, and siphon with warm, soapy water and rinse thoroughly. Then sterilize by rinsing with a mix of 1 tablespoon household bleach and 1 gallon water. Rinse a final time with clean water.
2. Pour 2½ to 3 gallons cold water in the pail.
3. Bring 7½ quarts of water to a boil in a large pot. Add malt extract very slowly, stirring, and then simmer uncovered for 20 minutes.
4. Add sugar and stir until dissolved.
5. Dump the hot mixture into the pail containing the cold water, splashing it in to increase the oxygen in the liquid (yeast needs oxygen to do its job).
6. Add ice water until mixture is about 70°F (water that is too hot can kill the yeast).
7. Add the yeast and stir well.
8. Cover loosely (if the lid is too tight, the pail could explode) and allow to sit in a moderate to cool place (around 62°F to 68°F) for 6 to 10

days. Don't open the pail, tip it, or shake it for at least 6 days.

9. Place the hydrometer in the beer and give it a spin to release air bubbles. The hydrometer should read about 1.008 for dark beers and 1.010 to 1.105 for light beers.

10. When the beer is ready, place the bucket on a bench or sturdy table and place the sterilized bottles on the floor below. Add about 2 teaspoons of white granulated sugar to each bottle to help carbonate the beer.

11. Use the siphon and clamp to siphon the beer into the bottles, screw on the lids, give the bottles a quick shake, and store the bottles in a warm, dark area for a few days, and then move into cool, dark area. Store at least three weeks before drinking.

Make Your Own Wine

Supplies
Colander or strainer
Large bowl or pot
1-gallon container with a secure lid
Spoon
Potato masher
Funnel

Ingredients
1 qt fruit
2 cups sugar
1 gallon water, divided
1 package active yeast

Directions
1. Thoroughly clean all your cooking utensils with warm, soapy water and rinse thoroughly. Then sterilize by rinsing with a mix of 1 tablespoon household bleach and 1 gallon water. Rinse a final time with clean water.
2. In a bowl, crush the fruit with a potato masher (or use a food processor) until smooth.

3. Dissolve the sugar in 1 cup of hot water. Allow to cool to room temperature and add to the fruit.
4. Dissolve the yeast in 2 cups of warm water and add to the fruit, along with the remaining water. Stir once every day for a week.
5. Strain through a colander into your 1-gallon container, close lid securely, and allow to rest in a cool, dark place for 6 weeks.
6. Strain the wine into your sterilized bottles (leaving one empty) and cork lightly. After three days, strain the wine from one bottle into the empty one, leaving about 1 inch headspace below the cork. Repeat until bottles are full.
7. Soak new corks in warm water for about 2 hours, rinse several times, place securely in bottles, and seal with paraffin.

Dandelion Wine

Ingredients
4 qts dandelion blossoms (use the full dandelion heads—not just the petals)
4 qts boiling water
2 oranges
2 lemons
4 lbs sugar
2 tbsp yeast

Directions
1. Wash dandelion blossoms and place them in a large pot. Pour 4 quarts of boiling water over them and let stand 24 hours.
2. Strain through cheesecloth and add grated rind and juice of two oranges and two lemons, four pounds of granulated sugar, and two tablespoonfuls yeast.
3. Let stand one week, then strain and fill bottles.

PART THREE   The Backyard Farm

The prospect of raising farm animals in your backyard does not need to be overwhelming. If you're concerned about not having enough land, keep in mind that a few chickens can be raised on less than an eighth of an acre; you may be able to have a beehive on your rooftop; and a couple of goats or sheep will be perfectly content on a quarter of an acre. Worried about the cost? With chickens, the small amount you will invest in buying chicks will quickly pay itself back in fresh eggs or meat, and since chicken feed is very inexpensive, the upkeep costs are minimal. If you sheer your sheep or llamas, you can spin the wool and sell it at a local market or online to make a profit. However, if time is your concern, you should stop to think before purchasing animals or rescuing them from shelters. Any animal you bring onto your property deserves a portion of your time every day. You certainly don't have to spend every waking moment with your animals, but you will need to provide food, water, shelter, and a few other necessities. If you don't have the time for this on a regular basis, consider helping out at a local farm or shelter, or simply support other farmers by shopping at farmer's markets. If you do have the time to care properly for animals, very often you will find that they give you far more than you give them.

Chickens

Raising chickens in your yard will give you access to fresh eggs and meat, and because chickens are some of the easiest creatures to keep, even families in very urban areas are able to raise a few in a small backyard. Four or five chickens will supply your whole family with eggs on a regular basis.

Housing Your Chickens

You will need to have a structure for your chickens to live in to protect them from predators and inclement weather, and to allow the hens a safe place to lay their eggs. See "Poultry Houses" on page 175 to see several types of structures you can make for housing chickens and other poultry.

Placing your henhouse close enough to your own home will remind you to visit it frequently to feed the chickens and to gather eggs. It is best to establish the house and yard in dry soil, away from areas in your yard that are frequently damp or moist, as this is the perfect breeding ground for poultry diseases. The henhouse should be well-ventilated, warm, protected from the cold and rain, have a few windows that allow the sunlight to shine in (especially if you live in a colder climate), and have a sound roof.

The perches in your henhouse should not be more than 2½ feet above the floor, and you should place a smooth platform under the perches to catch the droppings so they can easily be cleaned. Nesting boxes should be kept in a darker part of the house and should have ample space around them.

The perches in your henhouse can be relatively narrow and shouldn't be more than a few feet from the floor.

Selecting the Right Breed of Chicken

Take the time to select chickens that are well-suited for your needs. If you want chickens solely for their eggs, look for chickens that are good egg-layers. Mediterranean poultry are good for first-time chicken owners as they are easy to care for and only need the proper food to lay many eggs. If you are looking to slaughter and eat your chickens, you will want to have heavy-bodied fowl (Asiatic poultry) in order to get the most meat from them. If you are looking to have chickens that lay a good amount of eggs and that can also be used for meat, invest in the Wyandottes or Plymouth Rock breeds. These chickens are not incredibly bulky but they are good sources of both eggs and meat.

Wyandottes have seven distinct breeds: Silver, White, Buff, Golden, and Black are the most common. These breeds are hardy and they are very popular in the United States. They are compactly built and lay excellent dark brown eggs. They are good sitters and their meat is perfect for broiling or roasting.

Plymouth Rock chickens have three distinct breeds: Barred, White, and Buff. They are the most popular breeds in the United States and are hardy birds that grow to a medium size. These chickens are good for laying eggs, roost well, and also provide good meat.

Plymouth rock chickens are good all-around farm chickens with their docile dispositions, hardiness, tendency to be very productive egg-layers, and good meat.

Building a chicken coop close to your house will make it easier to tend the chickens and gather eggs in inclement weather.

Feeding Your Chickens

Chickens, like most creatures, need a balanced diet of protein, carbohydrates, vitamins, fats, minerals, and water. Chickens with plenty of access to grassy areas will find most of what they need on their own. However, if you don't have the space to allow your chickens to roam free, commercial chicken feed is readily available in the form of mash, crumbles, pellets, or scratch. Or you

A simple movable chicken coop can be constructed out of two-by-fours and two wheels. The floor of the coop should have open slats so that the manure will fall onto the ground and fertilize the soil. An even simpler method is to construct a pen that sits directly on the ground, making sure that it has a roof to offer the chickens suitable shade. The pen can be moved once the area is well-fertilized.

can make your own feed out of a combination of grains, seeds, meat scraps or protein-rich legumes, and a gritty substance such as bone meal, limestone, oyster shell, or granite (to aid digestion, especially in winter). The correct ratio of food for a warm, secure chicken should be 1 part protein to 4 parts carbohydrates. Do not rely too heavily on corn as it can be too fattening for hens; combine corn with wheat or oats for the carbohydrate portion of the feed. Clover and other green foods are also beneficial to feed your chickens.

How much food your chickens need will depend on breed, age, the season, and how much room they have to exercise. Often it's easiest and best for the chickens to leave feed available at all times in several locations within the chickens' range. This will ensure that even the lowest chickens in the pecking order get the feed they need.

Wyandottes originated in the United States and were first bred in the 1870s. This one is a golden laced wyandott.

This one is a barred Plymouth rock chicken.

Chickens that are allowed to roam freely ("free-range" chickens) will be able to scavenge most of the food they need, as long as there is plenty of grass or other vegetation available.

Chicken Feed

4 parts corn (or more in cold months)

3 parts oat groats

2 parts wheat

2 parts alfalfa meal or chopped hay

1 part meat scraps, fish meal, or soybean meal

2 to 3 parts dried split peas, lentils, or soybean meal

2 to 3 parts bone meal, crushed oyster shell, granite grit, or limestone

½ part cod-liver oil

You may also wish to add sunflower seeds, hulled barley, millet, kamut, amaranth seeds, quinoa, sesame seeds, flax seeds, or kelp granules. If you find that your eggs are thin-shelled, try adding more calcium to the feed (in the form of limestone or oystershell). Store feed in a covered bucket, barrel, or other container that will not allow rodents to get into it. A plastic or galvanized bucket is good, as it will also keep mold-causing moisture out of the feed.

Hatching Chicks

If you are looking to increase the number of chickens you have, or if you plan to sell some chickens at the market, you may want your hens to lay eggs and hatch chicks. To hatch a chick, an egg must be incubated for a sufficient amount of time with the proper heat, moisture, and position. The period for incubation varies based on the species of chicken. The average incubation period is around 21 days for most common breeds.

If you are only housing a few chickens in your backyard, natural incubation is the easiest method with which to hatch chicks. Natural incubation is dependent upon the instinct of the mother hen and the breed of hen. Plymouth Rocks and Wyandottes are good hens to raise chicks. It is important to separate the setting hen from the other chickens while she is nesting and to also keep the hen clean and free from lice. The nest should also be kept clean, and the hens should be fed grain food, grit, and clean, fresh water.

A nesting box should have plenty of clean hay or straw for the hen to rest in.

Bacteria Associated with Chicken Meat

- *Salmonella*—This is primarily found in the intestinal tract of poultry and can be found in raw meat and eggs.
- *Campylobacter jejuni*—This is one of the most common causes of diarrheal illness in humans and is spread by improper handling of raw chicken meat and not cooking the meat thoroughly.
- *Listeria monocytogenes*—This causes illness in humans and can be destroyed by keeping the meat refrigerated and by cooking it thoroughly.

It is important, when you are considering hatching chicks, to make sure your hens are healthy, have plenty of exercise, and are fed a balanced diet. They need materials on which to scratch and should not be infested with lice and other parasites. Free-range chickens, which eat primarily natural foods and get lots of exercise, lay more fertile eggs than do tightly confined hens. The eggs selected for hatching should not be more than 12 days old and they should be clean.

You'll need to construct a nesting box for the roosting hen and the incubated eggs. The box should be roomy and deep enough to retain the nesting material. Treat the box with a disinfectant before use to keep out lice, mice, and other creatures that could infect the hen or the eggs.

Make the nest of damp soil a few inches deep, placed in the bottom of the box, and then lay sweet hay or clean straw on top of that.

Place the nesting box in a quiet and secluded place away from the other chickens. If space permits, you can construct a smaller shed in which to house your nesting hen. A hen can generally sit on anywhere between 9 and 15 eggs. The hen should only be allowed to leave the nest to feed, drink water, and take a dust bath. When the hen does leave her box, check the eggs and dispose of any damaged ones. An older hen will generally be more careful and apt to roost than a younger female.

Once the chicks are hatched, they will need to stay warm and clean, get lots of exercise, and have access to food regularly. Make sure the feed is ground finely enough that the chicks can easily eat and digest it. They should also have clean, fresh water.

If an egg breaks, use it immediately or discard it. Once the egg is exposed to the air it spoils much more quickly

Storing Eggs

Eggs are among the most nutritious foods on earth and can be part of a healthy diet. Hens typically lay eggs every 25 hours, so you can be sure to have a fresh supply on a daily basis, in many cases. But eggs, like any other animal byproduct, need to be handled safely and carefully to avoid rotting and spreading disease. Here are a few tips on how to best preserve your farm-fresh eggs:

1. Make sure your eggs come from hens that have not been running with male roosters. Infertile eggs last longer than those that have been fertilized.
2. Keep the fresh eggs together.
3. Choose eggs that are perfectly clean.
4. Make sure not to crack the shells, as this will taint the taste and make the egg rot much more quickly.
5. Place your eggs directly in the refrigerator where they will keep for several weeks.

Wash fresh eggs and then refrigerate them immediately.

Ducks

Ducks tend to be somewhat more difficult than chicks to raise, but they do provide wonderful eggs and meat. Ducks tend to have pleasanter personalities than chickens and are often prolific layers. The eggs taste similar to chicken eggs, but are usually larger and have a slightly richer flavor. Ducks are happiest and healthiest when they have access to a pool or pond to paddle around in and when they have several other ducks to keep them company.

Breeds of Ducks

There are six common breeds of ducks: White Pekin, White Aylesbury, Colored Rouen, Black Cayuga, Colored Muscovy, and White Muscovy. Each breed is unique and has its own advantages and disadvantages.

1. White Pekin—The most popular breed of duck, these are also the easiest to raise. These ducks are hardy and do well in close confinement. They are timid and must be handled carefully. Their large frame gives them lots of meat, and they are also prolific layers.
2. White Aylesbury—This breed is similar to the Pekin but the plumage is much whiter and they are a bit heavier than the former. They are not as popular in the United States as the White Pekin duck.
3. Colored Rouens—These darkly plumed ducks are also quite popular and fatten easily for meat purposes.
4. Black Cayuga and Muscovy breeds—These are American breeds that are easily raised but are not as productive as the White Pekin.

Housing Ducks

You neither need a lot of space in which to raise ducks nor do you need water to raise them successfully, though they will be happier if you can provide at least a small pool of water for them to bathe and paddle around in. Housing for ducks is relatively simple. The houses do not have to be as warm or dry as for chickens but the ducks cannot be confined for as long periods as chickens

Ducks are social birds; they are happiest in groups.

White Pekins were originally bred from the Mallard in China and came to the United States in 1873.

Ducks should have access to a lake, pond, or at least a small pool.

can. They need more exercise out-of-doors to be healthy and to produce more eggs. A house that is protected from dampness or excess rain water and that has straw or hay covering the floor is adequate for ducks. If you want to keep your ducks somewhat confined, a small fence about 2½ feet high will do the trick. Ducks don't require nesting boxes, as they lay their eggs on the floor of the house or in the yard around the house.

Feeding and Watering Ducks

Ducks require plenty of fresh water to drink, as they have to drink regularly while eating. Ducks eat both vegetable

According to Mrs. Beeton in her *Book of Household Management*, published in 1861, "[Aylesbury ducks'] snowy plumage and comfortable comportment make it a credit to the poultry-yard, while its broad and deep breast, and its ample back, convey the assurance that your satisfaction will not cease at its death."

and animal foods. If allowed to roam free and to find their own foodstuff, ducks will eat grasses, small fish, and water insects (if streams or ponds are provided).

Ducks need their food to be soft and mushy in order for them to digest it. Ducklings should be fed equal parts corn meal, wheat bran, and flour for the first week of life. For the next fifty days or so, the ducklings should be fed that mixture in addition to a little grit or sand and some green foods (green rye, oats, clover) all mixed together. After this time, ducks should be fed on a mixture of two parts cornmeal, one part wheat bran, one part flour, some coarse sand, and green foods.

Hatching Ducklings

The natural process of incubation (hatching ducklings underneath a hen) is the preferred method of hatching ducklings. It is important to take good care of the setting hen. Feed her whole corn mixed with green food, grit,

A Black Cayuga (right) stands with two Saxony ducks.

and fresh water. Placing the feed and water just in front of the nest for the first few days will encourage the hen to eat and drink without leaving the nest. Hens will typically lay their eggs on the ground, in straw or hay that is provided for them. Make sure to clean the houses and pens often so the laying ducks have clean areas in which to incubate their eggs.

Caring for Ducklings

Young ducklings are very susceptible to atmospheric changes. They must be kept warm and from getting chilled. The ducklings are most vulnerable during the first three weeks of life; after that time, they are more

likely to thrive to adulthood. Construct brooders for the young ducklings and keep them very warm by hanging strips of cloth over the door cracks. After three weeks in the warm brooder, move the ducklings to a cold brooder as they can now withstand fluctuating temperatures.

Common Diseases

On a whole, ducks are not as prone to the typical poultry diseases, and many of the diseases they do contract can be prevented by making sure the ducks have a clean environment in which to live (by cleaning out their houses, providing fresh drinking water, and so on).

Two common ailments found in ducks are botulism and maggots. Botulism causes the duck's neck to go limp, making it difficult or even impossible for the duck to swallow. Maggots infest the ducks if they do not have any clean water in which to bathe, and are typically contracted in the hot summer months. Both of these conditions (as well as worms and mites) can be cured with the proper care, medications, and veterinary assistance.

Turkeys

Turkeys are generally raised for their meat (especially for holiday roasts) though their eggs can also be eaten. Turkeys are incredibly easy to manage and raise as they primarily subsist on bugs, grasshoppers, and wasted grain that they find while wandering around the yard. They are, in a sense, self-sustaining foragers.

If you are looking to raise a turkey for Thanksgiving dinner, it is best to hatch the turkey chick in early spring, so that by November, it will be about 14 to 20 pounds.

Breeds of Turkeys

The largest breeds of turkeys found in the United States are the Bronze and Narragansett. Other breeds, though not as popular, include the White Holland, Black turkey, Slate turkey, and Bourbon Red.

Bronze breeds are most likely a cross between a wild North American turkey and domestic turkey, and they have beautiful rich plumage. This is the most common type of turkey to raise, as it is the largest, is very hardy, and is the most profitable. The White Holland and Bourbon Red, however, are said to be the most "domesticated" in their habits and are easier to keep in a smaller roaming area.

Housing Turkeys

Turkeys flourish when they can roost in the open. They thrive in the shelter of trees, though this can become problematic as they are more vulnerable to predators than if they are confined in a house. If you do build a house for them, it should be airy, roomy, and very clean.

It is important to allow turkeys freedom to roam; if you live in a more suburban or neighborhood area, raising turkeys may not be the best option

What Do Turkeys Eat?

Turkeys gain most of their sustenance from foraging, either in lawns or in pastures. They typically eat green vegetation, berries, weed seeds, waste grain, nuts, and various kinds of acorns. In the summer months, turkeys especially like to eat grasshoppers. Due to their love of eating insects that can damage crops and gardens, turkeys are quite useful in keeping your growing produce free from harmful insects and parasites.

Turkeys may be fed grain (similar to a mixture given to chickens) if they are going to be slaughtered, in order to make them larger.

for you, as your turkeys may wander into a neighboring yard, upsetting your neighbors. Turkeys need lots of exercise to be healthy and vigorous. When turkeys are confined for long periods of time, it is more difficult to regulate their feeding (turkeys are natural foragers and thrive best on natural foods), and they are more likely to contract disease than if they are allowed to range freely.

Hatching Turkey Chicks

Turkey hens lay eggs in the middle of March to the first of April. If you are looking to hatch and raise turkey chicks, it is vital to watch the hen closely for when she lays the eggs, and then gather them and keep the eggs warm until the weather is more stable. Turkey hens generally aim to hide their nests from predators. It is best, for the hen's sake, to provide her with a coop of some sort, which she can freely enter and leave. Or, if no coop is available, encourage the hen to lay her eggs in a nest close to your house (putting a large barrel on its side and heaping up brush near the house may entice the hen to nest there). This way, you can keep an eye on the eggs and hatchlings.

Hens are well-adapted to hatch all of the eggs that they lay. It takes 27 to 29 days for turkey eggs to hatch. While the hens are incubating the eggs, they should be given adequate food and water, placed close to their nest. Wheat and corn are the best food during the laying and incubation period.

Raising the Poults

Turkey chicks, also known as "poults," can be difficult to raise and require lots of care and attention for their first few weeks of life. In this sense, a turkey raiser must be "on call" to come to the aid of the hen and her poults at any time during the day for the first month or so. Many times, the hens can raise the poults well, but it is important that they receive enough food and warmth in the early weeks to allow them to grow healthy and strong. The poults should stay dry, as they become chilled

easily. If you are able, encouraging the poults and their mother into a coop until the poults are stronger will aid their growth to adulthood.

Poults should be fed soft and easily digestible foods. Stale bread, dipped in milk and then dried until it crumbles, is an excellent source of food for the young turkeys.

Diseases

Turkeys are hardy birds but they are susceptible to a few debilitating or fatal diseases. It is a fact that the mortality rate among young turkeys, even if they are given all the care and exercise and food needed, is relatively high (usually due to environmental and predatory factors).

The most common disease in turkeys is blackhead. Blackhead typically infects young turkeys between 6 weeks and 4 months old. This disease will turn the head darker colored or even black and the bird will become very weak, will stop eating, and will have an insatiable thirst. Blackhead is usually fatal.

Another disease that turkeys occasionally contract is roup. Roup generally occurs when a turkey has been exposed to extreme dampness or cold drafts for long periods of time. Roup causes the turkey's head to swell around the eyes and is highly contagious to other turkeys. Nutritional roup is caused by a vitamin A deficiency, which can be alleviated by adding vitamin A to the turkey's drinking water. It is best to consult a veterinarian if your turkey seems to have this disease.

Slaughtering Poultry

If you are raising your own poultry, you may decide that you'd like to use them for consumption as well. Slaughtering your own poultry enables you to know exactly what is in the meat you and your family are consuming, and to ensure that the poultry is kept humanely before being slaughtered. Here are some guidelines for slaughtering poultry:

1. To prepare a fowl for slaughter, make sure the bird is secured well so it is unable to move (either hanging down from a pole or laid on a block that is used for chopping wood).
2. Killing the fowl can be done in two ways: one way is to hang the bird upside down and to cut the jugular vein with a sharp knife. It is a good idea to have a funnel or vessel available to collect the draining blood so it does not make a mess and can be disposed of easily. The other option is to place the bird's head on a chopping block and then, in one clean movement, chop its head off at the middle of the neck. Then, hang the bird upside down and let the blood drain as described earlier.
3. Once the bird has been thoroughly drained of blood, you can begin to pluck it. Have a pot of hot water (around 140 degrees Fahrenheit) ready, into which to dip the bird. Holding the bird by the feet, dip it into the pot of hot water and leave it for about 45 seconds—you do not want the bird to begin to cook! Then, remove the bird from the pot and begin plucking immediately. The feathers should come off fairly easily, but this process takes time, so be patient. Discard the feathers.
4. Once the bird has been completely rid of feathers, slip back the skin from the neck and cut the neck off close to the base of the body. Remove the crop, trachea, and esophagus from the bird by loosening them and pulling them out through the hole created by chopping off the neck. Cut off the vent to release the main entrails (being careful not to puncture the intestines or bacteria could be released into the meat) and make a horizontal slit about an inch above it so you can insert two fingers. Remove the entrails, liver (carefully cutting off the gallbladder), gizzard, and heart from the bird and set the last three aside if you want to eat them later or make them into stuffing. If you are going to save the heart, slip off the membrane enclosing it and cut off the veins and arteries. Make sure to clean out the gizzard as well if you will be using it later.
5. Wash the bird thoroughly, inside and out, and wipe it dry.
6. Cut off the feet below the joints and then carefully pull out the tendons from the drumsticks.
7. Once the carcass is thoroughly dry and clean, store it in the refrigerator if it will be used that same day or the next. If you want to save the bird for later use, place it in a moisture-proof bag and set it in the freezer (along with any innards that you may have saved).
8. Make sure you clean and disinfect any surface you were working on to avoid the spread of bacteria and other diseases.

Beekeeping

Beekeeping (also known as apiculture) is one of the oldest human industries. For thousands of years, honey has been considered a highly desirable food. Beekeeping is a science and can be a very profitable occupation it is also a wonderful hobby for many people in the United States. Keeping bees can be done almost anywhere—on a farm, in a rural or suburban area, and even in urban areas (even on rooftops!). Anywhere there are sufficient flowers from which to collect nectar, bees can thrive.

Apiculture relies heavily on the natural resources of a particular location and the knowledge of the beekeeper in order to be successful. Collecting and selling honey at your local farmers' market or just to family and friends can supply you with some extra cash if you are looking to make a profit from your apiary.

Why Raise Bees?

Bees are essential in the pollination and fertilization of many fruit and seed crops. If you have a garden with many flowers or fruit plants, having bees nearby will only help your garden flourish and grow year after year. Furthermore, nothing is more satisfying than extracting your own honey for everyday use.

How to Avoid Getting Stung

Though it takes some skill, you can learn how to avoid being stung by the bees you keep. Here are some ways you can keep your bee stings to a minimum:

1. Keep gentle bees. Having bees that, by sheer nature, are not as aggressive will reduce the number of stings you are likely to receive. Carniolan bees are one of the gentlest species, and so are the Caucasian bees introduced from Russia.
2. Obtain a good "smoker" and use it whenever you'll be handling your bees. Pumping smoke of any kind into and around the beehive will render your bees less aggressive and less likely to sting you.
3. Purchase and wear a veil. This should be made out of black bobbinet and worn over your face. Also, rubber gloves help protect your hands from stings.
4. Use a "bee escape." This device is fitted into a slot made in a board the same size as the top of the hive. Slip the board into the hive before you open it to extract the honey, and it allows the worker bees to slip below it but not to return back up. So, by placing the "bee escape" into the hive the day before you want to gain access to the combs and honey, you will most likely trap all the bees under the board and leave you free to work with the honeycombs without fear of stings.

Wearing a hat and veil will help to prevent stings on your face and head.

A smoker will help to relax your bees and make them less agressive.

What Type of Hive Should I Build?

Most beekeepers would agree that the best hives have suspended, movable frames where the bees make the honeycombs, which are easy to lift out. These frames, called Langstroth frames, are the most popular kind of frame used by apiculturists in the United States.

Whether you build your own beehive or purchase one, it should be built strongly and should contain accurate bee spaces and a close-fitting, rainproof roof. If you are looking to have honeycombs, you must have a hive that permits the insertion of up to eight combs.

Where Should the Hive Be Situated?

Hives and their stands should be placed in an enclosure where the bees will not be disturbed by other animals or humans and where it will be generally quiet. Hives should be placed on their own stands at least 3 feet from each other. Do not allow weeds to grow near the hives and keep the hives away from walls and fences. You, as the beekeeper, want to be able to easily access your hive without fear of obstacles.

Swarming

Swarming is simply the migration of honeybees to a new hive and is led by the queen bee. During swarming season (the warm summer days), a beekeeper must remain very alert. If you see swarming above the hive, take great care and act calmly and quietly. You want to get the swarm into your hive, but this will be tricky. It they land on a nearby branch or in a basket, simply approach and then "pour" them into the hive. Keep in mind that bees will more likely inhabit a cool, shaded hive than one that is baking in the hot summer sun.

Sometimes it is beneficial to try to prevent swarming, such as if you already have completely full hives Frequently removing the new honey from the hive before swarming begins will deter the bees from swarming. Shading the hives on warm days will also help keep the bees from swarming.

Bee Pastures

Bees will fly a great distance to gather food but you should try to contain them, as well as possible, to an area within 2 miles of the beehive. Make sure they have access to many honey-producing plants that you can grow in your garden. Alfalfa, asparagus, buckwheat, chestnut, clover, catnip, mustard, raspberry, roses, and sunflowers are some of the best honey-producing plants and trees. Also make sure that your bees always have access to pure, clean water.

Preparing Your Bees for Winter

If you live in a colder region of the United States, keeping your bees alive throughout the winter months is difficult. If your queen bee happens to die in the fall, before

Frame from a healthy beehive.

Raw honey is an anti-bacterial, anti-uiral, and anti-fungal substance—besides being delicious.

Bees thrive on sweet flowers, such as clover.

a young queen can be reared, your whole colony will die throughout the winter. However, the queen's death can be avoided by taking simple precautions and giving careful attention to your hive come autumn.

Colonies are usually lost in the winter months due to insufficient winter food storages, faulty hive construction, lack of protection from the cold and dampness, not enough or too much ventilation, or too many older bees and not enough young ones.

If you live in a region that gets a few weeks of severe weather, you may want to move your colony indoors, or at least to an area that is protected from the outside elements. But the essential components of having a colony survive through the winter season are to have a good queen; a fair ratio of healthy, young, and old bees; and a plentiful supply of food. The hive needs to retain a liberal supply of ripened honey and a thick syrup made from white cane sugar (you should feed this to your bees early enough so they have time to take the syrup and seal it over before winter).

To make this syrup, dissolve 3 pounds of granulated sugar in 1 quart of boiling water and add 1 pound of pure extracted honey to this. If you live in an extremely cold area, you may need up to 30 pounds of this syrup, depending on how many bees and hives you have. You can either use a top feeder or a frame feeder, which fits inside the hive in the place of a frame. Fill the frame with the syrup and place sticks or grass in it to keep the bees from drowning.

Extracting Honey

To obtain the extracted honey, you'll need to keep the honeycombs in one area of the hive or packed one above the other. Before removing the filled combs, you should allow the bees ample time to ripen and cap the honey. To uncap the comb cells, simply use a sharp knife (apiary suppliers sell knives specifically for this purpose). Then put the combs in a machine called a honey extractor to extract the honey. The honey extractor whips the honey out of the cells and allows you to replace the fairly undamaged comb into the hive to be repaired and refilled.

The extracted honey runs into open buckets or vats and is left, covered with a tea towel or larger cloth, to stand for a week. It should be in a warm, dry room where no ants can reach it. Skim the honey each day until it is perfectly clear. Then you can put it into cans, jars, or bottles for selling or for your own personal use.

Making Beeswax

Beeswax from the honeycomb can be used for making candles, can be added to lotions or lip balm, and can even be used in baking. Rendering wax in boiling water is especially simple when you only have a small apiary.

Collect the combs, break them into chunks, roll them into balls if you like, and put them in a muslin bag. Put the bag with the beeswax into a large stockpot and bring the water to a slow boil, making sure the bag doesn't rest on the bottom of the pot and burn. The muslin will act as a strainer for the wax. Use clean, sterilized tongs to occasionally squeeze the bag. After the wax is boiled out of the bag, remove the pot from the heat and allow it to cool. Then, remove the wax from the top of the water and then re-melt it in another pot on very low heat, so it doesn't burn.

Pour the melted wax into molds lined with wax paper or plastic wrap and then cool it before using it to make other items or selling it at your local farmers' market.

Extra Beekeeping Tips

General Tips

1. Clip the old queen's wings and go through the hives every 10 days to destroy queen cells to prevent swarming.
2. Always act and move calmly and quietly when handling bees.

Bees live off of the honey stored in the combs. In winter months they need a supply of ripe honey and benefit from extra sugary syrup.

A beekeeper carefully removes frames from the hive.

3. Keep the hives cool and shaded. Bees won't enter a hot hive.

When Opening the Hive

1. Have a smoker ready to use if you desire.
2. Do not stand in front of the hive while the bees are entering and exiting.
3. Do not drop any tools into the hive while it's open.
4. Do not run if you become frightened.

5. If you are attacked, move away slowly and smoke the bees off yourself as you retreat.
6. Apply ammonia or a paste of baking soda and water immediately to any bee sting to relieve the pain. You can also scrape the area of the bee sting with your fingernail or the dull edge of a knife immediately after the sting.

When Feeding Your Bees

1. Keep a close watch over your bees during the entire season, to see if they are feeding well or not.
2. Feed the bees during the evening.

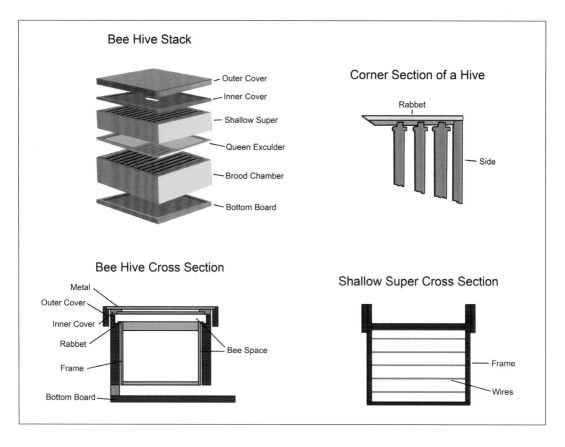

Bee Hive Stack

- Outer Cover
- Inner Cover
- Shallow Super
- Queen Exculder
- Brood Chamber
- Bottom Board

Corner Section of a Hive

Rabbet

Side

Bee Hive Cross Section

- Metal
- Outer Cover
- Inner Cover
- Rabbet
- Frame
- Bottom Board
- Bee Space

Shallow Super Cross Section

- Frame
- Wires

3. Make sure the bees have ample water near their hive, especially in the spring.

Making a Beehive

The most important parts of constructing a beehive are to make it simple and sturdy. Just a plain box with a few frames and a couple of other loose parts will make a successful beehive that will be easy to use and manipulate. It is crucial that your beehive be well-adapted to the nature of bees and also the climate in which you live. Framed hives usually suffice for the beginning beekeeper. Below is a diagram of a simple beehive that you can easily construct for your backyard beekeeping purposes.

Goats

Goats provide us with milk and wool and thrive in arid, semitropical, and mountainous environments. In the more temperate regions of the world, goats are raised as supplementary animals, providing milk and cheese for families and acting as natural weed killers.

Breeds of Goats

There are many different types of goats. Some breeds are quite small (weighing roughly 20 pounds) and some are very large (weighing up to 250 pounds). Depending on the breed, goats may have horns that are corkscrew in shape, though many domestic goats are dehorned early on to lessen any potential injuries to humans or other goats. The hair of goats can also differ—various breeds have short hair, long hair, curly hair, silky hair, or coarse hair. Goats come in a variety of colors (solid black, white, brown, or spotted).

Feeding Goats

Goats can sustain themselves on bushes, trees, shrubs, woody plants, weeds, briars, and herbs. Pasture is the lowest-cost feed available for goats, and allowing goats to graze in the summer months is a wonderful and economic way to keep goats, even if your yard is small. Goats thrive best when eating alfalfa or a mixture of clover and timothy. If you have a lawn and a few goats, you don't need a lawn mower if you plant these types of plants for your goats to eat. The one drawback to this is that your goats (depending on how many you own) may quickly deplete these natural resources, which can cause weed growth and erosion. Supplementing pasture feed with other food-stuff, such as greenchop, root crops, and wet brewery grains will ensure that your yard does not become overgrazed and that your goats remain well-fed and healthy. It is also beneficial to supply your goats with unlimited access to hay while they are grazing. Make sure that your goats have easy access to shaded areas and fresh water, and offer a-salt-and mineral mix on occasion.

Six Major U.S. Goat Breeds

Alpine—Originally from Switzerland, these goats may have horns, are short haired, and are usually white and black in color. They are also good producers of milk.

Alpine goat

Anglo-Nubian—A cross between native English goats and Indian and Nubian breeds, these goats have droopy ears, spiral horns, and short hair. They are quite tall and do best in warmer climates. They do not produce as much milk, though it is much higher in fat than other goats'. They are the most popular breed of goat in the United States.

Anglo-Nubian goat

LaMancha—A cross between Spanish Murciana and Swiss and Nubian breeds, these goats are extremely adaptable, have straight noses, short hair, may have horns, and do not have external ears. They are not as good milk producers as the Saanen and Toggenburg breeds, and their milk fat content is much higher.

La Mancha goats

Pygmy—Originally from Africa and the Caribbean, these dwarfed goats thrive in hotter climates. For their size, they are relatively good producers of milk.

Pygmy goat

Saanen—Originally from Switzerland, these goats are completely white, have short hair, and sometimes have horns. Goats of this breed are wonderful milk producers.

Saanen goat

Toggenburg—Originally from Switzerland, these goats are brown with white facial, ear, and leg stripes; have straight noses; may have horns; and have short hair. This breed is very popular in the United States. These goats are good milk producers in the summer and winter seasons and survive well in both temperate and tropical climates.

Toggenburg goat

Goats enjoy having objects to climb on.

Dry forage is another good source of feed for your goats. It is relatively inexpensive to grow or buy and consists of good quality legume hay (alfalfa or clover). Legume hay is high in protein and has many essential minerals beneficial to your goats. To make sure your forages are highly nutritious, be sure that there are many leaves that provide protein and minerals and that the forage had an early cutting date, which will allow for easier digestion of the nutrients. If your forage is green in color, it most likely contains more vitamin A, which is good for promoting goat health.

Goat Milk

Goat milk is a wonderful substitute for those who are unable to tolerate cow's milk, or for the elderly, babies, and those suffering from stomach ulcers. Milk from goats is also high in vitamin A and niacin but does not have the same amount of vitamins B6, B12, and C as cow's milk.

Lactating goats do need to be fed the best quality legume hay or green forage possible, as well as grain. Give the grain to the doe at a rate that equals ½ pound grain for every pound of milk she produces.

Common Diseases Affecting Goats

Goats tend to get more internal parasites than other herd animals. Some goats develop infectious arthritis, pneumonia, coccidiosis, scabies, liver fluke disease, and mastitis. It is advisable that you establish a relationship with a good veterinarian who specializes in small farm animals to periodically check your goats for various diseases.

Milking a Goat

Milking a goat takes some practice and patience, especially when you first begin. However, once you establish a routine and rhythm to the milking, the whole process should run relatively smoothly. The main thing to remember is to keep calm and never pull on the teat, as this will hurt the goat and she might upset the milk bucket. The goat will pick up on any anxiousness or nervousness on your part and it could affect how cooperative she is during the milking.

Supplies
- A grain bucket and grain for feeding the goat while milking is taking place
- Milking stand
- Metal bucket to collect the milk
- A stool to sit on (optional)
- A warm, sterilized wipe or cloth that has been boiled in water
- Teat dip solution (2 tbsp bleach, 1 quart water, one drop normal dish detergent mixed together)

Directions
1. Ready your milking stand by filling the grain bucket with enough grain to last throughout the entire milking. Then retrieve the goat, separating her from any other goats to avoid distractions and unsuccessful milking. Place the goat's head through the head hold of the milking stand so she can eat the grain and then close the lever so she cannot remove her head.
2. With the warm, sterilized wipe or cloth, clean the udder and teats to remove any dirt, manure, or bacteria that may be present. Then, place the metal bucket on the stand below the udder.
3. Wrap your thumb and forefinger around the base of one teat. This will help trap the milk in the teat so it can be squirted out. Then, starting with your middle finger, squeeze the three remaining fingers in one single, smooth motion to squirt the milk into the bucket. Be sure to keep a tight grip on the base of the teat so the milk stays there until extracted. Remember: The first squirt of milk from either teat should not be put into the bucket as it may contain dirt or bacteria that you don't want contaminating the milk.
4. Release the grip on the teat and allow it to refill with milk. While this is happening, you can repeat

this process on the other teat and alternate between teats to speed up the milking process.

6. When the teats begin to look empty (they will be somewhat flat in appearance), massage the udder just a little bit to see if any more milk remains. If so, squeeze it out in the same manner as above until you cannot extract much more.

7. Remove the milk bucket from the stand and then, with your teat dip mixture in a disposable cup, dip each teat into the solution and allow to air dry. This will keep bacteria and infection from going into the teat and udder.

8. Remove the goat from the milk stand and return her to the pen.

Making Cheese from Goat Milk

Most varieties of cheese that can be made from cow's milk can also be successfully made using goats' milk. Goats' milk cheese can easily be made at home. To make the cheese, however, at least one gallon of goat milk should be available. Make sure that all of your equipment is washed and sterilized (using heat is fine) before using it.

Cottage Cheese

1. Collect surplus milk that is free of strong odors. Cool it to around 40°F and keep it at that temperature until it is used.

2. Skim off any cream. Use the skim milk for cheese and the cream for cheese dressing.

3. If you wish to pasteurize your milk (which will allow it to hold better as a cheese) collect all the milk to be processed into a flat-bottomed, straight-sided pan and heat to 145°F on low heat. Hold it at this temperature for about 30 minutes and then cool to around 80°F. Use a dairy thermometer to measure the milk's temperature. Then, inoculate the cheese milk with a desirable lactic acid–fermenting bacterial culture (you can use commercial buttermilk for the initial source). Add about 7 ounces to 1 gallon of cheese milk, stir well, and let it sit undisturbed for about 10 to 16 hours, until a firm curd is formed.

4. When the curd is firm enough, cut the curd into uniform cubes no larger than ½ inch using a knife or spatula.

5. Allow the curd to sit undisturbed for a couple of minutes and then warm it slowly, stirring carefully, at a temperature no greater than 135°F. The curd should eventually become firm and free from whey.

6. When the curd is firm, remove from the heat and stop stirring. Siphon off the excess whey from the top of the pot. The curd should settle to the bottom of the container. If the curd is floating, bacteria that produces gas has been released and a new batch must be made.

7. Replace the whey with cold water, washing the curd and then draining the water. Wash again with ice-cold water to chill the curd. This will keep the flavor fresh.

8. Using a draining board, drain the excess water from the curd. Now your curd is complete.

9. To make the curd into a cottage cheese consistency, separate the curd as much as possible and mix with a milk or cream mixture containing salt to taste.

Domiati Cheese

This type of cheese is made throughout the Mediterranean region. It is eaten fresh or aged two to three months before consumption.

1. Cool a gallon of fresh, quality milk to around 105°F, adding 8 ounces of salt to the milk. Stir the salt until it is completely dissolved.

2. Pasteurize the milk as described in step 3 of the cottage cheese recipe.

3. This type of cheese is coagulated by adding a protease enzyme (rennet). This enzyme may be purchased at a local drug store, health food store, or a cheese maker in your area. Dissolve the concentrate in water, add it to the cheese milk, and stir for a few minutes. Use 1 milliliter of diluted rennet liquid in 40 milliliters of water for every 2½ gallons of cheese milk.

4. Set the milk at around 105°F. When the enzyme is completely dispersed in the cheese milk, allow the mix to sit undisturbed until it forms a firm curd.

5. When the desired firmness is reached, cut the curd into very small cubes. Allow for some whey separation. After 10 to 20 minutes, remove and reserve about ⅓ the volume of salted whey.

Cottage cheese

Damiati cheese

Feta cheese

6. Put the curd and remaining whey into cloth-lined molds (the best are rectangular stainless steel containers with perforated sides and bottom) with a cover. The molds should be between 7 and 10 inches in height. Fill the molds with the curd, fold the cloth over the top, allow the whey to drain, and discard the whey.

7. Once the curd is firm enough, apply added weight for 10 to 18 hours until it is as moist as you want.

8. Once the pressing is complete and the cheese is formed into a block, remove the molds and cut the blocks into 4-inch-thick pieces. Place the pieces in plastic containers with airtight seals. Fill the containers with reserved salted whey from step 5, covering the cheese by about an inch.

9. Place these containers at a temperature between 60°F and 65°F to cure for 1 to 4 months.

Feta Cheese

This type of cheese is very popular to make from goats' milk. The same process is used as the Domiati cheese except that salt is not added to the milk before coagulation. Feta cheese is aged in a brine solution after the cubes have been salted in a brine solution for at least 24 hours.

Angora Goats

Angora goats may be the most efficient fiber producers in the world. The hair of these goats is made into mohair: a long, lustrous hair that is woven into fine garments. Angora goats are native to Turkey and were imported to the United States in the mid-1800s. Now, the United States is one of the two biggest produces of mohair on earth.

Angora goats are typically relaxed and docile. They are delicate creatures, easily strained by their year-round fleeces. Angora goats need extra attention and are more high-maintenance than other breeds of goat. While these goats can adapt to many temperate climates, they do particularly well in the arid environment of the southwestern states.

Angora goats can be sheared twice yearly, before breeding and before birthing. The hair of the goat will grow about ¾ inch per month and it should be sheared once it reaches 4 to 6 inches in length. During the shearing process, the goat is usually lying down on a clean floor with its legs tied. When the fleece is gathered (it should be sheared in one full piece), it should be bundled into a burlap bag and should be free of contaminants. Mark your name on the bag and make sure there is only one fleece per bag. For more thorough rules and regulations about selling mohair through the government's direct-payment program, contact the USDA Agricultural Stabilization and Conservation Service online or in one of their many offices.

Shearing can be accomplished with the use of a special goat comb, which leaves ¼ inch of stubble on the goat. It is important to keep the fleeces clean and to avoid injuring the animal. The shearing seasons are in the spring and fall. After a goat has been sheared, it will be more sensitive to changes in the weather for up to six weeks. Make sure you have proper warming huts for these goats in the winter and adequate shelter from rain and inclement weather.

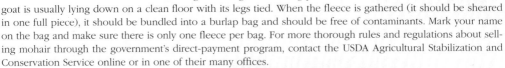

Sheep

Sheep were possibly the first domesticated animals and are now found all over the world on farms and smaller plots of land. Almost all the breeds of sheep that are found in the United States have been brought here from Great Britain. Raising sheep is relatively easy, as they only need pasture to eat, shelter from bad weather, and protection from predators. Sheep's wool can be used to make yarn or other articles of clothing and their milk can be made into various types of cheeses and yogurt, though this is not normally done in the United States.

Sheep are naturally shy creatures and are extremely docile. If they are treated well, they will learn to be affectionate with their owner. If a sheep is comfortable with its owner, it will be much easier to manage and to corral into its pen if it's allowed to graze freely. Start with only one or two sheep; they are not difficult to manage but do require a lot of attention.

Breeds of Sheep

There are many different breeds of sheep—some are used exclusively for their meat and others for their wool. Six quality wool-producing breeds are as follows:

1. Cotswold Sheep—This breed is very docile and hardy and thrives well in pastures. It produces around 14 pounds of fleece per year, making it a very profitable breed for anyone wanting to sell wool.
2. Leicester sheep—This is a hardy, docile breed of sheep that is a very good grazer. This breed has 6-inch-long, coarse wool that is desirable for knitting. It is a very popular breed in the United States.
3. Merino sheep—Introduced to the United States in the early twentieth century, this small- to medium-sized sheep has lots of rolls and folds of fine white wool and produces a fleece anywhere between 10 and 20 pounds. It is considered a fine-wool specialist, and though its fleece appears dark in color, the wool is actually white or buff. It is a wonderful foraging sheep, is hardy, and has a gentle disposition, but is not a very good milk producer.
4. Oxford Down sheep—A more recent breed, these dark-faced sheep have hardy constitutions and good fleece.
5. Shropshire sheep—This breed has longer, more open, and coarser fleece than other breeds. It is quite popular in the United States, especially in areas that are more moist and damp, as they seem to be better in these climates than other breeds of sheep.
6. Southdown sheep—One of the oldest breeds of sheep, these sheep are popular for their good quality wool and are deemed the standard of excellence for many sheep owners. Docile, hardy, and good grazing on pastures, their coarse and light-colored wool is used to make flannel.

Housing Sheep

Sheep do not require much shelter—only a small shed that is open on one side (preferably to the south so it can stay warmer in the winter months) and is roughly 6 to 8 feet high. The shelter should be ventilated well to reduce any unpleasant smells and to keep the sheep cool in the summer. Feeding racks or mangers should be placed inside of the shed to hold the feed for the sheep. If you live in a

Cotswold sheep

Merino sheep

Southdown sheep

colder region of the country, building a sturdier, warmer shed for the sheep to live in during the winter is recommended.

Straw should be used for the sheep's bedding and should be changed daily to make sure the sheep do not become ill from an unclean shelter. Especially for the winter months, a dry pen should be erected for the sheep to exercise in. The fences should be strong enough to keep out predators that may enter your yard and to keep the sheep from escaping.

What Do Sheep Eat?

Sheep generally eat grass and are wonderful grazers. They utilize rough and scanty pasturage better than other grazing animals and, due to this, they can actually be quite beneficial in cleaning up a yard that is overgrown with undesirable herbage. Allowing sheep to graze in your yard or in a small pasture field will provide them with sufficient food in the summer months. Sheep also eat a variety of weeds, briars, and shrubs. Fresh water should always be available for the sheep.

Especially during the winter months, when grass is scarce, sheep should be fed hay (alfalfa, legume, or clover hay) and small quantities of grain. Corn is also a good winter food for the sheep (it can also be mixed with wheat bran), and straw, salt, and roots can also be occasionally added to their diet. Good food during the winter season will help the sheep grow a healthier and thicker wool coat.

Shearing Sheep

Sheep are generally sheared in the spring or early summer before the weather gets too warm. To do your own shearing, invest in a quality hand shearer and a scale on which to weigh the fleece. An experienced shearer should be able to take the entire wool off in one piece.

You may want to wash the wool a few days to a week before shearing the sheep. To do so, corral the sheep into a pen on a warm spring day (make sure there isn't a cold breeze blowing and that there is a lot of sunshine so the sheep does not become chilled). Douse the sheep in warm water, scrub the wool, and rinse. Repeat this a few times until most of the dirt and debris is out of the wool. Diffuse some natural oil throughout the wool to make it softer and ready for shearing.

Leicester sheep   Shropshire sheep

Oxford down sheep

Sheer your sheep in the spring or early summer, before the weather gets hot.

The sheep should be completely dry before shearing and you should choose a warm—but not overly hot—day. If you are a beginner at shearing sheep, try to find an experienced sheep owner to show you how to properly hold and shear a sheep. This way, you won't cause undue harm to the sheep's skin and will get the best fleece possible. When you are hand-shearing a sheep, remember to keep the skin pulled taut on the part where you are shearing to decrease the potential of cutting the skin.

Once the wool is sheared, tag it and roll it up by itself, and then bind it with twine. Be sure not to fold it or bind it too tightly. Separate and remove any dirty or soiled parts of the fleece before binding, as these parts will not be able to be carded and used.

Carding and Spinning Wool

To make the sheared wool into yarn you will need only a few tools: a spinning wheel or drop spindle and wool-cards. Wool-cards are rectangular pieces of thin board that have many wire teeth attached to them (they look like coarse brushes that are sometimes used for dogs'

Wod-cards are used to soften and clean the wod fibers.

hair). To begin, you must clean the wool fleece of any debris, feltings, or other imperfections before carding it; otherwise your yarn will not spin correctly. Also wash it to remove any additional sand or dirt embedded in the wool and then allow it to dry completely. Then, all you need is to gather your supplies and follow these simple instructions:

Carding Wool

1. Grease the wool with rape oil or olive oil, just enough to work into the fibers.
2. Take one wool-card in your left hand, rest it on your knee, gather a tuft of wool from the fleece, and place it onto the wool-card so it is caught between the wired teeth of the card.

Spinning on a traditional spinning wheel

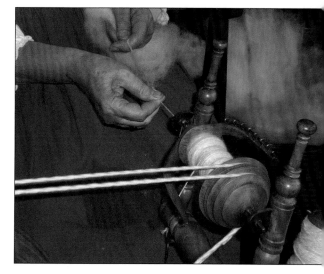

Note: If you are unable to obtain a spinning wheel of any kind, you can spin your carded wool by hand, although this will not produce the same tightness in your yarn as regular spinning. All you need to do is take the carded wool, hold it with one hand, and pull and twist the fibers into one, continuous piece. Winding the end of the yarn around a stick, spindle, or spool and securing it in place at the end will help keep your fibers tight and your yarn twisted.

If you want your yarn to be different colors, try dying it with natural berry juices or with special wool dyes found in arts and crafts stores.

Milking Sheep

Sheep's milk is not typically used in the United States for drinking, making cheese, or other familiar dairy products. Sheep do not typically produce milk year-round, as cows do, so milk will only be produced if you bred your sheep and had a lamb produced. If you do have a sheep that has given birth and the lamb has been sold or taken away, it is important to know how to milk her so her udders do not become caked. Some ewes will still have an abundance of milk even after their lambs have been weaned and this excess milk should be removed to keep the ewe healthy and her udder free from infection.

To milk an ewe, bring her rear up to a fence so she cannot step backwards and, placing two knees against her shoulders to prevent her from moving forward, reach under with both hands and squeeze the milk into a bucket. When the udder is still soft but the ewe has been partly milked out, set her loose and then milk her again a few days later. If there is still milk to be had, wait another three days and then milk her again. By milking the ewes in this manner, you can prevent their udders from becoming infected and the milk from spoiling.

Diseases

The main diseases to which sheep are susceptible are foot rot and scabs. These are contagious and both require proper treatment. Sheep may also acquire stomach worms if they eat hay that has gotten too damp or has been lying on the floor of their shelter. As always, it is best to establish a relationship with a veterinarian who is familiar with caring for sheep and have your flock regularly checked for any parasites or diseases that may arise.

3. Take the second wool-card in your right hand and bring it gently across the other card several times, making a brushing movement toward your body.

4. When the fibers are all brushed in the same direction and the wool is soft and fluffy to the touch, remove the wool by rolling it into a small, fleecy ball (roughly a foot or more in length and only 2 inches in width) and put it in a bag until it is used for spinning.

Note: Carded wool can also be used for felting, in which case no spinning is needed. To felt a small blanket, place large amounts of carded wool on either side of a burlap sack. Using felting needles, weave the wool into the burlap until it is tightly held by the jute or hemp fabrics of the burlap.

Spinning Wool

1. Take one long roll of carded wool and wind the fibers around the spindle.

2. Move the wheel gently and hold the spindle to allow the wool to "draw," or start to pull together into a single thread.

3. Keep moving the wheel and allow the yarn to wind around the spindle or a separate spool, if you have a more complex spinning wheel.

4. Keep adding rolls of carded wool to the spindle until you have the desired amount of yarn.

Llamas

Llamas make excellent pets and are a great source of wooly fiber (their wool can be spun into yarn). Llamas are being kept more and more by people in the United States as companion animals, sources of fiber, pack and light plow animals, therapy animals for the elderly, "guards" for other backyard animals, and good educational tools for children. Llamas have an even temperament and are very intelligent. Their intelligence and gentle nature make them easy to train, and their hardiness allows them to thrive well in both cold and warmer climates (although they can have heat stress in extremely hot and humid parts of the country).

Before you decide to purchase a llama or two for your yard, check your state requirements regarding livestock. In some places, your property must also be zoned for livestock.

Llamas come in many different colors and sizes. The average adult llama is between 5½ and 6 feet tall and weighs between 250 and 450 pounds. Llamas, being herd animals, like the company of other llamas, so it is advisable that you raise a pair to keep each other company. If you only want to care for one llama, then it would be best to also have a sheep, goat, or other animal that can be penned with the llama for camaraderie. Although llamas can be led well on a harness and lead, never tie one up as it could potentially break its own neck trying to break free.

Llamas tend to make their own communal dung heap in a particular part of their pen. This is quite convenient for cleanup and allows you to collect the manure, compost it, and use it as a fertilizer for your garden.

Feeding Llamas

Llamas can subsist fairly well on grass, hay (an adult male will eat about one bale per week), shrubs, and trees, much like sheep and goats. If they are not receiving enough nutrients, they may be fed a mixture of rolled corn, oats, and barley, especially during the winter season when grazing is not necessarily available. Make sure not to overfeed your llamas, though, or they will become overweight and constipated. You can occasionally give cornstalks to your llamas as an added source of fiber, and you may add mineral supplements to the feed mixture or hay if you want. Salt blocks are also acceptable to have in your llama pen, and a constant supply of fresh water is necessary. Nursing female llamas should receive a grain mixture until the cria (baby) is weaned.

Be sure to keep feed and hay off the ground. This will help ward off parasites that establish themselves in the feed and are then ingested by the llamas.

Housing Your Llamas

Llamas may be sheltered in a small stable or even a converted garage. There should be enough room to store feed and hay, and the shelter should be able to be closed off during wet, windy, and cold weather. Llamas prefer light, open spaces in which to live, so make sure your shed or shelter has large doors and/or big windows. The feeders for the hay and grain mixture should be raised above the ground. Adding a place where a llama can be safely restrained for toenail clippings and vet checkups will help facilitate these processes but is not absolutely necessary.

The llamas should be able to enter and exit the shelter easily and it is a good idea to build a fence or pen around the shelter so they do not wander off. A fence about four feet tall should be enough to keep your llamas safe and enclosed. If you happen to have both a male and female llama, it is necessary to have separate enclosures for them to stave off unwanted pregnancies.

Alpacas, like llamas, are social creatures and are happiest with other alpacas.

Toenail Trimming

Llamas need their toenails to be trimmed so they do not twist and fold under the toe, making it difficult for the llama to move around. Laying gravel in the area where your llamas frequently walk will help to keep the toenails naturally trimmed, but if you need to cut them, be careful not to cut too deeply or you may cause the tip of the toe to bleed and this could lead to an infection in the toe. Use shears designed for this purpose to cut the nails. Use one hand to hold the llama's "ankle" just above where the foot bends. Hold the clippers in your other hand, cutting away from the foot toward the tip of the nail. The nail's are easiest to clip in the early morning or after a rain, since the wetness of the ground will soften them.

Shearing

It is important to groom and shear your llama, especially during hot weather. Brushing the llama's coat to remove

Llamas enjoy hay, but keep it off the ground to help prevent your llamas from ingesting parasites.

dirt and keep it from matting will not only make your llamas look clean and healthy but it will also improve the quality of their coats. If you want to save the fibers for spinning into yarn, it is best to brush, comb, and use a hair dryer to remove any dust and debris from the llama's coat before you begin shearing.

Shearing is not necessarily difficult, but if you are a first-time llama owner, you should ask another llama farmer to teach you how to properly shear your llama. To shear your llama, you can purchase battery-operated shears to remove the fibers for sale or use. Different llamas will respond in different ways to shearing. Try holding the llama with a halter and lead in a smaller area to begin the shearing process. Do not completely remove the llama from any other llamas you have, though, as their presence will help calm the llama you are shearing. It is best to have another person with you to aid in the shearing (to hold the llama, give it treats, and offer any other help). When shearing a llama, don't shear all the way down to the skin. Allowing a thin coating of hair to cover the llama's body will help protect it from the sun and from being scratched when it rolls in the dirt.

Start by shearing a flat top the length of the llama's back. Next, taking the shears in one hand, move them in a downward position to remove the coat. Shear a strip the length of the neck from the chin to the front legs about 3 inches wide to help cool the llama. Shearing can take a long time, so it may be necessary for both you and the llama to take a break. Take the llama for a quiet walk and allow it to go to the bathroom so it will not become antsy during the rest of the shearing process.

Collect the sheared fibers in a container and make sure you are working on a clean floor so you can collect any excess fibers and use them for spinning. Do not store the fiber in a plastic bag, as moisture can easily accumulate, ruining the fiber and making it unusable for spinning.

Caring for the Cria

Baby llamas require some additional care in their first few days of life. It is important for the cria to receive the

Baby llamas and alpacas are called "Crias."

colostrum milk from their mothers, but you may need to aid in this process. Approach the mother llama and pull gently on each teat to remove the waxy plugs covering the milk holes. Sometimes, you may need to guide the cria into position under its mother for it start nursing.

Weigh the cria often (at least for the first month) to see that it's gaining weight and growing strong and healthy. A bathroom scale, hanging scale, or larger grain scale can be used for this.

If the cria seems to need extra nourishment, goat or cow milk can be substituted during times when the mother llama cannot produce enough milk for the cria. Feed this additional milk to the cria in small doses, several times a day, from a milking bottle.

Diseases

Llamas are prone to getting worms and should be checked often to make sure they do not have any of these parasites. There is special worming paste that can be mixed in with their food to prevent worms from infecting them. You should also establish a relationship with a good veterinarian who knows about caring for llamas and can determine if there are any other vaccinations necessary in order to keep your llamas healthy. Other diseases and pests that can affect llamas are tuberculosis, tetanus, ticks, mites, and lice.

Using Llama Fibers

Llama fiber is unique from other animal fibers, such as sheep's wool. It does not contain any lanolin (an oil found in sheep's wool); thus, it is hypoallergenic and not as greasy. How often you can shear your llama will depend on the variety of llama, its health, and environmental conditions. Typically, though, every year llamas grow a fleece that is 4 to 6 inches long and that weighs between 3 and 7 pounds. Llama fiber can be used like any other animal fiber or wool, making it the perfect substitute for all of your fabric and spinning needs.

Llama fiber is made up of two parts: the undercoat (which provides warmth for the llama) and the guard hair (which protects the llama from rain and snow). The undercoat is the most desirable part to use due to its soft, downy texture, while the coarser guard hair is usually discarded.

Gathering llama hair is easy. To harvest the fiber, you must shear the llama. However, the steps involved in shearing when you are gathering the fiber are slightly different than when you are simply shearing to keep the llama cooler in the summer months. To shear a llama for fiber collection:

1. Clean the llama by blowing and brushing until the coat is free from dirt and debris.
2. Wash the llama. Be sure to rinse out all of the soap from the hair and let the llama air-dry.
3. You can use scissors or commercial clippers to shear the llama. Start at the top of the back, behind the head and neck and work backwards. If using clippers, shear with long sweeping motions, not short jerky ones. If using scissors, always point them downward. Leave about an inch of wool on the llama for protection against the sun and insect bites. You can shear just the area around the back and belly (in front of the hind legs and behind the front legs) if your main purpose is to offer the llama relief from the heat. Or you can shear the entire llama—from just below the head, down to the tail—to get the most wool. Once the shearing is complete, skirt the fleece by removing any little pieces or belly hair from the shorn fleece.

The fiber can be hand-processed or sent to a mill (though sending the fibers to a mill is much more expensive and is not necessary if you have only one or two llamas). Processing the fiber by hand is definitely more cost-effective but you will initially need to invest in some

Llama fiber can be dyed and spun to be used for knitting.

Llamas should be washed and allowed to air dry before shearing.

equipment (such as a spinning wheel, drop spindle, or felting needle).

To process the fiber by hand:

1. Pick out any remaining debris and unwanted (coarse) fibers.

2. Card the fiber. This helps to separate the fiber and will make spinning much easier. To card the fiber, put a bit of fiber on one end of the cards (standard wool-cards do the trick nicely) and gently brush it until it separates. This will produce a rolag (log) of fiber.

3. Once the fiber is carded, you can use it in a few different ways:

a. Wet felting: To wet felt, lay the fiber out in a design between 2 pieces of material and soak it in hot, soapy water. Then, agitate the fiber by rubbing or rolling it. This will cause it to stick together. Rinse the fiber in cold water. When it dries, you will have produced a strong piece of felt that can be used in many crafting projects.

b. Needle felting: For this type of manipulation, you will need a felting needle (available at your local arts and crafts or fabric store). Lay out a piece of any material you want over a pillow or Styrofoam piece. Place the fiber on top of the material in any design of your choosing. Push the needle through the fiber and the bottom material and then gently draw it back out. Continue this process until the fiber stays on the material of its own accord. This is a great way to make table runners or hanging cloths using your llama fiber.

c. Spinning: Spinning is a great way to turn your llama fiber into yarn. Spinning can be accomplished by using either a spinning wheel or drop spindle, and a piece of fiber that is either in a batt, rolag, or roving. A spinning wheel, while larger and more expensive, will easily help you to turn the fiber into yarn. A drop spindle is convenient because it is smaller and easier to transport, and if you have time and patience, it will do just as good a job as the spinning wheel. To make yarn, twist two or more pieces of spun wool together.

d. Other uses: carded wool can also be used to weave, knit, or crochet.

If you become very comfortable using llama fiber to make clothing or other craft items, you may want to try to sell these crafts (or your llama fiber directly) to consumers. Fiber crafts may be particularly successful if sold at local craft markets or even at farmers' markets alongside your garden produce.

PART FOUR

Simple Structures for Your Land

"Regard it as just as desirable to build a chicken house as to build a cathedral."

—Frank Lloyd Wright

"Develop an infallible technique and then place yourself at the mercy of inspiration."

—Lao-Tzu

Even if you only have a small plot of land, it may be helpful to have a modest potting shed near your garden or a workshop where you can keep your tools. If you'll be raising animals, you'll need shelter for them—even a dog deserves a house it can call its own. Some of the projects in this chapter offer step-by-step instructions that will guide you through the entire building process. Others are meant to offer guidelines for a structure, which you can then alter to meet your own wants and needs. If you are new to woodworking, you may want to start off with one of the simpler projects, such as a birdhouse, and then progress to more complex structures as you build confidence. Follow the directions closely, measure materials carefully, and cross-reference with similar plans found online or in other books when needed. If you're an experienced builder, use the directions and illustrations here as inspiration to create your own unique masterpieces. Whatever your skill level, as with everything, try to enjoy the process as much as the end result.

Doghouses

Dog houses and kennels are easy to construct and are especially useful if you have dogs that primarily live out of doors. A dog kennel needs to protect the dog from harsh winds and heavy rains and should be spacious enough for the dog to move around in comfortably. Doghouses should be located near to your own house, so you can have easy access to your pet, and should be situated on a side of your house that creates a natural barrier from the wind and weather. Dogs should not be left outside overnight in very cold weather, even with access to a doghouse. Below are a couple of doghouses and kennels that can be easily constructed for your outdoor pet.

Standard Dog Kennel

This kennel is constructed to be warm and windproof, to direct the rain away from the base by creating large roof overhangs, and to be easily cleaned.

Materials

- Matched boards for the sides, ends, and bottom (standard measurements for the kennel are 30 inches long, 20 inches wide, and 30 inches tall)
- Weather boards for the roof
- Strip of sheet metal
- Wooden beading

Directions

1. Make the ends first by nailing lengths of matching boards across uprights of 2 x 1-inch batten *(f)*. At the top, halve the battens into the two roof pieces. Set the two outer uprights, X X, in about ¾ inch from the edges to allow the sides to be flush with the outside of the ends. Place these four uprights on the inside.

2. It is advisable to cut out the door—using a pad-saw for the semicircular top—before nailing on Y Y, which should be a little nearer to one another than are the rough edges of the door. Two short verticals on the outside, also projecting beyond the edges, prevent the dog injuring his coat on them. Pieces Z Z give the door a neat finish.

The dog house is wider and has the door set off to one side, which allows for even more protection from the elements.

3. The battens may be omitted from the back end of the kennel, but they ultimately help strengthen the structure and so are advisable to include.

4. When the ends are finished, the horizontal boards for the sides are nailed on to each end (b). Begin at the bottom, arranging the lowest board with its tongue pointing upwards and add the upper boards one by one. The direction in which the tongue points is an important detail—if the boards are put on the wrong way, water will leak more easily into the kennel, rotting the boards and making your dog wet.

5. Battens (d) and (e) are nailed inside along the sides of the kennel and a third is nailed across the back, at a distance above the bottom edge equal to the thickness of the bottom boards and of the battens (b) and (c), to which they are attached. At each end a 2 x 2-inch deal, (f), is screwed to (b) and (c) to raise the bottom clear off the ground.

6. The roof weather boards must be long enough to project at least 6 inches beyond the door end, to prevent rain from coming through the entrance. The eaves overhang 3 inches and are supported, as shown in (a), by three brackets cut out of hard wood. Begin laying on the boards, starting at the eaves and finishing at the ridge, which is closed with a 6-inch strip of sheet metal placed on top of a wooden beading.

7. Stain all the exterior surfaces, including the bottom, and fill in the cracks with caulking to keep the water from seeping through.

The inside part of the kennel should be exposed to the sun occasionally by being turned on its end, and the bottom should be cleaned often.

Modify the dog kennel plans here to fit your dog if it is a larger breed.

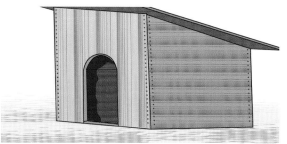

This kennel has a floor that is 2 feet square, is 3 feet 4 inches high in front, and the roof has an overhang of 8 inches.

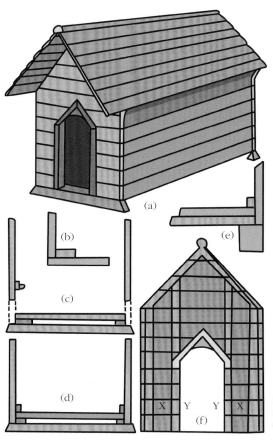

(a)

(b)

(c)

(d)

(e)

X   Y   Y   X

(f)

Refer to this illustration when making the dog kennel. The kennel raised off the ground is shown by (c); (d) illustrates the parts in contact; (e) is a vertical section of the back end.

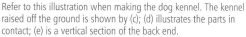

Birdhouses

If you are looking to attract birds to your yard during the spring, summer, and fall months, in particular, it is important to have shelter for the birds. Birdhouses do not need to be very elaborate and they should be rather inconspicuous so birds can easily come and go without attracting predators to their house and nest. All that is really required of a birdhouse is a good hiding place, with an opening just large enough for the bird to fit through, and a strong roof that keeps out the rain.

Birdhouses can be made from a variety of materials—even an old hat tacked to the side of a shed with a hole cut in the top can suffice for a birdhouse. Other usable materials include tin cans, barrels, flowerpots, wooden buckets, and small boxes (preferably wooden or metal).

Most standard birdhouses are made of wood pieces nailed together to look like a miniature house. If you are looking to have many birds nesting in your yard, you may want to build a few birdhouses during the winter so they can be ready for springtime, when birds are beginning to nest. To attract a particular kind of bird to your birdhouse, you must make the size of the hole appropriate for the type of bird. For wrens, make the hole about 1 inch; for bluebirds and tree-swallows, the hole should be 1½ inches; for martins, it should be 2½ inches. Below are a few examples of birdhouses you can easily make to attract beautiful birds to your yard.

Be creative with your birdhouse designs, experimenting with different shapes and materials.

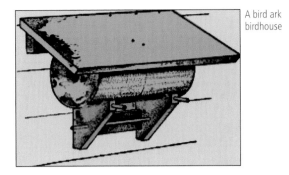

A bird ark birdhouse

Bird Ark Birdhouse

This birdhouse is constructed of three tin cans joined together. Both ends of the center can are removed, but the bottom is left on both end cans. To make the bird ark, simply:

1. Cut a hole into the side of the center can and another through the bottom of each can. Do not remove the pieces of tin but bend them out to serve as perches.

2. Cut the roof boards of the correct size to project over the ends and sides about 1 inch, nail them together, and then fasten them in place by nailing the boards to the connecting blocks between the cans.

3. Fasten the ark between the blocks on a platform or board and then mount the platform on post supports and brace it with brackets, as seen in the picture above. Attach several sticks for perches.

Log Cabin Birdhouse

This birdhouse can be made out of any sized box. Nail pieces together to form the roof, and then thatch the roofing itself to blend into the surrounding environment. The more sloped the roof, the easier the rain can fall off

and not penetrate into the house. This house is slightly more elaborate in the sense that the support pole passes through the house to form a "chimney." The windows can be cut out and fake doors painted on for aesthetic purposes. Small branches should be cut to the proper lengths, split, and then nailed all over the exterior of the house to produce a sort of "log cabin" look—this also helps the birdhouse to better blend into the surrounding trees and foliage in your yard.

Temple Birdhouse

This is a small birdhouse, perfect for wrens. This birdhouse hangs from a tree branch.

Materials
- Large tin can
- Wooden board about 7 inches square
- Carpet or upholstery tacks
- Earthen flowerpot
- Small cork to plug up the flowerpot hole
- Eye screw
- Short stick
- Wire
- Small nails

Cross section of a log cabin birdhouse

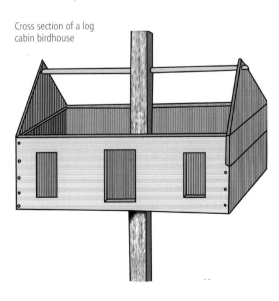

Temple birdhouse

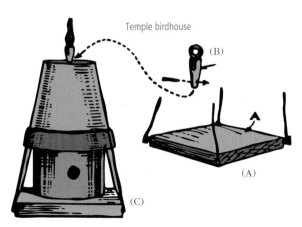

Directions

1. Mark the doorway on the side of the can and cut the opening with a can opener.
2. Fasten the can to the square baseboard (A) by driving large carpet tacks through the bottom of the can into the board.
3. Invert the flowerpot to make the roof. Plug up the drain hole to make the house waterproof (use a cork or other means of stopping up the hole) (B).
4. Screw the eye screw into the top of the plug to attach the suspending wire. Drill a small hole through the lower end of the plug so that a short nail can be pushed through after the plug has been inserted to keep it from coming out.
5. Fasten the flowerpot over the can with wire, passing the loop of wire entirely around the pot and then running short wires from this wire down to small nails driven into the four corners of the base, (C).
6. Now the bird temple can be painted and hung on a tree.

Birdhouses for Specific Bird Species

Species	Floor of cavity (inches)	Depth of cavity (inches)	Entrance above floor (inches)	Diam. of entrance (inches)	Height above ground (feet)
Bluebird	5 x 5	8	6	1½	5 to 10
Robin	6 x 8	8	(a)	(a)	6 to 15
Chickadee	4 x 4	8 to 10	8	1⅛	6 to 15
Tufted titmouse	4 x 4	8 to 10	8	1¼	6 to 15
White-breasted nuthatch	4 x 4	8 to 10	8	1¼	12 to 20
House wren	4 x 4	6 to 8	1 to 6	⅞	6 to 10
Bewick wren	4 x 4	6 to 8	1 to 6	⅞	6 to 10
Carolina wren	4 x 4	6 to 8	1 to 6	1⅛	6 to 10
Dipper	6 x 6	6	1	3	1 to 3
Violet-green swallow	5 x 5	6	1 to 6	1½	10 to 15
Tree swallow	5 x 5	6	1 to 6	1½	10 to 15
Barn swallow	6 x 6	6	(a)	(a)	8 to 12
Martin	6 x 6	6	1	2½	15 to 20
Song sparrow	6 x 6	6	(b)	(b)	1 to 3
House finch	6 x 6	6	4	2	8 to 12
Phoebe	6 x 6	6	(a)	(a)	8 to 12
Crested flycatcher	6 x 6	8 to 10	8	2	8 to 20
Flicker	7 x 7	16 to 18	16	2½	6 to 20
Red-headed woodpecker	6 x 6	12 to 15	12	2	12 to 20
Golden-fronted woodpecker	6 x 6	12 to 15	12	2	12 to 20
Hairy woodpecker	6 x 6	12 to 15	12	2	12 to 20
Downy woodpecker	4 x 4	8 to 10	8	1¼	6 to 20
Screech owl	8 x 8	12 to 15	12	3	10 to 30
Sparrow hawk	8 x 8	12 to 15	12	3	10 to 30
Saw-whet owl	6 x 6	10 to 12	10	2½	12 to 20
Barn owl	10 x 18	15 to 18	4	6	12 to 18
Wood duck	10 x 18	10 to 15	3	6	4 to 20

(a) One or more sides open
(b) All sides open

Simple Stables

If you are raising larger livestock—sheep, goats, horses, or llamas, for example—you will need a small stable where they can go for protection during inclement weather and especially during the winter months in cooler regions. Building stables can be done relatively easily and inexpensively, and doing it yourself means that you can customize the design to fit your and your animals' needs.

Stables should be built on relatively flat ground that does not become excessively wet or flooded during heavy rains. Laying down a thick bed of gravel or sand below the stable floor will help keep surface water drained. Also consider the positioning of the stable; try to find an area that is protected from strong winds but also near your own home so you don't have to go too far to tend the animals during bad weather. Facing the stable toward the south or west will help keep a nice breeze flowing through your stable while protecting it from harsh northerly winds. A place to store feed and hay for your animals is also a worthwhile addition when planning and building a simple stable.

General Stable Construction

When building a stable for your livestock, make sure that the interior walls are weatherproof and free of dampness. To keep moisture out of the stable, the building should be situated on slightly higher ground than that surrounding it. This will keep the ground from getting too damp, and vapors will not be as likely to rise through the floor and foundation walls. If possible, it is best to make the stable floor out of concrete between 4 and 6 inches thick.

The stable walls should be built solid. Brick and stone are preferable to wood, but wooden stables also do an adequate job of providing shelter and are much more common in the United States, due to the availability of wood. If you decide to build your stable using bricks, building the walls one brick (9 inches) thick should be suitable. Internal walls should be built solid, and the foundation must be deep and wide enough to give the whole structure stability. If one side of your stable gets the brunt of driving rain or moisture, it is a good idea to cover it with an extra layer of cement or stucco, or hang shingles to protect the wall.

The Dutch door on this stable can keep animals enclosed while allowing fresh air to circulate.

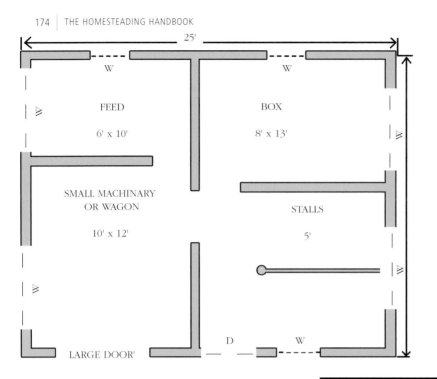

Plans for a small stable

The external angles of all of the doors and windows should be rounded. This can be done by using bull-nosed bricks. This way, horses and other livestock will not be injured by coming into contact with any sharp angles or ledges.

A Small Stable for Horses, Llamas, or Sheep

This simple stable is inexpensive to build and has plenty of room for two horses, llamas, or sheep, along with feed and tack. Hay and grain can be kept in the loft. Place the windows as high up as possible and hinge them at the bottom so they'll open inwardly to permit the air to pass over the animals without blowing directly on them. Make the stable door a "Dutch door"; that is, a door divided horizontally in the middle so that the upper half may be opened and the lower half remain closed.

A stable can be made out of a variety of materials, including brick and wood.

Poultry Houses

Poultry houses should be warm, dry, well-lighted, and ventilated shelters with convenient arrangements for roosts, feeding space, and nest boxes. In winter, if you're living in a cool climate, light and warmth are of the up most importance. Fowl will stop laying eggs and their health will suffer when confined in cold, wet, and dark conditions. Windows facing the south or southeast, large enough to admit the sun freely, should be provided and made to slide open to increase circulation during the summer.

Beyond these few requirements, houses for your poultry can be made in a variety of ways and are, generally, relatively easy to construct. Below are many different types of poultry houses that can be used to keep your fowl warm, dry, and healthy.

Simplest Poultry House

While poultry can survive in this type of cheaply and simply built coop, it is best used in warmer climates, where the winter months do not become incredibly cold and not much, if any, snow falls. Also, this type of coop is best suited for only one or two chickens or ducks.

Materials
- Four pieces of 1 x 2-inch boards for the studs and rafters
- Strong nails
- Wire netting
- Tarred paper

1. Take two of the boards and nail them together in a T shape. Repeat with the other two. Set these apart from each other about 2 feet 10 inches on the centers, and cover them with tightly drawn wire netting (cut to size).
2. Cover the wire netting with tarred paper, creating a barrier between the outside winds and weather and the fowl inside.

Young Poultry Coops

Chicks need extra warmth and protection from predators. This coop, if it houses small chicks, should not hold the other fowl, as they may bully or even harm the young chicks.

This pitched roof chicken coop consists of a pitched roof mounted on three boards, 6 feet high. This coop is 3 feet wide and 2 feet deep. Nail slats across the front to prevent the hen from getting out but to allow the chicks to enter and exit freely into a small fenced-in area surrounding the coop.

The coop pictured above is similar to the pitched roof chicken coop except that there is a canopy that keeps the rain out and shades the interior of the coop so it does not become too warm. This coop is 3 feet long, 2 feet wide, and 30 inches high at the front and 24 inches high in the back. The coop can be constructed from boards with matched edges and should be raised an inch or two above the ground to ensure the floor remains dry. Tack a piece of light canvas or muslin to the roof to serve as the awning.

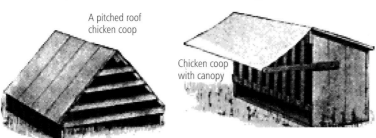

A pitched roof chicken coop

Chicken coop with canopy

This henhouse has a scratching shed, which allows the chickens access to the open air while still being protected from the elements.

You can build a simple ramp to give your chickens easy access to the coop

Practical Henhouse

This simple and efficient henhouse has a shed roof and, as most poultry houses should, faces toward the south. This house can be up to 10 feet wide and as long as you need to accommodate your chickens.

A scratching shed is in the center of the building and has windows that let sunlight in. The sleeping quarters should be kept warm. An open, wire-enclosed front for the scratching shed should be included, too. The roosts should be made moveable and fresh bedding should be kept on the floor of the henhouse.

The roof of the henhouse should project out 1 foot over the south, east, and west sides. It should also be 5 inches higher than the siding, allowing for free ventilation. Two large windows will admit light and warmth into the henhouse. A laying box should extend the entire length of the room and must be divided into compartments and covered with a hinged lid. This allows the eggs to be gathered simply by raising the lid from the outside. Make sure the floor is cleaned weekly to keep out disease. The inside of the walls should be whitewashed often to keep out moisture and pests.

Two-Room Henhouse

This two-room henhouse has a south-facing front to allow ample sunlight and warmth into the house. It can be made as large as 10 x 12 feet and should be constructed of wood or timber planks. It is divided into two rooms by a partition made out of wire netting. This henhouse can serve two separate yards. A fence con-

These pictures show how the perches can be moved to allow for easy cleaning

structed in the middle of the house yard should join the center of the front of the building (and at the back as well if you so desire). In this house, both hens and roosters can be kept and are easily separated while allowing each enough space and exercise.

The platform and perches should be constructed inside of each room. When the perches are in need of cleaning, they are raised up against the wall in the house, in a perpendicular position. To clean the trough, the perches and platform are raised perpendicular to the floor.

Duck Houses

Ducks, while they can survive rather well in any type of poultry house, are happiest when they have either a stream or pond in which to swim, bathe, and gather food. If you have a stream or pond on your property, situating a duck house nearby will help ensure that the duck eggs are safe and secure.

If you are raising a good number of ducks, your duck house should be about 30 feet long and 12 feet high. Doors should be situated in the front of the house and the house should have a few small windows that can be slid open to allow fresh air to circulate within the duck

A two-room henhouse with a south-facing front

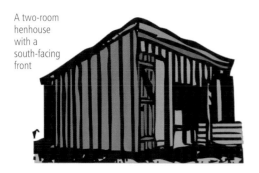

house. The rear of the house should hold the nests (boxes open at the front). A small door should be situated behind each nest so the eggs can be easily removed.

You can use a strip of wire netting to enclose a small, narrow yard in the front of the house. Do not use twine netting, however, as the ducks could get their heads twisted in it and strangle themselves.

Easy, Creative Coops

If you don't have much space in your yard and only have a few chickens to keep, very good coops can be made at a very small cost from items found around your house, yard, or at rummage sales:

1. Barrel Coop
   a. First, drive shingle nails through the hoops on both sides of each stave and clinch them down on the inside.
   b. Divide the barrel in half, if it is big enough, by cutting through the hoops and the bottom.
   c. Drive sticks into the ground to hold the coop in place, and drive a long stick at each side of the opened end just far enough from the coop to allow the front door to be slipped in and out.
   d. The night door can be made from the head of the barrel or any solid board, and the slatted door, used to confine the hen, can be made by nailing upright strips of lath to a cross-lath at top and bottom.
2. Box Coop
   a. Find a box that is roughly 2 to 2½ feet long, 16 inches deep, and 2 feet high and saw a hole, *d*, in one end.
   b. Strengthen the box with narrow strips of wood, *b*, *c*, on each side of the hole. This acts as a groove for the door, *a*, to slide in. By doing so, you will have a sliding door that opens and shuts easily.
   c. The front of the coop is enclosed with lath, or narrow strips, placed 2½ to 3 inches apart. The top should be covered with a good grade of roofing paper to make it completely waterproof.
3. Portable Coop—This type of coop will allow you to have a fresh yard for your chickens and other poultry to scrounge in and is easily transported to any place on your property.
   a. The coop is built of ordinary material on a base frame and with a V-shaped roof and side frames. The preferred length of the coop is about 2 feet and the yard should be around 3 to 4 feet.
   b. The ridge pole is extended, as shown at each end, to form a handle.
   c. If desired, the hen may be allowed to freely roam the yard or can be contained within the coop by slats, as is pictured in the drawing.

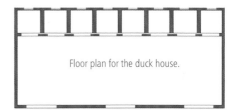
A barrel chicken coop

Floor plan for the duck house.

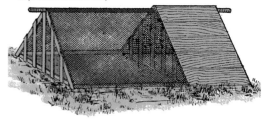
A portable chicken coop

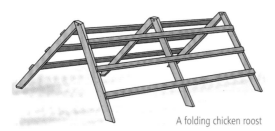
A folding chicken roost

A simple box coop

Poultry House Aids and Other Considerations

Folding Chicken Roost

This roost is made of 3-inch boards cut to any desired length that will fit within your poultry house. A small bolt fastens the upright pieces at their top ends and the horizontal pieces are fastened on with nails. This roost can be kept at any angle and may be quickly taken out of the house when it is time to clean. This sort of roost will accommodate more fowl in the same space than the flat kind.

Keeping Rats and Mice Out of the Poultry House

If you are building a permanent poultry house, you should try to make it as rodent-proof as possible. If rats and mice can easily enter your poultry house, they will not only steal eggs and spread diseases, but they could scare or even harm the fowl. Cheap and efficient walls can be made of small fieldstones in this way:

1. Dig trenches for the walls below the frost line.
2. Drive two rows of stakes into the trenches, one row at each side of the trench.
3. Set up boards in between the stakes. The boards will hold the stones and cement in place until the cement hardens. The top boards should have a straight upper edge and should be placed level to determine the top of the wall.
4. Place two or three layers of stone in the bottom of the trench, pour in thinly mixed cement, and pound it in. Repeat this until the desired height is reached.
5. The top of the wall should be smoothed off with a trowel and left until the cement completely hardens. The side boards can now be removed and the poultry house built.

Winter Care of Fowl

If chickens and other fowl are not kept warm in the winter, they will stop growing, cease laying eggs, and can become ill. There are several ways you can winterize chicken coops to ensure your birds' comfort and well-being.

Especially if you live in colder climates, having a house with hollow or double side walls will help keep your fowl warm during the winter season. Buildings with hollow side walls are warmer in the winter and are also cooler in the summer. They do not collect as much severe frost and result in less moisture seeping into the henhouse once the frost melts.

The outside walls of chicken coops can be plastered or lined with matched boards and the spaces between the boards filled with wood shavings, sawdust, or hay. The floor should be covered with several inches of dry sand, wood shavings, or straw, and the ventilating holes near the roof should be partly stopped up or shutters

arranged to close most of them in very cold weather. You don't want to seal the place up completely, though. Nothing is more important to the health of fowl than pure air. Birds breathe with great rapidity and maintain a relatively high body temperature, so they need plenty of oxygen.

Constructing a solid, insulated roof for your poultry house for the winter is very important. A roof can be built either by sealing the inside with material to exclude draughts or by placing roof boards close together and covering them thoroughly with tarred paper before shingling. An ordinary shingled roof allows too much wind to come into the house and could cause your fowl to get frosted combs or wattles. If this happens, there will not be much, if any, egg production in the winter months.

Hanging curtains in front of the perches is also a great way to keep your fowl warm during the winter months. Make these curtains of burlap and hang them from the roof in such a way that the perches are enclosed in a little room. Make sure the curtains are long enough to touch the floor all around, and sew the edges of the burlap together, except at the corners. At night, the corners can be pinned together to keep the birds from leaving their sheltered perches. This pseudo-sleeping room allows air to move in without creating drafts and it also helps retain the birds' body heat. This maintains a comfortable temperature for the birds during cold, winter nights.

A drinking fountain for your chickens can be made with a can or bucket and a tray. Cut out one end of the can and poke holes along the edge as shown. Fill with water, cover with a shallow tray, and turn the whole thing over quickly. Chicks will be able to drink water easily without risk of drowning.

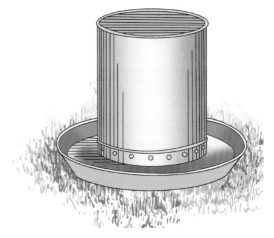

Fences, Gates, and Pens

Whether you are looking to add a lovely fence and gate around your garden plants or you have poultry or other livestock to keep in check, you may need to build a fence, gate, or animal pen. These structures can be attractive if well built and should be able to stand up to all kinds of weather and animals. Depending on your needs, here are some various fences, gates, and pens you can easily construct in your yard or on your property.

Fences

Fences are perfect for keeping animals or young children in a confined space or for drawing boundaries between yours and your neighbor's property lines—but check with your neighbors before you construct your fence to make sure they don't mind. Also call your local utility companies to make sure that you will not be digging up power or gas lines.

Wooden Fences

Wooden fences allow for good ventilation and an open, airy feel. They can provide protection for young shrubs and plants as well as keep animals and children safe within the yard or fenced-in space.

The most common type of wooden fence consists of horizontal rails nailed to posts or stakes that are placed vertically into the ground. These fences can be constructed with three or four horizontal rails that are made out of split wood, spruce, or pine wood planks. The posts are usually about 6 feet long and sharpened at the end that will be driven into the ground (to a depth of roughly 8 inches). These posts should be spaced about 6 feet apart.

In order to keep the pointed, earth-bound ends from rotting, dip them in melted pitch before inserting them into the ground. To do this, boil linseed oil and stir in pulverized coal until it reaches the consistency of paint. Brush a coat of this on the wooden post. Make sure the posts are completely dry before painting them. If properly done, this should keep moisture from seeping into the buried parts of the posts and will keep your fence upright for many, many years.

A simple wooden fence is enough to keep most animals in their pastures.

In order to drive the posts into the ground, you will need either a very good shovel or a heavy wooden mallet. For longer poles, use a post-hole borer. This saves lots of time and energy and will work with almost all types of soil.

To construct a basic wooden fence, you'll need:

Materials
- Post-hole diggers, a post-hole borer, or a shovel
- 4 x 4 wooden posts (wood that has been treated will last longer but is not necessary)
- 2 x 4 lumber (this too can be treated but does not need to be) or fence boards (which can be purchased at your local home and gardening center)
- Thick, long nails

Directions
1. Decide where the fence will be constructed and then lay a line of twine or string to mark out the border.
2. Decide how tall you want your fence to be. Take into consideration what the fence is being used for (if it's for larger animals, such as llamas, you may want a 6-foot-tall fence; if for decoration, a shorter fence may do the trick).
3. Dig holes for your end posts (in all four corners of your fence). Make sure the holes are deep enough to be able to support the end posts. Fill in dirt around the posts and pack in the soil very well.

You can nail wire mesh to the rails of a wooden fence for extra security or to allow vines or other climbing plants to grow up along the posts.

A hole borer lifts the soil from the hole without having to use spades. These borers can be used by hand or electric models can be purchased for the same purpose.

A picket fence is constructed by nailing two or more long boards to posts, and then nailing narrow vertical boards to the horizontal ones.

4. Start digging the remaining holes, trying to keep them in alignment with the end posts.
5. Insert the remaining posts into the holes, piling in the dirt and packing it down as before.
6. Nail on your fence boards, leaving a little space in between. Paint or stain the finished fence if you wish.

Note: If you want a privacy fence, you can nail thicker boards horizontally or vertically between each post, making sure the space in between is quite small.

Wire Fences

Wire fences are both portable and durable, making them convenient and economical to build. Wire fences usually have a longer staying power than wooden fences since they are less prone to deterioration or rot.

The most common type of wire fence is one that has wire lines strung between wooden posts. The wires are fastened to the posts by galvanized wire staples. The wooden posts should be spaced roughly 6 feet apart and should use five single wires.

A more substantial wire fence can be made with G-line wires. Each line consists of a three-ply strand. Instead of the wires being fastened to the post by staples, holes are bored through the posts and the lines

A wire netting fence

Drive your fence poles far enough into the ground that they stand firmly upright even when moderate pressure is applied to one side.

A G-line wire fence consists of three-ply strands of wire.

pass through. Straining eye bolts with nuts and washers are attached for tightening up the fence. This type of fence, however, is much more expensive to build and, unless you desire a fence that is incredibly strong, is probably not necessary.

[only one example below (and some pictures that have already been explained)]

Wire Netting Fence

Galvanized wire netting fences are used for enclosing root gardens and for poultry fences. The standard type of netting used when making this fence is 3-inch mesh netting that is 3 feet x 3 feet, and is rather inexpensive to buy.

A separate strip of 2-inch galvanized wire netting that is 6 inches wide can be laid flat on the ground on the side of the fence where the poultry are—this way they can not dig underneath, especially once grass and other natural materials hide the wire netting.

To dig in this type of fence, make a trench about 6 inches deep, drop the netting into it, and then fill the trench up with dirt, stones, or even concrete, depending on how permanent you want the fence to be.

Portable Fences

If you need a temporary fence or if you want to be able to easily move your livestock fence to new grazing areas on your property, you may want to consider one of these easily made moveable fences. Below are a few types of portable fences that can be tailored to your specific needs.

Convenient and Portable Fence

Often it is helpful to have a fence that can be quickly erected and disassembled. This fence is very cheap, strong, and convenient to use. It is built out of pine (any other wood can be substituted, but pine is typically lighter and easier to move), 1 x 6 inches for the bottom rail and 1 x 4 inches for the top rails. The braces that hold it upright are 2 x 4 inches and the base (cross piece) is 2 x 6 inches. The base is notched 2 inches and the bottom boards are notched with holes.

The base piece, which is more susceptible to rot, could be made out of a stronger wood, such as oak.

Make sure the panels aren't too long or they might warp out of shape. This fence can be put up very quickly and taken down again with ease if you want to move it to another part of your yard or get rid of it for a while.

Scotch Hurdle Fence

This moveable fence consists of two posts, each 2 x 3 inches and 4½ feet long. The lower ends are long and pointed—this allows them to easily enter the ground and prop up the fence. The brace and two diagonals are made of larch or fir wood. This fence is around 9 feet long and 4 feet high.

A portable fence

The Scotch Hurdle fence is easy to set up. The incline should be facing away from any livestock you might have contained inside of it. A stay should be placed between every two hurdles to keep them in position. One wooden peg should be fastened to one end of the hurdle and another peg driven through the other end and into the ground.

English Hurdle Portable Fence

This moveable fence is much lighter, cheaper, and more convenient than the Scotch hurdle fence. Usually made of split oak, this fence is tough and impenetrable. It consists of two upright end pieces that are joined by four or five mortised bars 7 to 9 feet long. These are strengthened by an upright bar in the middle and two

This Scotch hurdle fence is good for temporary use. If you live in a very windy area, however, this fence may not suit you well, as they do have a tendency to fall over in very strong gales.

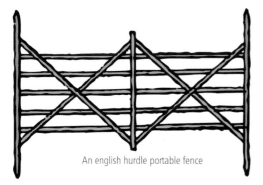

An english hurdle portable fence

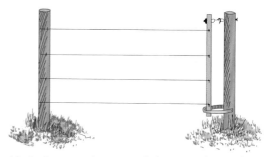

A basic wire gate can be constructed when you need an opening in your fence.

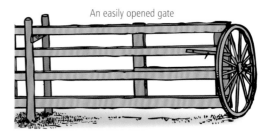

An easily opened gate

or more diagonals. The end pieces are long and pointed for setting into the ground. To set these into the earth, use an iron crowbar to avoid splitting the top of the wooden piece.

These fences are set erect and no stay is needed. The two adjoining ends of the fences are connected with a band that is passed over them.

Gates

Gates are a necessary part of any fence or pen and they can be situated in the fence wherever they can be easily accessed. If you have a field, your gate should be roughly 10 feet wide to allow small machinery through.

Most gates are made of either wood or iron (though iron is obviously much more expensive and more complicated to work with). Wooden gates will suffice for most of your homesteading needs. The following are a few simple gates that can be used for your garden, your backyard fences, and your pens housing livestock.

Inexpensive, Simple Gate

A light, useful, and durable gate can be made of sassafras poles (or other tall grass poles) and wire. Dig and place a strong post 4 feet in the ground in the middle of

Gates can be useful for entrances to a yard or walkway, as well as for animal pens or pastures.

the gateway and balance the gate on it. The lower rail is made of two forked sassafras poles securely nailed together so they can be coiled back over the post.

Easily Opened Gate

To construct this simple gate, take an old wheel (possibly found at an antique store or rummage sale) and fasten it to make a gate that you will be opening frequently. The piece of board (C) drops between the spokes of the wheel and holds the gate either open or closed.

Simple Gate

This is a simple and appealing gate, especially for fences leading into pastures. The materials required to make this gate vary depending on what purpose the gate will serve.

For a paddock or pasture gate, make it out of seasoned boards, 1 x 6 inches and 12 to 14 feet long. The posts supporting the gate should be placed about 5 inches apart, the one on the inside being about 8 inches ahead of the other. These are joined together by cleats

A simple sliding gate can be made for any modern or wire fence.

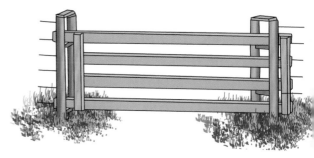

This wire gate is hung on ordinary iron posts. The heel of the gate, made of angle iron, is fitted with winding brackets for tightening the wire bars.

or rollers that support the gate and allow it to be pushed back and swing open. If rollers are not obtainable, cleats made of any hard wood are acceptable.

Pens

If you have built a simple stable to house your llamas, sheep, or other animals, it will be beneficial to build a small fence around it as an outdoor pen. A basic wooden fence or a simple wire fence will enclose most of your livestock in an area around the stable or shelter. If you have a llama or two, it is best to have at least a 4-foot

A bamboo fence or gate can be constructed by lashing the bamboo together with strong rope.

fence so they cannot escape. If you have ample space, having a pathway into a larger grazing field or pasture from your pen will allow your animals to come and go as they please. Or, if you want to keep them confined in the pen, a simple gate will suffice for when the animals need to be removed or relocated.

Basic Bridges

If you have a river or brook on your property, you may want to construct a simple bridge. Building these bridges can be quite easy, especially if you don't plan on transporting very heavy machinery or cars over them. Here are a few different ways to build basic bridges over streams, creeks, or other rather narrow waterways.

Footbridge

This natural-looking footbridge can be built between 8 feet and 12 feet long.

Excavate the banks of the stream or creek to allow for the building of a small, low rubble or stonewall. The sleepers will rest on this wall. The girders are formed of wooden spars (four are used in this plan). The girders should be between 8 and 10 inches in diameter. Lay the girders down and bolt them together in pairs with six ¾-inch-diameter coach bolts. Wedge the posts to fit mortises in the girders.

The posts and top rails should be roughly 4½ to 5½ inches in diameter and the intermediate rails 3 inches in diameter. Finally, join the rails to the posts.

The bridge should be anchored well if it's in a place where flooding is frequent, as you don't want your footbridge floating away in the stream. To do so, drive four short piles into the soil on the inside of the girders, near their ends. Fasten the girders to the piles with coach bolts. The pile tops are hidden by the ends of the floor battens.

Now, if you want to decorate your footbridge, you can use small twigs and nails to make patterns on your bridge.

Small Stream Bridge

If you have a small creek or stream on your property, you may want to construct a simple bridge for easy access to the other side. To build this bridge, you'll need lumber that is 6 inches wide and 2 inches thick, and additional lumber for the floor and four side braces.

Directions
1. Saw 11 pieces of wood the length required for the two sides.

Bridge can be fashioned in a range of shapes, styles, and sizes to meet your needs.

2. Bore bolt holes 1½ inches from each end. Use 5⁄8-inch bolts 8½ inches long for where four pieces come together, and use 6½-inch bolts where three pieces meet.

3. Bolt on the A-shaped supports and pieces for the approaches at one time, and then put on the side braces.

4. The sides of the bridge are made of triangles. The first triangle is made of pieces *a*, *b*, and *c*. The second triangle is made of pieces *b*, *d*, and *e*.

5. The piers for this bridge may be made of posts, stone, or even concrete, depending on how permanent you wish your small stream bridge to be.

A wooden footbridge

A cross section of the footbridge

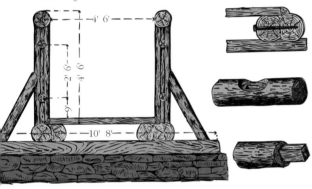

Join the rails of the footbridge to the posts as shown here.

A bridge for a small stream

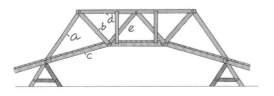

A Very Simple Bridge

Another very simple way of building a bridge across a creek or stream is to find a narrow part of the waterway and then find two logs that are longer than the creek is wide. These logs should be very sturdy (not rotted out) and thick. Place them across the creek, so they make a narrow beam over the water. Each log should have an extra foot at each end of the creek, so they can be securely walked upon with no danger of slipping into the creek bed. Place the logs roughly two feet apart.

If the water comes up close to the bottom of the logs, raise them so the bridge does not get washed away in heavy storms or during the course of the stream rising. To raise the bridge will require a bit more work, as each log will need to be set into another log on the edge of the streambed or even into stone to make it more permanent.

After you have the two base logs secured, find some sticks that are long enough (and relatively thick) to lay across the tops of the two logs. Or, if you have extra plywood or other boards, those can be used as well. Just make sure to place the sticks or boards fairly close to one another, leaving only little gaps between them. Then, once all the sticks have been laid down, secure these by tying twine or rope to them and the base logs.

If you'd like your bridge to last a little longer, you can pave it with clay or fine cement. Using a shovel, coat the bridge with the clay or cement until it's about 2 inches thick. Then shovel dirt onto the clay mixture, packing it down all over, and make the bridge as thick as you like. However, for just a simple bridge across a narrow stream or creek, the wooden sticks or boards will work just fine and won't require quite as much time and energy.

Tool Sheds and Workshops

Before building a tool shed, think about what you want to house in it. If you just need it for small tools, such as shovels, buckets, and a wheelbarrow, a smaller shed will be fine. However, if you plan to house your machinery there, such as a tractor, lawnmower, chainsaw, or rototiller, you'll need a larger shed and you may want to plan for a sliding garage door–style entrance. Will you want a workbench, space to pot plants, shelving, and drawers? Do you want electrical outlets for power tools and lights? Also consider location: It may be more convenient to have it close to your house, or you may prefer to have it nearer the garden. Below are a couple of examples of tool sheds that you can modify to meet your needs.

Medium-sized Tool Shed and Workshop

This shed is large enough to easily store your basic farm machinery. The shed is basically a giant umbrella with posts 30 feet apart in one direction and 12 or 16 feet apart in the other. There are no sides to this shed at all (though you could modify this if you want to store other tools here). If you park your main machinery (tractor, lawnmower, and so on) in the innermost part of the shed, you should still have an overhang of 10 feet. This shed would be most beneficial if it were 10 feet high—that way, most any kind of machine you want to house under it will fit well. Boarding up one, two, or three sides will help prevent snow from drifting in during the winter and rain from rusting your equipment. Making walls will also allow you to hang tools on the inside of the shed, such as clippers, weed whackers, or hoses.

The workshop housed above will hold a lot of smaller tools and is a good place to mend harnesses, make repairs, and store grain. The workshop gives about a 30-foot clearance space for the shed below. The entire building is built together using the following materials:

- 2 x 8-inch posts
- Three pieces of 2 x 12-inch wood materials (space these 2 inches apart)
- 2 x 10-inch box plates
- 6 x 6-inch bridge truss
- 2 x 4-inch or 2 x 6-inch beams for the rafters (depending on how much weight they must hold)

The floor of your shed should be either hard dirt or cement and the posts should be anchored firmly into the ground or on stone pillars. A shingle roof will ensure your smaller workshop tools are kept safe from the rain and snow.

Decide what you will want to store in your shed before you begin building so you know what size to make it.

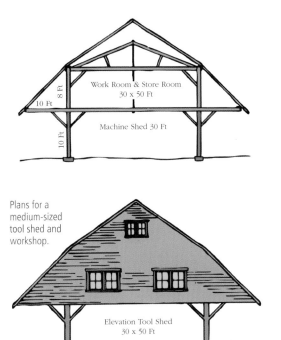

Plans for a medium-sized tool shed and workshop.

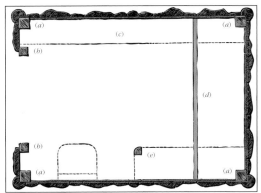

Plans for the inside of a rustic tool shed.

Small, Rustic Tool Shed

This small, rustic tool shed is made from "slabs" or "rough planks." If you are using trees from your own property to build the shed, you won't have to bother peeling the bark from the logs or cutting them as exactly. Slabs are cheap to buy (they can be found at saw mills and sometimes at home centers), and create an attractive, "woodsy" look. Although the boards are typically not uniform in size (some are wider than others), you can position them in such a way as to minimize the number of large cracks in your shed.

These boards may need to be straightened (especially the edges) with a saw or axe, and the interior of the tool shed should be lined with thin boards to cover up cracks and to keep out insects and animals.

When beginning construction on this type of shed, search for boards that lend themselves better to being end posts and those that are better suited for the walls. The corners of the four main posts (4 inches square) construct a building roughly 7 x 5 feet. Dig holes 2 feet into the ground and fit in the end posts.

On the tops of these posts, rest the wall plates—these should be 3 inches deep. These boards will be at the back and sides of the shed only. The sides will also need cross rails that are around 2 to 3 inches thick with ends flush to the corner posts. Nail the side and back boards to these cross boards to secure them.

Place two door posts in the front of the shed. They should stand 2 feet 8 inches apart and should be about

3 inches square. They should rise about 6 feet or so to attach to the rafters. Fill in the space between the door and corner posts with extra boards.

The roof for this tool shed can be thatched or made of boards and shingles, whichever you prefer. Make rafters and laths out of regular boards, arranging them about 1 foot apart, and the laths should be placed 6 inches apart for thatching. The shed can also be cheaply roofed with galvanized iron or tin roofing.

The door of the tool shed has the slabs nailed to it on the outside only, to make it aesthetically consistent. Attach hinges and the door should be ready. Inside the shed, sets of shelves may be hung in which tools and other items can be stored (c). A wheelbarrow can be stored upright at the back (d) and tools hung from hooks coming down from the rafters. Gardening tools and rakes can be stored on the right-hand side (e) and a chair can sit near the front of the door (f).

A finished small, rustic tool shed.

Smokehouses

If you are slaughtering your own poultry or other livestock, or if you just like the taste of smoked meat, try making your own smokehouse. Smokehouses help expose meats to the action of creosote and empyreumatic vapors resulting from the imperfect combustion of wood. The peculiar taste of smoked meat is from the creosote—this also helps preserve the meat. Other flavors are also imparted onto the meat by the choice of wood that is burned in the smokehouse, such as hickory.

To make a smokehouse you'll need a space (anything from the size of a barrel to a barn-sized area will work) that can be filled with smoke and closed up tightly. You'll also need a way to hang the meat that needs to be cured. In common smokehouses, a fire is made on a stone slab in the middle of the floor. In other instances, a pit is dug about a foot deep into the ground and the fire is built within it. Sometimes a stone slab covers the fire like a standard table. The possibilities are many, depending on your space and needs. Below are a few examples of smokehouses that can be built and used for smoking your own meats.

Standard Smokehouse

This smokehouse diffuses the rising smoke and prevents the direct heat of the fire from affecting the meats that are hung directly above it. In the picture, a section of the smokehouse is shown.

This standard smokehouse is 8 feet square and built of bricks—making it a somewhat permanent structure in your yard. If you want to make it out of wood, be sure to plaster is completely on the inside. The chimney, *(c)*, has an 8-inch flue and the fireplace, *(b)*, is outside, below the level of the floor. From this point, a flue, *(f)*, is carried underneath the chimney into the middle of the floor where it opens up under a stone table, *(e)*.

To kindle the fire, a valve is drawn to directly draft up through the chimney. The woodchips are thrown onto the fire and the valve is then placed so to direct the smoke into the brick smokehouse. There are openings, *(g, g)*, in both the upper and lower parts of the chimney that are closed by valves (these

Smokehouses can be made out of stucco, brick, or wood.

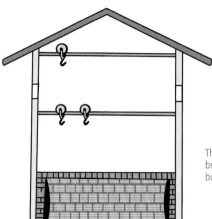

This is a sectional view of a brick smokehouse that can be built to any size.

can be manipulated from outside the smokehouse. The door of the smokehouse should be made to shut very tightly and, when building the smokehouse, be sure that there are not any cracks in the brick or mortar through which smoke can easily escape.

This type of smokehouse is nice because the smoke cools before it is pumped into the chamber and no ashes rise with the smoke. Meat may be kept in this smokehouse all year without tasting too smoky.

Another Brick Smokehouse

A smokehouse of this kind, built 7 x 9 feet, will be sufficient for private use. The bottom of this smokehouse has a brick arch with bricks left out sporadically. This is to allow the extraction of smoke from the house.

Located above the arch are two series of iron rods that have hooks with grooved wheels. You can find these at most local hardware stores. The open archway is for housing the fire and there is a door with steps leading up to it. A series of ventilating holes are situated above the lower bar and below the upper bar. These holes are meant to allow the smoke to escape from the house. By reinserting bricks into these holes, the smoke will stay mostly confined to the inside of the smokehouse.

The arch confines the fire and ashes, preventing any meat that might fall from being ruined or burned. The arch is made over a wooden frame of a few pieces of regular wood board, cut into an oval arch shape. Strips of wood are then nailed to this. When the brickwork is dry, the center is knocked out and removed. A small door can be fashioned to close up the arch when the fire is being kilned.

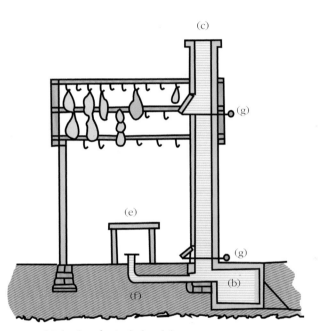

Interior view of a standard smokehouse

The drawing shows a common smokehouse that is built on a brick wall and over a brick arch. There are a number of holes left in it for smoke to escape. The ash pit is located beneath the arch, and there is also a door that opens to this pit. To reach the meat room door, use a sturdy ladder.

The interior of a smokehouse

A smoke barrel is a simple method for smoking meats.

Simple Way to Smoke Meats

If you don't want to commit to building a permanent smokehouse in your yard but you would like to smoke meats occasionally, you can used a large cask or barrel as a smokehouse substitute.

To make the barrel into an effective smokehouse, just follow these steps:

1. Dig a small pit and place a flat stone or a brick across it. This is where the edge of the cask will rest.
2. Making sure that half of the pit is beneath the barrel and half is outside, remove the head and bottom of the barrel (or cut a hole into the bottom slightly larger than the portion of the pit beneath it).
3. Remove the top of the barrel and then hang the meat on cross-sticks. Rest these cross-sticks on crossbars that are made to fit into holes bored into the sides of the barrel, close to the top.
4. Put the lid on top of the barrel and cover it with a sack to confine the smoke inside.
5. Put coals into the pit outside of the cask, and then feed the fire with damp corncobs or a fine brush.
6. Cover the pit with a flat stone that will help regulate the fire and can be removed when more fuel is needed.

Fish that are hung and ready to be smoked

Root Cellars

While most modern houses have basements or crawl spaces in which to keep fresh vegetables and preserves cool and dry, you may want to construct an additional root cellar if you'll be storing significant amounts of these items. A root cellar should be located near to your home and should be dry, well ventilated, and frost proof. Creating your own root cellar is not terribly expensive and will give your yard and property a true back-to-basics feel.

Root Cellar

If you have a hilly area in your yard, this is the perfect place to make a root cellar. To construct the root cellar, follow these simple steps:

1. Make an excavation in the side of the hill, determining how large you'd like your root cellar to be.
2. In the excavation, erect a sturdy frame of timber and planks, or even of logs. Put up planks to stand as side walls, and build a strong roof over the frame.
3. Throw the excavated earth over the structure until it is completely covered by at least 2 feet of soil.
4. On the exposed end, make a door that is large enough for you to enter without ducking. Or, if you like, you can make a sort of "manhole" through which you can enter—this will actually protect your root cellar from the frost much better than a full-sized door.

If the soil in the hill is composed of stiff clay, you may not even need to construct any side walls, and the roof can be fitted directly into the clay. Then build up the front of the cellar with planks, bricks, or stone, and create a door.

A root cellar can be built into the side of a hill using stone, bricks, or wood.

Root House

If you do not have a large hill on your property and would still like to construct a root cellar, find a knoll or other dry place and remove the soil over a space that is slightly larger than the size of the cellar (or root house if the structure is not built into a hill) and about 2 feet deep. To construct this root house:

1. Select poles or logs of two different sizes. The wider ones should be shorter than the other two.
2. Cut the ends of the logs very flat so they will fit closely together and make a very tight pen-like structure.
3. Cut two logs in each layer long enough to pass through and fit into the outer pen. This will help fasten the two walls together.
4. Build the doorway up with short logs passing from one layer of poles to the other. These serve as supports to the ends of the wall poles.
5. Fill in the space between these two walls with soil. It is important that these are filled in fully (sod may also be used to pack in spaces between the logs) to protect the inside storage items from frost and to keep the whole structure cool. Pack up the soil as you construct the walls so you can more easily compact it as you build up.
6. When the walls are about 5 or 6 feet on one side and 2 or 3 feet on the other, put the roof on. The roof is made of poles placed close together, secured to the logs, and covered with sod, then 18 inches of soil. It is then finished off with sod once again.

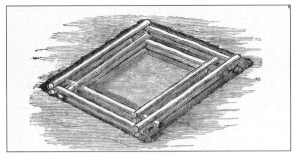

The base of the root house.

The finished root house.

Root cellars or houses are great for keeping vegetables like potatoes or carrots and for apples, which can keep for months in cool, dry storage.

PART FIVE   # Energy

With the extreme fluctuation in oil prices and ever-growing concerns about the state of our environment, it's no wonder that more and more people are turning to the natural elements for power. Sun, wind, water, and earth have provided for the basic needs of humanity since the beginning of time and it only makes sense to learn how to work with them more efficiently. The term "self-sufficiency," as it is commonly used, is something of a misnomer. We will never be able to meet all of our own needs alone. We don't create the natural world that supplies us with the light, heat, and other resources that we depend on. But we can learn how to make good use of those gifts. In these pages you will find both simple and advanced projects to do so, from fashioning and using solar cookers to building and installing wind turbines to utilizing geothermal systems. There's a lot here, but it's only a sampling of the methods available for harnessing natural energy. Look online or visit your library for more ideas, plans, and tips; you'll also find an extensive list of resources in the back of this book. Remember that the simplest and perhaps most effective way to be energy-efficient is to use less of it. The simple things, like turning off a light when you're not in the room—or even using candlelight in the evenings—can make a big difference. The more you understand about the process of turning the natural elements into usable energy, the more you'll appreciate the value of electricity and want to conserve it in any way you can.

Solar Energy

Solar energy is, in its simplest form, the sun's rays that reach the earth (also known as solar radiation). When you step outside on a hot, sunny summer day, you can feel the power of the sun's heat and light. Solar energy can be harnessed to do a variety of things in your home. These include:

- Heating your home through passive solar design or through active solar heating systems
- Generating electricity
- Heating water in your home
- Heating swimming pool water
- Lighting your home both inside and out
- Drying your clothes via a clothesline strung outside in direct sunlight

Solar energy can also be converted into thermal (heat) energy and used to heat water for use in homes, buildings, or swimming pools and also to heat spaces inside homes, greenhouses, and other buildings.

Photovoltaic energy is the conversion of sunlight directly into electricity. A photovoltaic cell, known as a solar or PV cell, is the technology used to convert solar energy into electrical power. A PV cell is a non-mechanical device made from silicon alloys. PV systems are often used in remote locations that are not connected to an electric grid. These systems are also used to power watches, calculators, and lighted road signs.

Solar Thermal Energy

Solar thermal (heat) energy is used most often for heating swimming pools, heating water to be used in homes, and heating specific spaces in buildings. Solar space heating systems are either passive or active.

Passive Solar Space Heating

Passive space heating is what happens in a car on a sunny summer day—the car gets hot inside. In buildings, air is circulated past a solar heat surface and through the building by convection—less dense, warm air tends to rise while the denser, cooler air moves downward. No mechanical equipment is needed for passive solar heating.

PV System Components.

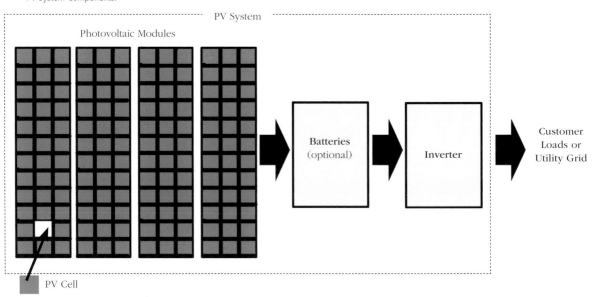

Advantages of Solar Energy

- It's free.
- Its supplies are unlimited.
- Solar heating systems reduce the amount of air pollution and greenhouse gases that result from using fossil fuels (oil, propane, and natural gas) for heating or generating electricity in your home.
- Solar heating systems reduce heating and fuel bills in the winter.
- It is most cost-effective when used for the entire year.

Disadvantages of Solar Energy

- The amount of sunlight that arrives at the earth's surface is not constant and depends on location, time of day and year, and weather conditions.
- A large surface area is required to collect the sun's energy at a useful rate.

Passive solar space heating takes advantage of the warmth from the sun through design features, such as large, south-facing windows and materials in the floors and/or walls that absorb warmth during the day and release it at night when the heat is needed most. Sunspaces and greenhouses are good examples of passive systems for solar space heating.

Passive solar systems usually have one of these designs:

1. Direct gain—This is the simplest system. It stores and slowly releases heat energy collected from the sun shining directly into the building and warming up the materials (tile or concrete). It is important to make sure the space does not become overheated.
2. Indirect gain—This is similar to direct gain in that it uses materials to hold, store, and release heat. This material is generally located between the sun and the living space, usually in the wall.
3. Isolated gain—This collects solar energy separately from the primary living area (a sunroom attached to a house can collect warmer air that flows through the rest of the house).

Active Solar Space Heating

Active heating systems require a collector to absorb the solar radiation. Fans or pumps are used to circulate the heated air or the heat-absorbing fluid. These systems often include some type of energy storage system.

There are two basic types of active solar heating systems. These are categorized based on the type of fluid (liquid or air) that is heated in the energy collectors. The collector is the device in which the fluid is heated by the sun. Liquid-based systems heat water or an antifreeze solution in a hydronic collector. Air-based systems heat air in an air collector. Both of these systems collect and absorb solar radiation, transferring solar heat to the interior space or to a storage system, where the heat is then distributed. If the system cannot provide adequate heating, an auxiliary or backup system provides additional heat.

Liquid systems are used more often when storage is included and are well suited for radiant heating systems, boilers with hot water radiators, and absorption heat pumps and coolers. Both liquid and air systems can adequately supplement forced air systems.

Active solar space heating systems are comprised of collectors that absorb solar radiation combined with electric fans or pumps to distribute the solar heat. These systems also have an energy-storage system that provides heat when the sun is not shining.

Another type of active solar space heating system, the medium temperature solar collector, is generally used for solar space heating. These systems operate in much the same way as indirect solar water heating systems but have a larger collector area, larger storage units, and much more complex control systems. They are usually configured to provide solar water heating and can provide between 30 and 70 percent of residential heating requirements. All active solar space heating systems require more sophisticated design, installation, and maintenance techniques than passive systems.

Passive Solar Water Heaters

Passive solar water heaters rely on gravity and on water's natural tendency to circulate as it is heated. Since these heaters contain no electrical components, passive systems are more reliable, easier to maintain, and work longer than active systems. Two popular types of passive systems are:

1. Integral-collector storage systems—These consist of one or more storage tanks that are placed in an insulated box with a glazed side facing the sun. The solar collectors are best suited for areas where temperatures do not often fall below freezing. They work well in households with significant

A combination of an indirect water heater and a highly efficient boiler can provide a very inexpensive method of water heating.

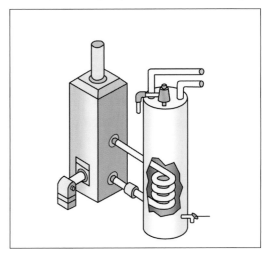

daytime and evening hot-water needs but they do not work as efficiently in households with only morning hot-water draws as they lose most of the collected energy overnight.

2. Thermospyhon systems—These are an economical and reliable choice particularly in newer homes. These systems rely on natural convection of warm water rising to circulate the water through the collectors and into the tank. As water in the collector heats, it becomes lighter and rises to the tank above it and the cooler water flows down the pipes to the bottom of the collector. In freeze-prone climates, indirect thermosyphons (using glycol fluid in the collector loop) can be installed only if the piping is protected.

Active Solar Water Heaters

Active solar water heaters rely on electric pumps and controllers to circulate the water (or other heat-transfer fluids). Two types of active solar water heating systems are:

1. Direct circulation systems—These use pumps to circulate pressurized potable water directly through the collectors. These systems are most appropriate for areas that do not have long freezes or hard/acidic water.

2. Indirect circulation systems—These pumps heat transfer fluids through the collectors. These heat exchangers then transfer the heat from the fluid to potable water. Some of these indirect circulation systems have overheat protectors so the collector and glycol fluid do not become superheated.

Common indirect systems include antifreeze, in which the heat transfer fluid is usually a glycol-water mixture, and drainback, in which pumps circulate the water through the collectors and then the water in the collector loop drains back into a reservoir tank when the pump stops.

Installing a Passive Solar Space Heater

A passive solar space heater works when the sun shines through the solar panels to heat the air inside a box. As the air heats up in the box, it rises and moves into the house. Cool air moves into the box and out of the house—in this way, the house is heated without the use of a mechanized heating system. Using a passive solar heater works best if you have a house that faces south and has both basement and first floor windows on that side of the house. If your house meets these requirements (and there aren't too many obstructions that would impede the sun from shining on the heater), then you can begin construction.

The passive solar space heater is made up of a floor and two triangular end walls, all of which can be made simply out of plywood. In between the open space, insulation can be placed. A lid can also be added to cover the heater in the summer.

To build such a solar space heater, first decide where on the southern wall your collector will be located. If you can place the heater in between windows, that is the best option. You may need to cut through the wall

A passive solar space heater.

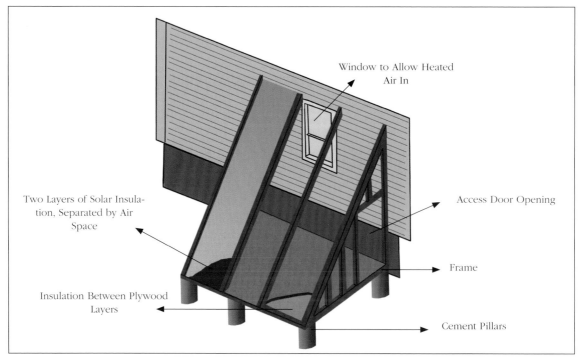

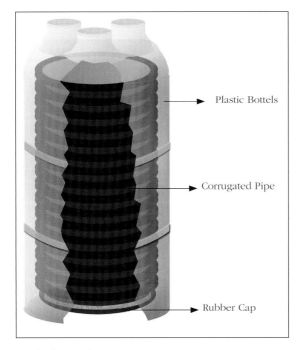

A solar water heater

near a window to allow for the proper ventilation but if you don't want to do this, you can also purchase a detachable plywood "chimney" to move the heated air into the house. Next, find the studs that will support the fiberglass panel and find a panel that will be of the appropriate size.

Next, make the base for your solar heating system. The base can be made of ⅜-inch plywood board. Nail the board to a 2 x 4 and level it. Next, add insulation (the kind found on rolls is best), nailing it to the plywood. Then, nail the whole board to the side of the house. Make sloping supports out of 2 x 4s. Make sure the end wall studding is nailed in, and then attach the outside panel to it.

Under the shingles, install flashing or something else that will keep water out of the top of the solar heater. Then, install the fiberglass panels, making sure the edges are caulked so no water can come in. Enclose the edges of the fiberglass with small strips of plywood. Then, install the outer fiberglass panel so that it is flush with the top surface and caulk it. To finish up, paint the inside of the plywood surfaces black to absorb the heat. The inside of the cover panel should be painted white to reflect the light.

Building Your Own Solar Water Heater

This very simple and basic solar water heater is a low-pressure system and so should not be combined with your home plumbing system. This type of heater is perfect for camping trips or other smaller water heating uses. Find the supplies online or at a hardware store.

Supplies

- Corrugated, high density polyethylene draining tube (4 inches is preferred)
- An EPDM rubber cap with clamp (available at hardware stores or online)
- Polyethylene terephthalate bottles (3-liter are preferred—soda bottles are fine)

To construct the water heater, simply stretch the EPDM rubber cap over one end of the draining tube and make certain the clamp is tight. Cut the ends off the bottles and fit them over the other end of the drainage pipe. This will serve as the glazing to heat the water. Each bottle should be able to fit tightly over the other bottle if you cut a small hole in the bottom of each. Fill the tube with water, place it in the sun, and allow the water inside the bottles and drainage tube to heat up. Once it's warm (around 120°F is the maximum it will heat the water), it can be used to wash dishes or clothes, or for a small bath.

Heating a Room Using Collectors

Air collectors can be installed on a roof or an exterior, south-facing wall to facilitate the heating of one or more rooms in a house. Factory-built collectors can be used but you can also make and install your own air collector, though note that this is not always cost-efficient.

The air collector should have an airtight and insulated metal frame and a black metal plate. This will absorb the heat through the glazing on the front. The sun's rays heat the plate, which then heats the air in the collector. A fan or blower can pull the air from the room through to the collector and blow it into the room.

Room Air Heating with Collectors

Air collectors can be installed on a roof or an exterior (south facing) wall for heating one or more rooms. Although factory-built collectors for on-site installation

Solar collectors on a roof

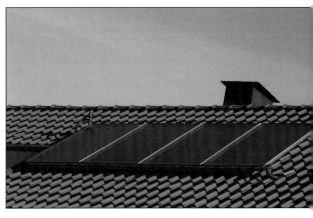

Roof Area Needed in Square Feet (shown in Bold Type)

PV module efficiency (¼)	PV capacity rating (watts)							
	100	250	500	1,000	2,000	4,000	10,000	100,000
4	30	75	150	300	600	1,200	3,000	30,000
8	15	38	75	150	300	600	1,500	15,000
12	10	25	50	100	200	400	1,000	10,000
16	8	20	40	80	160	320	800	8,000

*Although the efficiency (percent of sunlight converted to electricity) varies with the different types of PV modules available today, higher-efficiency modules typically cost more. So, a less-efficient system is not necessarily less cost-effective

are available, do-it-yourselfers may choose to build and install their own air collectors. A simple window air heat collector can be made for a few hundred dollars. Simple window box collector fans will fit in a window opening. These fans can be active or passive. A passive collector fan allows air to enter the bottom of the collector, rise as it heats, and enter the room. A damper keeps the room air from flowing back into the panel on overcast or cloudy days. Window box systems only provide a small amount of heat as the collectors are quite small.

Solar Collectors

Solar collectors are an essential part of active solar heating systems. These collectors harness the sun's energy and transform it into heat. Then, the heat is transferred to water, solar fluid, or air. Solar collectors can be one of two types:

1. Nonconcentrating collectors—These have a collector area that is the same size as the absorption area. The most common type is flat-plate collectors and these are used when temperatures below 200°F are sufficient for space heating.
2. Concentrating collectors—The area of these collectors gathering the solar radiation is much greater than the absorber area.

Solar thermal energy can be used for solar water heating systems, solar pool heaters, and solar space heating systems. There are many types of solar collectors, such as flat plate collectors, evacuated tube collectors, and integral collector storage systems.

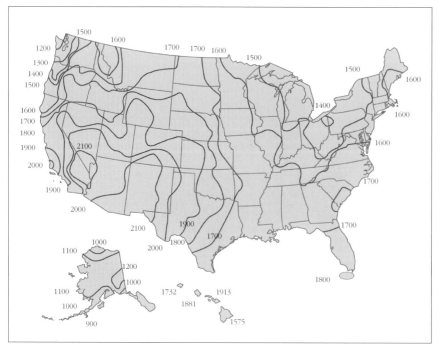

Calculating Electricity Bill Savings for a Net-Metered PV System

First determine the system's size in kilowatts (kW). A reasonable range is 1 to 5 kW. This value is the "kW of PV" input in the equations. Next, based on your geographic location, select the energy production factor from the map below for the kWh/kW-year input for the equations.

Energy from the PV system = (kW of PV) x (kWh/kW-year) = kWh/year. (Divide this number by twelve if you want to determine your monthly energy reduction.)

Energy bills savings = (kWh/year) x (Residential Rate)/100 = $/year saved. (Residential Rate in this above equation should be in dollars per kWh; for example, a rate of 10 cents per kWh is input as $0.10/kWh.)

For example, a 2-kW system in Denver, CO, at a residential energy rate of $0.07/kWh will save about $266 per year (1,900 kWh/kW-year x $0.07/kWh x 2kW = $266/year).

Including plenty of energy-efficient windows in your home will allow sunlight to warm your rooms naturally.

Another Form of Solar Heating: Daylighting

Solar collector panels are not the only way in which the sun's heat can be harnessed for energy purposes. Daylighting uses windows and skylights to bring sunlight into your home. Using energy-efficient windows, as well as carefully thought-out lighting design, reduces the need for artificial lighting during the daytime. These windows also cut down on heating and cooling problems.

The effectiveness of daylighting in your home will depend on your climate and the design of your house. The sizes and locations of window and skylights should be based on the way in which the sun hits your home and not on the outward aesthetics of your house. Facing windows toward the south is most advantageous for daylighting and for moderating seasonal temperatures.

A simple solar oven

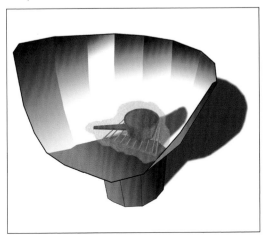

Placing windows that face toward the south will allow more sunlight into your home during the winter months. North-facing windows are also useful for daylighting as they allow a relatively even, natural light into a room, produce little glare, and capture no undesirable summer heat.

Make Your Own Solar Cooking Oven

This type of simple, portable solar oven is perfect for camping trips or if you want to do an outdoor barbeque with additional cooked foods in the summer. This homemade solar oven can reach around 350°F when placed in direct sunlight.

Supplies
- A reflective car sunshade or any sturdy but flexible material (such as cardboard) covered with tin foil and cut to the notched shape of a car sunshade
- Velcro
- A bucket
- A cooking pot
- A wire grill
- A baking bag

Directions
1. Place the car sunshade on the ground. Cut the Velcro into three separate pieces and stick on half of each piece onto the edge near the notch. Then, test the shade to see if the Velcro pieces, when brought together, form a funnel. Place the funnel atop the bucket.
2. Place the cooking pot on the wire grill. Put this all in the baking bag and put it inside the funnel. The rack should now be lying on top of the bucket. Now place the whole cooker in direct sunlight and angle the funnel in the direction of the sun. Adjust the angle as the sun moves.

Make Your Own Solar Panels

Making your own solar panels can be tricky and time-consuming, but with the right materials and lots of patience, you can certainly create an effective solar energy panel.

Supplies
- Pegboard
- Solar cells (quantity will be determined by how much power you want to get from your solar panel)
- Contact wire
- Wire cutters
- Solder
- Soldering iron
- Bolts with washers and wingnuts
- Plexiglass

Solar ovens can be fashioned in a variety of ways. The goal is to have as much surface area as possible reflecting the sun toward your food.

- Aluminum framing
- Silicone caulking
- Screws

Directions

1. Apply silicone caulking in vertical strips between the rows of holes on the peg board. Place the solar cells face up along the caulking in straight rows, carefully aligning them so that the wires poke through the holes. The solar cells should completely cover the board.
2. Place a soft sheet or blanket on the ground or table (to prevent the cells from scratching) and care-

Refer to these illustrations while constructing your own solar panel.

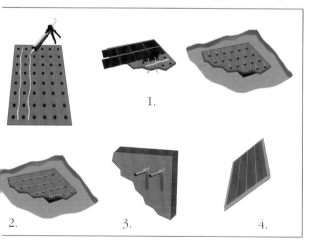

fully flip the baord so that it is face down. Solder together the wires coming out to create one thick wire stemming from each hole. Then use connecting wire or metal strips to connect the wires along horizontal lines. Be sure to connect all positive wires together and all negative wires together, without mixing the two.

3. Drill two holes in the back of your panel and attach a positive and negative bolt, washer, and wingnut. Solder the positive wires to the positive bolt and the negative wires to the negetaive bolt.
4. Build a watertight frame to size, using aluminum framing for the sides, plywood for the backing, and a plexiglass face to allow the sunlight to shine through. Seal all cracks and edges with silicone sealant.

Installing Your Heat Collector

If possible, install your own solar heat collector on the south side of your house (the side that receives the most sunlight during the day). It can be placed in a window to help minimize your heating costs during the winter months.

A solar heat collector can be made from heavy-duty foam insulation, window glass, sealant, aluminum foil, and heavy-duty tape. Paint the foam panel, or both sides of the aluminum sheets, black and then mount it on cubes that are cemented to the side of your house near a window. This will allow the air to come in on both sides of the heat collector.

All sides of the foam should be covered with aluminum foil and then adhered to the foam board. Then place and seal the glass panels over the foam, sealing it wirh the sealant and heavy-duty tape if needed. Another piece of foam can be utilized as a cover for the duct at night or

The more surface area you cover with solar panels, the more power you'll get. It's best to install your panels on the south side of your home.

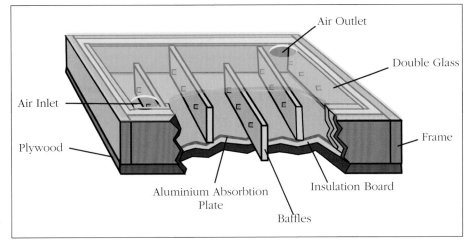

Alternate solar
heating panel

during the warm, sunny summer months. Hinge this on with hinge brackets or clasps.

An Alternative Solar Heating Panel

This type of solar panel is quite different from the expensive, manufactured panels you can purchase and have installed on your roof or the side of your house. It is great for heating air but cannot produce electricity. You can either situate this heater in a south-facing window of your home or place it on the outside, southern wall or on the roof. Heating panels that are on the outside of a house generally create more heat and are much more effective in heating a room or area of your home.

To start, you will need to purchase glass or Plexiglas for your solar heating panel. Either one should be double-paned to keep out moisture. To build the frame for your solar heating panel, use 2 x 4s and create a square or rectangle that will fit your pane of glass. Nail

plywood to the back of the frame. Next, take a piece of insulation board and put it at the back of the panel. Heat absorption can be gained through aluminum flashing or copper. After this is inserted, screw down the window frame, if you are using one, and make sure it is caulked well to keep out any leaking water.

Add the interior boards that line the frame and the baffles to seal the top of the glass. Screw these interior boards to the sides of the panel to keep them secure. Then, cut out the air openings using a jigsaw. One circular opening should be in the lower left and the other in the upper right of your heating panel. Before hanging the panel up, you will need to determine where the studs are in the wall or where the roof rafters are located (if you are installing on your roof). It is also important that your openings do not fall on top of a stud or rafter as this will defeat their ability to direct airflow. Screw in

Solar panels can be placed in a field or other sunny area to collect energy, which is stored and then used as needed.

Regulations for Installing and Building Solar Heating Systems

Before you install a solar energy system, it is important to learn about the local building codes, zoning, and neighborhood covenants as they apply to these systems. You will most likely need to obtain a building permit to install a solar energy system onto an existing building. Common problems you may encounter as a homeowner in installing a solar energy system are: exceeding roof load, unacceptable heat exchangers, improper wiring, tampering with potable water supplies, obstructing property and yards, and placing the system too close to the street or lot lines. There are also local compliances that must be factored in before installing your system. Contact your local jurisdiction zoning and building enforcement divisions and any homeowner's, neighborhood, or community associations before building and installing any solar heating equipment.

boards along the studs or rafters, on which you will then mount the panel.

Once the panel is secured to the wall or roof, begin to install the air delivery system so the hot air can be circulated throughout your home. You may want to add a small fan (one used in a computer will be fine) to your heating panel so you can better circulate the air through-out the system, though this is not necessary to operate your heating panel effectively. If you do choose to use a fan, it must be able to fit inside the wall plate. You will need to drill a hole in your wall where the panel holes are situated on the outside. Cut the hole and add the connector to the ductwork, sliding it through the hole into the room, and seal off the edges of the hole.

Place the fan within the wall plate in the room, and place an electrical box near the fan to turn it on and off. If you aren't familiar with electrical work, you may want to ask an electrician to help you with connecting the electrical wiring. Next, mount the solar panel so it faces to the south, running a wire into the electrical box inside the room. This will save you money and energy while running your fan. Now turn on the fan and feel the warm air starting to blow through your room.

To finish your outside panel, simply paint the inside black to absorb more heat, add some weather stripping to seal the glass tightly, and screw the glass piece to the panel.

Solar Greenhouse

Greenhouses collect solar energy on sunny days and then store the heat for use in the evening and on days when it is overcast. A solar greenhouse can be situated as a free-standing structure (like a shed or larger enclosure) or in an underground hole.

For gardeners who want to grow small amounts of produce, passive solar greenhouses are a good option and help extend the growing season. Active systems take supplemental energy sources to move the solar heated air from its storage facility to other parts of the greenhouse. Solar greenhouses can utilize many of the same features and installation techniques as passive solar heating systems used in homes to stay heated.

While standard greenhouses also rely on the sun's rays to heat their interiors, solar greenhouses are different because they have special glazing that absorbs large amounts of heat during the winter months and also use

materials to store the heat. Solar greenhouses have a lot of insulation in areas with little sunlight to keep heat loss at a minimum.

Types of Solar Greenhouses

Two common types of solar greenhouses are the attached solar greenhouse and the freestanding solar greenhouse. Attached solar greenhouses are situated next to a house or shed and are typically lean-to structures. They are limited in the amount of produce they can grow and have passive solar heating systems.

Freestanding solar greenhouses are large structures that are best suited for producing a large variety and quantity of produce, flowers, and herbs. They can be constructed in the form of either a shed structure or a hoop house. In a shed greenhouse, the south wall is glazed to maximize the heating potential and the north wall is extremely well insulated. Hoop house greenhouses are rounded instead of shaped like an elongated shed. Solar energy is collected and stored in earth thermal storage and in water. These systems, while common,

Both flowers and vegetables can thrive in greenhouses.

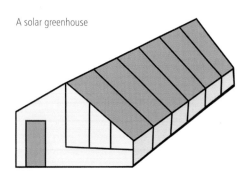

A solar greenhouse

are not as effective in utilizing solar energy as the shed and lean-to structures.

Sites for Solar Greenhouses

The glazing portion of the solar greenhouse should ideally face directly south to gain the maximum exposure to the sun's heat. Situating the solar greenhouse on a slight slope facing upward will maximize the amount of solar energy it can absorb.

Materials Used in Solar Greenhouse Construction

For a solar greenhouse to be able to collect, circulate, and maintain the greatest amount of heat, it is important that it is constructed out of the proper materials. Glazing materials need to allow photosynthetic radiation to get through so it can reach the plants. Clear glass allows direct light into the greenhouse and so should be used as a glazing material. It is also imperative that when the glazing materials are mounted on the greenhouse, there are no cracks or holes that can allow for heat to escape. Thus, glazing material should have high heat efficiency and be made of resistant material to hold up in inclement weather and hail.

Solar greenhouses also need to be able to store the heat that is collected for use on cloudy days or at night. The easiest method for storing heat is to situate rocks, concrete, and/or water in the path of the sunlight that is entering the greenhouse. These materials will absorb the heat during the day and release it during the evening hours. Pools of water, rocks, and concrete slabs or small walls should be large enough to absorb and emit enough heat to last for the night or for a few cloudy days.

Phase-change materials may also be used to effectively store heat in your solar greenhouse. These materials consist of paraffin, fatty acids, and Glauber's salt. These materials store heat as they change into liquid and release it as they turn back into a solid form. They are kept in sealed tubes and many are needed to provide enough heat.

Greenhouses can be made in a range of shapes and sizes and can be attached to your home or separate from it.

All areas of the greenhouse that are not glazed need to be insulated to keep in the maximum amount of heat. Weather stripping is helpful in sealing doors and vents; foam insulation is helpful for walls. Place a polyethylene film between the insulation and the greenhouse walls to keep these materials dry—if they become too wet or saturated, they will be less effective and may start to mold. The floors of a solar greenhouse can also lose heat so they should be made out of brick or flagstone (with insulation foam underneath) to keep the heat in.

The solar greenhouse needs outdoor insulation as well, which can be attained by placing hay bales along the edges of the greenhouse, or the greenhouse can be situated slightly underground (a pit greenhouse). Of course, if a greenhouse is dug into the soil, it needs to be in an area that is above the water level to minimize leakage.

A solar greenhouse, like any other greenhouse, also needs proper ventilation for the warmer summer months. Vents in the sides of the greenhouse will help create air flow. Ridge vents in the roof will allow the hottest air to escape out of the top of the greenhouse as well. If a greenhouse needs more ventilation, a solar chimney can be hooked up to the passive solar collectors to release extra heat out into the air.

Wind Energy

Wind energy is created naturally by circulation patterns in the Earth's atmosphere driven by the heat from the sun. These winds are caused by the uneven heating of the atmosphere by the sun, the irregularities of the earth's surface, and the rotation of the earth. Wind patterns are modified by the earth's terrain, bodies of water, and vegetation. Since the earth's surface is made of very different types of land and water, it absorbs the sun's heat at different rates. During the day, the air above the land heats up very quickly. The warm air over the land expands and rises and the heavier, cooler air rushes in to take its place, creating winds. At night, the winds are reversed as the air cools rapidly over land. This air flow is used for many purposes: sailing, flying kites, and generating electricity.

Small Wind Electric Systems

Small wind electric systems are one of the most cost-effective, home-based renewable energy systems. These systems are nonpolluting and are fairly easy to set up. A small wind electric system can effectively:

- Lower your electricity bills by 50 to 90 percent
- Help you avoid high costs of having utility power lines extended to a remote location
- Help uninterruptible power supplies ride through extended utility outages

How Do Small Wind Electric Systems Work?

When the wind spins a wind turbine's blades, a rotor captures the kinetic energy of the wind, converting it into rotary motion to drive the generator. Most turbines have automatic overspeed-governing systems to keep the rotor from spinning out of control on very windy days.

A small wind system can be connected to an electric distribution system (grid-connected) or it can stand alone (off-grid). To capture and convert

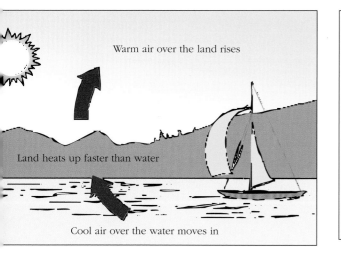

Warm air over the land rises

Land heats up faster than water

Cool air over the water moves in

A Brief History of Wind Energy

People have been harnessing energy from the wind since ancient times. Wind was used to sail ships and windmills were build to help grind wheat, corn, and other grains. Windmills were also used to pump water and to cut wood at sawmills in the formative years of the American colonies. Even into the early twentieth century, windmills were being used to generate electricity in rural parts of America. The windmill again gained national attention in the early 1980s when wind energy was finally considered a renewable energy source. It continues to be a growing industry throughout the United States.

the wind's kinetic energy into electricity, a home wind energy system must generally be comprised of the following:

1. A wind turbine—This consists of blades attached to a rotor, a generator/alternator mounted on a frame, and a tail
2. A tower
3. Balance-of-system components—i.e., controllers, inverters, and/or batteries

A wind-electric turbine generator, more commonly known as a "wind turbine," converts kinetic energy in the wind into mechanical power. This power can be used directly for specific tasks, like grinding grains or pumping water. A generator can also convert this mechanical power into a high-value, highly flexible and useful form of energy—electricity.

Wind turbines make electricity by working in the opposite way as a fan. Instead of using electricity to make wind, as a fan does, turbines use wind to make electricity. The wind turns the blades, spinning a shaft that connects to a generator, which makes electricity.

The basic parts of a small wind electric system

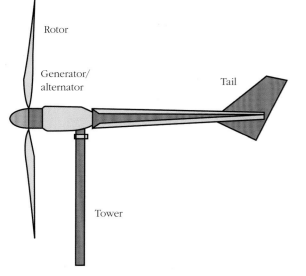

Rotor

Generator/
alternator

Tail

Tower

Installing a Small Electric Wind System

Small wind electric systems, with the proper installation and maintenance, can last over 20 years. Before installing your system, first find the best site, determine the appropriate size of your wind turbine, decide whether you want a grid-connected or stand-alone system, and find out about your local zoning, permitting, and neighborhood covenant requirements.

Many people decide to install these systems on their own (though the manufacturer and/or dealer should also be able to help you install the small wind electric system). However, before you attempt to install the wind turbine, make sure you can answer these do-it-yourself questions:

1. Can I pour a proper cement foundation?
2. Do I have access to a lift, ladder, or another way to erect the tower safely?
3. Do I know the difference between alternating current (AC) and direct current (DC) wiring?
4. Do I know enough about electricity to safely wire my turbine?
5. Do I know how to safely handle and install batteries?

If the answer to any of these questions is "No," then you should have someone help you install the system (contact the manufacturer or your state energy office).

Evaluating a Potential Site for Your Small Wind Turbine

The site on which you choose to install your system should meet the following criteria:

• Your property has a good wind resource—good annual wind speeds and a prevailing direction for the wind.

Inside a Wind Turbine

Parts of a wind turbine:

- Anemometer: measures the wind speed and transmits wind speed data to the controller.
- Blades: most turbines have either two or three blades and the wind blows over the blades, causing the blades to lift and rotate.
- Brake: a disc brake, applied mechanically, electrically, or hydraulically, and stops the rotor in emergencies.
- Controller: starts up the machine at wind speeds of about 8 to 16 mph and shuts off the machine at about 55 mph wind speeds. Turbines do not operate at wind speeds above 55 mph because they may be damaged.
- Gear box: gears connect the low-speed shaft to the high-speed shaft and increase the rotational speeds from about 30 to 60 rotations per minute (rpm) to about 1000 to 1800 rpm—the rotational speed required by most generators to produce electricity. The gear box is a costly and heavy part of the wind turbine.
- Generator: usually an off-the-shelf induction generator that produces 60-cycle AC electricity.
- High-speed shaft: drives the generator.
- Low-speed shaft: turned by the rotor at about 30 to 60 rpm.
- Nacelle: sits atop the tower and contains the gear box, low- and high-speed shafts, generator, controller, and brake. Some nacelles are large enough for a helicopter to land on.
- Pitch: Turns the blades out of the wind to control the rotor speed and keep the rotor from turning in winds that are too high or too low to produce electricity.
- Rotor: the blades and hub.
- Tower: made from tubular steel, concrete, or steel lattice. Since wind speed increases with height, taller towers enable turbines to capture more energy and generate more electricity.
- Wind direction: an "upwind" turbine operates facing into the wind while other turbines are designed to face "downwind" or away from the wind.
- Wind vane: measures wind direction and communicates with the yaw drive to orient the turbine properly with respect to the wind.
- Yaw drive: used to keep the rotor facing into the wind as the wind direction changes (not required for downwind turbines).
- Yaw motor: powers the yaw drive.

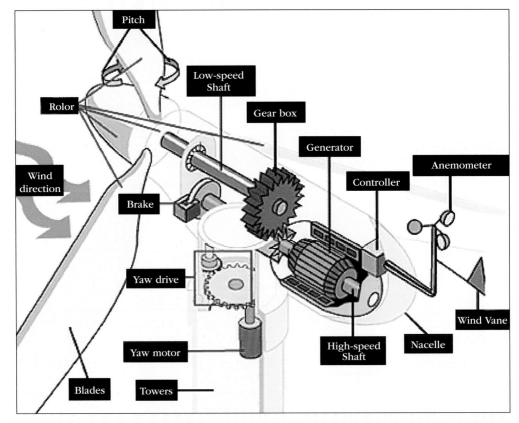

- Your home is located on at least one acre of land in a rural area.
- Your local zoning codes and covenants do not prohibit construction of a wind turbine.
- Your average electricity bill is $150 per month or more.

If you live in an area that has complex terrain, be careful when selecting an installation site. If you place your wind turbine on the top of a hill or on an exceptionally windy side, you will have more access to prevailing winds than in a gully or on the sheltered side of a hill. Additionally, it is important to consider any existing obstacles—trees, houses, sheds—that may be in the way of the wind's path. You should also plan for future obstructions, such as new buildings or landscaping. Your turbine needs to be positioned upwind of any buildings and trees, and it needs to be 30 feet above anything within 300 feet of its site.

When determining the suitability of your site for a small electric wind system, estimate your site's wind resource. Wind resource can vary significantly over an area of just a few miles because of local terrain's influence on wind flow. Use the following methods to help estimate your wind resource before installing your small electric wind system:

1. Consult a wind resource map. This is used to estimate the wind resource in your area. You can find a specific map for your state at the U.S. Department of Energy's Wind Powering America Program Web site. A general U.S. map is shown in the figure.
2. Obtain wind speed data. The easiest way to quantify the wind resource in your area is by obtaining the average wind speed information from a local airport. Airport wind data are typically measured 20 to 33 feet above ground. Average wind speeds increase with height and may be as much as 15 to 25 percent greater at a usual wind turbine hub (80 feet high) than those measured at airports.
3. Watch vegetation flagging. Flagging is the effect of strong winds on an area of vegetation. For example, if a group of trees on flat ground is leaning significantly in one direction, chances are they've become that way due to strong winds.
4. Use a measurement system. Direct monitoring using a measurement system at a certain site provides the best picture of the available wind resource. These are very expensive, however, and so may not be practical to use.
5. Obtain data from a local small wind system—if there is a small wind turbine near your area, you may be able to obtain information on the annual output of the system, as well as wind speed data.

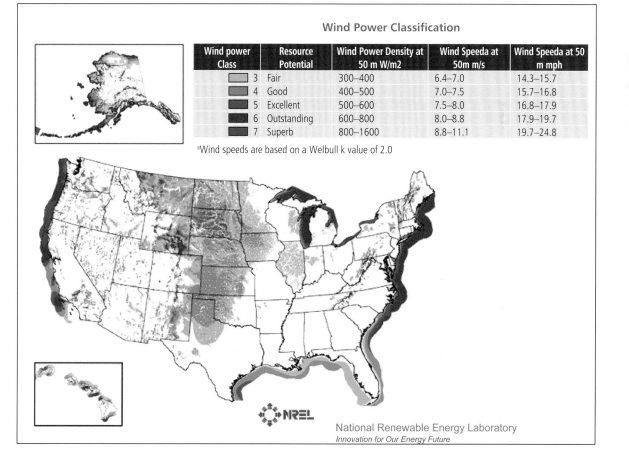

Wind Power Classification

Wind power Class		Resource Potential	Wind Power Density at 50 m W/m2	Wind Speed[a] at 50m m/s	Wind Speed[a] at 50 m mph
	3	Fair	300–400	6.4–7.0	14.3–15.7
	4	Good	400–500	7.0–7.5	15.7–16.8
	5	Excellent	500–600	7.5–8.0	16.8–17.9
	6	Outstanding	600–800	8.0–8.8	17.9–19.7
	7	Superb	800–1600	8.8–11.1	19.7–24.8

[a]Wind speeds are based on a Welbull k value of 2.0

National Renewable Energy Laboratory
Innovation for Our Energy Future

Small Wind Turbines Used for Homes

Single, small, stand-alone turbines that are sized below 100 kilowatts are used for homes, tele-communication dishes, and water pumping. Used in residential applications, these small wind turbines can range from 400 watts to 20 kilowatts. In addition to being used for generating electricity and pumping water, they can be used for charging batteries. Most U.S. manufacturers rate their small wind turbines by the amount of power they can safely produce at wind speeds between 24 and 36 mph.

An average home uses about 9,400 kilowatt-hours of electricity per year. Thus, a wind turbine rated in the 5- to 15-kilowatt range would make a significant contribution to this energy demand. Before deciding on a wind turbine you should:

1. Establish an energy budget. Try to reduce the electricity use in your home so you will only need a small turbine.
2. Determine an appropriate height for the wind turbine's tower so it will generate the maximum amount of energy.
3. Remember that a small home-sized wind machine has rotors that are between 8 and 25 feet in diameter and stand around 30 feet tall. If your property does not have enough space to accommodate this, you may not be able to have a powerful enough turbine to help significantly reduce your energy costs.

Windmill blades can vary in shape but should always be angled to catch the most wind.

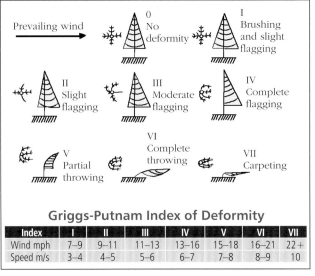

Griggs-Putnam Index of Deformity

Index	I	II	III	IV	V	VI	VII
Wind mph	7–9	9–11	11–13	13–16	15–18	16–21	22+
Speed m/s	3–4	4–5	5–6	6–7	7–8	8–9	10

Vegetation flagging is the effect of strong winds on vegetation. It's a good indicator of how strong the winds are in that area.

Maintaining Your Small Wind Turbine

In order to keep your turbine running smoothly and efficiently, do an annual check of the following:

- Check and tighten bolts and electrical connections as necessary.
- Check machines for corrosion.
- Check the guy wires for proper tension.
- Check for and replace any worn leading-edge tape on the turbine blades.
- Replace the turbine blades and/or bearings after 10 years.

Types of Wind Turbines

Modern wind turbines fall into two basic categories: horizontal-axis varieties and vertical-axis designs.

Horizontal-axis Wind Turbines

Most wind machines used today fall into this category. Horizontal-axis wind machines have blades like an airplane propeller. A standard horizontal wind machine stands about 20 stories tall and has three blades spanning 200 feet across. These are the machines most readily found in large fields and on wind farms.

The majority of small wind turbines made today are of the horizontal-axis style. They have two or three blades made of composite material, such as fiberglass. The turbine's frame is a structure to which the rotor, generator, and tail are all attached. The diameter of the rotor will determine the amount of energy the turbine will produce. The tail helps keep the turbine facing into the

Stand-Alone and Small Hybrid Systems

⩘ A solar and wind hybrid energy system

Hybrid power » systems combine multiple sources to deliver non-intermittent electric power.

Wind power can also be used in off-grid systems. These are called stand-alone systems because they are not connected to an electric distribution grid. In these systems, small wind turbines can be used in combination with other components, such as small solar electric systems, to create a hybrid power system. Hybrid power systems provide reliable off-grid power for homes (and even for entire communities in certain instances) that are far from local utility lines.

A hybrid electric system may be a practical system for you if:

• You live in an area with average annual wind speed of at least nine mph.
• A grid connection is not available or can only be made through a very costly extension.
• You would like to become independent from your energy utility company.
• You would like to generate clean power.

Small hybrid systems that combine wind and solar technologies offer several advantages over either single system. In many parts of the United States, wind speeds are low in the summer when the sun shines the brightest and for the longest hours. Conversely, the wind is stronger in the winter when less sunlight is available. These hybrid systems, therefore, are more likely to produce power when you need it.

If there are times when neither the wind nor the solar systems are producing energy, most hybrid systems will then provide power through batteries or an engine generator powered by diesel fuel (which can also recharge the batteries if they run low).

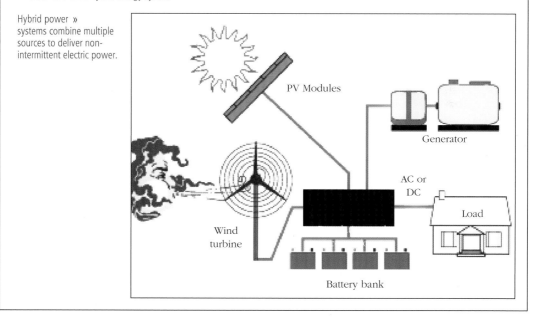

wind. Mounted on a tower, the wind turbine has better access to stronger winds.

These machines also require balance-of-system components. These parts are required for water pumping systems and other residential uses of your wind turbine. These also vary based on the type of system you are using: either a grid-connected, stand-alone, or hybrid.

For example, if you have a residential grid-connected wind turbine system, your balance-of-systems parts will include:

• A controller
• Storage batteries
• A power conditioning unit (inverter)
• Wiring

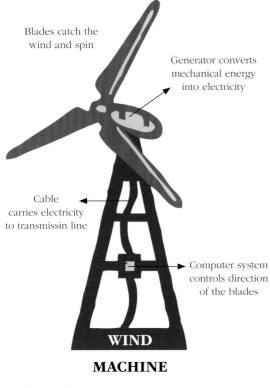

Blades catch the wind and spin

Generator converts mechanical energy into electricity

Cable carries electricity to transmissin line

Computer system controls direction of the blades

WIND MACHINE

A horizontal-axis wind turbine

A hybrid wind and solar energy system

- Electrical disconnect switch
- Grounding system
- Foundation for the tower

Vertical-axis Wind Turbines

These machines have blades that go from top to bottom. The most common type looks like a giant two-bladed egg beater. Vertical-axis wind machines are generally 100 feet tall and 50 feet wide. Though these wind turbines have the potential to produce a great deal of energy, they make up only a small percentage of the wind machines that are in use currently due to the cost and effort required to set them up. In addition, they produce a great deal of noise, can be unsightly, hurt the bird population, and require large roads and heavy-duty equipment to get them up and running.

Grid-Connected Small Wind Electric Systems

Small wind energy systems can be connected to the electricity distribution system to become "grid-connected systems." These wind turbines can help reduce your consumption of utility-supplied electricity for appliances, electric heat, and lighting. The utility will make up the difference for any energy that your turbine cannot make. Any excess electricity that is produced by the system, and cannot be used by the household, can often be sent or sold to the utility. One drawback to this system, however, is that during power outages, the wind turbine is required to shut down for safety reasons.

Grid-connected systems are only practical if:

- You live in an area with average annual wind speeds of at least 10 mph.
- Utility-supplied electricity is expensive in your area.
- The utility's requirements for connecting your system to its grid are not exceedingly expensive.
- There are good incentives for the sale of excess electricity.

Mounting Your Small Wind Electric System on a Tower

Since wind speeds increase with height, it is essential that your small wind turbine be mounted on a tower. The higher the tower, the more power the wind system will be able to produce. To determine the best height for your tower, you will need to know the estimated annual energy output and the size of your turbine.

There are two types of towers: self-supporting (free-standing) and guyed. Most home wind power systems use a guyed tower as it is the least expensive. Guyed towers consist of these parts:

- Lattice sections

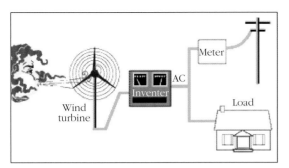

A grid-connected small wind electric system

- Pipe
- Tubing (depending on the design)
- Supporting guy wires

These towers are easier to install but they do require lots of space—the radius of the tower must be ½ to ¾ of the tower height.

Tilt-down towers, while more expensive, offer an easy way to maintain smaller, lightweight turbines that are less than 10 kilowatts. These towers can be lowered to the ground during severe weather or unusually high winds.

Generally, it is a good idea to install a small wind turbine on a tower with the bottom of the rotor blades around 30 feet above any obstacle that is within 300 feet from the tower.

Windmills

Windmills are used for pumping water, milling, and operating light machinery all around the world. They are constructed in a variety of shapes and some are quite picturesque. When set up properly, windmills cost nothing to operate and if the wheel is made well, it will last for many years without need for major repairs. To make a windmill requires a good understanding of carpentry and workmanship but it is not incredibly difficult or expensive to do.

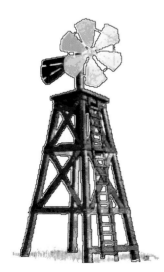

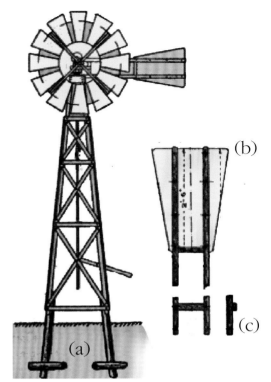

Details of the windmill. Figure (a) shows a general view with the tail turned to "off" position. Figure (b) shows details of the tail, and (c) shows a cross-piece of the tail.

Constructing a Windmill

Windmills can be of all sizes, though the larger the windmill, the more power it can generate. This windmill and tower can be easily constructed out of wood, an old wheel, and a few iron fittings you may be able to find at a hardware store or home center. Constructing the windmill in sections is the easiest way to create this structure. Simply follow these directions to make your own energy-producing windmill:

The Tower

1. The tower is the first part to be built and should be constructed out of four spruce sticks that are 16 feet long and 4 inches square, in a configuration that measures 30 inches square at the top and 72 inches square at the base.
2. The deck should be 36 inches square and should project 2 inches over the top rails.
3. The rails and cross braces can be spruce or pine strips and should measure 4 inches wide and 7/8 inch thick. Attach these to the corner posts with steel-wire nails.
4. Embed the corner posts 2 feet into the ground, leaving 14 feet above the surface. The rail at the bottom, which is attached to the four posts, should measure 3 feet above the ground. Midway between

Beveled cross braces fit snugly against the corners.

this and the top rail of the deck, run a middle rail around the post. Make sure that where your wheel will be attached, this point rises at least 2 feet above any obstructions (buildings, trees, etc.) so it can have access to the blowing wind.

5. The cross braces should be beveled at the ends so they fit snugly against the corner.
6. The posts, rails, and braces should be planed so they present a nice appearance at the end of the building. A ladder can also be constructed at one side of the tower to allow easy access to the mill.
7. Nail a board across two of the rails halfway up the tower. Secure the lower end of a trunk tightly here

if you are constructing a pumping mill. However, if a wooden mill is what you are after, you can use an old wheel from a wagon and six blades of wood.

The Turntable

1. The turntable holds the wheel and tail. It should be built of 2½ x 2-inch timber and 2-inch galvanized wrought iron "water" tube and flanges.
2. The upper flange supports the timber framing. It should be countersunk, using a half-round file, and screwed tightly onto the tube as far as possible. The end of the tube should project just slightly beyond the face of the flange so that it can be riveted over to fill the countersink.
3. Bolt the two loose flanges to the framework of the tower. Use them with 2-inch pipe with the thread filed away so they may slide freely onto the tube. The upper loose flange should form a footstep bearing and the lower flange a guide for the turntable.
4. Now mount the turntable on the ball bearing to make sure the mill head can turn freely. Screw on two back nuts to guard against any possibility of the turntable being lifted out of place by a strong wind.

The Head

1. This is the part that will carry the wheel spindle.
2. Notch the joints and secure them with 2-inch bolts.
3. The upright, which carries a bolt or pin for the spur-wheel to revolve upon, is kept in place in the front and at the sides by a piece of hoop iron.

The windmill turntable (d, e, and f) holds the wheel and tail. The flange (detailed drawings g and h) forms a support for the timber framing.

Details of the wheel shaft frame (i, j); front and side views, (k, l); axle of wheel (m); attachment of inner end of vane to inner ring of frame (n); vane on rings (o); attachment of vane to outer brackets by bracket (p).

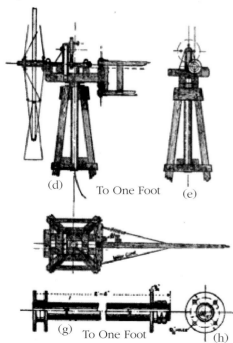

(d) To One Foot (e)

(g) To One Foot (h)

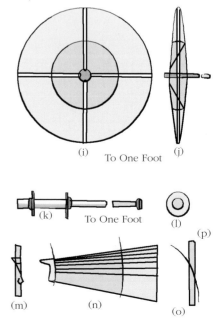

(i) To One Foot (j)

(k) To One Foot (l)

(p)

(m) (n) (o)

4. The tail vane swivel is a piece of 5-inch bore tube with back nuts and washers. Pass an iron bolt or other piece of iron through this, screw it to each end, and fit it with four nuts and washers.

The Wheel Shaft

1. Use wrought-iron tubing and flanges to create the wheel shaft. The bore of the tube is at least 5 inches, and the outside diameter should be roughly 1½ inches. Both the tube and the fittings should be of good quality and a thick gauge (steam quality is preferred).
2. If lathe is available, lightly skim it over the tubing. However, if it's not, a careful filing will do just as well to smooth down the edges.
3. Screw the tube higher up on one end to receive the flanges forming the hub. Screw these on and secure them on one side with back nuts and on the other with a distance piece made out of a 1½-inch bore tube. Fit a cap to close the open front end of the tube.
4. Grease two plummer blocks with some form of lubrication. These will be the bearings for the shaft.
5. A pinion is needed of at least 2½ inches in diameter at the pitch circle. Bore it to fit the wheel shaft. A spur wheel of 7 inches in diameter should follow that (gear wheels from a lawn mower can be used if available).

The Wheel

1. The wheel should be at least 5 feet in diameter to produce a good amount of energy. The framing consists of an inner and outer ring and four double arms with cross stays and diagonals (a regular wooden wheel will be sufficient, or you can find one made of galvanized steel).
2. Cut each spoke at an angle on one side so that the blades will have the necessary pitch to make the wind turn them.
3. The blades should be 18 inches long, 12 inches wide at the outer ends, and 6 inches wide next to the hub. Each blade should be only ¾ inch thick. Attach them to the spokes with simple screws.
4. If you desire, you can string a wire between the outer end of each blade to the end of the next spoke. This will help steady the blades.

The Tail

1. Run a fine saw cut up about 2 feet 6 inches from the outer end to receive the vane (optional).
2. Pass a cord over two pulleys and down the turntable tube. It is necessary to attach the end of the cord to a short cylinder of hard wood or metal (about 2 to 3 inches in diameter). This revolves with the turntable but can be slid up or down.

Each spoke should be cut at an angle so that the blades will have the pitch to make the wind turn them.

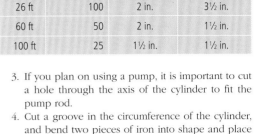

Total Lift	Gallons per Hour	Bore of Pump	Approximate Stroke
26 ft	100	2 in.	3½ in.
60 ft	50	2 in.	1½ in.
100 ft	25	1½ in.	1½ in.

3. If you plan on using a pump, it is important to cut a hole through the axis of the cylinder to fit the pump rod.
4. Cut a groove in the circumference of the cylinder, and bend two pieces of iron into shape and place them into the grooves. Now take the cords from the two bolts, untying the straps. Join these two cords to another cord, which acts as a reel or lever at the base of the tower. In this way, the position of the tail can be regulated from a stationary point.

Adding Pumps to Your Windmill

If you want to use this windmill to pump water, then you may need to do some experimenting with different lengths of pump stroke. Below is a table indicating what should be expected from the pump, and also providing the size of the single-action pump suitable for a given lift (using a ratio of 1 to 3).

Make sure that your pump is not too large; otherwise, it may not start in a light wind or breeze.

The pump is driven by a pin screwed into the side of the spur wheel and is secured with a lock nut. Drill and tap three or four holes at different distances from the center of the wheel so the length of the stroke can be adjusted. If the spokes on the wheel are too thin for drilling, you can use a clamp with a projecting pin instead.

A pump rod—a continuous wooden rod about 1 inch square and thicker at the top end—can be used in connecting the bottom end (by bolting) to the "bow" supplied with the pump. Intermediate joints, if needed, can be fashioned with 1 x ½-inch fish plates roughly 6 inches long. If the pump is no more than 12 feet below the crank pin, one guide will be adequate. The pump rod must be able to revolve with the head and will be need to be thickened up in a circular section where it passes through the guide. Make the guide in two halves and screw or bolt it to a bar running across the tower.

Final Touches

When construction is finished, paint all of the woodwork any color that complements your yard or property and, if desired, lacquer it to protect the wood from rain and snow. A windmill of this size will create at least a one quarter horsepower in a 15 mph wind.

Building a Small Wind Motor

This small wind motor can easily be made to generate energy for small machines, tool shed lightbulbs, and other small mechanics. The foundation for this wind-

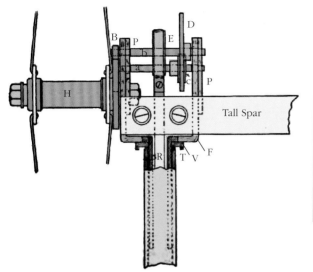

Details of small wind motor

Zoning, Permitting, and Covenant Requirements

Before you invest in or make your own small wind energy system, you should research any zoning and neighborhood covenant issues that may deter your installing a wind turbine system. You can find out about local zoning restrictions by contacting a local building inspector, board of supervisors, or planning board. They will inform you whether or not you'll need a building permit and will provide you with a list of other requirements. Further, your neighbors or homeowners' association may object to a wind machine that will block their view or a system that will be too noisy.

wheel can be made out of the front wheel of an old bicycle with the front spindle and cones completely intact.

Attach eight to 12 vanes of stout sheet tin to the rim. These sheets should be around 8 inches long and 4 to 6 inches wide and should lie at a 30-degree angle to the plane of the rim. The vanes will be much more efficient if they are curved in a circular arc about the same radius as the wheel. The concave side should be positioned to face toward the wind.

On the back of each vane, rivet a rib of strip iron ½ inch thick. This strip should project about ½ inch beyond the tip and 1½ inches at the other end. There, twist and bend it to make a bracket and then bolt the vane to the center line of the rim.

The illustration above shows a side view of the motor with its gearing and supports. *A* is the rim and part of the spokes of a toothed wheel that are attached at several points to the spokes of the bicycle wheel. It is loosely fixed and adjusted until it runs well when the wheel is moved. It should not wobble. *A* drives a smaller cog, *B*,

mounted on the same spindle, *a*. This spindle revolves around two plates, *PP*, screwed to *F*. *C* drives a large cog, *D*, and an eccentric, *E*, which moves the eccentric rod, *R*, up and down. This works the small pump at the foot of the mast that supports the windmill. *E* can be quickly made out of a thick disc with two larger discs soldered to it. *R* is a piece of stout brass strip bent around *E* and closed with a screw.

When all of the vanes are in position, connect the tips of the ribs and vanes together with rings of stout wire and solder them on at all the contact points. Screw one of the spindle nuts tightly against its cone. The other end of the spindle should pass through one arm of the stirrup (F) made out of ½-inch iron 1½ inches wide. This is then secured by a washer and nut on the inside. The stirrup and circular plate (V) are bored to accommodate the end of the iron pipe (T).

Close off the top of the hole (F) and heat the top of the pipe to expand it to fit into the chamber. Clean these parts well and weld them together. It is important that the *T* is square with the stirrup. Then, cut the pipe off 9 inches below *V*. Solder a small ring to the underside of *V* to prevent moisture from working its way along *T* and ruining your motor.

The tail spar is a wooden bar 1½ x 2½ inches wide and 40 inches long. It is notched to fit the stirrup and tapered off toward the tail. A sheet of sturdy iron, 15 x 12 inches, is then fitted into the saw cut. Two bolts clip the wings of the forked end tightly against the sides of the stirrup. The tail should be able to balance the wheel on the vertical pivot to avoid stressing the joint at the top of *T*.

A wind-wheel this size will spin quite effectively in a blustery wind but will probably only generate enough energy to power a small pump. This will do nicely to fill a watering can for your garden or for powering other light machinery.

A Pumping Windmill

A pumping windmill can help you pump water from a well or other underground reservoir into a suction-pump. This windmill has a simple wheel with spokes

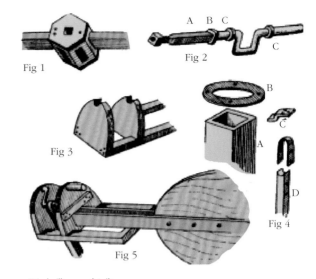

A pumping windmill

Windmill pump details

and sails. It consists of a hub, six spokes, a fan tail, and a trunk or pole for attaching the wheel.

The hub is a hexagon 6 x 6 inches. One spoke can be driven into a hole made on either side (Figure 1). The spokes should be 3 feet long, 3 x 1½ inches at the hub end, and 1 x 1½ inches on the outer end. The spokes are driven into the holes in the hub and pinned to hold them in place.

The hub should be made of hard wood and the holes may be cut with a mortise chisel and mallet. Make sure the holes are spaced evenly so the spokes will light up properly.

Attach triangular pieces of twilled muslin sheeting to the face of each spoke. The loose corner of each can be attached to the next spoke end with a piece of string. This creates an outlet between the leech and the spoke of each space between the spoke so that the wind can pass through. This, in effect, makes the wheel turn.

The wheel should be held in place at the top of the supporting post by a shaft passing through the hub and bolted to the front of the wheel with a nut. Figure 2 is a good example of what this should look like. The shaft should be about 1 inch square where it passes through the hub. At the front end, it should be tightened with a nut and washer. The square part, A, where the end of the hub will be, should be welded at B to hold the hub in the proper place. About an inch beyond the square shoulder, another one, C, should be welded to the shaft. This helps balance the wheel.

Now a crank can be formed, 2 inches wide and 3 inches out from the shaft. Another collar, C, C, should be welded onto the crank and then, beyond this point, the shaft should stick out about 6 inches.

The total length of the shaft is 15 inches, and the whole device can be painted. To attach the fan tail, a head made out of two blocks of wood should be

What would happen if we used more wind energy?

According to the American Wind Energy Association, if we increase our nation's wind energy capacity to 20 percent by 2030, it would have the following effects:

- *Reduce Greenhouse Gas Emission:* A cumulative total of 7,600 million tons of CO_2 would be avoided by 2030, and more than 15,000 million tons of CO_2 would be avoided by 2050.
- *Conserve Water:* Reduce cumulative water consumption in the electric sector by 8 percent or 4 trillion gallons from 2007 through 2030.
- *Lower Natural Gas Prices:* Significantly reduce natural gas demand and reduce natural gas prices by 12 percent, saving consumers approximately $130 billion.
- *Expand Manufacturing:* To produce enough turbines and components for the 20 percent wind scenario, the industry would require more than 30,000 direct manufacturing jobs across the nation (assuming that 30 to 80 percent of major turbine components would be manufactured domestically by 2030).
- *Generate Local Revenues:* Lease payments for wind turbines would generate well over $600 million for landowners in rural areas and generate additional local tax revenues exceeding $1.5 billion annually by 2030. From 2007 through 2030, cumulative economic activity would exceed $1 trillion or more than $440 billion in net present value terms.

The use of large scale windmills is often controversial. They can provide a significant amount of clean energy, but they also clutter ridgelines, produce a lot of noise, and hurt the bird population.

attached and fastened 5 inches apart on the lower rails (Fig. 3). The upper ends of the blocks should be cut so as to allow the shaft to enter them. The collars, *C* and *C*, *C*, are placed at the inside of the blocks. To hold the shaft in place, small iron straps can be screwed tightly over the top of each block.

This head rests on the top of a hollow square post through which the rod passes, connecting the crank with the piston-rod of the pump (Fig. 4 A). A flat iron collar, *B*, should be screwed tightly at the top. To keep the head properly secured, four iron cleats (Fig. 4 C) should be screwed tightly under the corners of the head to help grip the projecting edge of the collar. This will hold the head rigid while allowing it to move about with the force of the wind.

Apply a little bit of grease or Vaseline to the top of the collar so the head will move easily. The top of the connecting rod should be attached to the crank and bolted to the top of the hard wood rod (Fig. 4 D).

The tail, which is 33 inches long and 24 inches wide at the end, is made of boards that are ¾ inch thick. The tail should be attached to the head (Fig. 5).

To place the windmill over a pump, build a platform that is braced with pieces of wood (see the illustration). Wires can also be run from the upper part of the trunk down to pegs driven into the ground. This will add additional support and steadiness to the upright shaft.

To start the wheel, snap the ends of the sheets to the spoke ends. To stop the wheel, unsnap the ends and furl the sails around the spokes, tying them securely with a piece of yarn or a cotton cord.

Hydropower

Water is constantly moving through a vast global cycle, evaporating from lakes and oceans, forming clouds, precipitating, and then flowing back into the ocean. The energy of this water cycle, which is mainly driven by the sun, can be tapped to produce electricity or to power machines—a process called hydropower. Hydropower uses water as a type of fuel that is neither reduced nor used up in the process. Since the water cycle is endless and will constantly recharge the system, hydropower is considered a renewable energy.

Hydropower (also known as hydroelectric power) is made when flowing water is captured and turned into electricity. There are many types of hydroelectric facilities that are all powered by the kinetic energy derived from flowing water as it moves downstream. Generators and turbines convert this energy into electricity. This is then fed into the electrical grid for use in homes, businesses, and other industries.

Types of Hydropower Plants

There are three types of hydropower plants:

1. Impoundment—Impoundment facilities are the most common type of hydroelectric power plants. This facility, typically a large hydropower system, uses a dam to store river water in a reservoir. Water that is released from the reservoir flows through a turbine, spinning it. This activates a generator to produce electricity. The water may be released either to meet the changing electricity needs or to maintain a constant reservoir level.

2. Diversion—A diversion facility, sometimes referred to as a run-of-river facility, channels a portion of a river through a canal or penstock. This does not always require the use of a dam.

3. Pumped storage—A pumped storage facility stores energy by pumping water from a lower reservoir to an upper reservoir when electricity demands are low. During times when electrical demands are high, water is then released back into the lower reservoir to generate electricity.

Some hydropower plants use dams and others do not. Many dams were originally built for other purposes and then hydropower was added at a later date. In the United States, only 2,400 of the 80,000 dams produce power—the rest are used for recreation, farm ponds, flood control, water supply, and irrigation.

Size of Hydropower Plants

Hydropower plants range in size from small and micro systems, which are operated for individual needs or to sell the power to utilities, to larger projects that produce electricity for utilities, supplying many consumers with electricity.

Micro hydropower plants have a capacity of up to 100 kilowatts. Small hydropower plants have a capacity between

≈ Water's never ending cycle

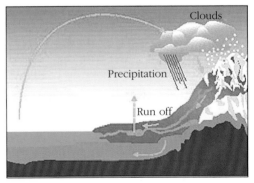

Clouds

Precipitation

Run off

A Brief History of Hydropower

Humans have been using water to help them perform work for thousands of years. Water wheels have been employed for grinding grains into flour, to saw wood, and to power textile mills. The technology to use running water to create hydroelectricity has been around for over a hundred years. The modern hydropower turbine was created in the middle of the eighteenth century and developed into direct current technology. Today, an alternating current is in use and came about when the electric generator was combined with the turbine. The first hydroelectric plant in the United States was built in Appleton, Wisconsin in 1882.

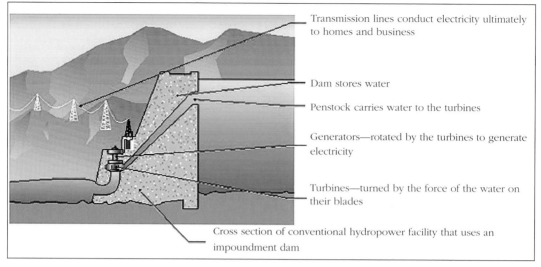

Transmission lines conduct electricity ultimately to homes and business

Dam stores water

Penstock carries water to the turbines

Generators—rotated by the turbines to generate electricity

Turbines—turned by the force of the water on their blades

Cross section of conventional hydropower facility that uses an impoundment dam

Diagram of a hydropower plant

100 kilowatts and 30 megawatts. Large hydropower plants have a capacity of more than 30 megawatts. The small and micro systems can produce enough electricity for a home, farm, or even a small village.

Hydropower Turbines

There are two main types of hydropower turbines: impulse and reaction. The type of turbine selected for a project is based on the height of the standing water (the "head") and the flow (volume) of the water at a particular site. It is also determined by how deep the turbine must be set, its efficiency, and its cost.

A micro hydropower plant.

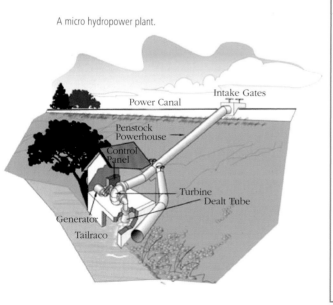

Impulse Turbine

An impulse turbine typically uses the velocity of water to move the runner and discharges to atmospheric pres-

Advantages of Hydropower

- It is fueled by water, making it a clean energy source.
- It does not pollute the air since it does not burn any fossil fuels.
- It is a domestic energy source.
- It relies on the water cycle and is a renewable energy source.
- It is usually available as needed.
- The water flow can be controlled through the turbine to produce energy on demand.
- The plants provide reservoirs for recreation (fishing, swimming, boating), water supply, and food control.

Disadvantages of Hydropower

- It can negatively impact fish populations by hampering fish migration upstream past dams, though there are ways to allow for passage both up- and downstream.
- It can impact the quality and flow of water, causing low dissolved oxygen levels that can negatively impact the riverbank habitats.
- The plants can be impacted by drought, and if they are not receiving adequate water, they cannot produce electricity.
- The plants compete for land use and can cause humans, plants, and animals to lose their natural habitat.

sure. The water stream then hits each bucket on the runner. The water flows out of the bottom of the turbine after hitting the runner. These turbines are suitable for high head, low flow applications.

Reaction Turbine

A reaction turbine generates power by the combined action of pressure and moving water. The runner is placed in the water stream, which flows over the blades instead of striking each one separately. These turbines are used for sites with lower head and higher flows.

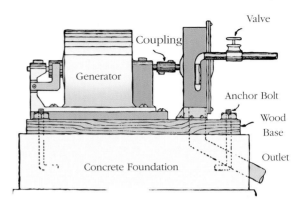

Diagram of a hydroelectric motor

Even a small waterfall can provide a lot of power.

Geothermal Energy

Geothermal energy (the heat from the Earth) is accessible as an alternative source of heat and power. Geothermal energy can be accessed by drilling water or steam wells using a process much like drilling for oil. This resource is enormous but is sadly underused as an energy source. When it is employed, though, it proves to be clean (emitting little or no greenhouse gases), reliable, economical, and domestically found (geothermal energy can be harnessed from almost anywhere and thus makes countries less dependent on foreign oil).

Wells a mile or more deep can be drilled into underground reservoirs to tap steam and very hot water. This can then be brought to the surface and used in a variety of ways—such as to drive turbines and electricity generators. In the United States, most geothermal reservoirs are located in the western states, in Alaska, and in Hawaii. People in more than 120 locations in the United States are using geothermal energy for space and district heating.

Geothermal resources can range from shallow ground water to hot water found in rocks several miles below the surface of the earth. It can even be harnessed, in some cases, from magma (hot molten rock near the earth's core). Geothermal reservoirs of low to moderate temperature (roughly 68 to 302°F) can be used to heat homes, office, and greenhouses. Curiously, the dehydration of onions and garlic comprises the largest industrial use of geothermal energy in the United States.

Three Main Uses of Geothermal Energy

Some types of geothermal energy usage draw from the earth's temperatures closer to the surface and others require, as noted above, drilling miles into the earth. The three main uses of geothermal energy are:

1. Direct Use and District Heating Systems—These use hot water from springs and reservoirs near the earth's surface.
2. Electricity Generation—Typically found in power plants, this type of energy requires high-temperature water and steam (generally between 300 and 700°F). Geothermal power plants are built where reservoirs are positioned only a mile or two from the earth's surface.
3. Geothermal Heat Pumps—These use stable ground or water temperatures near the earth's surface to control building temperatures above the ground.

A geothermal power plant in action

Additional Resources

The U.S. Department of Energy, in conjunction with the Geo-Heat Center, conducts research, provides technical support, and distributes information on a wide range of geothermal direct-use applications. Some information that is provided revolves around greenhouse informational packages, cost comparisons of heat pumps, low temperature resource assessments, cost analysis for homeowners, and information directed to aquaculture developers.

The greenhouse informational package provides information for people who are looking to develop geothermal greenhouses. This package includes crop market prices for vegetables and flowers, operating costs, heating system specifications, greenhouse heating equipment selection spreadsheets, and vendor information.

Groundwater heat pumps have also been identified as offering substantial savings over other types of pump systems. Informational packets about heat pump systems are provided to answer frequently asked questions concerning the application and usage of geothermal heat pumps.

The Geo-Heat Center examined the costs associated with the installation of district heating systems in single-family residential sectors. They discovered that cost-saving areas included installation in unpaved areas, using non-insulated return lines, and installation in areas that are unencumbered by existing buried utility lines.

Direct Use Geothermal Energy

Since ancient times, people have been directly using hot water as a source of energy. The Chinese, Native Americans, and Romans used hot mineral springs for bathing, cooking, and heating purposes. Currently, a number of hot springs are still used for bathing and many people believe these hot, mineral-rich waters possess natural healing powers.

You can combine solar and geothermal energy to produce more consistent power in your home.

Besides bathing, the most common direct use of geothermal energy is for heating buildings. This is through district heating systems—these types of systems provide heat for roughly 95 percent of the buildings in Reykjavik, Iceland. District heating systems pipe hot water near the earth's surface directly into buildings in order to provide adequate heat.

Direct use of geothermal resources is a proven, economic, and clean energy option. Geothermal heat can be piped directly into facilities and used to heat buildings, grow greenhouse plants, heat water for fish farming, and even pasteurize milk. Some northern U.S. cities pipe hot water under roads and sidewalks to melt the snow.

Geothermal Heat Pumps

Even though temperatures above the surface of the earth change daily and seasonally, in general, temperatures in the top 10 feet of the Earth's surface stay fairly constant

A horizontal closed-loop heat pump system

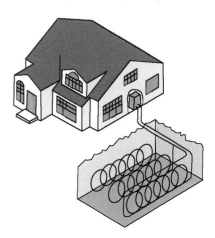

A geothermal power plant

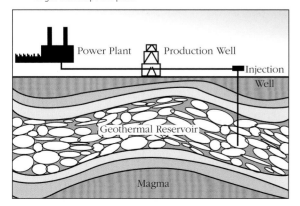

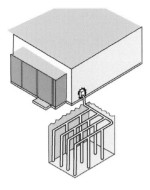

A vertical closed-loop heat pump system

at around 50 to 60°F. This means that, in most places, soil temperatures are typically warmer than air temperatures in the winter and cooler in the summer. Geothermal heat pumps (GHPs) use this constant temperature to heat and cool buildings. These pumps transfer heat from the ground (or underground water sources) into buildings during the winter and do the reverse process in the summer months.

Geothermal heat pumps, according to the U.S. Environmental Protection Agency (EPA), are the most energy-efficient, environmentally clean, and cost-effective systems for maintaining a consistent temperature control. These pumps are becoming more popular, even though most homes still use furnaces and air conditioners. Sometimes referred to as earth-coupled, ground-source, or water-source heat pumps, GHPs use the constant temperature of the earth as the exchange medium (using ground heat exchangers) instead of the outdoor air temperature. In this way, the system can be quite efficient on cold winter nights in comparison to air-source heat pumps.

Geothermal heat pumps can heat, cool, and, in some cases, even supply hot water to a house. These pumps are relatively quiet, long-lasting, need little to no maintenance, and do not rely on outside temperatures to function effectively. While geothermal systems are initially more expensive to install, these costs are quickly returned in energy savings in about five to 10 years. Systems have a life-span of roughly 25 years for inside components and more than 50 years for ground loop systems. Each year, about 50,000 geothermal heat pumps are installed in the United States.

Types of Geothermal Heat Pump Systems

There are four basic types of ground loop heat pump systems: horizontal, vertical, pond/lake, and open-loop systems. The first three are closed-loop systems while the fourth is, as its name suggests, open-loop. The type of system used is generally determined based on the climate, soil conditions, land availability, and local installation costs of the site for the pump. All four types of geothermal heat pump systems can be used for both residential and commercial building applications.

Horizontal Heat Pump System

This closed-loop installation is extremely cost-effective for residential heat pumps and is well suited for new construction where adequate land is available for the system. Horizontal heat pump systems need 4-foot trenches to be installed. These systems are typically laid out using two pipes—one buried 6 feet and the other buried 4 feet below the ground—or by placing two pipes side by side at 5 feet underground in a 2-foot-wide trench.

Vertical Heat Pump System

Schools and larger commercial buildings use vertical heat pump systems because they require less land to be effectively used. These systems are best used where the soil is too shallow for trenching. They also minimize any disturbance to established landscaping. To install a vertical system, holes that are roughly 4 inches in diameter are drilled about 20 feet apart and 100 to 400 feet deep. Two pipes are inserted into these holes and are connected at the bottom with a U-bend, forming a loop. The vertical loops are then connected with a horizontal pipe, placed in the trenches, and connected to the heat pump in the building.

Pond/Lake Heat Pump System

Another closed-loop system is the pond/lake heat pump system. If a site has enough water—usually in the form of a pond or even a lake—this system may be the most cost-effective. This heat pump system works by running a supply line pipe underground from a building to the water source. The piping is coiled into circles no less than 8 feet under the surface—this prevents the water in the pipes from freezing. The coils should be placed only in a water source that meets the minimum volume, depth, and quality criteria.

Open-Loop Heat Pump System

An open-loop system uses well or surface body water as the heat exchange fluid that will circulate directly through the geothermal heat pump system. Once this water has circulated through the system, it is returned to the ground through a recharge well or as surface discharge. The system is really only practical where there is a sufficient supply of clean water. Local codes and regulations for proper groundwater discharge must also be met in order for the heat pump system to be utilized.

Selecting and Installing a Geothermal Heat Pump System in Your Home

The heating efficiency of commercial ground-source and water-source heat pumps is indicated by their coefficient of performance (COP)—the ratio of heat provided in Btu per Btu of energy input. The cooling efficiency is measured by the energy efficiency ratio (EER)—the ratio of heat removed to the electricity required (in watts) to run the unit. Many geothermal heat pump systems are approved by the U.S. Department of Energy as being energy efficient products and so, if you are thinking of

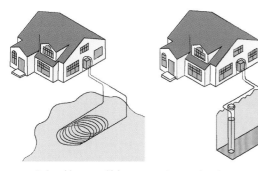

A closed-loop pond/lake heat pump system

An open-loop heat pump system

purchasing and installing this type of system, you may want to check to see if there is any special financing or incentives for purchasing energy efficient systems.

Evaluating Your Site

Before installing a geothermal heat pump, consider the site that will house the system. The presence of hot geothermal fluid containing low mineral and gas content, shallow aquifers for producing the fluid, space availability on your property, proximity to existing transmission lines, and availability of make-up water for evaporative cooling are all factors that will determine if your site is good for geothermal electric development. As a rule of thumb, geothermal fluid temperature should be no less than 300°F.

In the western United States, Alaska, and Hawaii, hydrothermal resources (reservoirs of steam or hot water) are more readily available than the rest of the country. However, this does not mean that geothermal heat cannot be used throughout the country. Shallow ground temperatures are relatively constant throughout the United States and this means that energy can be tapped almost anywhere in the country by using geothermal heat pumps and direct-use systems.

To determine the best type of ground loop systems for your site, you must assess the geological, hydrological, and spatial characteristics of your land in order to choose the best, most effective heat pump system to heat and cool your home:

1. Geology—This includes the soil and rock composition and properties on your site. These can affect the transfer rates of heat in your particular system. If you have soil with good heat transfer properties, your system will require less piping to obtain a good amount of heat from the soil. Furthermore, the amount of soil that is available also contributes to which system you will choose. For example, areas that have hard rock or shallow soil will most likely benefit from a vertical heat pump system instead of a system requiring large and deep trenches, such as the horizontal heat pump system.

2. Hydrology—This refers to the availability of ground or surface water, which will affect the type of system to be installed. Factors such as depth, volume, and water quality will help determine if surface water bodies can be used as a source of water for an open-loop heat pump system or if they would work best with a pond/lake system. Before installing an open-loop system, however, it is best to determine your site's hydrology so potential problems (such as aquifer depletion or groundwater contamination) can be avoided.

3. Available land—The acreage and layout of your land, as well as your landscaping and the location of underground utilities, also play an important part in the type of heat pump system you choose. If you are building a new home, horizontal ground loops are an economical system to install. If you have an existing home and want to convert your heat and cooling to geothermal energy, vertical heat pump systems are best to minimize the disturbance to your existing landscaping and yard.

Installing the Heat Pumps

Geothermal heat pump systems are somewhat difficult to install on your own—though it can certainly be done. Make sure, before you begin any digging, to contact your local utility company to make sure you will not be digging into gas pipes or electrical wires.

The ground heat exchanger in a geothermal heat pump system is made up of closed- or open-loop pipe—depending on which type of system you've determined is best suited for your site. Since most systems employed are closed-loop systems, high density polyethylene pipe is used and buried horizontally at 4 to 6 feet deep or vertically at 100 to 400 feet deep. These pipes are filled with an environmentally friendly antifreeze/water solution that acts as a heat exchanger. You can find this at your local home store or contact a contractor to see where it is distributed. This solution works in the winter by extracting heat from the earth and carrying it into the building. In the summertime, the system reverses, taking heat from the building and depositing it into the ground.

Air delivery ductwork will distribute the hot or cold air throughout the house's ductwork like traditional, conventional systems. An air handler—a box that contains the indoor coil and fan—should be installed to move the house air through the heat pump system. The air handler contains a large blower and a filter, just like standard air conditioning units.

A vertical closed-loop system

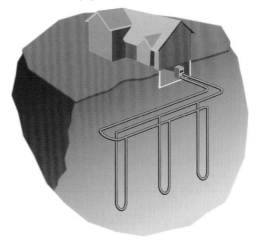

Cost-Efficiency of Geothermal Heat Pump Systems

By installing and using a geothermal heat pump system, you will save on the costs of operating and maintaining your heating and cooling system. While these systems are generally a bit pricier to install, they prove to be more efficient and thus save you money on a monthly and yearly basis. Especially in the colder winter months, geothermal heat pump systems can reduce your heating costs by about half. Annual energy savings by using a geothermal heat pump system range from 30 to 60 percent.

Benefits of Using Geothermal Energy

- It is clean energy. Geothermal energy does not require the burning of fossil fuels (coal, gas, or oil) in order to produce energy.
- Geothermal fields produce only about ⅙th of the carbon dioxide that natural gas-fueled power plants do. They also produce little to no sulfur-bearing gases, which reduces the amount of acid rain.
- It is available at any time of day, all year round.
- Geothermal power is homegrown, which reduces dependence on foreign oil.
- It is a renewable source of energy. Geothermal energy derives its source from an almost unlimited amount of heat generated by the earth. And even if energy is limited in an area, the volume taken out can be reinjected, making it a sustainable source of energy.
- Geothermal heat pump systems use 25 to 50 percent less electricity than conventional heating and cooling systems. They reduce energy consumption and emissions between 44 and 72 percent and improve humidity control by maintaining about 50 percent relative humidity indoors (GHPs are very effective for humid parts of the country).
- Heat pump systems can be "zoned" to allow different parts of your home to be heated and cooled to different temperatures without much added cost or extra space required.
- Geothermal heat pump systems are durable and reliable. Underground piping can last for 25 to 50 years and the heat pumps tend to last at least 20 years.
- Heat pump systems reduce noise pollution since they have no outside condensing unit (like air conditioners).

Alternate "Geothermal" Cooling System

True geothermal energy systems can be very expensive to install and you may not be able to use one in your home at this time. However, here is a fun alternative way to use the concepts of geothermal systems to keep your house cooler in the summer and your air conditioning bills lower. All you need are a basement, small window fan, and dehumidifier.

Your basement is a wonderful example of how the top layers of earth tend to remain at a stable temperature throughout the year. In the winter, your basement may feel somewhat warm; in the summer, it's nice and refreshingly cool. This is due to the temperature of the soil permeating through the basement walls. And this cool basement air can be used to effectively reduce the temperature in your home by up to five degrees during the summer months. Here are the steps to your alternative "geothermal" cooling system:

1. Run the dehumidifier in your basement during the night, bringing the humidity down to about 60 percent.
2. Keep your blinds and curtains closed in the sunniest rooms in your home.
3. In the morning, when the temperature inside the house reaches about 77°F, open a small window in your basement, just a crack, and open one of the upstairs windows, placing a small fan in it and directing the room air out of the window.
4. With all other windows and outside doors closed, the fan will suck the cool basement air through your home and out the open window. Doing this for about an hour will bring down the temperature inside your home, buying you a couple of hours of reprieve before switching on the AC.

The hot springs at Yellowstone are a natural example of geothermal heating.

Composting Toilets

Toilets come in three common varieties: siphon-jet flush valve toilets (common in most homes), pressurized tank toilets, and gravity flow. These toilets, generally speaking, use up large amounts of water and the waste is flushed into a sewer system and then dumped in a variety of locations. Composting toilets require little to no water, which provides a solution to sanitation and environmental problems in areas that are rural, without sewers, and in the suburbs throughout the world. Although composting toilets are rare in private homes—they are generally found in park facilities and small highway rest stops—these waterless toilets can be utilized by the regular homeowner.

It is astonishing that Americans flush about 4.8 billion gallons of water down toilets every day, according to the U.S. Environmental Protection Agency. Just replacing all existing U.S. toilets with 1.6-gallon-per-flush, ultra-low-flow (ULF) models would save about 5,500 gallons of water per person per year! So, if you are unable to install a composting toilet in your home or on your property, you may choose to install ULF models in your home to help conserve water usage.

The Basics of the Composting Toilet

Composting (or biological) toilet systems contain and process excrement, toilet paper, carbon additive, and, at times, food wastes. These systems rely on unsaturated conditions where aerobic bacteria break down waste—unlike septic systems—much like a compost heap for your gardening necessities. The resulting soil-like material—humus—must be buried or removed. It's a good idea to check state and local regulations regarding proper handling methods.

In many parts of the country, public health officials are realizing that there is a definite need for environmentally sound human waste treatment and recycling methods, and compost toilets are an easy way to work toward these needs. Because they don't require any water to be used, composting toilets are ideal for remote areas and places that have high water tables, shallow soil, and rough terrain. These systems save water and allow for valuable plant nutrients to be recycled in the process.

Composting toilets are being used more regularly in parks around the world.

A composting toilet

Factors that Affect the Rate of Composting

1. Microorganisms—A mix of bacteria and fungi need to be present in order for the excrement to turn into composted material.
2. Moisture—This helps the microorganisms to make simpler compounds before they are metabolized. Moisture should be kept between 40 and 70 percent.
3. pH—The best pH for the composting toilet material should be between 6.5 and 7.5.
4. Carbon to nitrogen ratio—It is important to balance out the nitrogen found in urine with added carbon in your composting toilet.
5. Proper care—Managing your composting toilet well will help keep it efficient and productive.

There are a few key components for establishing a composting toilet:

- Composting reactor that is connected to a micro-flush toilet
- Screened air inlet and exhaust system to remove odors and heat, plus CO_2 and other decomposition byproducts
- Mechanism to provide proper ventilation that will help aerobic organisms in the compost heap
- Process controls
- Access door for the removal of the end product

It is important that the composting toilet separates the solid from the liquid waste and produces a humus-like material with less than 200 MPN per gram of fecal coliform. The compost chamber can be solar or electrically heated to maintain the right temperature for year-round use and bacterial decomposition.

Main Objective of the Composting Toilet

These systems are designed to contain, immobilize, and destroy pathogens. This reduces the risk of human infection and ensures that the toilets do not pollute the environment. If done correctly, the composted material should be able to be handled with little to no risk of harming the individual working with it.

A composting toilet consists of a well-ventilated container that breeds a good environment for unsaturated, moist human excrement that can be decomposed under sanitary conditions. A composting toilet can be large or small, depending on the space and its use. Organic matter is transformed into a humus-like product through the natural breaking down from bacteria and fungi. Most systems like this use the process of continuous composting, which includes a single chamber where the excrement is added to the top and the end product is taken from the bottom.

Advantages of Using a Composting Toilet

Composting toilets can be used practically anywhere a flush toilet can be. They are most likely to be used in homes in rural areas, seasonal cabins, recreation areas, and other places where flush toilets are either unnecessary or impractical. They are more cost-effective than establishing a central sewage system and there is no water wasted. These systems—since they aren't using copious amounts of water—also reduce the quantity of wastewater that is disposed of on a daily basis. These toilets can also be used to recycle and compost food wastes, thus reducing the amount of household garbage that is dumped every day. Finally, these toilet systems are beneficial to the environment as they divert nutrient and pathogen-containing effluent from the soil, surface water, and the groundwater.

Disadvantages of Using a Composting Toilet

Composting toilets are a big responsibility; the owner of a composting toilet must be committed to maintaining the system. Removing the compost can be unpleasant if the toilet is not properly set up and they could end up having odor issues.

Successful Management of the Composting Toilet

Composting toilets do not require highly trained people to deal with the sewage as it is relatively harmless to handle. But it is important to maintain your composting toilet so it can be effective and safe. Some composting toilets may need organic bulking agents added

Compost will enrich the soil in your garden to help grow healthier plants.

to aid the composting process. Adding grass clippings, sawdust, and leaves to your composting toilet reservoir will help aid the process. The end product should be removed every three months for smaller systems and, if composted correctly, should not smell and should not be toxic to humans or animals. Be sure to dispose of the waste materials in accordance with your particular state and local regulations.

Making Your Own Composting Toilet

Building your own composting toilet can be quite inexpensive and takes only a short amount of time to assemble. In order to construct a composting toilet, you will need the following materials:

- Two or three 5-gallon buckets with lids
- A standard toilet seat (a used one will work just fine) with lid
- ¾ x 3 x 18-inch plywood sheets
- Boards to be cut and used for the sides of the toilet box and for the legs
- Two hinges
- Screws
- Saw and measuring tape
- Bag of sawdust, to be used for soaking up excess moisture in the compositing bucket

To begin, cut a hole in one of the pieces of plywood so that it fits the size of the bucket. Then, attach the pieces of plywood together using the hinges. Build a box with the boards and then screw in the solid piece of plywood to the box, allowing for the part with the hole to remain on the top. Attach legs to the box, allowing the bucket to lift just slightly above the hole cut in the top piece of plywood. Then, attach the toilet seat to the plywood top, making sure that it fits securely over the rim of the bucket. Finally, stain or paint the entire composting toilet so it will last longer and match the décor of your bathroom.

Before using your homemade composting toilet, sprinkle 1 to 2 inches of sawdust into the bottom of the bucket. This will help absorb extra moisture and will also add a necessary carbon element that is useful in composting. Sprinkle sawdust into the toilet after each use to facilitate the composting process and to minimize odors. When the first bucket is full, remove and cover (allowing the composting process to continue), insert another bucket, and continue use. When both buckets are full, remove them to your composting pile in your yard. Make a small indent in the center of your composting pile and dump the new compost into the depression, laying old compost and other organic materials on top of the new addition. If used properly, your composting toilet will be odorless and your compost will be rich and ready for use in your garden.

Greywater

Greywater is just wastewater. Greywater, however, does not include toilet wastewater, which is known as blackwater. These two different kinds of water should not be mixed together for basic health reasons. The main differences between greywater and blackwater are:

- Greywater contains less nitrogen than blackwater (and about half of the nitrogen that is found in greywater is organic nitrogen that can be filtered out and used by plants).
- Greywater contains fewer pathogens than blackwater and thus is not as likely to spread organisms that could be potentially harmful to humans.
- Greywater decomposes faster than blackwater and is less likely to cause water pollution because of this factor.

Greywater is not necessarily sewage to begin with, but if left untreated for a couple of days, it will become like blackwater and thus will be unusable. Therefore, it is important to know how best to treat and manage greywater so it can be successfully and safely reused.

What is Greywater?

Simply speaking, greywater is wash water—bath, dish, and laundry water that is free from toilet waste and garbage disposal remnants. Greywater, when it is managed properly, can be quite useful for growing things in your garden or yard. Greywater, in effect, is an excellent source of nutrients for plants when used properly.

Greywater Irrigation Systems

The practice of irrigating with greywater is common in areas where the water supply is short. To have effective greywater irrigation that successfully utilizes the nutrients in the greywater, it is important to take precautions before using it in irrigation.

Planning a greywater system requires either an assumption that the system is right for you and your family or an understanding that the system is needed for the house independent of who lives in it.

To assess whether your household could benefit from a greywater system, it is important to take inventory of all the sources of greywater in the house. Look at how many gallons of water you use, per person, per day, when doing the laundry, running the dishwasher, and taking a bath or shower, and then add up these numbers. Remember that the typical washing machine uses 30 gallons of water per cycle, a dishwasher uses between 3 and 5 gallons per cycle, and simply washing your hands and brushing your teeth daily wastes about 1 to 5 gallons of water per day. If you are able to recycle and reuse all of that wasted water, you can effectively reduce the amount of water consumption your family has every day and every year.

Once you've decided to use your greywater, it is important to check with your local authorities to see if there are any state or local regulations for greywater usage in your area. Once you have the go-ahead to proceed, you can begin reusing your greywater to the benefit of your garden and household.

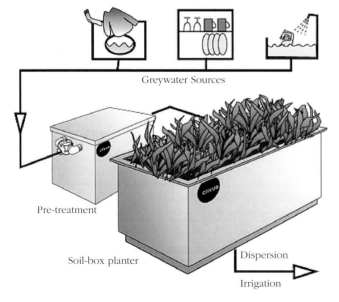

The pretreatment of greywater

Greywater Sources

Pre-treatment

Soil-box planter

Dispersion

Irrigation

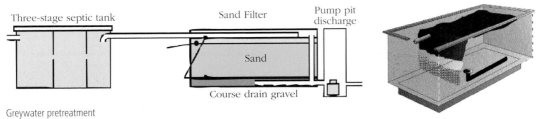

Greywater pretreatment

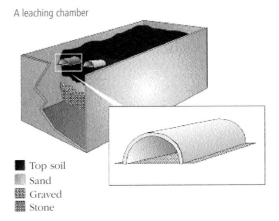

A planter soil box

Aerobic Pretreatment

This type of greywater treatment is suitable for shower, hand-washing, and laundry water. Aerobic pretreatment is a stretch filter technique that removes large particles and fibers to protect the pipes from clogging and transfers the greywater into a biologically active, aerobic soil-zone environment. Here microorganisms can survive and flourish. Stretch filters retain fibers and large particles and allow the rest of the materials to travel to the next processing stage. The filter is good for sinks and showers at public water facilities.

Anaerobic to Aerobic Pretreatment

If you have food waste entering the water system from dishwashers and kitchen sinks, this is the better option for treating your greywater. This system should have a three-stage septic tank to separate the sludge and grease from the water. This waste can then be removed easily. The outgoing water will be anaerobic and will need a sand filter to restore the aerobic conditions to the greywater. The final treatment leads the purified water to be treated in a planter bed. The system, while not inexpensive, is quite effective and is simple to maintain. A plan for this system can be seen above.

Planter Soil Box

Since 1975, soil boxes have been used to purify greywater. When using a soil box, however, it is vital that the planter bed be well drained to prevent water-logged zones from forming. Therefore, the bottom of the soil box should contain a layer of polyethylene pea gravel to provide for effective drainage. A layer of plastic mosquito netting should be placed over the gravel to prevent the layer of coarse sand from falling through. Atop the coarse sand should be a layer of concrete-mix sand and the top 2 feet should consist of humus-rich topsoil. Clay soils should not be used in soil boxes as they do not effectively allow water to pass through and drain.

Piping can usually be found in 5-foot sections.

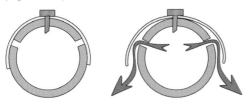

Pressure infiltration pipes should be designed to allow for the even distribution of water in both level and uneven terrain. These pipes are easy to clean and should be placed on the soil surface after planting. Then, they should be covered by a 2- to 4-inch layer of wood chip mulch. The pressure infiltration pipes consist of two concentric pipes that expand slightly due to the water pressure when the system is turned on. This causes the water to run out along the slot at the bottom of the soil box. When the water pressure is turned off, this causes the sleeve to close and prevents worms, insects, and roots from entering and clogging the pipe.

Gravity/Pressure Leaching Chambers

Leaching chambers can be successful in loading and receiving 2.4 gallons per square foot per day of greywater from a three-bedroom home. Using half of a PVC pipe that is 6 inches in diameter, this leaching chamber can be placed within a trench on a 1- to 2-inch mesh plastic netting to prevent the walls from sinking into the soil. No pre-filtration is used in these chambers. All that is required is a dosing pump chamber to pump every eight hours. The trench should have a minimum surface area of about 100 square feet—this will allow for a loading rate of around 2 to 2½ gallons per square foot per day for an average-sized home.

Gravity and Automatic Switch

The illustration below shows an example of an automatic switch system from a shallow leach chamber to one that is below the frost line—an important feature of

A leaching chamber

■ Top soil
▨ Sand
▨ Graved
▨ Stone

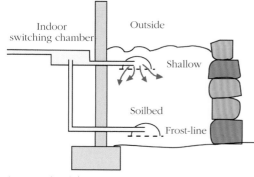

An automatic switch system

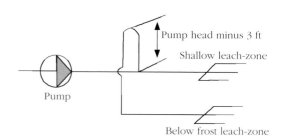

About 3 feet of water is a good margin for this automatic switch system.

any greywater system in the northern United States. If a shallow trench freezes and becomes clogged with ice, the water will back up and spill over into the pipe to the deeper, below-the-frost-line trench. It is worth noting that greywater is typically warmer than combined sewage and that the shallow leach zones that are operating in your system tend to stay freer of ice for longer periods of time than in places with combined waste water.

Automatic switching using pump pressure is different than gravity pressure switching. In an automatic switch system, a loop must be arranged indoors where the pressure needed for the shallow infiltration is normally lower than the pressure required to force the water up to the top of the loop. The top of the loop must, then, be no higher than the shut-off head of the pump. About 3 feet of water is a good margin for this system. The system can also be designed to be switched manually by the opening and closing of the valves that feed the different zones and levels of the greywater box.

An active cooling/passive heating greywater-irrigated greenhouse

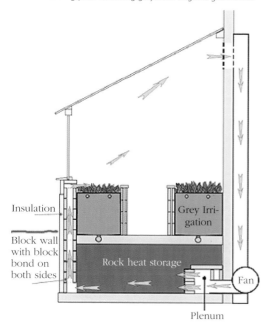

Options for Using Greywater in Cold Weather

Throughout New England, there are several greywater-irrigated greenhouses that feature a combination of automatically irrigated and fertilized growing beds that provide effective greywater treatment. Since these greenhouses are found in colder, northern states, it is important that these soil beds be deeper to store heat from both the sun and the greywater.

The greenhouse shown here provides enough salad greens for a family of four to six people throughout the long, cold northeastern winters. Growing broccoli, spinach, lettuce, mustard greens, and sorrel in these colder-climate greywater systems can be quite effective and profitable. To facilitate better distribution of greywater in the soil bed, a pipe-loop system can also be simply constructed to feed the bed from both sides.

Outdoor Planters

There are many variations of outdoor raised soil beds that are effective in replacing the soil needed for successful leach field treatment of greywater. Houses on ledges or in very sandy soils can be fitted with masonry soil boxes that serve to build up the site's soil profile. Such a strategy has been used in mounds or evapo-transpiration beds (a name derived from the assumption that all of the water will evaporate to the atmosphere even in wet and cold climates).

In parts of the country where construction density makes it very difficult to build a large mound or to locate planters for treating a significant volume of greywater, two adjacent neighbors can agree to build property dividers and plant hedges in their leaching area. This alternative combines privacy, landscaping aesthetics, and good environmental protection. Greywater gardens offer the added benefit of being able to garden at a higher elevation and in a raised garden bed.

Outdoor planters will have a less effective treatment during the winter seasons and during deep freezes. Yet,

Greywater is especially useful in areas that are very dry.

when relatively warm greywater is injected into the soil, increased biological activity as well as warming of the soil tends to keep the injection area unfrozen for longer periods of time than the surrounding area. Raised beds or planters can also be ideal for compost bins in the fall. The decomposing leaves and grasses act as an insulator as well as a composting fuel source that further insures that the soil beneath does not go into a deep freeze.

Shallow Subsoil Irrigation

This type of irrigation (2 to 6 inches below the soil level) is preferable to surface irrigation when these factors are in play:

- The water used is "grey" (neither clean nor free of salts)
- The irrigation system is located in a high evaporation locale with water shortages
- It is desired to produce leaf or garden waste compost quickly
- Selective irrigation is needed (for a flower border, shrub, bush, tree, etc.)
- You want to automatically irrigate a drained planter indoors or outdoors

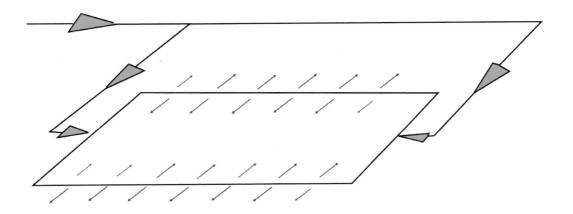

An injector pipe fork in the soil bed. Use 1-inch piping and drill ¼-inch holes on each side. Cover with canvas and a layer of soil to hide the pipe arrangement.

PART SIX   Crafts

"Crafts make us feel rooted, give us a sense of belonging, and connect us with our history. Our ancestors used to create these crafts out of necessity, and now we do them for fun, to make money and to express ourselves."

—Phyllis George

"The artist must create a spark before he can make a fire and before art is born, the artist must be ready to be consumed by the fire of his own creation."

—Auguste Rodin

Many people think of arts and crafts as something involving markers and construction paper that the kids do at summer camp. Certainly, the creativity that children express with scissors, tape, colored pencils, or clay is at the heart of crafting, but there's more to it than that. Most craft projects done for pleasure now were once done out of necessity—making candles, soaps, or baskets, for example—and many are still useful today. Beyond that, making things with your hands can be soothing, stimulating, or even enlightening, depending on the project and your frame of mind. Many people find knitting especially relaxing, and potters often discover within their art philosophical principles of intentionality, change, flexibility, and acceptance. In addition, crafting can become a lucrative and fulfilling business; handmade items are sought-after gifts and can be sold for significantly more than their factory-produced counterparts. In these pages you'll find an introduction to several diverse forms of crafting, from making soap and candles to pottery and even tying knots. Use the directions, descriptions, and images as a jumping-off point for your own creative endeavors, altering the projects as you're inspired in order to create one-of-a-kind pieces to use, give away, or sell . . . or just because they're fun to do.

Handmade Candles

Before the days of electricity, candles were a necessity in every home. Now they are enjoyed primarily for the unique way that they create ambience, or, for candles made with essential oils, for their aromatic properties. Turning off the lights for a few hours and enjoying the evening by candlelight can save money on your electric bill, too, and is a pleasant reminder of days gone by.

When making candles out of hot wax, it's a good idea to keep some baking soda nearby. If wax lights on fire, it reacts similarly to a grease fire, which is only aggravated by water. Douse a wax fire with baking soda, and it will extinguish quickly. Rather than pouring leftover wax down the drain (which will clog your drain and is bad for the environment), dump it into a jar and set it aside. If you continue to make candles, eventually your leftovers will become a unique layered jar candle.

Rolled Beeswax Candle

This is the simplest type of candle you can make and one that is great to do with children. Beeswax candles are cheap, eco-friendly, non-allergenic, dripless, and non-toxic, and they burn cleanly and beautifully. And you can make a beeswax candle in about 20 minutes! So, if you are pressed for time and want to make a nice homemade gift—or you'd just like to have sweet-smelling candles in your home—making beeswax candles is the way to go.

Materials
Sheets of beeswax, any color you want (you can find this at your local arts and crafts store or even from a beekeeper or at a farmers' market)
Wick (you can purchase candle wicks at your local arts and crafts store)

Supplies
Scissors (to cut the wick and excess beeswax)
Hair dryer (optional)

Directions
1. Take one sheet of beeswax and fold it in half. Cut along the folded edge so you have two separate pieces.
2. Cut your wick to be about 2 inches longer than the length of the beeswax sheet.

Beeswax candles are easy to make, non-allergenic, and dripless.

Purchase beeswax in sheets from crafts stores or gather them from your own hives.

3. Lay the wick on the edge of the beeswax sheet, closest to you. Make sure the wick hangs off of each end of the sheet.
4. Start rolling the beeswax over the wick, making sure it is tucked tightly around the wick. The tighter you begin rolling the beeswax, the more sturdy your candle will be and the better it will burn.
5. Carefully roll up the wick in the beeswax (as you would roll modeling clay). Stop about 2 inches from the other side and make sure the ends are smooth and straight. Apply slight pressure as you roll to keep the wax tightly bound.
6. When you reach the end, you must seal off your candle. To do so, start in the middle of the edge and gently press it into the candle, letting your body heat melt the wax into the rolled candle.
7. Trim the wick on the bottom (you may also want to cut the bottom slightly so it will stand up straight) and then cut the wick to about ½ inch at the top.

Note: If you are having trouble using the beeswax and want to facilitate the adhering process, you can use a hair dryer to soften the wax and to help you roll it. Start at the end with the wick and, moving the hair dryer over the wax, heat it up. Keep rolling until you reach a section that is not as warm, heat that up, and continue all the way to the end.

Taper Candles

Taper candles are perfect for candlesticks, and they can be made in a variety of sizes and colors.

Materials
Wick (be sure to find a spool of wick that is made specifically for taper candles)
Wax (paraffin is ideal for making taper candles)
Candle fragrances and dyes (optional)

Supplies
Pencil or chopstick (to wind the wick around to facilitate dipping and drying)
Weight (such as a fishing lure, bolt, or washer)
Dipping container (this should be tall and skinny. You can find these containers at your local arts and crafts store, or you can substitute a spaghetti pot)
Stove
Large pot for boiling water
Small trivet or rack
Newspaper (to prevent spills)
Glass or candle thermometer
Drying rack

Directions
1. Cut the wick to the desired length of your candle, leaving about 5 additional inches that will be tied onto the pencil or chopstick for dipping and drying purposes. It's also a good idea to put a weight on the dipping end of the wick (a fishing lure, bolt, or heavy metal washer) to help with the first few dips into the wax.
2. Ready your dipping container. Put the wax (preferably in smaller chunks to speed up the melting process) into the container and set aside.
3. In a large pot, start to boil water. Before putting the dipping container full of wax into the larger pot, place a small trivet, rack, or other elevating device into the bottom of the larger pot. This will keep the dipping container from touching the bottom of the larger pot and will prevent the wax from burning and possibly combusting.
4. Put the dipping container into the pot and start to melt the wax, keeping a thermometer in the wax at all times. The wax should be heated and melted between 150°F and 165°F. Stir frequently to keep the chunks of paraffin from burning and to ensure all the wax is thoroughly melted. (If you want to add fragrance or dye, do so when the wax is completely melted and stir until the additives are dissolved.)
5. Once your wax is completely melted, it's time to start the dipping process. Removing the container from the stove, take your wick that's tied onto a stick and dip it into the wax, leaving it there for a few minutes. Continue to lower the wick in and out of the dipping container, and by the eighth or ninth dip, cut off the weight from the bottom of the wick—the candle should be heavy enough now to dip well on its own.

6. To speed up the cooling process—and to help the wax continue to adhere and build up on the wick—blow on the hot wax each time you lift the candle out of the dipping pot.

7. When the candle is at the desired length and thickness, you may want to lay it down on a very smooth surface (such as a countertop) and gently roll it into shape.

8. On a drying rack (which can be made from a box long enough so the candles do not touch the bottom or from another device), carefully hang your taper candle to dry for a good 24 hours.

9. Once the candle is completely hardened, trim the wick to just above the wax.

Jarred Soy Candles

Soy candles are environmentally friendly and easy candles to make. You can find most of the ingredients and materials needed to make soy candles at your local arts and crafts store—or even in your own kitchen!

Materials
1 lb soy wax (either in bars or flakes)
1 ounce essential oil (for fragrance)
Natural dye (try using dried and powdered beets for red, turmeric for yellow, or blueberries for blue)

Supplies
Stove
Pan to heat wax (a double boiler is best)
Spoon
Glass thermometer
Candle wick (you can find this at your local arts and crafts store)
Metal washers
Pencils or chopsticks
Heatproof cup to pour your melted wax into the jar(s)
Jar to hold the candle (jelly jars or other glass jars work well)

Directions

1. Put the wax in a pan or a double boiler and heat it slowly over medium heat. Heat the wax to 130°F to 140°F or until it's completely melted.

2. Remove the wax from the heat. Add the essential oil and dye (optional) and stir into the melted wax until completely dissolved.

3. Allow the wax to cool slightly, until it becomes cloudy.

4. While the wax is cooling, prepare your wick in the glass container. It is best to have a wick with a metal disk on the end—this will help stabilize it while the candle is hardening. If your wick does not already have a metal disk at the end, you can easily attach a thin metal washer to the end of the wick, tying a knot until the wick can no longer pass through the washer. Position the wick in the glass container and, using a pencil or chopstick, wrap the excess wick around the middle and then, laying the pencil or chopstick on the rim of the container, position the wick so it falls in the center.

5. Using a heat proof cup or the container from the double boiler, carefully pour the cloudy wax into the glass container, being careful not to disturb the wick from the center.

6. Allow the candle to dry for at least 24 hours before cutting off the excess wick and using.

Jelly jars work well for poured candles.

Making Your Own Soap

Making your own soap can be a very rewarding process. It does, however, require a good amount of time, patience, and caution, because you'll be using some caustic and potentially dangerous ingredients—the main one being lye (sodium hydroxide). It is important, whenever you are making soap, that you are careful to avoid coming into direct contact with the lye. Wear goggles, rubber gloves, and long sleeves, and work in a well-ventilated area. Be sure, as well, that you never breathe in the fumes produced by the lye and water mixture.

Soap is made up of three main ingredients: water, lye, and fats or oils. While lard and tallow were once used exclusively for making soaps, it is perfectly acceptable to use a combination of pure oils for the "fat" needed to make soap. For these ingredients to become soap, they must go through a process called saponification, in which the mixture becomes completely blended and the chemical reactions between the lye and the oils, over time, turn the mixture into a hardened bar of usable soap.

Once you've become comfortable with the basic soap-making process, you can experiment with adding different colored dyes, essential oils, and other ingredients to make a personalized and interesting bar of soap—perfect for your own use or for giving as a gift.

Basic Recipe for Cold-Pressed Soap

Ingredients
6.9 ounces lye (sodium hydroxide)
2 cups distilled water, cold (from the refrigerator is the best)
2 cups canola oil
2 cups coconut oil
2 cups palm oil

Supplies
Goggles, gloves, and mask to wear while making the soap
Mold for the soap (a cake or bread loaf pan will work just fine; you can also find flexible plastic molds at your local arts and crafts store)
Plastic wrap or wax paper to line the molds
Glass bowl to mix the lye and water
Wooden spoon for mixing

You can pour your soap into molds, use stamps, or carve the finished bars to make them unique.

2 thermometers (one for the lye and water mixture and one for the oil mixture)

Stainless steel or cast iron pot for heating oils and mixing in lye mixture

Handheld stick blender (optional)

Directions

1. Put on the goggles and gloves and make sure you are working in a well-ventilated room.
2. Ready your mold(s) by lining with plastic wrap or wax paper. Set them aside.
3. Add the lye to the cold, distilled water in a glass bowl (never add the water to the lye) and stir continually for at least a minute, or until the lye is completely dissolved. Place one thermometer into the glass bowl and allow the mixture to cool to around 110°F (the chemical reaction of the lye mixing with the water will cause it to heat up quickly at first).
4. While the lye is cooling, combine the oils in a pot on medium heat and stir well until they are melted together. Place a thermometer into the pot and allow the mixture to cool to 110°F.
5. Carefully pour the lye mixture into the oil mixture (make sure you pour the lye solution in a small, steady stream), stirring continuously so that the lye and oils mix properly. Continue stirring, either by hand (which can take a very long time) or with a handheld stick blender, until the mixture traces (has the consistency of thin pudding). This may take anywhere from 30 to 60 minutes or more, so just be patient. It is well worth the time invested to make sure your mixture traces. If it doesn't trace all the way, it will not saponify correctly and your soap will be ruined.
6. Once your mixture has traced, pour carefully into the mold(s) and let sit for a few hours. Then, when the mixture is still soft but congealed enough not to melt back into itself, cut the soap with a table knife into bars. Let sit for a few days, then take the bars out of the mold(s) and place on brown paper (grocery bags are perfect) in a dark area. Allow the bars to cure for another 4 weeks or so before using.

If you want your soap to be colored, add special soap-coloring dyes (you can find these at the local arts and crafts store) after the mixture has traced, stirring them in. Or try making your own dyes using herbs, flowers, or spices.

To make a yummy-smelling bar of soap, add a few drops of your favorite essential oils (such as lavender, lemon, or rose) after the tracing of the mixture and stir in. You can also add aloe and vitamin E at this point to make your soap softer and more moisturizing.

To add texture and exfoliating properties to your soap, you can stir some oats into the traced mixture, along with some almond essential oil or a dab of honey. This will not only give your soap a nice, pumice-like quality but it will also smell wonderful. Try adding bits of lavender, rose petals, or citrus peel to your soap for variety.

To make soap in different shapes, pour your mixture into molds instead of making them into bars. For round soaps, you can take a few bars of soap you've just made, place them into a resealable plastic bag, and warm them by putting the bag into hot water (120°F) for 30 minutes. Then, cut the bars up and roll them into balls. These soaps should set in about an hour or so.

Natural Dyes for Soap or Candles

Light/Dark Brown	Cinnamon, ground cloves, allspice, nutmeg, coffee
Yellow	Turmeric, saffron, calendula petals
Green	Liquid chlrophyll, alfalfa, cucumber, sage, nettles
Red	Annatto extract, beets, grape-skin extract
Blue	Red cabbage
Purple	Alkanet root

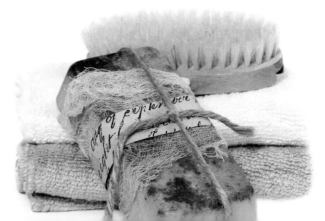

Pottery Basics

Pottery is enjoyable to make because of its flexibility and simplicity as a means of art expression, its utility, and its timelessness.

Clay is the basic ingredient for making pottery. Clay is decomposed rock containing water (both in liquid and chemical forms). Water in its liquid form can be separated from the clay by heating the mass to a boiling point—a process that restores the clay to its original condition once dried. The water in the clay that is found in chemical forms can also be removed by ignition—a process commonly referred to as "firing." After being fired, clay cannot be restored to any state of plasticity—this is what we term "pottery." Some clay requires greater heat in order to be fired, and these are known as "hard clays." These types of clay must be subjected to a "hard-firing" process. However, in the making of simple pottery, soft clay is generally used and is fired in an over-glaze (soft glaze) kiln.

Pottery clays can either be found in certain soils or bought from craft stores. If you have clay soil available on your property, the process of separating the clay from the other soil materials is simple. Put the earthen clay into a large bucket of water to wash the soil away. Any rocks or other heavy matter will sink to the bottom of the bucket. The milky fluid that remains—which is essentially water mixed with clay—may then be drawn off and allowed to settle in a separate container, the clear water eventually collecting on the top. Remove the excess water by using a siphon. Repeating of this process will refine the clay and make it ready for use.

You can also purchase clay at your local craft store. Usually, clay sold in these stores will be in a dry form (a grayish or yellowish powder), so you will need to prepare it before using it your pottery. To prepare it for use, you must mix the powder with water. If there are directions on your clay packet, then follow those closely to make your clay. In general, though, you can make your clay by mixing equal parts of clay powder and water in a bowl and allowing the mixture to soak for 10 to 12 hours. After it has soaked, knead the mixture thoroughly to disperse the water evenly throughout the clay and pop any air bubbles. Air bubbles, if left in the clay, could be detrimental to your pottery once kilned, because the bubbles would generate steam and possibly crack your creation. However, be careful not to knead your clay mixture too much,

A potter carefully forms a bowl which will eventually be glazed and fired in a kiln.

Making pottery takes patience and practice, but the process can be very enjoyable.

or you may increase the chance of air bubbles becoming trapped in the mixture.

If, after kneading, you find that the clay is too wet to work with (test the wetness of the clay on your hands and if it to slips around your palm very easily, it is probably too wet), the excess water can be removed by squeezing or blotting out with a dry towel or dry board.

The main tools needed for making pottery are simply your fingers. There are wooden tools that can be used for adding finer detail or decoration, but typically, all you really need are your own two hands. A loop tool (a piece of fine, curved wire) may also be used for scraping off excess clay where it is too thick. Another tool has ragged edges and this can be used to help regulate the contour of the pottery. Remember that homemade pottery will not always be symmetrical, and that is what makes it so special.

Sticks and other tools can be used to help you form and decorate your pottery.

Basic Vase or Urn

Try making this simple vase or urn to get used to working with clay.

1. Take a lump of clay. The clay should be about the size of a small orange and should be elastic feeling. Then, begin to mold the base of your object—let's say it is either a bowl or a vase.

2. Continue molding your base. By now, you'll have a rather heavy and thick model, hollowed to look a little like a bird's nest. Now, using this base as support, start adding pieces of clay in a spiral shape. Press the clay together firmly with your fingers. Make sure that your model has a uniform thickness all around.

3. Continue molding your clay and making it grow. As you work with the clay, your hands will become more accustomed to its texture and the way it molds, and you will have less difficulty making it do what you want. As you start to elongate and lengthen the model, remember to keep the walls of the piece substantial and not too thin—it is easier to remove extra thickness than it is to add it.

4. Don't become frustrated if your first model fails. Even if you are being extra careful to make your bowl or vase sturdy, there is always the instance when a nearly complete vase will fall over. This usually happens when one side of the structure becomes too thin or the clay is too wet. To keep this from happening, it is sometimes helpful to keep one hand inside the structure and the other outside. If you are building a vase, you can extract one finger at a time as you reach closer and closer to the top of the model.

5. The clay should be moist throughout the entire molding process. If you need to stop molding for an extended period of time, cover the item with a moist cloth to keep it from drying out.

6. When your model has reached the size you want, you may turn it upside down and smooth and refine the contours of the object. You can also make the base much more detailed and shaped to a more pleasing design.

7. Allow your model to air dry.

Embellishing Your Clay Models

You may eventually want to make something that requires a handle or a spout, such as a cup or teapot. Adding handles and spouts can be tricky, but only if you don't remember some simple rules. Spouts can be modeled around a straw or any other material that is stiff enough to support the clay and light enough to burn out in the firing. In the designing of spouts and handles, it is still important to keep them solid and thick. Also, keeping them closer to the body of your model is more practical, as handles and spouts that are elongated

are harder to keep firm and can also break off easily. Although more time-consuming and difficult to manage, handles and spouts can add a nice aesthetic to your finished pottery.

The simplest way to decorate your pottery is by making line incisions. Line incision designs are best made with wooden, finger-shaped tools. It is completely up to you as to how deep the lines are and into what pattern they are made.

Wheel-working and Firing Pottery

If you want to take your pottery-making one step further, you can experiment with using a potters' wheel and also glazing and firing your model to create beautiful pottery. Look online or at your local craft store for potters' wheels. Firing can leave your pottery looking two different ways, depending on whether you decide to leave the clay natural (so it maintains a dull and porous look) or to give it a color glaze.

Colored glazes come in the form of powder and are generally metallic oxides, such as iron oxides, cobalt oxide, chromium oxide, copper oxide, and copper carbonate. The colors these compounds become will vary depending on the atmosphere and temperature of the kiln. Glazes often come in the form of powder and need to be combined with water to be applied to the clay. Only apply glaze to dried pottery, because it won't adhere well to wet clay. Use a brush, sponge, or putty knife to apply the glaze. Your pottery is then ready to be fired.

There are various different kinds of kilns in which to fire your pottery. An over-glaze kiln is sufficient for all processes discussed here, and you can probably find a kiln in your surrounding area (check online and in your telephone book for places that have kilns open to the public). For schools that have pottery classes, over-glaze kilns may be installed there. It is important, whenever you are using a kiln, that you are with a skilled pottery maker who knows how to properly operate a kiln.

After the pottery has been colored and fired, a simple design may be made on the pottery by scraping off the surface color so as to expose the original or creamy-white tint of the clay.

Unglazed pottery may be worked with after firing by rubbing floor wax on the outer surface. This fills up the pores and gives a more uniform quality to the whole piece.

Pottery offers so many opportunities for personal experimentation and enjoyment; there are no set rules as to how to make a piece of pottery. Keep a journal about the different things you try while making pottery so you can remember what works best and what should be avoided in the future. Note the kind of clay you used and its consistency, the types of colors that have worked well, and the temperature and positioning within the kiln, if you use firing. Above all, enjoy making unique pieces of pottery!

Making Jars, Candlesticks, and Bowls

Making pottery at home is simple and easy, and is a great way for you to make personalized, unique gifts for family and friends. Clay can be purchased at local arts and crafts stores. Clay must always be kneaded before you model with it because it contains air that, if left in the clay, would form air bubbles in your pottery and spoil it. Work out this air by kneading it the same way that you knead bread. Also guard against making the clay too moist, because that causes the pottery to sag, and sagging, of course, spoils the shape.

To make your own pottery, you need modeling clay, a board on which you can work, a pie tin on which to build, a knife, a short stick (one side should be pointed), and a ruler.

Keep spouts and handles thick so they will not crack or break off. Use a stick or dowel to create line incisions like these.

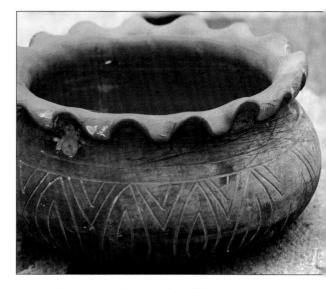

Using different glazes will give your pottery variances in odor and texture.

Jars

To start a jar, put a handful of clay on the board, pat it out with your hand until it is an inch thick, and smooth off the surface. Then, take a coffee cup, invert it upon the base, and, with your stick, trim the clay outside the rim.

To build up the walls, put a handful of clay on the board and use a knife to smooth it out into a long piece, ¼ inch thick. With the knife and a ruler, trim off one edge of the piece and cut a number of strips ¾ inch wide. Take one strip, stand it on top of the base, and rub its edge into the base on both sides of the strip. Take another strip and add it to the top of the first one, and continue building in this way, placing one strip on another, joining each to the one beneath it, and smoothing over the joints as you build. Keep doing this until the walls are as high as you want them to be. Remember to keep one hand inside the jar while you build, for extra support. Fill uneven places with bits of clay and smooth out rough spots with your fingers, having moistened your fingers with water first. When you are finished, you may also add decorations, or ornaments, to your jar.

Candlestick

Making a pottery candlestick requires a round base ½ inch thick and 4 inches in diameter. After preparing the base, put a lump of clay in the center, work it into the base, place another lump on top, work it into the piece, and continue in this way until the candlestick has been built as high as you want it. Then, force a candle into the moist clay, twisting it around until it has made a socket deep enough to place a candle into.

A cardboard "templet", with one edge trimmed to the proper shape, will make it easy to keep the walls of the candlestick symmetrical and the projecting cap on the top equal on all sides. Run the edge of the templet around the walls as you work, and it will show you exactly where and how much to fill out, trim, and straighten the clay.

If you want to make a candlestick with a handle, make a base just as described earlier. Then cut strips of clay and build up the wall as if building a jar, leaving a center hole just large enough to hold a candle. When the desired height for the wall has been reached, cut a strip of clay ½ inch wide and ½ inch thick, and lay it around the top of the wall with a projection of ¼ inch over the wall. Smooth this piece on top, inside, and outside with your modeling stick and fingers. For the handle, prepare a strip 1 inch wide and ³⁄8 inch thick, and join one end to the top band and the other end to the base. Use a small lump of clay for filling around where you join the piece, and smooth off the piece on all sides.

When the candlestick is finished, run a round stick the same size as the candle down into the hole, and let it stay put until the clay is dry, to keep the candlestick straight.

Bowls

Bowls are quite easy to make. Starting with a base, lay strips of clay around the base, building upon each strip as you did when making a jar. Once the bowl reaches its desired height and width, allow it to dry.

Glazing and Firing

Most pottery that you buy is glazed and then fired in a pottery kiln, but firing is not necessary to make beautiful, sturdy pottery. The clay will dry hard enough, naturally, to keep its shape, and the only thing you must provide for is waterproofing (if the pottery will be holding liquids). To do this, you can take bathtub enamel and apply it to the inside (and outside, if desired) of the pottery to seal off any cracks and keep the item from leaking.

If you do want to try glazing and firing your own pottery, you will need a kiln. Below are instructions for making your own.

Pottery may be ornamented by scratching a design on it with the end of a modeling stick. You can do a simple, straight-line design by using a ruler to guide the stick in drawing the lines.

Sawdust Kiln

This small, homemade kiln can be used to bake and fire most small pottery projects. It will only get up to about 1200 degrees Fahrenheit, which is not hot enough to fire porcelain or stonewear. However, it will suffice for clay pinch pots and other decorative pieces.

You will need:

- Sawdust
- 20–30 red or orange bricks
- Chicken wire
- Sheet metal
- Newspaper and kindling

1. Choose a spot outdoors that is protected from strong winds. Clear away any dried branches or other flammables from the immediate area. A concrete patio or paved area makes an ideal base, but you can also place bricks or stones on the ground.
2. Stack bricks in a square shape, building each wall up at least four bricks high. Fill the kiln with sawdust.
3. Place the chicken wire on top of the bricks and add another layer or two of bricks. Carefully place your pottery n the center of the mesh, spacing the pieces at least ½ inch apart. Cover the pottery with sawdust.
4. Add another piece of chicken wire, add bricks and pottery, and cover with sawdust. Repeat until your kiln is the desired height.
5. Light the top layer of sawdust on fire, using kindling and newspaper if needed. Cover with the sheet metal, using another layer of bricks to hold it in place.
6. Once the kiln stops smoking, leave it alone until it completely cools down. Then carefully remove the sheet metal lid.

Permanent Homemade Pottery Kiln

As you continue to create pottery, you may find that you enjoy the art enough that you would like to continue this craft for years to come. In that case, and if you have enough space in your yard, you may think about constructing a permanent kiln for all of your pottery needs.

This kiln requires some intense construction, but having your own wood-burning pottery kiln will make firing your creations easier and more effective.

The essentials of this kiln are: a fire box, an oven, and a chimney. The kiln works by allowing the fire to pass up from the fire box through the oven floor, between the bricks (spaced about 1½ inches apart), and out through the chimney at the top of the oven.

The Construction of the Kiln

1. Begin by laying out a space for the foundation of the kiln. This should be on solid, dry ground. It is advisable to make an excavation a few inches below the surface and fill it in with cinders or broken brick. The place you choose for your kiln should also allow water to run off and not collect underneath.
2. Build the walls of the kiln three bricks deep on each of the sides and the back. Leave the front of the kiln open for the fire mouths.
3. Halfway between the two side walls, build a thin, central support, made of three courses of brick on the edge. This will leave a narrow ledge where the grates of the fire boxes can rest. Build the other edge of each grate into the side wall.

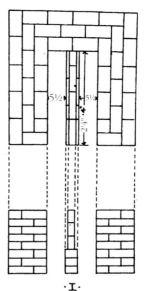

The top illustrations shows plan and front view of the kiln foundation up to the oven floor. The walls are three bricks thick on each side and the front is left open. The bottom illustration shows the bricks that rest on the side walls and on the central support. These should be made of fire bricks, since they'll be subjected to the most extreme heat.

·I·

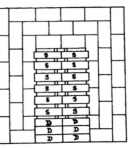

·II·

The size of the kiln will be dependent on the amount of bricks you lay. Lay bricks endwise to make a stronger wall.

4   Make the mortar of common clay (or you can buy it if you desire). Mix the clay with water into a mortar. You can add some regular sand to give the mortar better working qualities, and this will also help prevent shrinkage.

5.   Spread the mortar over the cinder foundation and start to lay the bricks. In building the walls and central support, make the joints between the bricks as tight and thin as possible. Tap the bricks into place so there will be no settling of the wall later on.

6.   Build the walls and central support up to the point where the oven floor will be. To make the oven floor, arrange the bricks on their edges about 1½ inches apart from the front to the back of the kiln. These bricks should rest on the side walls and central support. Since this oven floor is going to be subjected to high heat, use fire bricks. Also be sure to project the bricks out in the front for the oven door to sit on.

7.   Continue to build the side and back walls up nine more bricks. Then, you can start to taper the bricks into a chimney formation. Lay the next two levels of bricks (on the side walls only) in toward the center of the kiln about 1½ inches or so. The space between the walls at the top should not be more than 9 inches. Bridge the opening at the top across the front and back of the kiln, leaving an opening in the center just large enough for the chimney (about 8 or 9 inches square). You can do this by using large pieces of terra cotta flue lining (purchased at any hardware or home center store). The size of the flue lining should be about 2 feet x 8 inches x 6 inches.

8.   Carefully cut lines in the flue lining from end to end, until the side falls away. Cut this in two and use the two halves for closing in the top of the kiln. Put these bricks in place with plenty of mortar and finish out the rest of the bricking over the walls with other pieces of flue lining, making them level.

9.   Build two more levels of brick all around, leaving the chimney opening 9 inches by 9 inches.

10. Now build the chimney straight up with a single layer of bricks (or two bricks to each layer, if you desire). The inside diameter of the chimney should not be less than 7 inches by 7 inches. When complete, the chimney should be about 3 feet high.

11. You can also build the chimney 1 foot high and then let one brick on each side project into the chimney cavity about 2 inches. Then, fit ordinary stovepipe with a square end to rest on these projections inside the chimney. This is a lighter method than building brick all the way up.

12. Install grates to produce a better and cleared fire. You can find grates at your local hardware store or use old stove grates. Build these grates into the walls of the fire box and central support. Leave the front end of the oven open.

14. Place pottery in the oven. Brick up the front of the oven without any mortar and fill in the joints with wet sand.

15. The kiln will now need to be heated with wood. You should begin with a very simple fire lasting about an hour or two. This is extremely important, as the flame comes into contact with the raw clay, which, unless it is heated very gradually, could crack and split apart. After thoroughly warming the kiln, increase the heat more rapidly. After the firing is well underway (three or so hours later), close the doors of the fire boxes with pieces of sheet iron or bricks piled up in front. Only allow air in through the grates. Only remove the temporary doors to add fuel to the fire.

Cross section of the finished kiln. The space between the walls at the top should not be more than nine inches.

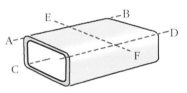

Cut lines in the flue lining from end to end at AB and CD. Then cut in two at EF and use the two halves for closing in the top of the kiln.

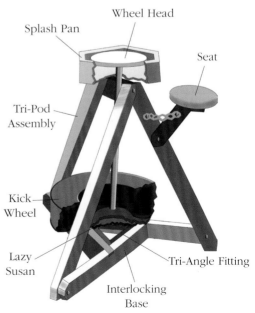

Knitting

The art of knitting was supposedly invented by the Spanish nobility as a means of relaxation for noble women in the country. The Scottish also claim to have developed knitting, and King Henry VII was the first to wear knitted stockings in England. Queen Elizabeth also wore knitted silk stockings made by Mistress Montegue.

Whenever and wherever knitting was first "discovered," it is useful, relaxing, and can be done while enjoying a good conversation with a friend.

Knitting Basics

Stitches

Knitting can be done in rows of plain or purl stitches or by incorporating a variety of stitches and knitting techniques in one project. However, the simpler stitches are better when first starting to knit. Just be sure not to pull the thread too tight or keep it too loose—as you continue to knit, you will learn the proper amount of tension to apply to your string so you create a perfect, knitted item.

Tools Needed for Knitting

1. **Gauge**—This measures the knitting needles. Most needles already have their gauge listed on them, but if your needles do not, you should find this measuring tool at your local arts and crafts store.
2. **Knitting needles**—These are made of steel, wood, or plastic and are used to knit your material together.
3. **Knitting shields**—Although these are not a necessary tool for knitting, you may find that you want these so the material does not slip off of your needle.
4. **Material to be knitted**—Beginners should use thicker yarn in their knitted items. When you have become more proficient in knitting, you can experiment with different types of threads and materials to create your various knitted items.

Knitting Terminology

To bring the thread forward—This means to pass the thread between the needles toward the knitter's body.

To cast off—You do this by knitting two stitches, passing the first over the second, and proceeding in this manner until the last stitch, which is secured by passing the thread through it.

To cast on the loops or stitches—Take the material in your right hand and twist it around the little finger, bringing it under the next two fingers, and passing it over the pointer finger. Then, take the end of the material in your left hand (holding the needle with your right), wrap it around the little finger, and then bring it over the thumb and around the second and third fingers. By doing so, you will have formed a loop. Now, bring the needle under the lower thread of the material and above the material that is over the right-hand pointer finger under the needle. The thread in the left hand should be pulled tightly, completing this step. You can repeat this process as many times as needed until you've cast the amount of stitches you want.

To cast over—This means to bring the material around the needle (bringing it forward).

To fasten on—This refers to fastening the end of the material when it's needed during the process of knitting. The best way to fasten on is to place the two ends in opposite directions and knit a few stitches with both.

Knitting stitch—In this stitch, the needle must be put through the cast-on stitch and the material should be turned over. This will be taken up and under the loop (or stitch) and then let off. This is also known as a plain stitch and will be continued until an entire round is complete.

A loop stitch—This is made by passing the thread before the needle.

Narrowing—This is to decrease the number of stitches by knitting two together, so you only form one loop.

Purl stitch—This is also known as a seam, ribbed, or turn stitch. It is formed by knitting with the material before the needle and instead of bringing the needle over the upper thread, the material is brought under it. This is the opposite of a knitting stitch.

Raising—This is to increase the number of stitches and is made by knitting one stitch in the usual way and then omitting to slip out the left-hand needle. Then, the material is passed forward, and a second stitch is formed by pulling the needle under the stitch. The material must be put back to its normal place when the extra stitch is completed.

To rib—To alternately knit plain and purled stitches (three plain then three purl, etc.).

A round—This is all of the stitches on two, three, or more needles.

A row—This refers to the stitches from one end of the needle to the other.

To seam—To knit a purl stitch every alternate row.

A slip stitch—This is made by passing the thread from one needle to another without knitting.

To turn—To change the type of stitch.

Welts—These are alternating plain and ribbed stitches and are used for anything that you don't want to twist or curl up.

How to Knit

1. To cast on, hold the two needles loosely in your hands. Pass a loop over the left-hand needle near the end of the yarn and hold the right-hand needle loosely. Put the right-hand needle into the loop, passing it from left to right and keeping the right-hand needle under the left needle. Pass the string over this needle—between it and the left-hand needle—and pull the loop up toward the right. Now, bring the right needle up and pass the stitch on it to the left needle by putting the left needle through the left side of the loop, keeping the right needle in the loop. It is ready to begin the next stitch. Repeat.

2. Knitting stitch: After you have made the correct number of stitches, hold the needle that has the stitches on it in your left hand and pass the right needle into the first stitch from left to right. Put the yarn around between the two needles, pull the loop through the other loop on the left needle, and slip that loop off the left needle. Repeat.

3. Purling stitch: Keep the yarn in the front of the work and put the right needle into a stitch from right to left, passing it upward through the front loop of the stitch. The right needle should be resting on the left. Pass the yarn around the front of the needle and bring it back between the two needles. Pull the right needle slightly back, so as to secure the loop on the right needle and then draw off the loop on the left needle. Repeat. Note: This is basically the knitting stitch, only backwards.

4. Slipping a stitch: This is done by passing a stitch from one needle to another without knitting it at the beginning of a row. This should always been done when using two needles at the beginning of each row, so the rows remain even.

5. Casting (binding) off: Knit two stitches, passing the first stitch over the second, and then knit a third stitch, passing the second over the third. Continue in this way until all the stitches are off the needle.

Two Simple Knitting Patterns

1. Patent Knitting, or Brioche Knitting

Cast on any number of stitches divisible by three.

Yarn forward, slip one, knit two together. Work every row in the same way.

2. Cane-work Pattern

Cast on any number of stitches divisible by four.

General Tip for Beginning Knitters

Hold the needles loosely in your hands and close to the points. To knit easily and quickly, your hands should neither move too much nor should you make large gestures with the needles.

Hold the needles loosely in your hands with the loose yarn wrapped around your pointer finger.

Slip the right needle into the top loop on the left needle, keeping the left needle above the right needle. To do a purl stitch, the right needle would go on top of the right needle.

Wrap the loose strand of yarn over and behind the right needle. For a purl stitch, wrap the yarn behind first and then over the needle. Slip the loop off of the left needle to finish the stitch.

First Row: make one, knit one, make one, knit three. Repeat.

Second Row: purl.

Third Row: knit three, make one, slip one, knit two together, pass the slip-stitch over the two knitted together, make one. Repeat.

Fourth Row: purl.

Fifth Row: make one, slip one, knit two together, pass the slip-stitch over, make one, knit three. Repeat.

Sixth Row: purl.

Seventh Row: repeat the third row.

Eighth Row: purl.

Ninth Row: make one, slip one, knit two together, pass the slip-stitch over, make one, knit three. Repeat.

Tenth Row: purl.

Repeat from the third row until the item is complete.

Simple Scarf

Materials

Mid-weight or 4-ply yarn of any color (use at least one full bundle of yarn)

Knitting needles (size 8 to 10.5 are best for knitting scarves)

Alternating rows of knit and purl stitches.

Directions

1. Decide how wide you want your scarf to be (26 to 35 stitches are the standard width for a scarf).
2. First row: knit 26 to 36 stitches
3. Second row: knit 26 to 35 stitches (if you want something a little more challenging, purl this row instead)
4. Continue knitting (or knitting and purling alternately) until you reach the desired length (60 inches is a good length for a scarf).
5. At the end, cast (bind) off the stitches.

Hat

Materials

Yarn of a medium-heavy weight, any color of your choosing

Knitting needles (depending on the head size for the hat, use No. 6 or No. 8 needles)

Directions

1. Cast on 72 stitches.
2. First row: knit 72 stitches.
3. Second row: purl 72 stitches.

This hat shows the "knit one row, purl one row" pattern. You can also follow this pattern for six or eight rows and then switch to just knitting to give your hat a differentiated band around the bottom. If desired, use round needles (two knitting needles that are attached by a plastic or rubber cord) to avoid having to sew a seam at the end.

4. Continue in this fashion until your hat is about 9 inches tall.

5. To begin to cast (bind) off your hat, follow this pattern:

   a. Knit five stitches, knit two together, and continue to the end of the row.

   b. Purl the next row.

   c. Knit four stitches, knit two together, and continue to the end of the row.

   d. Purl the next row.

   e. Knit three stitches, knit two together, and continue to the end of the row.

   f. Purl the next row.

   g. Knit two stitches, knit two together, and continue to the end of the row.

   h. Purl the next row.

   i. Knit every two stitches together.

7. Take the excess yarn, pull it through the last stitches, and cut off so only about an inch and a half remains. Sew a seam, put the remaining yarn through the loops, and fold your hat inside out.

Fingerless Mittens

Fingerless mittens are wonderful to use if your hands are cold but you still need to have complete access to things, such as typing on a computer or making a meal. They make wonderful gifts for friends and family members.

Materials

150 yards of worsted-weight yarn or wool/yarn blend
Double-pointed knitting needles, No. 8

Directions

1. To make the cuff, cast on 28 stitches, making sure these stitches are even. Then, begin to knit in the round. Do not twist the stitches. Use the yarn tail to keep track of the round ends. Knit three rounds. Switching to the twisted rib pattern, knit one stitch through the back loop in order to twist it. Purl one, and repeat this pattern until the cuff measures roughly 2½ inches.

2. Using a stocking stitch, begin the hand and thumb portion of the mitten.

3. First row: knit one, purl one, make one (increase the stitch), knit one, make one, purl one, knit until the end of the round.

4. Second row: knit one, purl one, knit until you reach the next purl stitch in the row above, purl one, knit until the end of the round.

5. Third row: knit one, purl one, make one, knit until the next purl, make one, purl one, knit until the end of the round.

6. Repeat the second and third rows until you have nine stitches between the purls. The glove should now measure about 5½ inches from the edge of the cast-off point.

7. Place two purl and nine thumb gore stitches on a piece of scrap yarn. Cast off three stitches and knit four rounds of stocking stitch. Change to twisted rib stitch and make six rounds. Bind this off very loosely.

You can easily modify the pattern described here to include these individual finger openings and the finger "hood." Simply follow the steps to make the thumb hole (steps 8–10) for each of the additional finger openings. For the "hood," follow the directions for making a hat (only make it much smaller) and sew it onto the mitten above the knuckles.

8. To make the thumb, put 11 stitches on hold for the thumb onto an extra knitting needle. Pick up three stitches at the base of the thumb and make 14 stitches.

9. Knit one round of only 12 stitches.

10. Using the twisted rib stitch, make six more rounds and bind off loosely.

11. To finish up, weave in the yarn ends and, if necessary, sew closed any holes at the sides of the thumb base.

Knitted Square Blanket

Materials

Thick yarn, any color you like (if you want a multicolored blanket, feel free to use different-colored yarn for each individual square)
Knitting needles, No. 6

Directions

1. Begin by making smaller squares that will be sewn together to form a larger blanket.

2. Cast on any number of stitches divisible by three. For a square of 6 inches, you'll need 45 stitches.

3. First row: Slip one, knit two. Turn the yarn around the needle and bring it again in front. Then, slip one, knit two together. Purl the last two stitches.

4. Second row: Turn the yarn around the needle, bringing it to the front. Slip one, knit two together. Knit the last two stitches in the row.

5. Continue the pattern in step 4 (alternating purled and knitted last two stitches) until you reach the end and cast off your square.

6. Continue making as many squares as you want to get the desired size of your blanket.

7. When you have all your knitted squares, take a knitting needle and sew each square together.

Tying Knots

Knowing how to tie different types of knots is a useful skill to have, especially if you are involved in boating, rock climbing, fishing, or other outdoor activities.

Strong knots are typically those that are neat in appearance and are not bulky. If a knot is tied properly, it will almost never loosen and will still be easy to untie when necessary.

The best way to learn how to tie knots effectively is to sit down and practice with a piece of cord or rope. Practice, in this case, definitely makes tying knots much faster and easier. Listed below are a few common knots that are useful to know:

- **Bowline knot:** Fasten one end of the line to some object. After the loop is made, hold it in position with your left hand and pass the end of the line up through the loop, behind and over the line above, and through the loop once again. Pull it tightly and the knot is now complete.

- **Clove hitch:** This knot is particularly useful if you need the length of the running end to be adjustable.

- **Halter:** If you need to create a halter to lead a horse or pony, try this knot.

- **Sheepshank knot:** This is used for shortening ropes. Gather up the amount to be shortened and then make a half hitch around each of the bends.

- **Slip knot:** Slip knots are adjustable, so that you can tighten them around an object after they're tied.

- **Timber hitch:** If you need to secure a rope to a tree, this is the knot to use. It is easy to untie, too.

- **Two half hitches:** Use this knot to secure a rope to a pole, boat mooring, washer, tire, or similar object.

- **Square/reef knot:** This is the most common knot for tying two ropes together.

PART SEVEN   Well-Being

On some level, we all know what we need for optimum health. Our bodies are built to give us clues, from simple ones—if we're tired, we probably need rest—to ones that require a little more attention to discern, such as a headache or stomachache, which can stem from a wide range of issues. Many of us consistently ignore the clues, masking exhaustion with caffeine, or popping an aspirin every time a pain begins to surface without even considering the cause. Well-being begins with taking the time to listen to ourselves, being honest about what needs healing or improvement, and nurturing the desire to reach a healthier level of being. Once the desire for health is strong, you will find a myriad of channels for achieving it. This section offers suggestions for finding well-being through natural means, from herbal medicine to natural spa products. There are times when the best thing to do is to go straight to a doctor, whether a doctor of Western medicine, a homeopath, or another type of medical practitioner. But part of leading a self-sufficient life is learning to recognize and meet your own needs, even in the areas of health and safety. From there, you can begin to help those around you, too. So start paying attention to your physical, mental, and spiritual state, and find out what you can do to be the best version of who you already are.

Herbal Medicine

An herb is a plant or plant part used for its scent, flavor, or therapeutic properties. For centuries herbs have been used in various forms for their health benefits. Many are now sold as tablets, capsules, powders, teas, extracts, and fresh or dried plants. However, some have side effects and may interact with other drugs you are taking.

To use an herbal product as safely as possible:
- Consult your doctor first.
- Do not take a bigger dose than the label recommends.
- Take it under the guidance of a trained medical professional.
- Be especially cautious if you are pregnant or nursing.

Herbal supplements are sold in many forms: as fresh or dried products; liquid or solid extracts; and tablets, capsules, powders, and tea bags. For example, fresh ginger root is often found in the produce section of food stores; dried ginger root is sold packaged in tea bags, capsules, or tablets; and liquid preparations made from ginger root are also sold. A particular group of chemicals or a single chemical may be isolated from a botanical and sold as a dietary supplement, usually in tablet or capsule form. Common preparations include teas, decoctions, tinctures, and extracts:

A *tea*, also known as an *infusion*, is made by adding boiling water to fresh or dried botanicals and steeping them. The tea may be drunk either hot or cold.

Some roots, bark, and berries require more forceful treatment to extract their desired ingredients. They are simmered in boiling water for longer periods than teas, making a *decoction*, which also may be drunk hot or cold.

A *tincture* is made by soaking a botanical in a solution of alcohol and water. Tinctures are sold as liquids and are used for concentrating and preserving a botanical. They are made in different strengths that are expressed as botanical-to-extract ratios (i.e., ratios of the weight of the dried botanical to the volume or weight of the finished product).

An *extract* is made by soaking the botanical in a liquid that removes specific types of chemicals. The liquid can be used as is or evaporated to make a dry extract for use in capsules or tablets.

Herbs can be utilized medicinally in the form of teas, tincture, extracts, or as an addition to soaps, lotions, or salves.

Add several drops of your tincture to tea or juice to receive the healing benefits without the strong flavor.

Make Your Own Herbal Tincture

Tinctures help to concentrate and preserve the health benefits of your herbs. To use, mix 1 teaspoon of tincture with juice, tea, or water and drink no more than three times a day.

1. Pick the fresh herbs, removing any dirty, wilted, or damaged parts. Do not wash. Be sure you know whether it is the stems, leaves, roots, or flowers that have the health benefits, and use only those parts.
2. Coarsely chop the plant parts. Flowers can be left whole.
3. Clean and dry a small glass jar with an airtight lid and put the herbs inside. Fill the jar with 100-proof vodka or warm cider vinegar until plant parts are fully immersed. Screw the lid on securely and label the jar.
4. Store for 6 to 8 weeks, gently shaking a few times a week.
5. Strain out the herbs and store the liquid tincture in a clean, dry bottle. Be sure to label the jar with the ingredients, and date and store it in a safe place away from children's reach.

Common Herbal Remedies

Here is a list of common herbs that can be used to cure or alleviate the symptoms of conditions ranging from cancer to acne to the common cold. If you are taking any other medications or supplements, check with your doctor before trying any herbs. As with any medication, every body is unique and certain herbs can have adverse side effects for certain people, so pay attention to your body and cease taking any herbs that make you feel worse in any way. It's a good idea to try one herb at a time per condition and to keep a journal documenting what you take when and how you feel. This way you'll be able to tell more easily what effects the herbs are having.

Aloe Vera

Uses: The clear gel in aloe is used topically to treat osteoarthritis, burns, and sunburn. The green part can be made into a juice or dried and taken orally to treat a variety of conditions, such as diabetes, asthma, epilepsy, and osteoarthritis.

Cautions: Using aloe vera on surgical wounds may inhibit their healing. If taken orally, aloe vera can produce abdominal cramps and diarrhea, which can decrease the absorption of many drugs.

If you have diabetes and take glucose-lowering medication, you should be careful of taking aloe orally, as studies suggest that aloe may decrease blood glucose levels.

Aloe vera can be used topically to treat and soothe a variety of skin irritations.

Bilberries are a close relative of blueberries and can be eaten whole or made into an extract.

Chamomile flowers can be used to make a relaxing tea.

Echinacea is beautiful as well as useful medicinally. It grows well in moderately dry soil.

Astragalus

Uses: Astragalus was traditionally used in Chinese medicine in combination with other herbs to help boost the immune system. It is still used widely in China for chronic hepatitis and as an additional cancer therapy. Astragalus is commonly used to boost the immune system to help colds and upper respiratory infections and has also been used to fight heart disease. The astragalus plant root is used in soups, teas, extracts, and capsules and is generally used with other herbs, like ginseng, angelica, and licorice.

Cautions: Astragalus may interact with medications that suppress the immune system (such as those taken by cancer patients or organ transplant recipients).

Bilberry

Uses: Bilberry fruit is used to treat diarrhea, menstrual cramps, eye problems, varicose veins, and circulatory problems. The leaf of a bilberry is used to treat diabetes. It's claimed that bilberry fruit also helps improve night vision, but this is not clinically proven. The bilberry fruit can be eaten or made into an extract. Likewise, its leaves can be used in tea or made into an extract.

Cautions: Though bilberry fruit is considered safe, high doses of the leaf or leaf extract may have possible toxic side effects.

Chamomile

Uses: Chamomile has a calming effect and is often used to counteract sleeplessness and anxiety, as well as diarrhea and gastrointestinal conditions. Topically, chamomile is used in the treatment of skin conditions and for mouth ulcers (particularly due to cancer treatment). The chamomile plant has flowering tops, which are used to make teas, extracts, capsules, and tablets. It can also be applied as a skin cream or ointment or even be used as a mouth rinse.

Cautions: Some people have developed rare allergic reactions from eating or coming into contact with chamomile. These reactions include skin rashes, swelling of the throat, shortness of breath, and anaphylaxis. People allergic to related plants, such as daisies, ragweed, or marigolds, should be careful when coming into contact with chamomile.

Cranberry

Uses: Cranberry fruit and leaves are used in healing many conditions, including wounds, urinary disorders, diarrhea, diabetes, and stomach and liver problems. Cranberries are often used in treating urinary tract infections and stomach ulcers. They may also be useful in preventing dental plaque and in preventing *E.coli* bacteria from adhering to cells along the urinary tract wall. Cranberry fruit can be eaten straight; made into juice; or used in the form of extracts, tea, or tablets and taken as a dietary supplement.

Cautions: Drinking copious amounts of cranberry juice can cause an upset stomach and diarrhea.

Dandelion

Uses: Dandelions, throughout history, have been most commonly used to treat liver and kidney diseases and spleen problems. Dandelions are sometimes used in liver and kidney tonics, as a diuretic, and for simple digestive issues. The dandelion's leaves and roots (and sometimes the entire plant) are used in teas, capsules, and extracts. The leaves are used in salads or are cooked, and the flowers are used to make wine.

Cautions: While using dandelions is typically safe, there are a few instances of upset stomach and diarrhea caused by the plant, as well as allergic reactions. If your gallbladder is inflamed or infected, you should avoid using dandelion products.

Echinacea

Uses: Traditionally, echinacea has been used to boost the immune system to help prevent colds, flu, and various infections. Echinacea can also be used for wounds, acne, and boils. The roots and exposed plant are used, either fresh or dried, for teas, juice, extracts, or in preparations for external use.

Cautions: Echinacea, taken orally, generally does not cause any problems. Some people do have allergic reactions (rashes, increased asthma, anaphylaxis), but typically only gastrointestinal problems are experienced. If you are allergic to any plants in the daisy family, it may be best to steer clear of echinacea.

Evening Primrose Oil

Uses: Since the 1930s, evening primrose oil has been used to fight eczema and recently, it has been used for other inflammatory conditions. Evening primrose oil is also used in the treatment of breast pain during the menstrual cycle, symptoms of menopause, and premenstrual issues. It may also relieve pain associated with rheumatoid arthritis.

The oil is extracted from the evening primrose seeds. You'll find it in capsule form at many health food stores.

Cautions: There may be some mild side effects, such as gastrointestinal upset or headache.

Flaxseed and Flaxseed Oil

Uses: Flaxseed is typically used as a laxative and to alleviate hot flashes. Flaxseed oil is used for treating arthritis pain. Both herbs are used to fight high cholesterol and can be beneficial for those with heart disease. Flaxseed, in either its whole or crushed form, may be mixed with water or juice and ingested. It is also available as a powder. Flaxseed oil can be taken in either a liquid or capsule form.

Cautions: It is essential to take flaxseed with lots of water, or constipation could worsen. Further, flaxseed fiber may decrease the body's ability to absorb other oral medications and so should not be taken together.

Garlic

Uses: Garlic is typically used as a dietary supplement for those with high cholesterol, heart disease, and high blood pressure. It may help decrease the hardening of the arteries and is also used in the prevention of stomach and colon cancer. It is also used topically or orally to heal some infections, including ear infections. Garlic cloves may be eaten either raw or cooked, or they may be dried or powdered and used in capsules. Oil and other extracts can be obtained from garlic cloves.

Cautions: Some common side effects of garlic are breath and body odor, heartburn, upset stomach, and allergic reactions. Garlic can also thin blood and so should not be used before surgeries or dental work, especially if you have a bleeding disorder. It also has an adverse effect on drugs used to fight HIV.

Garlic grows best in soil that is pH 6.5 to 7.0.

Ginger

Uses: Ginger is commonly used in Asian medicines to treat stomachaches, nausea, and diarrhea. Many U.S. dietary supplements containing ginger are used to help fight cold and flu and can be used to relieve post-surgery nausea or nausea related to pregnancy. It has also been used for arthritis and other joint and muscle pain. Ginger root can be found fresh or dried, in tablets, capsules, extracts, and teas.

Cautions: Side effects are rare but can include gas, bloating, heartburn, and, for some people, nausea.

Ginkgo

Uses: Traditionally, extract from ginkgo leaves has been used in the treatment of illnesses such as asthma, bronchitis, fatigue, and tinnitus. People use gingko leaf extract in the hopes that it will help improve their memory (especially in the treatment of Alzheimer's disease and dementia). It is also taken to treat sexual dysfunction, multiple sclerosis, and other health issues. Ginkgo leaf extracts are made into tablets, capsules, or teas. Sometimes the extracts can also be found in skin care products.

Cautions: Some common side effects are headache, nausea, gastrointestinal upset, diarrhea, dizziness, or skin irritations. Ginkgo may also increase bleeding risks, so those having surgery or with bleeding disorders should consult a doctor before using any ginkgo products. Uncooked ginkgo seeds are toxic and can cause seizures.

Ginkgo leaves can be made into an extract and ingested for a wide range of health benefits.

Ginseng (Asian)

Uses: Ginseng is used to help boost the immune system and contribute to the overall health of an individual. It has been used traditionally and currently for improving those who are recovering from illnesses, increasing stamina and mental and physical performance, treating erectile dysfunction and symptoms of menopause, and lowering blood glucose levels and blood pressure. In some studies, ginseng has been proven to lower blood glucose levels and boost immune systems. The ginseng root is dried and made into tablets, capsules, extracts, and teas. It can also be made into creams for external use.

Cautions: Limiting ginseng intake to three months at a time will most likely reduce any potential side effects. The most common side effects are headaches and sleep issues, along with some allergic reactions. If you have diabetes and are taking blood-sugar lowering medications, it is advisable not to use ginseng, as it too lowers blood sugar.

Grape Seed Extract

Uses: Grape seed extract is used for treating heart and blood vessel conditions, such as high blood pressure, high cholesterol, and low circulation. It is also used for those struggling with complications from diabetes, such as nerve and eye damage. Grape seed extract is also used in treating vision problems, reducing swelling after surgery, and cancer prevention. Extracted from grape seeds, it is readily available in tablets and capsules.

Cautions: Common side effects of prolonged grape seed oil use are headaches; dry, itchy scalp; dizziness; and nausea.

Green Tea

Uses: Green tea and its extracts have been used in preventing and treating breast, stomach, and skin cancers, as well as improving mental alertness, aiding weight loss, lowering cholesterol, and preventing the sun from damaging the skin. Green tea is typically brewed and drunk. Extracts can be taken in capsule form and sometimes green tea can be found in skin care products.

Cautions: While green tea is generally safe for most adults, there have been a few reports of liver problems occurring in those who take green tea extracts. Thus, these extracts should always be taken with food and should not be taken at all by those with liver disorders. Green tea also contains caffeine and can cause insomnia, anxiety, irritability, nausea, diarrhea, or frequent urination.

Lavender

Uses: Lavender, in the past, has been used as an antiseptic and to help with mental health issues. Now it is more commonly taken for anxiety, restlessness, insomnia, and depression, and can also be used to fight headaches, upset stomach, and hair loss.

Lavender has a soothing, relaxing aroma. It can also be ingested in the form of tea or extracts, or even in baked goods.

Most commonly used in aromatherapy, lavender essential oil can also be diluted with other oils and rubbed on the skin. When dried, lavender flowers can be made into teas or liquid extracts and ingested.

Cautions: Lavender oil applied to the skin may cause some irritation and is poisonous if ingested. Lavender tea may cause headache, appetite change, and constipation. If used with sedatives, it may increase drowsiness.

Licorice Root

Uses: Traditionally, licorice root is used as a dietary supplement for the treatment of stomach ulcers, bronchitis, and sore throat. It is also used to help cure infections caused by viruses. When licorice root is peeled, it can be dried and made into powder. It is available in capsules, tablets, and extracts.

Cautions: If taken in large doses, licorice root can cause high blood pressure, water retention, and low potassium levels, leading to heart conditions. Taken with diuretics, it could cause the body's potassium levels to fall to dangerously low levels. If you have heart disease or high blood pressure, you should practice caution when taking licorice root. Large doses of licorice root may cause preterm labor in pregnant women.

Milk Thistle

Uses: Milk thistle is used as a protective measure for liver problems and in the treatment of liver cirrhosis, chronic hepatitis, and gallbladder diseases. It is also used to lower cholesterol, reduce insulin resistance in those with type 2 diabetes, and reduce the growth of cancerous cells in the breast, cervix, or prostate. Milk thistle seeds are used to make capsules, extracts, and strong teas.

Milk thistle grows in a wide range of soil types and will thrive in sunny or partly shady areas.

Cautions: Occasionally, milk thistle may cause diarrhea, upset stomach, or bloating. It may also cause allergic reactions, especially in those with allergies to the daisy family.

Mistletoe

Uses: For hundreds of years, mistletoe has been used to treat seizures and headaches. In Europe, mistletoe is used to treat cancer and to boost the immune system. The shoots and berries of mistletoe are used in oral extracts. In Europe, these extracts are prescription drugs, available only by injection.

Cautions: Eating raw and unprocessed mistletoe may cause vomiting, seizures, a slowing of the heart rate, and even death. American mistletoe cannot be used for medical purposes. Injected mistletoe extract can irritate the skin and produce low-grade fevers or flu-like symptoms. There is also a slight risk for severe allergic reactions that could cause breathing difficulty.

Peppermint Oil

Uses: Usually, peppermint oil is used to treat nausea, indigestion, and cold symptoms and it can also be used to allay headaches, muscle and nerve pain, and irritable bowel syndrome. Peppermint essential oil can be taken orally in small doses. It can also be diluted with other oils and applied to the skin.

Cautions: Common side effects include allergic reactions and heartburn, though peppermint oil is relatively safe in small doses.

Red Clover

Uses: Red clover has been used for treating cancer, whooping cough, asthma, and indigestion. It is also used to allay menopausal symptoms, breast pain, high cholesterol, osteoporosis, and enlarged prostate. The red clover flower is used in preparing extracts in tablets and capsules as well as teas.

Cautions: No serious side effects have been reported, though it is unclear if it is safe for use by pregnant women, women who are breastfeeding, or women with breast or other hormonal cancer. The estrogen in red clover may also increase a woman's chance of contracting cancer in the uterus.

Soy

Uses: Soy products are typically used for treating high cholesterol, menopausal symptoms, osteoporosis, problems with memory, breast and prostate cancer, and high blood pressure. Available in dietary supplements, soy can be found in tablet or capsule form. Soybeans may be cooked and eaten, or made into tofu, soy milk, and other foods.

Cautions: Using soy supplements or eating soy products can create minor stomach and bowel problems, and in rare cases, allergic reactions causing breathing difficulties and rashes. While there is no conclusive evidence linking soy with increased risk of breast cancer, women who have or are at risk of getting breast cancer should consult a doctor about using soy products.

St. John's Wort

Uses: St. John's wort has been used for hundreds of years to treat mental illness and nerve pain. It has also been used as a sedative; in malaria treatment; and as a balm for wounds, burns, and insect bites. It is commonly used to treat depression, anxiety, and sleep disorders. The flowers are used, in extract form, for tea and capsules.

Cautions: A possible side effect of using St. John's wort is increased light sensitivity. Other common side effects are anxiety, dry mouth, dizziness, gastrointestinal symptoms, fatigue, headache, and sexual dysfunction. St. John's wort also interacts with drugs and may interfere with the way the body breaks down those drugs. It may affect antidepressants, birth control pills, cyclosporine, digoxin, indinavir and other HIV drugs, irinotecan and other cancer drugs, and anticoagulants.

If you are taking antidepressants, be careful if also taking St. John's wort, as it may increase the likelihood of nausea, anxiety, headache, and confusion.

Turmeric

Uses: Traditionally used in Chinese medicine, turmeric was supposed to aid digestion and liver function and to relieve arthritis pain. It was also taken to regulate the menstrual cycle. Applied directly to the skin, it was used to treat eczema and wounds. Now, turmeric is used in the treatment of heartburn, stomach ulcers, and gallstones. Turmeric is also used to reduce inflammation and in the prevention and treatment of certain cancers.

The underground stems of the turmeric plant are dried and taken orally in capsules, teas, or liquid extracts. It can also be made into a paste to be used on the skin.

Cautions: Considered safe for most adults, long-term use of turmeric may cause indigestion. Those with gallbladder problems should avoid turmeric, however, as it may worsen the condition.

Make St. John's wort flowers into tea and drink to boost your mood and ease tension.

Valerian

Uses: For many years, valerian has been used for sleep disorders and to treat anxiety. Valerian has also been used to alleviate headaches, depression, irregular heartbeat, and trembling. The roots and underground stems of the valerian plant are usually made into supplements in capsule, tablet, or liquid extract form. It can also sometimes be made into teas.

Cautions: Valerian is typically safe to use for short periods of time (no more than six weeks) but there is no proof about its long-term effectiveness. Some common side effects of valerian use are headaches, dizziness, upset stomach, and grogginess the morning after use.

Homemade Herbal Teas

Herbal teas can be very tasty and deliver between 50 and 90 percent of the medicinal qualities of the herbs used. Teas you make yourself will be more potent and flavorful than those you can buy at the store, and much less expensive. Try experimenting with different herbal combinations, but be careful to avoid any plants you cannot confidently identify as edible, or any plants sprayed with pesticides. If using dried herbs, you can store your tea mixes in sealed containers for months. Be sure to label each container with the name of the tea.

Use 1 to 2 teaspoons of dried herbs per cup of hot water or 3 teaspoons of fresh herbs per pint of water. Steep the herbs for about 10 minutes and then strain. The following plants can all be safely used in teas:

Flowers

Alliums, bee balm, carnations, echinacea (roots and flowers), hibiscus, hollyhocks, honeysuckle (avoid the poisonous berries), lavender, marshmallow (use the roots), red clover, nasturtiums, roses (flowers or hips), violets.

Herbs

Basil, chamomile flowers, chives, dill, eucalyptus, ginger root, lemon balm, lemongrass, marjoram, mint, oregano, parsley, peppermint, linden leaves, mint, rosemary, sage, thyme, valerian root, verbena.

Bushes and Trees

Birch leaves, blackberry leaves, citrus blossoms, elderberry flowers, gardenia, pine needles, raspberry leaves.

Weeds

Chickweed, chicory, dandelions, goldenrod, stinging nettle.

Tea for the Common Cold

Combine the following herbs in any proportion you like. Boil for 10 minutes, strain, and add honey to taste.

Marshmallow root (eases body aches, reduces inflammation)

Peppermint (reduces congestion, eases headaches, soothes stomach)

Echinacea roots and flowers (boosts the immune system)

Thyme (reduces chest and nasal congestion, increases circulation)

Cinnamon (reduces inflammation and fights infection)

Rosehips, finely chopped (full of vitamin C, which boosts the immune system and energizes)

Ginger root, peeled and finely chopped (warms from the inside out)

Lavender, crushed (eases migraines)

Lemon peel, finely grated (full of vitamin C)

Herbal teas are also delicious served cold in the summer months.

Red clover blossoms promote estrogen and nourish the uterus.

Calming Tea

Combine the following calming herbs, using about ¼ as much valerian as the other herbs (valerian can be very potent). Boil for 10 minutes, strain, and add honey to taste.

Lemon balm leaves
Chamomile flowers
Valerian root, crushed
Ginger root, peeled and finely chopped

Fertility Tea

Drink one cup of fertility tea a day to help balance your hormones and to get nutrients that can aid in becoming pregnant. Combine the herbs in equal proportion, boil for 10 minutes, strain, and add honey to taste.

Red clover blossoms (nourishes the uterus, promotes estrogen, rich in magnesium and calcium)

Nettle leaves (rich in calcium, potassium, phosphorous, iron, and sulfur)

Red raspberry leaves (aids the fertilized egg in attaching to the uterine lining, rich in minerals, helps to tone muscles in the pelvic region)

Peppermint (aids in absorption of red raspberry leaf nutrients)

Cleansing Tea

The herbs in this tea will improve your digestion, help your body in its natural detoxification process, and give you more energy. Combine the herbs in any proportion (go easy on the cayenne), boil for 10 minutes, strain, and add honey if desired.

Peppermint leaves
Dandelion root
Whole allspice berries
Ginger root, peeled and finely chopped
Licorice root, crushed
Cayenne pepper

Natural Cosmetics

Homemade Lip Gloss

You only need a few ingredients to make your own lip gloss, though once you understand the basic recipe you can begin to experiment by adding different essential oils, aloes, and food products to create your own, unique type of gloss.

Homemade lip gloss containers can be any small glass jar or tin, or you can reuse an old lip gloss container (just make sure all the old gloss is out of the container). To sterilize the container, wash with soap and hot water, dunk the container in a jar of rubbing alcohol, rinse clean, and then allow the container to completely dry before pouring in your melted gloss. Allow the gloss mixture to cool completely before using (you can speed

up this process by placing the container of gloss into the refrigerator for a few hours).

Honey Lip Gloss

Ingredients
1 tsp beeswax (you can find this at a craft store or at your local farmers' market)
½ tsp honey
2 tsp almond oil (optional)
Vitamin E oil from a capsule (optional)

Directions
1. Melt the beeswax and honey in a heat-proof jar in the microwave or use a double boiler method.
2. When the wax and honey are just melted, remove from the heat source and whisk in the almond oil and vitamin E oil, if you so desire. To remove the vitamin E oil from the capsule, simply prick the end of the capsule with a safety pin and squeeze it out.
3. Pour the mixture into the containers and allow to cool fully before using.

Note: If you want to add a citrus flavoring to this lip gloss, you can add a few drops of lemon or lime essential oil during the whisking stage.

"Make-up" Lip Balm

If you have leftover make-up (such as blush, lipstick, or shimmering eye shadow), don't let it go to waste. You can use it in this "recycled" lip balm.

Ingredients
Petroleum jelly
Blush, mineral eye shadow with shimmer, lipstick (only use one or two of these for your balm)
Essential oil for flavoring (optional)

Directions
1. Mix together the petroleum jelly and either the blush (add a little at a time until the desired color is attained), eye shadow, or the last remnants of any lipstick. Add essential oil and mix thoroughly.
2. Scoop the mixture into containers and put in the refrigerator to harden.

Note: You can also experiment by melting the jelly with some beeswax and then adding in the leftover makeup. The possibilities are endless.

Homemade Bath Products

Lavender Bath Salt

Pour several tablespoons of this into your bath as it fills for an extra-soothing, relaxing, and cleansing experience. You can also add powdered milk or finely ground old-fashioned oatmeal to make your skin especially soft. Toss in a few lavender buds if you have them.

Ingredients
2 cups coarse sea salt
½ cup Epsom salts
½ cup baking soda
4 to 6 drops lavender essential oil
Red and blue food coloring, if desired (use more red than blue to achieve a lavender color)

Mix all ingredients thoroughly and store in a glass jar or other airtight container.

Citrus scrub

Citrus Scrub

Use this invigorating scrub to wake up your senses in the morning. The vitamin C in oranges serves as an astringent, making it especially good for oily skin.

Ingredients
½ orange or grapefruit

3 tbsp cornmeal

2 tbsp Epsom salts or coarse sea salt

Squeeze citrus juice and pulp into a bowl and add cornmeal and salts to form a paste. Rub gently over entire body and then rinse.

Healing Bath Soak

This bath soak will relax tired muscles, help to calm nerves, and leave skin soft and fragrant. You may also wish to add blackberry, raspberry, or violet leaves. Dried or fresh herbs can be used.

2 tbsp comfrey leaves

1 tbsp lavender

1 tbsp evening primrose flowers

1 tsp orange peel, thinly sliced or grated

2 tbsp oatmeal

Combine herbs and tie up in a small muslin or cheesecloth sack. Leave under faucet as the tub fills with hot water. If desired, empty herbs into the bath water once the tub is full.

Rosemary Peppermint Foot Scrub

Use this foot rub to remove calluses, soften skin, and leave your feet feeling and smelling wonderful.

Ingredients
1 cup coarse sea salt

¼ cup sweet almond or olive oil

2 to 3 drops peppermint essential oil

1 to 2 drops rosemary essential oil

2 sprigs fresh rosemary, crushed, or ½ tsp dried rosemary

Combine all ingredients and massage into feet and ankles. Rinse with warm water and follow with a moisturizer.

Minty Cucumber Facial Mask

1 tbsp powdered milk

1 tsp plain yogurt (whole milk yogurt is best)

1 tsp honey

1 tsp fresh mint leaves

½ cucumber, peeled

Blend ingredients thoroughly, using a food processor or blender if available. Apply to face, avoiding eyes. Leave on for 10 to 15 minutes, then rinse.

After-Sun Comfrey Lotion

Comfrey root soothes skin and minimizes inflammation. Apply this lotion to sunburned skin for immediate relief and faster healing.

Ingredients
3 tbsp fresh comfrey root

1 cup water

1 tbsp beeswax, unrefined

¾ cup sweet almond oil or light cooking oil

¼ cup cocoa butter

4 vitamin E capsules

¼ cup aloe vera gel

1 tsp borax powder

12 to 16 drops essential oil (peppermint, lavender, or sandalwood are all good choices)

Directions
1. Place the comfrey root and water in a small pot and bring to a boil, simmering for about 30 minutes. Strain, retaining the water. Discard the root.
2. In a double boiler, combine beeswax, oil, and cocoa butter, stirring over low heat until melted. Remove from heat. Pierce the vitamin E capsules and add the oil from inside, stirring to combine.
3. In a separate saucepan, combine the comfrey water, aloe vera gel, and borax powder, stirring over low heat until the borax is fully dissolved. Allow to cool.
4. Once both mixtures are cooled to room temperature, pour the beeswax and oil mixture in a thin stream into the comfrey water mixture, whisking vigorously to combine (or use a food processor). Add the essential oils and continue mixing until thoroughly combined.
5. Cover and store in a cool, dark place.

Shampoo

Cleaning your hair can be as simple as making a baking soda and water paste, scrubbing it into your hair, and rinsing well. However, if you enjoy the feel of a sudsy, soapy, scented shampoo, try this recipe. You can substitute homemade soap flakes for the castile soap, if desired.

Ingredients
4 ounces liquid castile soap

3 tbsp fresh or dried herbs of your choice, boiled for 30 minutes in 2 cups water and strained

Pour the soap and herbal water into a jar, cover, and shake until well combined.

Hair Conditioner

This conditioner will add softness and volume to your hair. Avocado, bananas, and egg yolks are also great hair conditioners. Apply conditioner, allow to sit in hair a minimum of five minutes (longer for a deeper conditioning), and then rinse well. You may wish to shampoo a second time after using this conditioner.

Ingredients

1 cup olive oil
1 tsp lemon juice
1 tsp cider vinegar
2 tsp honey
6 to 10 drops essential oils, if desired

Whisk all ingredients together or blend in a food processor. Store in an airtight container.

Herbs for Your Hair

Herbs for dry hair	Burdock root, comfrey, elderflowers, lavender, marshmallow, parsley, sage, stinging nettle
Herbs for oily hair	Calendula, horsetail, lemon juice, lemon balm, mints, rosemary, witch hazel, yarrow
Herbs to combat dandruff	Burdock root, garlic, onion, parsley, rosemary, stinging nettle, thyme
Herbs for body and luster	Calendula, catnip, horsetail, licorice, lime flowers, nasturtium, parsley, rosemary, sage, stinging nettle, watercress
Herbs for shine	Horsetail, parsley, nettle, rosemary, sage, calendula
Herbs for hair growth	Aloe, arnica, birch, burdock, catmint, chamomile, horsetail, licorice, marigold, nettles, parsley, rosemary, sage, stinging nettle
Herbs for coloring	Brown: henna (reddish brown), walnut hulls, sage Blonde: calendula, chamomile, lemon, saffron, turmeric, rhubarb root

Papaya is ofen used in face creams for its anti-aging anti-acne properties.

Fruits and Vegetables for Your Skin

These fruits and vegetables can be applied directly to your face or blended together to make a mask. Leave on skin for 20 to 30 minutes and then rinse thoroughly with clean water.

Beneficial for Oily Skin	Beneficial for Normal Skin	Beneficial for Dry Skin
Lemons, grapes, limes, strawberries, grapefruits, apples	Peaches, papayas, tomatoes, apricots, bananas, persimmons, bell peppers, cucumbers, kiwi, pumpkins, watermelons	Carrots, iceberg lettuce, honeydew melons, avocados, cantaloupes

Tropical Face Cleanser

The vitamin C in kiwi has enzymatic and cleansing properties, and the apricot oil serves as a moisturizer. The ground almonds act as an exfoliant to remove dead skin cells. Yogurt has cleansing and moisturizing properties.

1 kiwi
¾ cup avocado, banana, apricot, peach, strawberry, or papaya (or some of each)
2 tbsp plain yogurt (whole milk is best)
1 tbsp apricot oil (almond oil also works well)
1 tbsp honey
1 tsp finely ground almonds

Purée all ingredients together. Massage into face and neck and rinse thoroughly with cool water. Store excess in refrigerator for one to two days.

First Aid

It's impossible to predict when an accident will occur, but the more you educate yourself ahead of time, the better you'll be able to help should the need arise. The first step in an emergency situation should always be to call for help, but there are many things you can do to help the victim while you're waiting for assistance to arrive. The most important procedures are described in this section.

Drowning

1. As soon as the patient is in a safe place, loosen the clothing, if any.
2. Empty the lungs of water by laying the body breastdown and lifting it by the middle, with the head hanging down. Hold for a few seconds until the water drains out.
3. Turn the patient on his breast, face downward.
4. Give artificial respiration: Press the lower ribs down and forward toward the head, then release. Repeat about twelve times to the minute.
5. Apply warmth and friction to extremities, rubbing toward the heart.
6. Don't give up! Persons have been saved after hours of steady effort, and after being underwater for more than twenty minutes.
7. When natural breathing is reestablished, put the patient into a warm bed, with hot-water bottles, warm drinks, fresh air, and quiet.

Sunstroke

1. Move the patient to a cool place, or set up a structure around the patient to produce shade.
2. Loosen or remove any clothing around the neck and upper body.
3. Apply cold water or ice to the head and body, or wrap the patient in cold, damp cloths.
4. Encourage the patient to drink lots of water.

Burns and Scalds

1. Cover the burn with a thin paste of baking soda, starch, flour, petroleum jelly, olive oil, linseed oil, castor oil, cream, or cold cream.
2. Cover the burn first with the paste, then with a soft rag soaked in the paste.
3. Shock always accompanies severe burns, and must be treated.

Keep a buoy nearby whenever spending time in or near the water.

A simple hand bandage can be made from any square cloth or handkerchief.

Shock or Nervous Collapse

A person suffering from shock has a pale face, cold skin, feeble breathing, and a rapid, feeble pulse, and will appear listless or half-dead.

1. Place the patient on his back with head low.
2. Give stimulants, such as hot tea or coffee.
3. Cover the patient with blankets.
4. Rub the limbs and place hot-water bottles around the body.

Cuts and Wounds

1. After making sure that no dirt or foreign substance is in the wound, apply a tight bandage to stop the bleeding.
2. Raise the wound above the heart to slow the bleeding.
3. If the blood comes out in spurts, it means an artery has been cut. For this, apply a tourniquet: Make a big knot in a handkerchief, tie it around the limb, with the knot just above the wound, and twist it until the flow is stopped.

Hemorrhage or Internal Bleeding

Internal bleeding usually comes from the lungs or stomach. If from the lungs, the blood is bright red and frothy, and is coughed up; if from the stomach, it is dark, and is vomited.

1. Help the patient to lie down, with head lower than body.
2. Encourage the patient to swallow small pieces of ice, and apply ice bags, snow, or cold water to the place where the bleeding is coming from.
3. Hot applications may be applied to the hands, arms, feet, and legs, but avoid stimulants, unless the patient is very weak.

Fainting

Fainting is caused by a lack of blood supply to the brain and is cured by getting the heart to correct the lack.

1. Have the person lie down with the head lower than the body.
2. Loosen the clothing. Give fresh air. Rub the limbs. Use smelling salts.
3. Do not let the person get up until fully recovered.

Snake Bite

1. Put a tight cord or bandage around the limb between the wound and the heart. This should be loose enough to slip a finger under it.
2. Keep the wound lower than the heart. Try to keep the patient calm, as the faster the heart beats, the faster the venom will spread.
3. If you cannot get to a doctor quickly, suck the wound many times with your mouth or use a poison suction kit, if available.

Insect Stings

1. Wash with oil, weak ammonia, or very salty water, or paint with iodine.
2. A paste of baking soda and water also soothes stings.

Poison

1. First, get the victim away from the poison. If the poison is in solid form, such as pills, remove it from the victim's mouth using a clean cloth wrapped around your finger. Don't try this with infants because it could force the poison further down their throat.
2. If the poison is corrosive to the skin, remove the clothing from the affected area and flush with water for 30 minutes.
3. If the poison is in contact with the eyes, flush the victim's eyes for a minimum of 15 minutes with clean water.

How to Make a Tourniquet

The tourniquet is an appliance used to check severe bleeding. It consists of a bandage twisted more or less lightly around the affected part. The bandage—a cloth, strap, belt, necktie, neckerchief or towel—should be long enough to go around the arm or leg affected. It can then be twisted by inserting the hand, and the blood stopped.

If a stick is used, there is danger of twisting too tightly.

The tourniquet should not be used if bleeding can be stopped without it. When used it should be carefully loosened every 15 to 20 minutes to avoid permanent damage to tissues.

For elbow, arm, or wrist injuries, a simple sling can be made out of a piece of cloth or clothing.

How to Put Out Burning Clothing

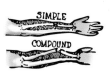

A compound fracture is one that breaks through the flesh.

1. If your clothing should catch fire, do not run for help, as this will fan the flames.
2. Lie down and roll up as tightly as possible in an overcoat, blanket, rug, or any woolen article—or lie down and roll over slowly, at the same time beating the fire with your hands. Smother the fire with a coat, blanket, or rug. Remember that woolen material is much less flammable than cotton.

Ice Rescue

1. Always have a rope nearby if you're working or playing on ice. This way, if someone falls through, you can tie one end to yourself and one to a tree or other secure anchor onshore before you attempt to rescue the person.
2. You could also throw one end to the victim if his head is above water.
3. Do not attempt to walk out to victim. Push out to him or crawl out on a long board or rail or tree trunk.
4. The person in the water should never try to crawl up on the broken ice, but should try merely to support himself and wait for help, if it is at hand.

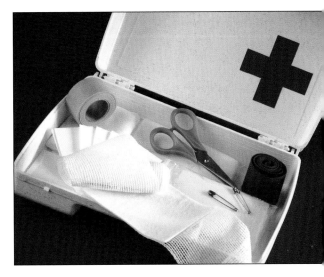

Broken Bone

A simple fracture is one in which the bone is broken but does not break the skin. In a compound fracture, the bone is broken and the skin and tissue are punctured or torn. A simple fracture may be converted into a compound fracture by careless handling, as a broken bone usually has sharp, saw-tooth edges, and just a little twist may push it through the skin.

1. Do not move the patient without supporting broken member by splints.
2. In a compound fracture, bleeding must be checked—by bandage over compress, if possible, or by tourniquet in extreme cases. Then splints may be applied.
3. Where skin is broken, infection is the great danger, so exercise care that compress or dressing is sterile and clean.

Dislocation

A dislocation is an injury where the head of a bone has slipped out of its socket at a joint.

1. Do not attempt to replace the joint. Even thumb and finger dislocations are more serious than usually realized.
2. Cover the joint with cloths wrung out in very hot or very cold water. For the shoulder—apply padding and make a sling for the arm.
3. Seek medical assistance.

There are many ways to carry someone with an injury. If neck or spine injury is suspected, do not attempt to move the victim if you can get help to come to the victim instead. If the victim must be moved, the head and neck must first be carefully stabilized.

Grip to form basket seat

Two-handed chair carry

Chair carry

"Three bearers' position for lift"

"Three bearers' lift"

Arm carry

Horseback carry

First Aid Checklist

To administer effective first aid, it is important to maintain adequate supplies in each first aid kit. A first aid kit should include:

- Adhesive bandages: These are available in a large range of sizes for minor cuts, abrasions, and puncture wounds.
- Butterfly closures: These hold wound edges firmly together.
- Rolled gauze: These allow freedom of movement and are recommended for securing a wound dressing and/or pads. These are especially good for hard-to-bandage wounds.
- Nonstick sterile pads: These are soft, super-absorbent pads that provide a good environment for wound healing. These are recommended for bleeding and draining wounds, burns, or infections.
- First aid tapes: Various types of tapes should be included in each kit. These include adhesive, which is waterproof and extra strong for times when rigid strapping is needed; clear, which stretches with the body's movement and is good for visible wounds; cloth, recommended for most first aid taping needs, including taping heavy dressings (less irritating than adhesive); and paper, which is recommended for sensitive skin and is used for light and frequently changed dressings.
- Items that can also be included in each kit are tweezers, first aid cream, thermometer, an analgesic or equivalent, and an ice pack.

Witch hazel bark can be brewed and used to soothe irritated skin or eyes.

Nature's First Aid

Antiseptic or *wound-wash*: A handful of salt in a quart of hot water.

Balm for wounds: Balsam fir. The gum can be used as healing salve, usually spread on a piece of linen and laid over the wound for a dressing.

Cough remedy: Slippery elm or black cherry inner bark boiled, a pound to the gallon, boiled down to a pint, and given a teaspoonful every hour.

Linseed can be used the same way; add honey if desired. Or boil down the sap of the sweet birch tree and drink it on its own or mixed with the other remedies.

Diuretic: A decoction of the inner bark of elder is a powerful diuretic.

Inflammation of the eyes or skin: Wash with a strong tea made of the bark of witch hazel.

Lung balm: Infusion of black cherry bark and root is a powerful tonic for lungs and bowels. Good also as a skin wash for sores.

Poison ivy: Wash every hour or two with hot soapy water, then with hot salt water.